INTRODUCTION TO INDUSTRIAL ORGANIZATION

INTRODUCTION TO INDUSTRIAL ORGANIZATION

LUÍS M. B. CABRAL

THE MIT PRESS

CAMBRIDGE, MASSACHUSETTS · LONDON, ENGLAND

This book was set in Melior and MetaPlus by Windfall Software using ZzTEX and was printed and bound in the United States of America.

Library of Congress Cataloging-in-Publication Data

Cabral, Luís M. B.
  Introduction to industrial organization / Luís M. B. Cabral
    p. cm.
  Includes bibliographical references and index.
  ISBN 0-262-03286-4
    1. Industrial organization (Economic theory)   I. Title.
  HD2326.C33 2000
  338.6—dc21   00—038666
                                                CIP

10 9 8 7 6 5

CONTENTS

PREFACE

Why yet another text on industrial organization (IO)? IO texts are not in short supply, and so the question is only fair and natural. Accordingly, this preface provides a convincing answer to this opening question.

Industrial organization has changed a great deal over the past two decades. Most importantly, it has evolved from a niche area in economics to an independent discipline that is studied by most economists and by students and scholars in areas such as finance, marketing, and strategy. This shift has resulted from two factors: (1) IO is the first economics discipline to incorporate the developments in game theory that took place during the late 1960s and 1970s, and (2) the analysis of imperfectly competitive markets (a possible definition of IO) is an inherently interesting and important task.

The evolution of the status of IO has not been reflected in the supply of new IO texts. Although the latter have increased in number, one cannot avoid the feeling that most texts have been written primarily for an audience of advanced undergraduate economics students; and in some cases for students who intend to pursue an academic career in economics. Why do I say this? First, because the *level* at which they are written is somewhat advanced for a student who does not have economics as a primary field of study. Second, many of these texts are *methodology* driven rather than *issue* driven: They introduce readers to a collection of models and econometric regressions as if to initiate them in the activity of research in IO—which is a natural bias, given that most authors are well-known IO researchers.

This text fills the perceived gap: Here, then, is a text that will appeal to a wide audience of readers, including economics students as well as students from other areas who are interested in economics as part of their education. Accordingly, the two main objectives of this book are the following:

1. The book is an *introduction*. This is naturally reflected by its length, between one third and one half of the size of most other texts. However, brevity is achieved not so much through superficiality in the treatment of each issue, but rather through greater selectivity in the list of topics addressed.[a]

2. The book is *issue* driven rather than *methodology* driven or *literature* driven. Although I make extensive use of models (because I think they are a useful way of understanding reality), I introduce a new model only when this is justified in terms of the marginal benefit in understanding an issue.[b]

Studying this book will not make the reader an expert in industrial organization; nor will it provide a complete or even representative view of two decades of research in the field. However, it *will* give an idea of the main issues involved in the analysis

[a] G. K. Chesterton once wrote a long letter to the editor of a newspaper. Asked why he wrote such a long letter, he allegedly answered, "Because I didn't have the time to write a short one." I consider its relatively short length as one of the accomplishments of this text.

[b] In particular, I should emphasize that the list of references in the book does *not* reflect a balanced survey of the IO literature. To stress this point, I have chosen not to make direct reference to sources in the text, leaving bibliographic references to notes at the end of the text. (These are the notes marked with numbers, as opposed to footnotes such as this one, which are marked with letters.)

of market competition, and in applying these ideas to the understanding of relevant problems reported in the *Wall Street Journal, Financial Times, Economist,* and related publications:[c] How should Nintendo react to Sony's cutting the price of its PlayStation? Was the Department of Justice right in suing Microsoft for bundling Windows with Internet Explorer? How will the proposed merger between British Airways and American Airlines impact on transatlantic airfares? Should the European Union allow the merger? And so forth.

This text is as up-to-date as possible. Although most of the developments in IO occurred during the 1980s, it is surprising how many are still not included in textbooks. Although their original treatment is rather technical, the basic ideas are sufficiently important to warrant a simplified textbook treatment. Examples include the analysis of price competition with capacity constraints, dynamic models of collusive behavior, competitive selection, endogenous entry costs, and vertical restraints.

The text strikes a balance in terms of the relative weight of ideas and examples and of the relative weight of U.S. and non–U.S. examples (the latter mostly European). Some of the examples are presented in separate boxes, of which there are more than thirty in the book; most are introduced in the main text.

Readers should be familiar with basic economics, at the level of Economics 1. Those less familiar with the background concepts necessary for IO can start with chapter 2, a primer in microeconomics that covers the necessary concepts for the purpose of this book. The basic text consists mostly of graphical analysis. This is complemented by a series of supplemental materials (posted on the web) that make more extensive use of algebra and calculus. In this way, the book is sufficiently flexible to accommodate readers of different technical backgrounds. Although the basic text is self-contained without the mathematical sections, readers familiar with algebra and differential calculus will find the supplemental sections helpful.

The exercises at the end of each chapter are divided into "Revision and Practice" exercises and "Extension" exercises. The titles are self-explanatory. Extension exercises typically consider generalizations of results presented in the main text. Exercises are classified from (no asterisk) to ***, according to level of difficulty.

The book's website may be accessed at the following address:

http://luiscabral.org

[c] The number of citations to newspaper articles in this book is approximately equal to the number of citations to scholarly articles.

At this site, readers will find advanced mathematical sections, additional examples and case studies, solutions to exercises, and other materials of interest. The site also includes sections especially designed to help instructors.

ACKNOWLEDGMENTS

Several people helped me with comments on previous drafts of several chapters: Dan Ackerberg (Boston), Mark Armstrong (Nuffield College), Helmut Bester (Berlin), Bruno Cassiman (Pompeu Fabra), Pascal Courty (LBS), Joe Farrell (Berkeley), David Genesove (Jerusalem), Ben Hermalin (Berkeley), Francine LaFontaine (Michigan), Ramiro Tovar Landa (ITAM, Mexico), Frank Mathewson (Toronto), Michael Peitz (Frankfurt), Rob Porter (Northwestern), Michael Riordan (Columbia), John Small (Auckland), John Sutton (LSE), Frank Verboven (Antwerp), Reinhilde Veugelers (Leuven), Len Waverman (LBS), and Peter Zemsky (Insead). To this list, I should add the various anonymous reviewers who also took their time to read previous drafts. I thank them all for their comments and encouragement. Unfortunately, I alone am responsible for remaining errors and omissions.

Some of the exercises at the end of each chapter have been adapted from economics problem sets used at Stanford and Berkeley while I taught there. I thank Severin Borenstein, Tim Bresnahan, Ben Hermalin, Johnatan Leonard, and Carl Shapiro for allowing me to use these.

Finally, I would like to thank all of my graduate and undergraduate students at London Business School, London School of Economics, and Berkeley, who studied from previous versions of the book. Many of the examples contained in the text originated from their suggestions.

PART ONE

INTRODUCTION

CHAPTER 1

WHAT IS INDUSTRIAL ORGANIZATION?

What is industrial organization? It might help to start by clarifying the meaning of "industrial." According to *Webster's New World Dictionary,* "industry" refers to "manufacturing productive enterprises collectively, especially as distinguished from agriculture" (definition 5a). "Industry" also means "any large-scale business activity," such as the tourism industry, for example (definition 4b).

This double meaning is a frequent source of confusion regarding the object of industrial organization. For our purpose, "industrial" should be interpreted in the sense of Webster's definition 4b. That is, industrial organization applies equally well to the steel industry and to the tourism industry; as far as industrial organization is concerned, there is nothing special about manufacturing.

Industrial organization is concerned with the *workings of markets and industries, in particular the way firms compete with each other.* The study of how markets operate, however, is the object of microeconomics; it has been said that "there is no such subject as industrial organization," meaning that industrial organization is nothing but a chapter of microeconomics.[1] The main reason for considering industrial organization as a separate subject is its emphasis on the study of the firm strategies that are characteristic of market interaction: price competition, product positioning, advertising, research and development, and so forth. Moreover, whereas microeconomics typically focuses on the extreme cases of monopoly and perfect competition, industrial organization is concerned primarily with the intermediate case of oligopoly, that is, competition between a few firms (more than one, as in monopoly, but not as many as in competitive markets). For the preceding reasons, a more appropriate definition of the field would be something like "economics of imperfect competition." But the term "industrial organization" was adopted and we are not going to change it.

1.1 AN EXAMPLE

Examples are often better than definitions. In this section, we examine the case of a pharmaceutical firm, Glaxo Wellcome. This example touches on a number of issues of interest to industrial organization. It thus provides a useful introduction to the next section, where we look in a more systematic way at the main questions addressed by industrial organization.

Zantac, the well-known ulcer and heartburn medicine produced by Glaxo Wellcome, is the largest-selling prescription drug in the world, with sales of $1.6 billion. It costs relatively little to produce Zantac. However, the drug is sold at a very high price—that is, the price margin set by Glaxo Wellcome is very high. Why? An obvious answer is that the seller wants to maximize profits and is able to do so by increasing price.

This begs a second question: Why is Glaxo Wellcome able to increase prices without losing a significant number of customers? One possible answer is that there are relatively few substitutes for Zantac. In other words, Glaxo Wellcome has a significant degree of market power in its therapeutical area (ulcers).

If Glaxo Wellcome's Zantac is so successful, why have other firms not imitated it? In part, because Glaxo Wellcome holds a number of patents that protect its blockbuster drug—or better, used to hold. As the following news item suggests, the years of Zantac's exclusivity have gradually come to an end.

Novopharm has won permission from the U.S. Federal Court of Appeals to market a generic version of Glaxo Wellcome's ulcer drug Zantac. The court ruled against Glaxo Wellcome's claim that Novopharm's drug infringes its patent rights.

Glaxo Wellcome is fighting seven other cases against generic versions of Zantac.[2]

A generic is a chemically equivalent drug that is sold under the generic chemical name (ranitidine, in the case of Zantac) rather than under the brand name. Notwithstanding innumerous claims that generic Zantac has the same effect as branded Zantac, the latter still manages to command a large market share while selling at a much higher price. In July 1999, RxUSA, a discount drug seller, was quoting a 30-tablet box of 300-mg Zantac at $85.95. For a little more than that, $95, one could buy a 250-tablet box of 300-mg generic Zantac (ranitidine)—that is, for 7.5 times less per tablet.

Zantac, moreover, is not the only drug in its therapeutical area; there are several alternatives to Zantac, such as SmithKline's Tagamet. Reviews of clinical trials indicate that there is little difference in the success rates of one drug over the others; in other words, one drug can easily be substituted for any of the others. Why then isn't price competition more intense? The following quote offers a possible answer.

BELLYACHE BATTLES. We knew that the battle for your bellyaches would be big, but we had no idea it would be so bloody. Hundreds of millions of dollars are being poured into advertising designed to establish brand loyalty for either Tagamet HB or Pepcid AC. Zantac 75 will join the fray shortly.

These drugs were blockbusters as prescription ulcer treatments; now that they are available over-the-counter for heartburn, their manufacturers have really taken off the gloves.[3]

In other words, advertising plays a very important role. In fact, the advertising budgets of large pharmaceutical companies are of the same order of magnitude as their research budgets. It is not the product's worth that matters, but rather what consumers—and doctors, who frequently act as agents for the final consumer—think the product is worth.

Glaxo Wellcome may complain about the advance of generics producers who are gradually eroding Zantac's market share. But Zantac itself was also, to a great extent, a so-called "me-too" drug. Tagamet, introduced by SmithKline in 1977, was the truly revolutionary drug in ulcer therapy. Zantac, which came a few years later, was sufficiently different that it did not infringe SmithKline's patent rights, but was sufficiently similar to allow Glaxo to compete head-to-head with Tagamet.

At the time of the introduction of Zantac, Glaxo was an independent company. Since then, it has merged with Wellcome to form Glaxo Wellcome. The merger was heralded as the creator of important synergies: It linked up similar avenues of research into prescription drugs previously sought by both companies.

We have very complementary product lines, with Glaxo's strength in respiratory and gastrointestinal medications and Wellcome's in antiviral remedies. So there's the chance for synergies.

More specific synergy has emerged recently. Glaxo has reported that a combination of Wellcome's AZT and Glaxo's 3TC, an anti–hepatitis B drug now in clinical trials, works better against AIDS than either drug alone.[4]

The Glaxo Wellcome Zantac example illustrates several issues that industrial organization is concerned with (see following, in italics): Glaxo Wellcome is a firm that commands a significant degree of *market power* in the anti-ulcer and heartburn therapeutical segment (the relevant *market definition*). Glaxo Wellcome, which resulted from the *merger* of Glaxo and Wellcome, established its position by means of a clever *R&D strategy* that allowed it to enter an industry already dominated by SmithKline; and by means of an aggressive *marketing strategy* that increased its market share. For a time, Zantac's position was protected by *patent rights*. This is no longer the case, meaning that *differentiating the product* with respect to the incoming rivals (generics producers) is now a priority.

In the next section, we consider these and other important issues, organizing them into a set of central questions addressed by industrial organization.

1.2   CENTRAL QUESTIONS

The example in the previous section suggests a number of issues, all centered around the notion of market power. In this section, we attempt to formulate the object of industrial organization in a more systematic way. One can say that the goal of industrial organization is to address the following four questions: (1) Is there market power? (2) How do firms acquire and maintain market power? (3) What are the implications of market power? (4) Is there a role for public policy regarding market power?

Because all of these questions revolve around the notion of market power, it may be useful to make this notion more precise. **Market power** may be defined as the ability to set prices above cost, specifically above incremental or marginal cost, that is, the cost of producing one extra unit.[a] So, for example, if Glaxo Wellcome spends $10 to produce a box of Zantac and sells it for $50, then we say that it commands a substantial degree of market power.

IS THERE MARKET POWER?

Understandably, this is an important question, in fact, a crucial one. If there is no market power, then there is little point in the study of industrial organization.

Over the years, many empirical studies have attempted to measure the extent of market power. Assuming that costs are proportional to output, a good approximation of the extent of market power can be obtained from data on prices, output, and profit rates.[b] One famous study along these lines found that the extent of market power in the American economy is very low, a conclusion that follows from observing relatively low profit rates.[5] This finding is consistent with one of the central tenets of the Chicago school: As long as there is free entry into each industry, the extent of market power is never significant. If a firm were to persistently set prices above cost, a new firm would find it profitable to enter the market and undercut the incumbent. Therefore, market power cannot persist, the argument goes.[c]

Not every economist agrees with this view, either at a theoretical or at an empirical level. From an empirical point of view, an alternative approximation to the value of marginal cost is obtained by dividing the increase in cost from year t to year $t + 1$ by the increase in output in the same period. Based on this approach, a study estimates that prices may be as much as three times higher than marginal cost.[7]

Evidence from particular industries also suggests that the extent of market power may be significant. Take, for example, the U.S. airline industry. A 1996 U.S. government report analyzed average fares in 43 large airports. In ten of these airports, one or a few airlines hold a tight control over takeoff and landing slots. The report found that, on average, fliers were paying 31% more at these airports than at the remaining 33 airports.[8] In other words, the report provides evidence that airlines that manage to control the critical asset of airport access hold a significant degree of market power. More recently, in response to a proposed merger between Staples and Office Depot, the Federal Trade Commission examined prices of office supplies in areas with one, two, or more competing

[a] A rigorous definition of marginal cost and other cost concepts is given in chapter 2. If costs are proportional to output, then marginal cost is equal to unit cost.

[b] The profit rate is given by revenues minus cost divided by costs: $r = (R - C)/C$. If costs are proportional to output, then costs are given by unit cost times output, $UC \cdot Q$ (Q is output), whereas revenues are given by $R = P \cdot Q$ (P is price). It follows that $r = (P - UC)/UC$, so r is a good measure of the gap between price and unit cost (which in this case is also equal to marginal cost).

[c] The theory of **contestable markets** formalizes this argument.[6]

superstores. In areas where only one chain operates, the study concludes, prices can be up to 15% higher than in other areas.

Further examples could be supplied. These would not necessarily be representative of what takes place in every market. To be sure, in a large number of industries, firms hold little or no market power (see chapter 6). The point is that there are *some* industries where market power exists to a significant extent.

How Do Firms Acquire and Maintain Market Power?

Market power translates into higher profits. Creating and maintaining market power is therefore an important part of a firm's value-maximization strategy.

How do firms acquire market power? One way is through legal protection from competition, so that high prices can be set without new competitors entering the market. For example, in the 1960s, Xerox developed the technology of plain-paper photocopying and patented it. Given the legal protection provided by Xerox's patents, it could raise prices to a significant level without attracting competition (see box 16.1).

Firm strategy may also play an important role in establishing market power. Take, for example, the case of the British Sky Broadcasting Group (BSkyB). BSkyB, which broadcasts by satellite, is one of the contenders for the British digital TV market. Its competitors include ONdigital, which is based on terrestrial broadcasting, and a consortium of cable operators. In May 1999, BSkyB introduced an aggressive package that includes a free set-top decoder box, free Internet access, and a 40% discount on telephone charges.[9] The idea of BSkyB's marketing plan is to preempt its rivals by creating an early lead in installed base of subscribers, a lead that eventually will give BSkyB a persistent advantage over the competition. In fact, following the announcement of the new package, BSkyB's shares were up by 12%, whereas ONdigital's slid by 1.8%. Still, there is concern that BSkyB's move may trigger a price war that could hurt the profits of every firm in the industry. In fact, ONdigital reacted by saying it also will provide free set-top boxes.

Creating market power is only one part of the story. A successful firm also must be able to maintain market power. Patents expire. Imitation takes place. Protected industries are deregulated. What can incumbents do to maintain their position? The airline industry provides an example. In 1998, Japan deregulated its airline industry. Skymark Airlines and Air Do entered a market that, for 35 years, was dominated by incumbents Japan Airlines (JAL) and All Nippon Airlines (ANA). The latter have responded to this entry by engaging in an aggressive price war—to the delight of consumers. But the incumbents' response goes beyond this. ANA and JAL carry out maintenance of the upstarts' planes, for there are no independent servicing companies in Japan. There is a fear that ANA and JAL will refuse to service additional planes introduced by Skymark and Air Do and that, eventually, the industry will return to its old ways—high fares and high profits.[10]

In the United States, American Airlines is fighting a court battle over alleged predatory pricing against entrants into its Dallas/Forth Worth hub. American did manage to drive out three competitors: Vanguard, Sun Jet, and Western Pacific. Fares on the route between Dallas and Kansas City, for example, fell from \$108 to \$80 when Vanguard entered the market. After Vanguard exited, American gradually raised fares to up to \$147 in 1996.[11] Joel Klein, head of the antitrust division at the Justice Department, thinks American's strategy achieved more than just driving current rivals out of the market—it also sent a clear signal to potential future entrants: "A sophisticated economist compared it to choosing between two fields with 'no trespassing' signs. One has two dead bodies in it, the other has no dead bodies in it. Which field would you feel ready to trespass?" Reputation for toughness is a reliable means of maintaining a position of market power.

In different chapters of this text, especially in chapters 10 to 17, we examine a large set of strategies that firms may deploy to create and maintain their market power.

WHAT ARE THE IMPLICATIONS OF MARKET POWER?

From the firm's point of view, market power implies greater profits and greater firm value. From a social welfare point of view—or from a policymaker point of view, if we believe policymakers pursue the collective good—the implications are more complicated.

The first-order effect of a high price is a transfer from consumers to firms:[d] For each extra dollar in price, each buyer is transferring one extra dollar to the seller. If regulators put a greater weight on consumer welfare than on profits, then this transfer should be seen as a negative outcome. In fact, antitrust and competition policies are to a great extent motivated by the goal of protecting consumers from these transfers (see the next section).

In addition to a transfer effect, however, a high price implies an inefficient allocation of resources. High airfares, for example, mean that there are potential fliers who refrain from buying tickets even though the cost of carrying them as passengers would be very low. From a social point of view, it would be efficient to fly many of these potential travelers: Although the value they derive from flying is lower than the price (hence they don't fly), that value is greater than the cost of flying (which is much lower than price). The loss that results from the absence of these sales is the *allocative inefficiency* implied by market power.[e]

"The best of all monopoly profits is the quiet life":[12] A monopolist does not need to be bothered with competition. More generally, firms with greater market power have less incentive to be cost efficient, one may argue. For example, European airlines are known to be less efficient than North American airlines. To a great extent, this efficiency gap results from the more intense competition in the North American market. In other words, market power implies a second type of inefficiency—*productive inefficiency,* which we define as the increase in cost that results from market power.[f]

When market power is artificially maintained by government intervention, a third type of inefficiency may result—rent seeking. By **rent seeking,** we mean the unproductive resources spent by firms in attempting to influence policymakers. Consider, for example,

[d] By "first-order," we mean the effect that is quantitatively most significant.

[e] A rigorous definition of this concept is given in chapter 2.

[f] Again, we defer the more precise definition to the next chapter. The discussion of the preceding hypothesis (market power leads to productive inefficiency) can be found in chapter 3.

the following news article regarding AT&T's effort to maintain its position in the cable television market:

> *This summer, AT&T Corp. faced the specter of cities around the country requiring it to open its cable television lines to rival Internet companies. . . . The threat never really materialized. Why not? It depends on whom you ask.*
>
> *AT&T attributes its success to its ability to explain the issues to local officials . . . [Others have a different opinion:] "It comes down to bribery or threats," says Greg Simon, co-director of Opennet Coalition, a group of companies that has launched its own lobbying effort to promote open access.*[13]

Another example of large amounts of resources spent in attempting to influence decision makers is the recent Microsoft case. Netscape, Sun Microsystems, and Microsoft itself would not have spent the vast amounts that they did if the operating system industry were not as profitable as it is—thus the idea that rent seeking is a consequence of market power.

The preceding discussion supports the view that market power, good as it might be for firms, is bad for society. First, it makes firms richer at the expense of consumers. Second, it decreases economic efficiency (allocative and productive efficiency). Third, it induces firms to waste resources to achieve and maintain market power. However, from a *dynamic* point of view, an argument can be made in favor of market power:

> *As soon as we go into the details and inquire into the individual items in which progress was most conspicuous, the trail leads not to the doors of those firms that work under conditions of comparatively free competition but precisely to the doors of the large concerns.*[14]

This argument is one of the central points of the Austrian school, led by its greatest exponent, J. Schumpeter, author of the preceding quotation. It is examined in greater detail in chapter 16. Like the Chicago school, the Austrian school is quite radical when it comes to market power. However, whereas a Chicago economist would argue that market power does not exist, a Schumpeterian would rather say that market power exists—and it's a good thing that it does, for market power is a precondition for technical progress.

IS THERE A ROLE FOR PUBLIC POLICY REGARDING MARKET POWER?

In the context of industrial organization, the primary role of public policy is to avoid the negative consequences of market power. Public policy in this area can be broadly divided into two categories: regulation and antitrust (or competition policy).[g] Regulation refers to the case in which a firm detains monopoly or near-monopoly power, and its actions (e.g., the price it sets) are directly under a regulator's oversight. For example, until 1996,

[g] The terminology "antitrust" is more common in the United States, whereas "competition policy" is the corresponding European term.

AT&T needed regulatory approval each time it changed its long-distance telephone rates. Antitrust policy (or competition policy) is a much broader field. The idea is to prevent firms from taking actions that increase market power in a detrimental way. A couple of examples may help.

In May 1999, shareholders of Exxon Corp. and Mobil Corp. overwhelmingly approved the plan to merge the two companies. Lee Raymond and Lucio Noto, the two chairmen and chief executives, claim that size and market power are not the motivation for the merger, rather it's the cost savings that will be achieved—$2.8 billion annually, they estimate.[15] *"If anybody thinks that this company will have monopolistic power in this environment, when we have less than 4% of world production and 11% of world sales, they are dreaming," says Mr. Noto. U.S. antitrust regulators don't seem to share the same opinion. They are expected to require Exxon and Mobil to divest some refineries and retail outlets, especially in areas where the two companies hold a greater market share.*

On the other side of the pond, U.K.'s Office of Fair Trading (OFT), one of Britain's competition watchdogs, has recently examined the actions taken by The Times *newspaper. Over a period of six or seven years,* The Times *followed very aggressive pricing strategies that nearly drove some of its rivals to bankruptcy. Although the "victims"—The Independent, The Daily Telegraph, and* The Guardian—*survived the alleged predatory attacks,* The Times' *market share increased significantly. The OFT decided not to impose any penalty, as there was insufficient evidence of intent to drive rivals out of the market. However, it mandated* The Times *to inform the OFT of future plans to reduce prices, and to justify the rationale for such price cuts.*

The previous two examples provide an idea of the variety of situations that may fall under the scope of public policy. The overall rationale is to prevent and remedy situations where market power may reach unreasonable levels, to the detriment of society—consumers in particular. Over the course of the next chapters, we examine several other areas for policy intervention motivated by the goal of curbing market power.

As was stated before, the Chicago school takes a very different approach. The claim is that, in a world of free competition, market power is never very significant. In fact, the few situations where market power does exist result precisely from government intervention. In other words, the Chicago school reverses the order of causation: It's not that market power prompts government intervention but the exact opposite—government intervention creates market power, protecting the interests of firms and not those of consumers. As Milton Friedman, a leader of the Chicago school, stated:

Because we all believed in competition 50 years ago, we were generally in favor of antitrust. We've gradually come to the conclusion that, on the whole, it does more harm than good. [Antitrust laws] tend to become prey to the special interests. Right now, who is promoting the Microsoft case? It is their competitors, Sun Microsystems and Netscape.[16]

Industrial Policy

In addition to regulation and antitrust (or competition policy), some countries have followed policies targeted at particular firms or groups of firms. Of particular importance is **industrial policy**. The goal of industrial policy is very different from that of regulation and antitrust. Whereas the latter attempt to promote competition, the former is geared toward strengthening the market position of a firm or industry, particularly with respect to foreign firms. For example, much of the success of Airbus Industrie, a consortium backed by four European countries, is the result of the support it has received from the respective governments over the past three decades. Starting from a market share of less than 10% in the 1970s, Airbus is now competing head-to-head with Boeing, the industry's main competitor.

Industrial policy is generally not favored by economists. In practice, it amounts to governments picking winners among a number of potential firms and industries. But why should governments know better than the market who the promising firms and industries are? A frequent argument in support of industrial policy is the example of MITI, the Japanese Ministry of Industry and Foreign Trade. True, the prowess of the Japanese export sector is a success story and owes a great deal to the role played by MITI. For example, MITI's support was an important factor in the emergence of Japan as a leader in semiconductors. But together with the success stories, there is also a fair number of flops: For example, the 1980's project to develop a "fifth generation computer," which would leapfrog the American competitors, led to very poor results.[17] For these reasons, and as a matter of consistency, when talking about public policy we will restrict our attention in this text to regulation and antitrust.

1.3 COMING NEXT

There are sixteen chapters to come, divided into six different parts.

Parts one and two are introductory in nature. Part one provides some of the tools required for the study of IO: basic microeconomics (chapter 2), a brief introduction to the theory of the firm (chapter 3), elements of game theory (chapter 4). Part two deals with the extreme cases of monopoly and perfect competition. As suggested at the beginning of the chapter, these models are normally treated in microeconomics courses. For readers with a background in the field, some of the material treated in chapters 5 and 6 may already be familiar.

Insofar as industrial organization is the study of imperfect competition, parts three through six constitute the core of the text. Within these, part three plays a central role, as it introduces the basic theory of oligopoly competition—static models (chapter 7), dynamic models (chapter 8), and the study of the relation between market structure and market power (chapter 9). Part four extends the analysis by considering firm strategies beyond the simple pricing and output decisions examined in part three. These include price discrimination (chapter 10), vertical relations (chapter 11), product differentiation (chapter 12), and advertising (chapter 13).

Throughout most of the text, we assume a *given* industry structure. Part five takes one step back and looks at the endogenous determinants of industry structure. We begin by looking at how technology and demand conditions influence market structure (chapter 14), and then move on to examine the role played by firm strategy (chapter 15). Part six concludes the text by focusing on technology-intensive industries. In chapter 16, we study how firms compete in research and development (R&D) and how this influences market structure. In chapter 17, we examine industries where networks and standards play an important role.

A Note on Methodology

Most economists analyze industries with reference to a framework known as the **structure-conduct-performance (SCP) paradigm**.[18] First, one looks at the aspects that characterize market structure: the number of buyers and sellers, the degree of product differentiation, and so forth. Second, one pays attention to the typical conduct of firms in the industry: pricing, product positioning and advertising, and so forth. Finally, one attempts to estimate how competitive and efficient the industry is.

Underlying this system is the belief that there is a causal chain between the preceding different components: Market structure determines firm conduct, which in turn determines industry and firm performance. For example, in an industry with very few competitors, each firm is more likely to increase prices or collude with its rivals. And higher prices have the performance implications discussed in the previous section.

Causality also works in the reverse direction. For example, a firm that does not perform well exits the market, so performance influences market structure. Likewise, a firm may price very low to drive a rival out of the market, an instance where conduct influences structure. Finally, government intervention and basic demand and supply conditions also influence the different components of the SCP paradigm.

In chapters 9 and 14, we look at the relation between the different components in the structure-conduct-performance paradigm. However, most of the text centers on the analysis of firm conduct and how it influences firm and industry performance as well as market structure.[h]

[h] It should be clear that the SCP paradigm is not a model that directly provides answers to the questions listed previously. It is best thought of as a guide that allows one to analyze and understand the workings of different industries. Alternative frameworks have been proposed for the same or similar purposes. Examples include Michael Porter's **five-forces framework** for the analysis of industry competition. The five forces are suppliers, buyers, substitute products, potential entrants, and competition between incumbent firms.[19]

SUMMARY

- Industrial organization is concerned with the workings of markets and industries, in particular, the way firms compete with each other.

- Specifically, the central questions addressed by industrial organization are (1) Is there market power? (2) How do firms acquire and maintain market power? (3) What are the implications of market power? (4) Is there a role for public policy as regards market power?

KEY CONCEPTS

- market power
- efficiency
- regulation
- rent seeking
- antitrust and competition policy
- industrial policy
- Chicago school
- Austrian school
- structure-conduct-performance paradigm

REVIEW AND PRACTICE EXERCISE

1.1* Empirical evidence from a sample of more than 600 U.K. firms indicates that, when controlling for the quantity of inputs (i.e., taking into account the quantity of inputs), firm output is increasing in the number of competitors and is decreasing in market share and industry concentration.[20] How do these results relate to the ideas presented in the chapter?

CHAPTER 2

BASIC MICROECONOMICS

Industrial organization is a branch of microeconomics. Although this text is an introduction to industrial organization, it assumes some familiarity with the basic concepts of microeconomics. In this chapter, we summarize the main points that are relevant for the chapters that follow.

2.1   DEMAND

Before going to watch a movie, you stop at a fast-food pizza store and place your order. Pizza comes at a dollar a slice. Imagine what would be the maximum price you would pay for one pizza slice. Perhaps three dollars, especially if you are very hungry and there is no alternative restaurant in the neighborhood. Consumers don't usually think about this; all they need to know is that they are willing to pay *at least* one dollar for that pizza slice. But, for the sake of argument, let us suppose that the maximum you would be willing to pay is three dollars.

How about a second slice of pizza? Although one slice is the minimum necessary to survive through a movie, a second slice is an option. It makes sense to assume you would be willing to pay less for a second slice than for the first slice; say, one dollar and 50 cents. How about a third slice? For most consumers, a third slice would be superfluous. If you are going to watch a movie, you might not have the time to eat it, anyway. If you were to buy a third slice, you would probably eat only the topping and little else. You wouldn't be willing to pay more than, say, 20 cents. Putting all of this information together, we have your demand curve for pizza. Figure 2.1 illustrates this. On the horizontal axis, we have the number of pizza slices you buy. On the vertical axis, we measure the **willingness to pay**, that is, the maximum price at which you would still want to buy (in dollars).

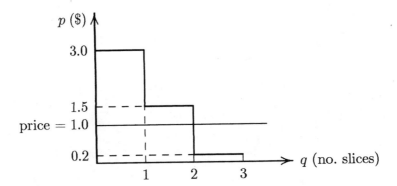

FIGURE 2.1 **CONSUMER DEMAND FOR PIZZA SLICES.**

There are two things we can do with a demand curve. First, knowing what the price is (one dollar per slice), we can predict the number of slices bought. This is the number of slices such that willingness to pay is greater than or equal to price. Or, to use the demand curve, the quantity demanded is given by the point where the demand curve crosses the line $p = 1$: two slices.

A second important use of the demand curve is to measure the consumer's surplus. You would be willing to pay up to three dollars for one slice of pizza. That is, had the price been $3, you would have bought one slice of pizza anyway. In fact, you only paid $1 for that first slice. Because the pizza is the same in both cases, you are $3−$1 = two dollars better off than you would have been had you bought the slice under the worst possible circumstances. Likewise, you paid 50 cents less for the second slice than the maximum you would have been willing to pay.

The sum of these values ($2 plus 50 cents) is your surplus in the consumption of pizza. Specifically, the **consumer's surplus** is the *difference between willingness to pay and price for all units purchased.* In terms of figure 2.1, the consumer surplus would be given by the area between the demand curve and the line $p = 1$.

From the individual demand curves of each consumer, we can obtain the market demand curve. We can to do this in the following way. We start with the highest price for which anyone is willing to buy a slice of pizza and determine how many consumers would be willing to pay that much. Then we consider a slightly lower price and ask the same question again, and so forth. The result is a curve like the one in figure 2.2. Because the number of consumers is typically large, the demand curve is normally a continuous— or nearly continuous—line. As in the case of an individual demand curve, we measure the consumer's surplus as the area between the demand curve and the price level: This is given by area *CS* in figure 2.2.

The preceding analysis suggests that we can read the market demand curve in two ways. Taking q as the dependent variable and p as the independent variable, the demand

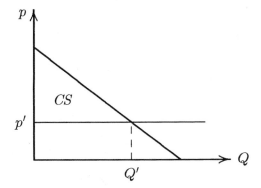

FIGURE 2.2 MARKET DEMAND.

curve $D(p)$ gives the total quantity demanded by consumers for a given price. This is the "normal" way of reading the demand curve. Alternatively, we can take p as the dependent variable and q as the independent variable. Then the demand curve $P(q)$ (the inverse of $D(p)$) gives the willingness to pay for the qth output unit.

DEMAND ELASTICITY

The demand curve indicates the quantity demanded at a given price. One practical question of interest is how much demand changes as a result of a price change. This is given by the slope of the demand curve, that is, the derivative of q with respect to p (that is, the variation of q divided by the variation of p).[a] One problem with measuring the slope of the demand curve is that the value depends on the units used for p and q. For example, the slope of the demand for oil depends on whether we measure price in dollars or in euros, and on whether output is measured in millions of barrels a day or thousands of barrels a day.

The concept of demand elasticity allows the determination of how quantity demanded depends on price in a way that is not dependent on units of measurement. The **demand elasticity** is defined as the percent variation of quantity demanded divided by the percent variation in price. Because quantity demanded decreases when price increases—and vice versa—it is common to append a minus sign before the value of the ratio given earlier. Formally,

$$\epsilon \equiv -\frac{d\,q}{d\,p} \cdot \frac{p}{q} \approx -\frac{\Delta q/q}{\Delta p/p}$$

The first part of the preceding equation gives the exact definition of demand elasticity— the derivative of quantity demanded with respect to price multiplied by the ratio of price over quantity. For small changes in p, a reasonable approximation to the value of the derivative is the ratio between the percent variation in output ($\Delta q/q$) and the percent variation in price ($\Delta p/p$).

[a] The slope of the demand curve is a frequent source of confusion. For historical reasons, the demand curve is represented with price on the vertical axis and quantity on the horizontal axis, even though the "normal" way of reading the demand curve is to think of quantity as the dependent variable. This implies that a greater derivative of q with respect to p—a steeper demand curve— looks flatter under the usual representation of the demand curve.

2.2   COSTS

At the risk of oversimplification, we can think of a firm as a process of transforming inputs into outputs.[b] An interesting question is then how efficiently the firm transforms inputs into outputs. The answer is given by the firm's **cost function**, which shows the total cost of inputs the firm needs to pay to produce output q.

Cost analysis is important for a second reason. Decision making is, to a great extent, a process of comparing costs and benefits. A correct evaluation of the former is therefore the first step in sound economic decision making. We begin this section by listing a number of important cost concepts:

- **Fixed Cost** (FC): The cost that does not depend on the output level.

- **Variable Cost** (VC): That cost which would be zero if the output level were zero.

- **Total Cost** (TC): Sum of fixed cost and variable cost.

- **Average Cost** (AC) (also "unit cost"): Total cost divided by output level.

- **Marginal Cost** (MC): The cost of one additional unit. In other words, total cost of producing $q + 1$ units minus total cost of producing q units of output.[c]

To illustrate all of these cost concepts, let us consider a very simple example, that of a small T-shirt factory. To produce T-shirts, a manager leases one machine at the rate of $20 per week. The machine must be operated by one worker. The hourly wage paid to that worker is as follows: $1 during weekdays (up to 40 hours), $2 on Saturdays (up to 8 hours), and $3 on Sundays (up to 8 hours). Finally, the machine—operated by the worker—produces one T-shirt per hour. Assuming that current output (q) is 40 T-shirts per week, we have the following:

- The fixed cost is given by the machine weekly lease. We thus have FC=$20.

- The variable cost is given by 40 T-shirts times one hour per T-shirt times $1 per hour, which equals $40.

- The average cost is (20+40)/40 = $1.5.

- The marginal cost is $2. In fact, producing the 41st T-shirt in a given week would imply asking the worker to work on Saturday, which would be paid at the hourly rate of $2; moreover, producing a T-shirt requires one hour of work.

[b] In chapter 3, we will go beyond this simplified view of the firm.

[c] Strictly speaking, this is the definition of *incremental cost*. The rigorous definition of *marginal cost* is the derivative of total cost with respect to the output level.

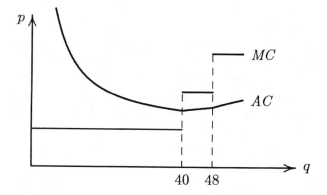

FIGURE 2.3 MARGINAL COST AND AVERAGE COST IN THE T-SHIRT FACTORY EXAMPLE.

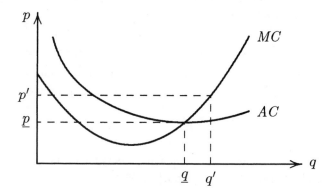

FIGURE 2.4 MARGINAL COST AND AVERAGE COST: GENERAL CASE.

These cost values were computed for a particular value of output. However, both average cost and marginal cost depend on the value of output. By computing the values of marginal cost and average cost for each value of output, we get the marginal cost and average cost functions. Figure 2.3 depicts these functions for the particular case of the T-shirt factory. The more general case is given by figure 2.4. What is the use of all of these cost concepts? Consider the following application. Suppose that Benetton, the sole buyer of T-shirts from our small factory, is offering a price of $p = \$1.8$ per T-shirt. Moreover, Benetton is willing to buy as many T-shirts as the factory wants to sell at that price. Given this offer, should the factory operate on Saturday?

At the current output of $q = 40$ T-shirts per week, average cost is given by \$1.5 (see earlier). This means that, at $p = \$1.8$, the factory is making money. It might seem that, for this reason, it is worth it to operate on Saturdays as well: "If you are making money at the current output level, produce more and you will make more money." As it turns out, this is wrong. What is relevant for the decision of whether or not to operate on Saturdays is the comparison between price and *marginal* cost, not the comparison between price and average cost. Because the marginal cost of operating on Saturdays is \$2, it is not worth pursuing that strategy given that the selling price is only \$1.8.

In other words, although the factory is making money at an output level of $q = 40$ (because price is greater than average cost), profits would be lower if output were increased (because price is lower than marginal cost); the factory would lose money at the margin.[d]

Suppose now that Benetton (still the sole buyer) offers a price $p = \$1.3$ per T-shirt. It can be checked that, no matter what the output level is, price is below average cost. That is, no matter how much the factory produces, it will lose money. In fact, $p < AC$ implies that $p \cdot q < AC \cdot q$, that is, revenues ($p \cdot q$) are less than total cost ($AC \cdot q$). It follows that the optimal decision would be to not produce at all.[e]

To summarize:

> Marginal cost is the appropriate cost concept to decide how much to produce, whereas average cost is the appropriate cost concept to decide whether to produce at all.

The misuse of the concepts of average and marginal cost may easily lead to incorrect decisions, especially in multi-product firms. Box 2.1 presents a particularly extreme case of this.

The T-shirt factory example is a bit special in that there are only two factors of production, and there isn't much flexibility in production. In general, the marginal cost and average cost functions would be continuous functions—or nearly continuous functions—as in figure 2.4. In this figure, $\underline{p}$ denotes the minimum of the average cost function. For prices below this minimum, the firm would prefer not to produce at all. For values of p greater than $\underline{p}$, the optimal output level is given by the marginal cost function. For example, if $p = p'$, then optimal output is q'. More generally, the firm's **supply function** is given by the marginal cost function for values of price greater than the minimum of average cost.[f]

OPPORTUNITY COST AND SUNK COST

Opportunity cost is a very important concept in decision making. Although it is seldom considered explicitly, it is part of everyone's way of thinking and acting. The **opportunity cost** of using time, money, or any resource for a given purpose is defined as *the*

[d] By "lose money at the margin," we mean lose money by producing an additional—a marginal—unit of output.

[e] This comparison is based on the assumption that the firm still has not paid for the weekly lease of the machine. More on this in the next section.

[f] Notice that this characterization is valid only in competitive markets, that is, when the firm is a price taker. More on this in section 2.3.

Box 2.1 Fixed Costs, Variable Costs, and the Shut-Down Decision[21]

Consider a firm that sells red pens and blue pens. Each pen costs 15¢ in labor and raw materials. In addition, each pen must be run through a machine that costs $1000 a day to use, regardless of how many pens it processes. The first 5000 red pens are sold at 30¢ per pen; additional red pens can be sold at 20¢ each. Blue pens, in contrast, are sold for 25¢ per pen regardless of quantity. The total capacity of the machine is 8000 pens per day (red or blue).

Initially, the firm was selling 5000 red pens and 3000 blue pens for a daily profit of $50 (5000 red pens at a 15¢ margin plus 3000 blue pens at a 10¢ margin minus $1000 of fixed cost). At this point, an accounting consultant was hired to create a system of cost allocation across product lines. The consultant decided to allocate shared overheads (fixed costs) on the basis of output. Thus the $1000 running costs of the machine were allocated as $625 to the red-pen production line and $375 to the blue-pen production line. Based on this new accounting system, the blue-pen production line showed a loss of $75 a day (3000 pens at a 10¢ margin minus a fixed cost of $375). Accordingly, the firm decided to shut down the blue-pen production line and increase the output of red pens to 8000 per day. Revenues were now 5000 pens at 30¢ plus 3000 pens at 20¢, or $2100. However, total costs were 8000 times 15¢ (labor and raw materials) plus $1000 (to run the machine), implying a loss of $100 per day. The firm thus decided to shut down the red-pen production line.

In summary, the firm started with a profit of $50 and ended up with a profit of zero. What went wrong in the shutdown decisions? How do the concepts presented in section 2.2 apply to this problem?

foregone benefit from not applying the resource in the best alternative use. The concept of opportunity costs is also referred to as **imputed cost**.

Suppose that retail company X owns some real estate in downtown Chicago and is planning to use it to open a new store. In comparing the costs and benefits of opening a new store, should the real estate cost be included? Because company X already owns the property, no actual payment will be made. However, by opening a store on that piece of real estate, the benefit of using it for a different purpose is foregone. Such alternative benefit, which might be the revenue from leasing or selling the property, is the opportunity cost of allocating it to the new store. From an economic point of view, such *opportunity costs should be taken into account when making a decision.* Box 2.2 presents a real-world example where the concept of opportunity cost plays a central role.

Another important cost concept in economics—and particularly in industrial organization—is that of sunk cost. A **sunk cost** is an investment in an asset with no

BOX 2.2   REDSYKE QUARRY[22]

One of Britain's main freeways, the M6, was upgraded in 1986. The work required the extended use of a quarry, the Redsyke quarry, to provide stone for the freeway's foundations. The quarry's extension, in turn, took place over an 8-hectare plot that was being used for grazing. The owner of the plot did not own the rights to the minerals—the quarry did—but was entitled to a compensation for the loss of use of the land.

The quarry offered the farmer a compensation based on the value of the land used. Neighboring farmland had recently been sold for £233 (approximately $370). The quarry offered £775 (approximately $1240), adding that this was a particularly generous offer as the quarry would need the land for only a few years, whereas the value £233 corresponded to freehold.

The farmer's lawyer suggested that he could demand a higher offer based on an estimate of foregone earnings. The farmer was making an average profit of £84 per cow and £12 per sheep per year. The loss of the grazing land forced the farmer to reduce his cattle and sheep flocks by 20 and 100, respectively. This adds up to a total loss of £2880 per year, or £11,520 after four years (the estimated period of full use of the land by the quarry). This value exceeds the quarry's offer of £6200 (8 times £775).

The farmer further argued that this value *underestimated* his loss. The argument is that the average profit includes many fixed costs that he'd need to incur even with a lower animal count. His lawyer, in turn, cautioned that the value may have *overestimated* the relevant loss because the profit estimate was gross of income tax. The quarry, on the other hand, maintained that the farmer was using the wrong basis for compensation.

No agreement was reached. The dispute was taken to arbitration and the tribunal ruled in favor of the quarry. The farmer did not accept the decision, however, and decided to take the case to court.

What would your evidence be if you were called as an expert witness trained in economics?

alternative use (also referred to as "specific asset"). In other words, a sunk cost is an asset with no opportunity cost.

From the point of view of decision making, the main point is that *sunk costs should not be taken into consideration in economic decisions.* For example, suppose that a dam was built at a very high cost. At the time of construction, the estimated cost of energy produced by the dam was 10. Of these 10, 5 correspond to the amortization of the initial investment, and the remaining 5 to variable, recurrent cost.

Now suppose that, after completion of the investment, a new energy source is discovered that allows the production of energy at a cost of 7 per unit. Should the dam be abandoned in favor of this alternative energy source? At first, it might seem that the answer is "yes." In fact, the unit cost of energy produced by the dam is 10, whereas the new energy source costs only 7 per unit. However, half the cost of 10 corresponds to a sunk cost: The cost of construction of the dam has already been incurred. For the purpose of actual decision making, the only relevant cost is the variable cost of 5 per unit. Because this is lower than 7, the dam should be used instead of the new energy source.

To summarize:

> Economic decisions should be based on the concept of **economic cost**. Economic cost differs from actual expenditures in that it includes opportunity costs that do not correspond to actual expenditures, and excludes expenditures that correspond to sunk costs.

It should be noted that whether a given cost is or is not sunk depends crucially on the time frame under consideration. Let us go back to the T-shirt factory example. It was said that, if price were $1.3, then the firm should shut down, for average cost is less than price. In computing average cost, we have included the weekly machine lease. Suppose, however, that news of the $1.3 price arrived on Monday, shortly after the weekly lease had been paid. Should the firm shut down immediately? The answer is "no": Because the weekly lease is now a sunk cost, only the cost of labor should be included. Taking only this cost into account, average cost is $1 up to 40 units, so the firm should remain active until the end of the week. Only then, when the decision of whether to renew the lease comes up, should the firm shut down. More generally, it is important to distinguish between the short-run average cost function (that excludes costs that are sunk in the short run) and the long-run average cost function (that includes all recurrent costs). Which one to use depends on the nature of each particular decision.

To conclude this subsection, it should be noted that, in the context of industrial organization, sunk costs are also important for their strategic commitment value. For example, in industries where production capacity is largely a sunk cost, making such an investment may provide a credible commitment to be an industry player. The idea of commitment value is introduced in chapter 4. A specific application in an industrial organization context is presented in chapter 15.

ECONOMIES OF SCALE AND ECONOMIES OF SCOPE

A good characterization of the typical cost function in a given industry goes a long way toward enabling understanding of the structure of that industry. Why is it that the plumbing services industry is very fragmented (many small firms), whereas the newspaper publishing industry is very concentrated (few large ones)? To a great extent, this is driven by the technologies of plumbing and newspaper publishing: In newspaper publishing, size is an important factor for efficiency, whereas the same is not true of plumbing services.[8]

The concept of scale economies captures this idea. We say there are **scale economies** if average cost declines with output. If average cost is constant, we have **constant returns to scale**. Finally, **diseconomies of scale** is the case where average cost is increasing in output. Empirically, a common pattern is for average cost to be decreasing up to output level q'; constant for $q' < q < q''$; and increasing for output levels greater than q''—a "saucer-shaped" AC curve. Thus, we have economies of scale for low output levels, diseconomies of scale for high output levels, and constant returns to scale for intermediate output levels.

A related cost concept is that of **minimum efficient scale** (MES), the lowest output level at which the minimum average cost is attained (q' in our example). The value of MES is frequently expressed as a fraction of market size, Q. A large value of MES/Q indicates that, on account of technological considerations, one should expect a relatively concentrated industry. So, for example, the value of MES/Q for newspaper publishing is likely to be greater than that for plumbing services.

Finally, another important related cost concept is that of economies of scope. We say there are **economies of scope** when the cost of producing outputs q_1 and q_2 together is lower than the cost of doing so separately. Formally, this corresponds to the equation $C(q_1, q_2) < C(q_1, 0) + C(0, q_2)$. For example, it is cheaper to have one firm fly New York to London and London to New York than to have two separate firms, one flying New York to London only, and the other one flying London to New York only.

2.3 PROFIT MAXIMIZATION

In the previous section, we looked at some general principles of economic decision making. Let us now consider, more specifically, the firm's choice of price and output. First notice that, even if in practice the firm decides on price and not on output level, we can—and will—treat its decision as one of choosing output level. In fact, given a demand curve $D(p)$, an output level implies a given price level. It is as if the firm were choosing an output level and then setting the price that would lead to that output level.

Firm profits are given by revenue, $R(q)$, minus cost, $C(q)$, where q is the output level: $\Pi(q) = R(q) - C(q)$. What is the optimal output level, that is, the output level that maximizes profit? It may help to think of the profit function as a "hill" in a graph where output is on the horizontal axis and profit on the vertical axis. The profit-maximizing output level then corresponds to the top of the hill. One important characteristic of the top of a hill is that the terrain is level. In terms of the graph, this means that the *slope*

[8] The study of the relation between cost functions and market structure is continued in chapters 3 and 14.

of the hill is zero, that is, *the derivative of profit with respect to output is zero.*[h] If that were not the case, one could always climb up a little more, implying that we would not be at the top of the hill. Because profit is given by $\Pi(q) = R(q) - C(q)$, saying that the derivative of profit is zero amounts to saying that the derivative of revenue minus cost is zero, that is, the derivative of revenue is equal to the derivative of cost:

$$MR = MC, \tag{2.1}$$

where MR is **marginal revenue**, the derivative of revenue with respect to output; and MC is marginal cost, a concept introduced in the previous section. In summary:

> Profit maximization implies that marginal revenue is equal to marginal cost.

Revenue is given by price times output: $R = pq$. Marginal revenue, the derivative with respect to output level q, is then $MR = (d\,p/d\,q)q + p$. Simplifying this expression, we get

$$MR = p\left(1 - \frac{1}{\epsilon}\right), \tag{2.2}$$

where ϵ is the value of demand elasticity, a concept introduced in Section 2.1. Because ϵ is greater than zero, it follows that *marginal revenue is lower than price.* Why? When a firm sells an extra unit of output, it gets p for it. However, to sell the extra unit of output, the firm must lower price by an amount that is greater the lower the demand elasticity. Increasing output by one unit thus implies that all units of output are sold at a lower price, a negative effect that makes marginal revenue less than the revenue from the marginal unit of output.

In competitive markets, firms are price takers: Increasing price would imply a drop in firm demand from a positive value to zero; decreasing price would imply an increase in demand from a small positive value (the firm's demand) to a large positive value (the market demand). In other words, a competitive market is the limit case when the firm's demand curve has an infinite elasticity: Even the smallest change in price would imply a very large change in (firm) demand. From equation (2.2) and the fact that ϵ is infinity, it follows that marginal revenue is equal to price. This is intuitive: In a competitive market, each (small) firm can sell as much as it wants at the ongoing market price; consequently, the revenue from selling an extra unit equals the price at which that unit is sold: $MR = p$. Finally, (2.1) implies that, *in competitive markets, firms set output at the level where price is equal to marginal cost,* as we saw in section 2.2.

[h] Zero derivative is a *necessary*, but not sufficient, condition. In fact, at the bottom of a valley, the terrain is also level. If a function is concave, however, then a zero derivative implies that the point is a maximum. The condition that the derivative is equal to zero is referred to as the *first-order condition for profit maximization.*

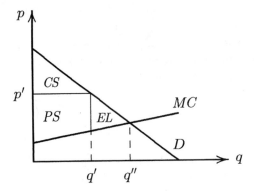

FIGURE 2.5   CONSUMER'S SURPLUS, PRODUCER'S SURPLUS, AND EFFICIENCY LOSS.

2.4   EFFICIENCY

In section 2.1, we introduced the concept of consumer's surplus. Let us restate it using a different example. Consider a potential buyer of a personal computer who purchases an iMac. The consumer would be willing to pay up to $3000 for the iMac. In fact, the price is only $1600. This means the consumer receives a surplus of 3000 minus 1600, or $1400, from purchasing the computer—the consumer's surplus.

But it is not only the consumer who gains from the transaction. In fact, one of the fundamental points of economics is that (free) exchange leads to bilateral gains from trade. Specifically, although Apple Computer is getting $1600 for the sale of an iMac, in fact it costs the firm only, say, $900 to produce it. This implies that the firm receives a variable profit of 1600 minus 900, or $700, per unit that it sells. This variable profit we refer to as **producer's surplus**.

If we aggregate the surplus of each consumer who makes a purchase, we obtain the total consumer's surplus. As we saw before, this is measured by the area between the demand curve and price (see figure 2.2). Likewise, we can aggregate the seller's surplus for all units sold, obtaining the total producer's surplus.[i] This is measured by the area between price and marginal cost, as illustrated in figure 2.5.[j] Finally, by adding the consumer's and producer's surpluses we obtain the **total surplus**. The total surplus measures the increase in value that results from production and trade. In other words, it measures how much better the economy is because of the existence of the particular industry under analysis.

Just as justice is to law and health is to medicine, efficiency is a central concept in economics, in particular, microeconomics. In this section, we introduce three notions of efficiency used in industrial organization (and, more generally, in microeconomics). The first concept is that of allocative efficiency. As the name suggests, **allocative efficiency** requires that resources be allocated to their most efficient use. Let us go back to the

[i] There is an interesting analogy between producer's and consumer's surplus. The firm's marginal cost can be interpreted as its "willingness to sell" of each unit, that is, the minimum the firm would require to sell that unit. This is analogous to the consumer's willingness to pay. One important difference, however, is that the firm's "willingness to sell" is normally increasing when the number of units increases, whereas the consumer's willingness to pay is decreasing.

[j] As suggested previously, the producer's surplus is nothing but the value of variable profit. By subtracting fixed costs from producer's surplus, we get net profits.

iMac example and assume that figure 2.5 provides a good approximation of this market. At price p', only q' units are sold. This implies that there are a number of disgruntled consumers who would be willing to buy an iMac but do not because the price is too high—specifically, those consumers whose willingness to pay is less than p'. Of these consumers, some would be willing to pay more than it costs to produce an iMac. This is specifically the case of the consumers of units q' to q'', where q'' is the output level such that marginal cost equals willingness to pay.

If resources were allocated from other sectors in the economy to the production of more iMacs, allocative efficiency would be greater.[k] That is, for each additional iMac produced, the additional gain (measured by the consumer willingness to pay) would be greater than the additional cost (measured by the production marginal cost).

From the preceding analysis, we may conclude that *allocative efficiency is measured by total surplus*. In fact, so long as the demand curve (willingness to pay) lies above the marginal cost curve ("willingness to sell"), an increase in output increases the total surplus, as well as allocative efficiency. Maximum allocative efficiency is achieved at the point where marginal cost equals willingness to pay (output level q'' in figure 2.5). By comparison with this point of maximum allocative efficiency, the case when price is p' represents an efficiency loss given by the area EL, the difference in total surplus between output levels q'' and q'.

EFFICIENCY IN PRODUCTION

It is often said that the European airline industry is less efficient than its American counterpart. This was especially true before the European deregulation process was initiated in the early 1990s, but it is still true to a great extent. In part, inefficiency results from the fact that fares are higher in Europe than they are in the United States. This is the type of inefficiency we considered previously—allocative inefficiency. However, a second source of inefficiency is that productivity is lower in Europe than in the United States.

Low productivity results from using excessive amounts of certain inputs or from using the wrong input mix. In graphical terms, low productivity implies a high marginal cost curve. This is illustrated in figure 2.6, where two marginal cost curves are depicted. The area between the high marginal cost curve and the low marginal cost curve, which we assume is the lowest possible, measures the extent of inefficiency in production associated with MC_H. More generally, **productive efficiency** refers to how close the actual production cost is to the lowest cost achievable. X-inefficiency, which refers to the phenomenon of waste in production, and efficiency in the choice of production techniques also fall under the general concept of productive efficiency.

DYNAMIC EFFICIENCY

So far, we have been concerned only with static efficiency effects. In some cases, however, dynamic efficiency is at least as important as static efficiency. Take the case of personal computers. More important than having the right number of iMacs produced and sold,

[k] This assumes that there are resources elsewhere in the economy yielding a small gain at the margin. This is an implicit assumption when we consider a *partial equilibrium* analysis, as we do most of the time in industrial organization. A rigorous treatment of the concept of allocative efficiency would require a *general* equilibrium analysis. For most practical applications, however, partial equilibrium analysis provides a reasonable first-order approximation.

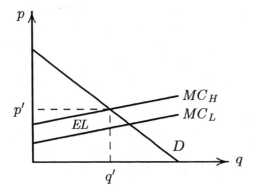

FIGURE 2.6 INEFFICIENCY IN PRODUCTION.

and more important than efficiency in the production of the iMac, is the fact that the iMac exists at all. More generally, the rate of introduction of new products, as well as improvement in the production techniques of existing ones, is the result of an industry's **dynamic efficiency**.

Unlike allocative efficiency and efficiency in production, dynamic efficiency is difficult to measure. It is even more difficult to compare the relative magnitude of static inefficiencies (allocative or productive) with that of dynamic inefficiencies. For this reason, industrial economists have tended to pay more attention to static efficiency than to dynamic efficiency.

The bias toward static efficiency is not innocuous. As we will see in the following chapters, different forms of industrial organization imply different levels of static and dynamic efficiency. Moreover, there is often a trade-off between static and dynamic efficiency. In particular, it can be shown that perfect competition implies the maximum allocative and productive efficiency possible, that is, the maximum static efficiency. However, this may not count much in industries where technology evolves rapidly, such that static efficiency is a second-order effect with respect to dynamic efficiency.

We can summarize the preceding discussion by stating:

> *Allocative efficiency* requires that output be at the appropriate level. *Productive efficiency* requires that such output be produced in the least expensive way given the available set of technologies. *Dynamic efficiency* refers to the improvement over time of products and production techniques.

One should also mention that, strictly speaking, productive efficiency and dynamic efficiency are also components of allocative efficiency. For example, a firm that lacks efficiency in production is a firm that fails to allocate the right mix of production inputs, which in turn results in a higher cost than the minimum necessary for producing a given output level. However, we normally use the term allocative efficiency—or simply efficiency—to characterize the output level as it compares to the surplus-maximizing output level. More on this in chapters 16 and 17.

Summary

- The demand curve measures the quantity demanded at a given price. It also measures the willingness to pay for the qth unit consumed.

- Consumer's surplus is the difference between willingness to pay and the price actually paid. Producer's surplus is variable profit. Total surplus, the measure of allocative efficiency, is the sum of the consumer's and producer's surpluses.

- Marginal cost is the appropriate cost concept to decide how much to produce, whereas average cost is the appropriate cost concept to decide whether to produce at all.

- Opportunity costs should be taken into account in economic decisions. By contrast, sunk costs should not be part of the cost-benefit balance.

- Optimal output is obtained by equating marginal revenue to marginal cost. In competitive markets, this corresponds to equating price to marginal cost.

- Economic efficiency may be divided into static efficiency (allocative and productive) and dynamic efficiency.

Key Concepts

- willingness to pay
- consumer's surplus, producer's surplus, and total surplus
- demand elasticity
- average cost and marginal cost
- economies of scale, economies of scope, and minimum efficient scale
- opportunity cost and sunk cost

- economic cost

- marginal revenue

- allocative efficiency and productive efficiency

- static efficiency and dynamic efficiency

REVIEW AND PRACTICE EXERCISES

2.1 "A price-taking firm selling in a market with a price greater than the firm's average cost should increase its output level." Comment.

2.2* Consider the following values of the price elasticity of demand:

Cigarettes	0.5
U.S. luxury cars in the United States	1.9
Foreign luxury cars in the United States	2.8

Based on these values, provide an estimate of the impact on revenues of a 10% increase in the price of each of the above three products.

2.3 You own and operate a facility located in Taiwan that manufactures 64-megabyte dynamic random-access memory chips (DRAMs) for personal computers (PCs). One year ago you acquired the land for this facility for $2 million, and used $3 million of your own money to finance the plant and equipment needed for DRAM manufacturing. Your facility has a maximum capacity of 10 million chips per year. Your cost of funds is 10% per year for either borrowing or investing. You could sell the land, plant, and equipment today for $8 million; you estimate that the land, plant, and equipment will gain 6% in value over the coming year. (Use a one-year planning horizon for this problem.)

In addition to the cost of land, plant, and equipment, you incur various operating expenses associated with DRAM production, such as energy, labor, raw materials, and packaging. Experience shows that these costs are $4 per chip, regardless of the number of chips produced during the year. In addition, producing DRAMs will cause you to incur fixed costs of $500,000 per year for items such as security, legal services, and utilities.

a. What is your cost function, $C(q)$, where q is the number of chips produced during the year?

Assume now that you can sell as many chips as you make at the going market price per chip of p.

b. What is the minimum price, p, at which you would find it profitable to produce DRAMs during the coming year?[23]

2.4   Consider the following 1988 data on the costs of a Sprinter (Class 150/2) train:[24]

Capital cost	525,000
Annual costs (per unit)	
Depreciation (20 years)	26,300
Overhaul and maintenance	32,600
Stabling and cleaning	9,400
Total annual cost of	
2 drivers	20,200
2 guards	15,600
Mileage costs of rolling stock (per unit mile)	
Maintenance	0.15
Fuel	0.126

(Notes: [1.] Annual costs assume a 90,000-mile benchmark annual use. [2.] There are 145 seats on the train.)

Based on these numbers, answer the following questions:

a. What is the average cost per train mile?

b. What is the average cost per passenger mile? (*Note:* the average number of passengers during this time period was 45.)

c. What is the marginal cost per train mile?

d. What is the marginal cost per passenger mile?

2.5   You are considering opening your own restaurant. To do so, you will have to quit your current job, which pays $46 thousand per year, and cash in your life savings of $200 thousand, which have been in a certificate of deposit paying 6% per year. You will need this $200 thousand to purchase equipment for your restaurant operations. You estimate that you will have to spend $4 thousand during the year to maintain the equipment so as to preserve its market value at $200 thousand. Fortunately, you own a building suitable for the restaurant. You currently rent out this building on a month-by-month basis for $2500 per month. You anticipate that you will spend $50 thousand for food, $40 thousand for extra help, and $14 thousand for utilities and supplies during the first year of operations. There are no other costs involved in this business. What are the economic costs of operating the restaurant during the first year? In other words, what level of revenues will you need to achieve in the first year to make the first year profitable in an economic sense?[25]

2.6   Eurotunnel, the company that owns the tunnel linking England and France, earned an operating profit of £46 million during the first six months of 1998. However, subtracting interest payments (mainly from the construction of the tunnel), its bottom line was a loss of £130 during the same period.[26] Is it optimal to continue operating the tunnel, given all these losses?

2.7*   1998 was a turning point for Old McDonald's farm. Until then, the farm produced unprocessed tomato exclusively, selling its 100,000 tons for a profit margin of $2.1/ton. In January 1998, however, Old McDonald decided to start exporting processed tomato (tomato pulp) to Europe. At that time, the price of tomato pulp was $6/ton. In order to produce tomato pulp, Old McDonald bought a machine capable of processing 100,000 tons per year. The machine cost $200,000 and was paid for with retained earnings that had been earning an 8% rate of return. This machine has a useful lifetime of 2 years. The market value of this machine drops to $50,000 after one year of use (and zero after two years of use). In addition to the machine cost, there is a $2.2/ton harvesting and processing cost (mostly labor cost).

a. Determine Old McDonald's average cost, marginal cost, and profit margin.

A few months later, things turned bad for Old McDonald. In December 1998, the European Union increased its tariffs on imported tomato pulp, implying that the net price received by American exporters is now only $5/t. It is not expected that this price will change in the future. One accountant consulting for Old McDonald stated that as margins have declined drastically the farmer had better sell the machine right away and go back to producing unprocessed tomato. Old McDonald is trying to decide whether to take this consultant's advice.

b. What would you advise Old McDonald to do?

c. Would your advice change if the price of unprocessed tomato were expected to be $0.50/ton higher than described? Explain why or why not.

2.8*   Las-O-Vision is the sole producer of holographic TVs, 3DTVs. The daily demand for 3DTVs is $D(p) = 10200 - 100p$. The cost of producing q 3DTVs per day is $q^2/2$ (note this implies that $MC = q$).

a. What is Las-O-Vision's total revenue schedule?

b. What is Las-O-Vision's marginal revenue schedule?

c. What is the profit-maximizing number of 3DTVs that Las-O-Vision must produce each day? What price does Las-O-Vision charge per 3DTV? What is its daily profit?[27]

2.9* You own a private parking lot near University of California at Berkeley with a capacity of 600 cars. The demand for parking at this lot is estimated to be $Q = 1000 - 2p$, where Q is the number of customers with monthly parking passes and p is the monthly parking fee per car.

a. Derive your marginal revenue schedule.

b. What price generates the greatest revenues?

Your fixed costs of operating the parking lot, such as the monthly lease paid to the landlord and the cost of hiring an attendant, are $25,000 per month. In addition, your insurance company charges you $20 per car per month for liability coverage, and the City of Berkeley charges you $30 per car per month as part of its policy to discourage the use of private automobiles.

c. What is your profit-maximizing price?[28]

EXTENSION EXERCISE

2.10** You are one of two companies bidding to try to win a large construction project. Call your bid B. You estimate that your costs of actually performing the work required will be $800,000. You are risk neutral.[l] You will win if and only if your bid is lower than that of the other bidder. You are not sure what bid your rival will submit, but you estimate that the rival's bid is uniformly distributed between $1 million and $2 million.[m] What bid should you submit?

[l] We say that an agent is risk neutral if he or she is indifferent between receiving 100 for sure and receiving 0 or 200 with probability 50% each. Generally, a risk-neutral agent cares only about the expected value of each outcome.

[m] By "uniformly distributed between a and b," we mean that all values between a and b are equally likely.

CHAPTER **3**

THE FIRM

The firm is the central element in any industry. It is therefore surprising that much of the analysis in industrial organization treats the firm as a sort of "black box": a function that produces outputs from inputs in a predictable, mechanistic way, that way being profit maximization. Is this a realistic assumption? Do firms indeed maximize profits? We start this chapter by examining the arguments in favor of and against this basic assumption. We then move on to two other important questions regarding the nature of the firm: (1) What determines the firm's boundaries, both horizontally and vertically? (2) Why are firms different?[a]

3.1 DO FIRMS MAXIMIZE PROFITS?[29]

One of the beliefs of the "black-box" view of the firm is that firms maximize profits. How realistic is this assumption? In most modern corporations, management is separated from ownership, that is, the recipients of the firm's profits (owners) are not the agents whose decisions ultimately determine the firm's profit level (managers). Although we would expect managers to be motivated by the firm's success, profits are only one aspect of firm success. In general, the managers' objectives differ from those of the shareholders. Does this imply that the assumption of profit maximization is wrong?

INTERNAL DISCIPLINE
Recognizing this difference in objectives, one thing shareholders can do is to appoint a manager with a contract that induces the latter to act in the former's interest. However, many corporations are owned by a large number of small shareholders. This considerably

[a] The first two questions—profit maximization and firm boundaries—have been extensively examined by industrial economists over the past two decades or so. Much less so the third question, although one can argue that it is the most important of the three questions.

decreases the incentives for shareholders to act: The effort necessary to determine how to instruct managers is very high compared with the benefits a small shareholder would gain from better management.[b]

Boards of directors are supposed to solve, or at least attenuate, this problem. The board of directors has the discretion to appoint managers, fire them, set their salaries, correct them when and if necessary, and in doing so, to represent the interests of shareholders. But just as managers don't necessarily have the same objectives as shareholders, so too boards of directors may have goals other than maximizing shareholder value. In fact, anecdotal evidence suggests that boards of directors are seldom independent and frequently defend the interests of the CEOs, not those of the shareholders. On the independence of boards of directors, see box 3.1.

Even if shareholders can and are willing to control managers, there is still the problem that managers normally know better than shareholders what is best for the firm. In other words, there is a problem of asymmetric information. **Agency theory** is the area of economics that deals with this class of strategic interaction, that is, a principal who wants an agent to act in the principal's interest but who possesses less information than the agent.

A critical result from agency theory is that, if the agent—the manager, in our case—is risk neutral, then the optimal solution is for the manager to pay the shareholders an initial fee and then retain all of the profits—a management buyout.[c] In other words, the optimal solution is for ownership and management to be unified. Under this solution, the manager's decisions will be optimal from the owner's point of view.

The reason we observe separation between management and ownership is that managers are subject to financial constraints, and, more importantly, managers are risk averse. The optimal contract between shareholders and managers is therefore one that balances the benefits from insuring the manager against risk, on the one hand, and the benefits from providing the manager with the right incentives, on the other hand. At one extreme, we have the solution outlined earlier (shareholders sell the firm to the manager), which entails maximum risk and maximum incentives. At the opposite extreme, we have a fixed wage or salary, which entails minimum risk and minimum incentives.

From a theoretical point of view, the optimal contract—the optimal balance between risk and incentives—is typically very complicated. Moreover, the solution turns out to depend greatly on the precise assumptions regarding the environment in which the firm operates. For these reasons, it is not surprising that actual contracts tend to be simple: Normally, they are a combination of fixed wage and a profit-contingent compensation (e.g., stock options). Such contracts attenuate the agency problem of separation between ownership and management, but clearly do not completely solve it.

LABOR MARKET DISCIPLINE

Even if shareholders are unable to "punish" a manager for poor performance, the manager cannot avoid the negative reputation that follows poor performance. Because managers

[b] This argument suggests that monitoring by shareholders is more frequent when ownership is more concentrated. However, anecdotal evidence suggests that German banks, which own significant shares in other firms, do not monitor CEOs to any significant extent. Evidence from the U.S. banking industry (see box 3.2) also suggests that shareholder concentration has little effect.

[c] We say that an agent is risk neutral if he or she is indifferent between receiving 100 for sure and receiving 0 or 200 with probability 50% each. Generally, a risk-neutral agent cares only about the expected value of each outcome. By contrast, a risk-averse agent would prefer a safe outcome to another outome with the same expected value but greater risk. In the preceding example, a risk-averse agent would prefer 100 for sure to the 0 or 200 gamble.

Box 3.1   What Determines the Composition of Boards of Directors?[30]

Boards of directors are composed of "insider" and "outsider" members. Insiders are those who either work in the company (as managers) or are otherwise close to the CEO. Outsiders are those who bear no relation to the company or the CEO. A board of directors is more independent the lower the number of insiders it includes. What determines the relative composition of boards of directors? Consider the following empirical results:

Likelihood of Departure of a Board Member

Explanatory variable	Insider	Outsider
CEO has held his or her job for less than 4.5 years*	.257	***
Recent stock market return**	−.493	***
Stock market return lagged one year**	−.287	−.308

* Difference with respect to CEOs with more than 10 years of tenure

** Compared to other firms in same industry

*** Not significantly different from zero

So, for example, if the CEO has held his or her job for less than 4.5 years, then the probability that an insider member leaves the board of directors is 25.7% higher than if the CEO has held his or her job for longer than 10 years.

Broadly speaking, these results indicate that the probability that board changes take place is lower the better the firm's past performance has been (third row)—"if it ain't broke don't fix it." In particular, the probability that *insider* members exit the board is decreasing with respect to the firm's past performance (second row). Moreover, the probability of an insider exit also declines as the CEO's tenure increases (first row).

These results are consistent with the following interpretation. The independence of the board of directors is the result of a negotiation process between the CEO and the shareholders. As the CEO's tenure increases and the firm's performance improves, the CEO's bargaining power increases and he or she is able to "impose" on shareholders a less independent board of directors.

don't stay with the same firm forever, they are interested in creating a reputation for being good managers. This reputation effect may help to provide managers with the proper incentives.

PRODUCT MARKET DISCIPLINE

Product market competition may also contribute to aligning shareholders' and manager's objectives. The idea is that, when product market competition is intense, firms cannot survive unless they maximize profits. Under intense market competition, if the manager does not actively seek to maximize firm profits, the likelihood that the firm goes out of business—and the manager loses his or her job—is high. We should therefore expect the manager to put more effort into profit maximization in a situation where product market competition is tougher.[d]

A second reason why product market competition may increase the incentives for profit maximization is that competitors provide useful signals about the firm's productivity. In other words, they reduce the shareholders' informational disadvantage with respect to the manager. In a monopoly situation, a manager can always blame poor performance on a number of exogenous industry factors. Such strategy is less effective when there are competing firms and the latter perform well.

CAPITAL MARKET DISCIPLINE

One of the most compelling arguments in favor of the assumption of profit maximization is the role played by capital markets, namely the role played by mergers and acquisitions. The idea is quite simple: If a manager does not maximize profits, then the value of the firm is lower than its potential. In that case, a **raider** could acquire the firm, change management to maximize profits, and thus make a capital gain.[e] Notice that, for the disciplining effect of takeovers to occur, it is not necessary for takeovers to actually take place—it is sufficient for the *threat* of takeover to be in place. Box 3.2 presents some empirical evidence from the U.S. banking industry.

Although the effect of takeovers on efficiency is a controversial issue (not all empirical evidence points in the same direction), the anecdotal evidence suggests that firms that are efficient are less prone to be taken over than less efficient firms. An example of this (also from the banking industry, this time the U.K. banking industry) is given by Lloyds TSB. Lloyds TSB has acquired the reputation for being the most thrifty large bank in the world. For example, the bank normally will not refund taxi fares to its employees, expecting them to choose cheaper means of transportation. As a result of this cost-cutting policy, Lloyds received a net return of 33.5% in the first half of 1999; although it is only the 40th largest bank in terms of assets, it ranks fourth in stock-market value. In addition to its outstanding financial performance,

Lloyds's efficiency lends it a certain takeover protection. That's because it would be hard for a raider either to fault management's performance or to make a case for a lot of cost cuts in the event of a merger. Indeed, both of the bidders for [a rival bank] . . . have pointed to Lloyds as an example of what they would like to achieve.[31]

[d] Exercise 3.10 formalizes this intuition.

[e] This argument is not free from criticism, however. If a raider can change management in a profit-increasing way, why can't current shareholders do the same? One possible answer is that the raider possesses information that shareholders do not: For example, the raider may be a firm from the same or a related industry. But if that is the case, then why would an individual shareholder sell his or her shares to the raider? Surely, if the raider is to change management and increase firm value, then the optimal strategy is to not sell the shares.

Box 3.2 Firm Monitoring and Firm Performance: Evidence from the U.S. Banking Industry[32]

Banking regulation varies considerably throughout the United States. In particular, some states are "takeover-friendly," whereas others are not. This fact provides a natural experiment on the effect of takeovers and the threat of takeover on firm performance. Based on a cross section of states, the following results are obtained:

Explanatory variable	Explained variable	
	Profit margin	Stock options*
Takeovers are allowed in state (1 if yes, 0 if no)	.112	−4.77
Percentage of shares controlled by five largest nonmanagement shareholders	**	**
Common stock and stock options owned by most highly paid officer divided by annual cash compensation	−.023	

* Same as third variable in row
** Not statistically different from zero

The .112 coefficient indicates that, everything else constant, profit margins are 11.2% higher in states that allow takeovers than in states that do not. This result suggests that the threat of takeovers significantly disciplines managerial behavior. Shareholder concentration, by contrast, seems to have no effect on firm profitability (second row variable). Performance pay (third variable in row) has a *negative* effect on profitability (the opposite of what one might expect), although the effect is low in absolute value. Finally, stock options are less common in states where takeovers are allowed (second coefficient in first row). This suggests that stock options are a "substitute" for takeovers as a mechanism to induce value-maximizing behavior on the part of managers.

In summary:

> Although management and ownership are normally separated, there are reasons to believe that deviations from profit maximization cannot be too large. These reasons include management incentive contracts, labor market discipline, product market discipline, and capital market discipline.

The precise meaning of "not too large," that is, the extent to which profit maximization is a good approximation, remains an unresolved empirical question.

3.2 WHAT DETERMINES THE FIRM'S BOUNDARIES?

Why should firms be of the size they are; why not smaller or bigger? What does economic analysis have to say about firm size? It may be useful to divide this into two questions: (1) What determines the horizontal extension of the firm? and (2) What determines the degree of vertical integration? By horizontal extension, we mean how much of a given product a firm produces and how many different products it offers. By vertical integration, we mean how many stages of the production process take place within the firm. So, for example, by acquiring Skoda, SEAT, and Bentley, Volkswagen increased its horizontal stretch. Volkswagen would increase the degree of vertical integration if it were to acquire a tire manufacturer, for example (tires being one of the inputs into car manufacturing).

The horizontal size of the firm is largely determined by costs. If average cost is U-shaped and there is free entry into the industry, then firms tend to produce at the level where average cost is minimized (see chapter 6). For example, there is an optimal size for a cement plant that minimizes cost. Plants of much smaller size or much larger size would probably incur a higher average cost and be unable to survive for very long.

We should point out, however, that empirical evidence suggests average cost functions are U-shaped with a flat bottom (that is, "saucer"-shaped). This implies that there is a range of output levels that attain the minimum average cost. In other words, costs may not entirely allow us to pin down the size of the firm.

The problem becomes more complicated if we consider the distinction between plant and firm. Production costs are related to plant operation. Suppose there is a unique output level that minimizes plant average costs, and that a given firm owns two plants. It is possible that the firm's average cost may be similar to the average cost of a firm owning one plant only. If so, then multi-plant firms create a new dimension of indeterminacy of firm size.

THE VERTICAL BOUNDARIES OF THE FIRM[33]

Perhaps a more interesting question regarding the boundaries of the firm is: Why do we observe a great degree of vertical integration in some industries and very little in others? One of the most important decisions that a firm has to make is how to obtain its inputs—to make or to buy? In other words, to use the market (vertical separation) or to use the firm (vertical integration). The degree of vertical integration in a given industry results from the aggregation of these micro decisions at each stage of the production process. Understanding the nature of the make-or-buy decision contributes to understanding the nature of the firm as well as the determinants of industry structure.

Let us start with a classical case study, that of Fisher Body.[34] Very early in the twentieth century, the technology of car manufacturing moved from wooden bodies to metal ones. Unlike wooden bodies, metal bodies require large investments that are *specific* to the particular body that is manufactured. That is, once those investments are made, the resulting assets can be used only for the specific type of car body for which they were created. We refer to these as **specific assets**.

During the wooden-body era, General Motors (GM) bought car bodies from Fisher Body on a short-term contractual basis. It was clear to both parties that the switch to metal bodies, with all the specific investments it involved, opened the door for opportunistic behavior: Once Fisher Body invested in machinery for producing GM bodies, it would have a high cost of switching to a different car manufacturer. It becomes, as it were, "hostage" to GM. For this reason, the parties agreed in 1919 to enter into a long-term (ten year) contractual relationship.

As it turned out, the demand for GM cars was significantly higher than was initially forecasted. General Motors was unhappy with the contractual terms and proposed to renegotiate them. The strain in the contractual relationship between Fisher Body and GM was further increased when the latter urged the supplier to locate its plant next to GM's plant. The idea was that, with adjacent plants, there would be no need for loading docks. This would be a much more efficient solution, but it would further increase the scope for **post-contractual opportunism**: The cost for Fisher Body to switch to a different buyer would now be enormous. Understanding that this situation could not be sustained, General Motors decided to acquire Fisher Body, which it gradually did between 1924 and 1926.

The GM–Fisher Body example suggests a theory of when firms would be vertically integrated, that is, when transactions should take place inside the firm and not through the market. The key elements of this theory are the occurrence of specific assets and the resulting possibility of opportunistic behavior once those investments are made—a situation known as the **hold-up problem**.

But vertical integration does not solve all incentive problems. In fact, it creates new incentive problems. Continuing with the example of GM, one of the problems the company has experienced in the past is that of quality. Typically, parts supplied by GM subsidiaries are of lower quality than those supplied by independent suppliers. An independent supplier knows that by lowering quality it risks losing its business with GM, whereas a GM affiliate expects to continue supplying GM cars even if quality standards slip away.

The extremes of both complete vertical integration and complete vertical separation imply incentive problems. Sometimes, the optimal solution may lie between the extremes. One possibility is that of **tapered integration**, whereby a given input is bought from an affiliated supplier *and* from an independent one. Examples of tapered integration include soft-drink bottling for the Coca-Cola and Pepsi-Cola companies, and crude oil supply to oil refineries. A second intermediate system is that of **franchising**, a system that has been used in a variety of industries, from fast food (e.g., McDonald's) to designer clothing (e.g., Stefanel). Franchising combines the benefits of vertical integration (specific investments are paid by the mother company) with the benefits of vertical separation (franchisees retain most of the profit they generate, and thus have strong incentives to be efficient). Finally, the Japanese system of supplier contracting also corresponds to an intermediate solution: The firm and its suppliers establish a long-term, informal relationship that falls short of full-scale vertical integration but goes a long way toward providing suppliers with the right incentives to invest in assets specific to the relationship with their customers.

In other words, the definition of the boundaries of the firm is far from being a well-defined problem with a well-defined answer. For example, is a Japanese *keiretsu* a firm in and of itself?[f] Probably not—but neither is it a simple collection of independent firms. Moreover, it is not uncommon to find two otherwise similar firms that differ significantly in the way they are organized. For example, the Italian clothes manufacturer Benetton depends largely on a franchise system for its retail sales, whereas Spanish rival Zara is completely vertically integrated. Examples like this suggest that there may be other determinants of firm structure that lead some firms to choose differently from others.

Although the problems of firm organization are extremely complex, both in theory and in practice it seems safe to summarize that:

> The horizontal boundaries of the firm are largely determined by cost considerations. The vertical boundaries result from the balance between investment incentives (specific assets) and performance incentives.

3.3 WHY ARE FIRMS DIFFERENT?

Casual observation of the real world reveals that firms are different from each other—different in size, different in scope, and so forth. In particular, we observe that firm performance (e.g., profit rate) varies enormously across firms. This is not entirely surprising if we consider that different firms may be of different size or may belong to different

[f] A *keiretsu* is a family of firms, typically from related industries, with cross shareholdings.

industries. Why should we expect the profit rate of Boeing to be the same as that of a coffee shop?

Empirical observation suggests, however, that firms in the same industry and of similar dimension also perform differently. Only 20% of the variance in firm profit rates can be explained by variables that relate to firm size, the type of industry in which the firm operates, and so forth.[35] Moreover, differences in firm performance seem to be very persistent. If we consider a set of firms that are twenty or more years old, we will observe that the firms that are more profitable today were, on average, more profitable twenty years ago.[36]

What is the source of the 80% variability in firm performance that is left to explain? Why do some firms hold a **sustained competitive advantage**? It may be useful to consider the analogy with car racing, say, Formula One racing. It is quite clear that there are significant differences between different Formula One teams and that those differences seem to persist from race to race. One rather obvious explanation is that not all drivers have the same ability. In order for the Arrows team to match the performance of the Ferrari team, the former might need to recruit a driver like Michael Schumacher (who currently races for Ferrari). But such a driver seems difficult to find. Likewise, in the world of business, there may be **impediments to imitation** that allow some firms to perform persistently better than others.[37] An obvious limit to imitation is imposed by legal restrictions. In the late 1960s and early 1970s, Xerox was the dominant player in the photocopier industry thanks to its patent on plain-paper photocopying. Once Xerox started licensing its technology, differences in performance with respect to competitors decreased significantly (see box 16.1).

If Arrows cannot find another Michael Schumacher, it should at least be able to imitate the best features of the Ferrari car (which seems to be faster than the Arrows car, even controlling for driver skills). Most features of Formula One cars are not patented. However, there are so many aspects in which a Ferrari car differs from an Arrows car that it would be difficult to understand which one is responsible for the superior performance of the former. Something similar occurs with firms as organizations. Toyota's superior performance in the world of car manufacturing—in particular, Toyota's superior procurement system—involves so many different aspects that it is difficult to pin down what the crucial success factors are. In fact, the problem is even more serious: Most of the features of any given organization are *tacit knowledge*, capabilities that are developed by experience and are rarely written down—capabilities that are difficult to express formally as an algorithm or a set of rules. Even if one of Toyota's rivals were to recruit some key employees and managers from Toyota, the latter would have difficulty in expressing their knowledge in the new organization, let alone implementing it. In strategy jargon, we say this is a case of **causal ambiguity**.[38]

Finally, even at times when the Ferrari car/driver duo is slower than rivals, the Ferrari team has frequently turned out to be the winner. In these cases, success is largely due to **strategy**. Strategic or tactical decisions include whether to stop once or twice during the race, when to stop, what kind of tires to use, and so forth, as well as how to react to the choices made by rival teams. In a business context, there are many dimensions in which strategy can have a lasting effect on firm performance: entry timing, capacity expansion, mergers and acquisitions, technological improvement, special contracts with customers and suppliers, not to mention pricing and advertising.

Of the three sources of competitive advantage listed earlier, strategy is the one we will focus on in the next chapters. This is not to say that the other ones are not important. In fact, the argument can be made that firm **culture**—a broad term that would include tacit knowledge and other aspects that cannot be easily imitated—is an equally important source of competitive advantage. But the focus of industrial organization is on competition between firms, rather than the way a firm is internally organized.

In conjunction with all of the preceding factors, one must also stress the importance of **history** in determining firm performance—and the persistence of differences in firm performance. Let us consider an example. The 1970s witnessed a fierce battle for dominance of the market for wide-body aircraft. The three competitors were Boeing (B747), McDonnell Douglas (DC10), and Lockheed (L1011). One important aspect of competition in this industry is the existence of a steep **learning curve**: The more aircraft units a firm produces, the lower the cost of producing an aircraft unit. The name of the game is therefore to move down the learning curve as quickly as possible.

At the start, all three competitors maintained approximately equal market shares. But in the early 1970s, Lockheed's main engine supplier, Rolls-Royce, began to experience a series of technical and financial difficulties. This slowed up Lockheed's production rate and the speed at which it moved down the learning curve. When Lockheed tried to get back in the game, later in the 1970s, it was too late, for its competitors were already too competitive. McDonnell Douglas did not have much better luck. A series of crashes in 1980 severely hit consumer confidence in the DC10. In retrospect, this turned out to be a statistical coincidence, not the result of a fundamental problem with the DC10 design. But again, by the time McDonnell Douglas tried to get back in the game it was too late: Boeing had reached a superior degree of cost efficiency that allowed it to enjoy a sustainable competitive advantage over its rivals.[8]

This is an example of historical events (Rolls-Royce's problems in the early 1970s, the DC10 crashes in 1980) having an effect that lasted beyond the time when they occurred. In particular, these are events that, together with the learning curve phenomenon, have led to a persistent asymmetry in firm performance between Boeing and its rivals. Other examples could be found, involving network externalities (see box 17.1), consumer switching costs, and so forth. The point is that sometimes, instead of insisting on a general theory of firm heterogeneity, one simply has to accept the importance that history has in shaping an industry and the firms that it includes. We resume this discussion in chapter 14. For now, we conclude with a summary of the preceding main points:

[8] Eventually, Lockheed exited from the civil aviation market. McDonnell Douglas, in turn, was acquired by Boeing. In the meantime, Airbus appeared in the scene, challenging Boeing's dominance.

> Firm performance varies a great deal. Firms are different because of impediments to imitation, causal ambiguity, firm strategy, and historical events.

SUMMARY

- Although management and ownership are normally separated, there are reasons to believe that deviations from profit maximization cannot be too large. These reasons include management incentive contracts, labor market discipline, product market discipline, and capital market discipline.

- The horizontal boundaries of the firm are largely determined by cost considerations. The vertical boundaries result from the balance between investment incentives (specific assets) and performance incentives.

- Firm performance varies a great deal. Firms are different because of impediments to imitation, causal ambiguity, firm strategy, and historical events.

KEY CONCEPTS

- principal-agent problem
- specific assets
- hold-up problem
- tapered integration
- franchising
- sustainable competitive advantage
- impediments to imitation
- causal ambiguity

REVIEW AND PRACTICE EXERCISES

3.1 Explain why the assumption of profit maximization is or is not reasonable.

3.2 Should firms have their own catering services, or should they outsource this? What are the main trade-offs? Are there other alternatives in addition to "make or buy"?

3.3 Two parts in an automobile taillight are the plastic exterior cover and the light bulb. Which of these parts is a car company more likely to manufacture in-house? Why?[39]

3.4   There are three main suppliers of commercial jet engines—Pratt & Whitney, General Electric, and Rolls-Royce. All three maintain extensive support staff at major (and many minor) airports throughout the world. Why doesn't one firm service each airport? Why do all three feel they need to provide service and support operations worldwide themselves? Why don't they subcontract this work? Why don't they leave it entirely to the airlines?[40]

3.5   The Smart car was created as a joint venture between Daimler-Benz AG and Swatch Group AG. Although Micro Compact Car AG (the name of the joint venture) was originally jointly owned, in November of 1998 Daimler-Benz AG took complete control by buying Swatch's share.[41] The deal put an end to a very stressed relationship between Daimler and Swatch. What does section 3.2 suggest as to what the sources of strain might have been?

3.6   Why do television networks have a few "owned and operated" stations but work through independent affiliates in most geographic locations?[42]

3.7   Empirical evidence from franchise retailing suggests that, even when stores have similar characteristics, the mother company resorts to a mix between company-owned stores and franchised ones.[43] How can this be justified?

3.8   The U.K. Body Shop franchise network consists of three types of stores—franchised, company-owned, and partnership stores. All stores that are distant from headquarters by more than 300 miles are franchised. More than half of the company-owned stores are within 100 miles of headquarters.[44] How can you explain these facts?

3.9   Explain why Intel has maintained, if not increased, its competitive advantage with respect to rivals. Indicate the explanatory power of the different causes considered in the text (impediments to imitation, causal ambiguity, strategy, history).

EXTENSION EXERCISES

3.10[***]   Suppose that a firm's profits are given by $\pi = \alpha + \phi(e) + \epsilon$, where α denotes the intensity of product market competition, e effort by the manager, and ϵ a random shock. The function $\phi(e)$ is increasing and concave, that is, $\phi' > 0$ and $\phi'' < 0$.

For the firm to survive, it must be that profits are greater than $\underline{\pi}$. The manager's payoff is $\beta > 0$ if the firm survives and zero if it is liquidated, that is, if profits fall short of the minimum target. The idea is that if the firm is liquidated, then the manager loses his job and the rents associated with it.

Suppose that ϵ is normally distributed with mean μ and variance σ^2, and that $\mu > \underline{\pi}$. Show that increased product market competition (lower α) induces greater effort by the manager, that is, $\frac{\partial e}{\partial \alpha} < 0$.

CHAPTER 4

GAMES AND STRATEGY

Suppose *Time* magazine is considering which cover story to publish next week. It has two alternatives to choose from: "Impeachment" or "Financial Crisis." "Impeachment" seems like a more promising story. However, it is important for *Time* not to choose the same cover story as *Newsweek*: If that happens, some readers will buy only one of the magazines when they would otherwise buy both. *Time's* dilemma illustrates the problem of *interdependent decision making*: *Time's* payoff depends not only on its own decision but also on the decision of another player, *Newsweek*. Economists study this type of situations as if Time and Newsweek were playing a *game*.

A **game** is a stylized model that depicts situations of strategic behavior, where the payoff for one agent depends on its own actions *as well as* on the actions of other agents.[a] The application of games to economic analysis is not confined to magazine publishing. For example, in a market with a small number of sellers, the profits of a given firm depend on the price set by that firm *and on the prices set by the other firms*. In fact, price competition with a small number of firms is a typical example of the world of strategic behavior—and games.

This type of situation introduces a number of important considerations. The optimal choice for a player—its optimal strategy—depends on what it conjectures other players will choose. Because other players act in a similar way, when conjecturing what another player will do, I may need to conjecture what the other player's conjecture regarding my behavior is, and so forth. Moreover, if the strategic interaction evolves over a number of periods, I should also take into account that my actions today will have an impact on the other players' conjectures and actions in the future. In summary, payoff interdependence introduces a host of possibilities for strategic behavior—the object of game theory.

[a] Economic analysis is based on the use of models. Models are stylized representations of reality, highlighting the particular aspects of interest to the economist. Being stylized is not a defect of models, rather it should be seen as a requisite: A completely realistic model would be as useful as an exceedingly detailed description of reality, so complete that the main points would be buried in the abundance of detail.
It is important to keep this point in mind when judging the very stylized nature of some of the games and models presented in this text.

Player 2

	L	R
T	5 ⟋ 5	6 ⟋ 3
B	3 ⟋ 6	4 ⟋ 4

FIGURE 4.1 THE "PRISONER'S DILEMMA" GAME.

The basic element of game theory and applied game theory is a game. A game consists of a set of players, a set of rules (who can do what when), and a set of payoff functions (the utility each player gets as a result of each possible combination of strategies).

Figure 4.1 depicts a simple game that exemplifies these ideas. There are two players, Player 1 and Player 2. Player 1 has two possible strategies, T and B, which we represent as Player 1 choosing a row in the matrix represented in figure 4.1. Player 2 also has two possible strategies, L and R, which we represent by the choice of a column in the matrix in figure 4.1.

For each combination of strategies by each player, the respective matrix cell shows the payoffs received by each player—In the lower left corner, the payoff received by Player 1; in the top right corner, the payoff received by Player 2. A crucial aspect of a game is that each player's payoff is a function of the strategic choice by *both* players. In figure 4.1, this is represented by a matrix, where each cell corresponds to a combination of strategic choices by each player. This form of representing games is know as **normal form**. Later, we will consider alternative forms of representing a game.

One final point regarding the game in figure 4.1 is the rule that both players choose their strategies simultaneously. This rule will be maintained throughout a number of examples in this chapter—in fact, throughout much of the book. It is therefore important to clarify its precise meaning. In real life, very seldom do agents make decisions at *precisely* the same time. A firm will make a strategic investment decision this week, its rival will do it in two or three weeks' time. So how realistic is the assumption that players choose strategies at the same time?

Suppose that there is an observation lag, that is, suppose that it takes time for Player 2 to observe what Player 1 chooses; and likewise, suppose that it takes time for Player 1 to observe what Player 2 chooses. In this context, it is perfectly possible that players make decisions at different times but that, when decisions are made, neither player knows what the other player's choice is. In other words, *it is as if players were simultaneously choosing strategies*. Naturally, the assumption that observation lags are long does not always hold true. Later in the chapter, we will find examples in which an explicit assumption of sequential decision making is more appropriate.

4.1   DOMINANT STRATEGIES, DOMINATED STRATEGIES, AND NASH EQUILIBRIUM

Consider again the game in figure 4.1. What strategies would we expect players to choose? Take Player 1's payoffs, for example. If Player 1 expects Player 2 to choose L, then Player 1 is better off by choosing B instead of T. In fact, B would yield a payoff of 6, which is more than the payoff from T, 5. Likewise, if Player 1 expects Player 2 to choose R, then Player 1 is better off by choosing B instead of T. In this case, payoffs are given by 3 and 4, respectively. In summary, Player 1's optimal choice is B, *regardless of what Player 2 chooses*.

Whenever a player has a strategy that is strictly better than any other strategy regardless of the other players' strategy choices, we say that the first player has a **dominant strategy**. If a player has a dominant strategy and if the player is rational, we should expect the player to choose the dominant strategy. Notice that all we need to assume is that the player is rational. In particular, we do not need to assume that the other players are rational. In fact, we do not even need to assume that the first player knows the other players' payoffs. The concept of dominant strategy is very robust.

The structure of the game presented in figure 4.1 is common in economics, in particular in industrial organization. For example, strategies T and L might correspond to setting a high price, whereas B and R correspond to setting a low price. What is interesting about this game is that (1) both players are better off by choosing (T, L), which gives each player a payoff of 5; (2) however, Player 1's dominant strategy is to play B and Player 2's dominant strategy is to play R; (3) for this reason, players choose (B, R) and receive (4, 4), which is less than the desired outcome of (5, 5).

In other words, the game in figure 4.1, which is commonly known as the **prisoner's dilemma**, depicts the *conflict between individual incentives and joint incentives.* Jointly, players would prefer to move from (B, R) to (T, L), boosting payoffs from (4, 4) to (5, 5). However, individual incentives are for Player 1 to choose B and for Player 2 to choose R. Chapters 7 and 8, show that many oligopoly situations have the nature of a "prisoner's dilemma." They also discuss in what ways firms can escape the predicament of lowering payoffs from the "good" outcome (5, 5) to the "bad" outcome (4, 4).

Consider the game in figure 4.2. There are no dominant strategies in this game. In fact, generally, few games have dominant strategies. We thus need to find other ways of "solving" the game. Consider Player 1's decision. Although Player 1 has no *dominant* strategy, Player 1 has a *dominated* strategy, namely M. In fact, if Player 2 chooses L, then Player 1 is better off by choosing B than M. The same is true for the cases when Player 2 chooses C or R. That is, M is dominated by B from Player 1's point of view (in fact, M is also dominated by T).

More generally, we define a **dominated strategy** as one whose payoff is inferior to that of another strategy, *regardless of what the other player does*. The idea is that, if a given player has a dominated strategy and that player is rational, then we should expect the player not to choose such a strategy.

Player 2

		L		C		R	
			1		0		1
	T	1		2		1	
			0		1		0
Player 1	M	0		0		0	
			1		0		2
	B	2		1		2	

FIGURE 4.2   ITERATED ELIMINATION OF DOMINATED STRATEGIES.

The concept of dominated strategies has much less "bite" than that of dominant strategies. If Player 1 has a dominant strategy, we know that Player 1 will choose that strategy; whereas if Player 1 has a dominated strategy all we know is that it will not choose that strategy; in principle, there could still be a large number of other strategies Player 1 might choose. Something more can be said, however, if we successively eliminate "dominated" strategies. (The justification for quotation marks around "dominated" will soon become clear.)

Suppose that Player 2 knows Player 1's payoffs and, moreover, knows that Player 1 is rational. By the reasoning presented above, Player 2 should expect Player 1 not to choose M. *Given that Player 1 does not choose M,* Player 2 finds strategy C to be "dominated" (by either L or R). Notice that, strictly speaking, C is not a dominated strategy: If Player 1 chooses M, then C is better than L or R. However, C is dominated by L or R *given* that M is not played by Player 1.

We can now take this process one step further. If Player 1 is rational, believes that Player 2 is rational, and believes that Player 2 believes that Player 1 is rational, then Player 1 should find T to be a "dominated" strategy. In fact, if Player 2 does not choose C, then strategy T is "dominated" by strategy B: If Player 2 chooses L, Player 1 is better off with B (2 instead of 1); if Player 2 chooses R, again, Player 1 is better off with B (2 instead of 1). Finally, if we take this process one step further, we conclude that L is a "dominated" strategy for Player 2. This leaves us with the pair of strategies (B, R).

As in the first example, we have reached a single pair of strategies, a "solution" to the game. However, the assumptions necessary for iterated elimination of dominated strategies to work are much more stringent than in the case of dominant strategies. Whereas in the first example, all we needed to assume was that players are rational, utility-maximizing agents, we now assume that each player believes that the other player is rational and believes that the other player believes that the first player is rational.

To understand the importance of these assumptions regarding rationality, consider the simple game in figure 4.3. Player 2 has a dominated strategy, L. In fact, it has a

Player 2

		L	R
		0	1
T	1	1	
		0	1
B	−100		2

Player 1

FIGURE 4.3 DUBIOUS APPLICATION OF DOMINATED STRATEGIES.

dominant strategy, too (*R*). If Player 1 believes that Player 2 is rational, then Player 1 should expect Player 2 to avoid *L* and instead play *R*. Given this belief, Player 1's optimal strategy is to play *B*, for a payoff of 2. Suppose, however, that Player 1 entertains the possibility, unlikely as it might be, that Player 2 is not rational. Then *B* may no longer be its optimal choice, because there is a chance of Player 2 choosing *L*, resulting in a payoff of −100 for Player 1. A more general point is that, in analyzing games,

> It is not only important whether players are rational. It is also important whether players believe the other players are rational.

Consider now the game in figure 4.4. There are no dominant or dominated strategies in this game. Is there anything we can say about what to expect players will choose? In this game, more than in the previous games, it is apparent that each player's optimal strategy depends on what the other player chooses. We must therefore propose a conjecture by Player 1 about Player 2's strategy and a conjecture by Player 2 about Player 1's strategy.

Player 2

		L	C	R
		1	2	1
T	2	2	0	
		1	1	1
M	1	1	1	
		1	0	2
B	0	0	2	

Player 1

FIGURE 4.4 NASH EQUILIBRIUM.

Player 2

		L		R	
			2		0
Player	T	1		0	
1			0		1
	B	0		2	

FIGURE 4.5 MULTIPLE NASH EQUILIBRIA.

A natural candidate for a "solution" to the game is then a situation whereby (1) players choose an optimal strategy given their conjectures of what the other players do, and (2) such conjectures are consistent with the other players' strategy choices.

Suppose that Player 1 conjectures that Player 2 chooses R, and that Player 2 conjectures that Player 1 chooses B. Given these conjectures, Player 1's optimal strategy is B, whereas Player 2's optimal strategy is R. In fact, if Player 1 conjectures that Player 2 chooses R, then B is Player 1's optimal choice; any other choice would yield a lower payoff. The same is true for Player 2. Notice that, based on these strategies, the players' conjectures are consistent: Player 1 expects Player 2 to choose what in fact Player 2 finds to be an optimal strategy, and vice versa. This situation is referred to as a Nash equilibrium.[45]

Although the concept of Nash equilibrium can be defined with respect to conjectures, it is simpler—and more common—to define it with respect to strategies.

> A pair of strategies constitutes a **Nash equilibrium** if no player can unilaterally change its strategy in a way that improves its payoff.

It can be checked that, in the game in figure 4.4, (B, R) is a Nash equilibrium and no other combination of strategies is a Nash equilibrium. For example, (M, C) is not a Nash equilibrium because, given that Player 2 chooses C, Player 1 would rather choose T.

Contrary to the choice of dominant strategies, application of the Nash equilibrium concept always produces an equilibrium.[b] In fact, there may exist more than one Nash equilibrium. One example of this is given by the game in figure 4.5, where both (T, L) and (B, R) are Nash equilibria. A possible illustration for this game is the process of standardization. Strategies T and L, or B and R, correspond to combinations of strategies that lead to compatibility. Both players are better off under compatibility. However, Player 1 prefers compatibility around the standard $(B\text{-}R)$, whereas Player 2 prefers compatibility over the other standard. More generally, this example is representative

[b] For the sake of rigor, two qualifications are in order: First, existence of Nash equilibrium applies to most games but not to all. Second, equilibria sometimes require players to randomly choose one of the actions (mixed strategies), whereas we have considered only the case when one action is chosen with certainty (pure strategies).

of a class of games in which (1) players want to coordinate, (2) there is more than one point of coordination, and (3) players disagree over which of the two coordination points is better. (Problems of standardization are further discussed in chapter 17.)

4.2 SEQUENTIAL GAMES: COMMITMENT AND BACKWARD INDUCTION[c]

In the previous section, we justified the use of simultaneous-choice games as a realistic way of modeling situations where observation lags are so long that it is as if players were choosing strategies simultaneously. When the time between strategy choices is sufficiently long, however, the assumption of sequential decision making is more realistic. Consider the example of an industry that is currently monopolized. A second firm must decide whether or not to enter the industry. Given the decision of whether or not to enter, the incumbent firm must decide whether to price aggressively or not. The incumbent's decision is taken *as a function* of the entrant's decision. That is, first the incumbent observes whether or not the entrant enters, and then decides whether or not to price aggressively. In such a situation, it makes more sense to consider a model with sequential rather than simultaneous choices. Specifically, the model should have the entrant—Player 1—move first and the incumbent—Player 2—move second.

The best way to model games with sequential choices is to use a game tree. A **game tree** is like a decision tree except that there is more than one decision maker involved. An example is given in figure 4.6, where strategies and payoffs illustrate the case of entrant and incumbent described earlier. In figure 4.6, a circle denotes a **decision node**. The game starts with decision node 1. At this node, Player 1 (entrant) makes a choice between e and $\bar{e}$, which can be interpreted as "enter" and "not enter," respectively. If the latter is chosen, then the game ends with payoffs $\Pi_1 = 0$ (entrant's payoff) and $\Pi_2 = 50$ (incumbent's payoff). If Player 1 chooses e, however, then we move on to decision node 2. This node corresponds to Player 2 (incumbent) making a choice between r and $\bar{r}$, which can be interpreted as "retaliate entry" or "not retaliate entry," respectively. Games which, like figure 4.6, are represented by trees are also referred to as games in **extensive form**.[d]

This game has two Nash equilibria: $(e, \bar{r})$ and $(\bar{e}, r)$. Let us first check that $(e, \bar{r})$ is indeed a Nash equilibrium, that is, that no player has an incentive to change its strategy given what the other player does. First, if Player 1 chooses e, then Player 2's best choice is to choose $\bar{r}$ (it gets 20, it would get −10 otherwise). Likewise, given that Player 2 chooses $\bar{r}$, Player 1's optimal choice is e (it gets 10, it would get 0 otherwise).

Let us now check that $(\bar{e}, r)$ is an equilibrium. Given that Player 2 chooses r, Player 1 is better off by choosing $\bar{e}$: this yields Player 1 a payoff of 0, whereas e would yield −10. As for Player 2, given that Player 1 chooses $\bar{e}$, its payoff is 50, regardless of which strategy it chooses. It follows that r is an optimal strategy (though not the only one).

[c] Sections 4.2 and 4.3 cover relatively more advanced material, which may be skipped in a first reading of the book.

[d] From this and the previous sections, one might erroneously conclude that games with simultaneous choices must be represented in the normal form, and games with sequential moves in the extensive form. In fact, both simultaneous and sequential choice games can be represented in both the normal and extensive forms. However, for simple games such as those considered in this chapter, the choice of game representation considered in the text is the more appropriate.

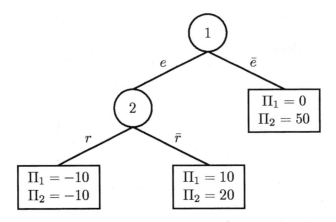

FIGURE 4.6 EXTENSIVE-FORM REPRESENTATION: THE SEQUENTIAL-ENTRY GAME.

Although the two solutions are indeed two Nash equilibria, the second equilibrium does not make much sense. Player 1 is not entering because of the "threat" that Player 2 will choose to retaliate. But, is this threat credible? If Player 1 were to enter, would Player 2 decide to retaliate? Clearly, the answer is "no": By retaliating, Player 2 gets −10, compared with 20 from no retaliation. We conclude that $(\bar{e}, r)$, although it is a Nash equilibrium, is not a reasonable prediction of what one might expect to be played.

One way of getting rid of this sort of "unreasonable" equilibria is to solve the game backward, that is, to apply the principle of **backward induction**. First, we consider node 2, and conclude that the optimal decision is $\bar{r}$. *Then,* we solve for the decision in node 1 *given the decision previously found for node 2*. Given that Player 2 will choose $\bar{r}$, it is now clear that the optimal decision at node 1 is e. We thus select the first Nash equilibrium as the only one that is intuitively "reasonable."

Solving a game backward is not always this easy. Suppose that, if Player 1 chooses e at decision node 1 we are led not to a Player 2 decision node but rather to an entire new game, say, a simultaneous-move game as in figures 4.1 to 4.5. Because this game is a part of the larger game, we call it a **subgame** of the larger one. In this setting, solving the game backward would amount to first solving for the Nash equilibrium (or equilibria) of the subgame, and then, given the solution for the subgame, solving for the entire game. Equilibria that are derived in this way are called **subgame-perfect equilibria**.[46]

In the game of figure 4.6, the equilibrium $(\bar{e}, r)$ was dismissed on the basis that it requires Player 2 to make the "incredible" commitment of playing r in case Player 1 chooses e. Such threat is not credible because, *given* that Player 1 has chosen e, Player 2's best choice is $\bar{r}$. But suppose that Player 2 writes an enforceable and non renegotiable contract whereby, if Player 1 chooses e, Player 2 chooses r. The contract is such that,

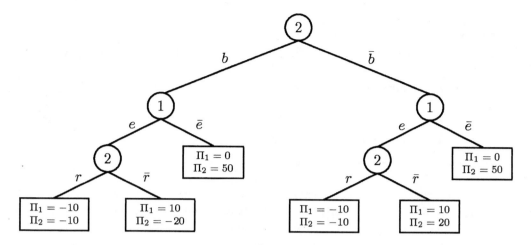

FIGURE 4.7 THE VALUE OF COMMITMENT.

were Player 2 not to choose r and chose $\bar{r}$ instead, Player 2 would incur a penalty of 40, lowering its total payoff to -20.[e]

The situation is illustrated in figure 4.7. The first decision now belongs to Player 2, who must choose between writing the bond described above (strategy b) and not doing anything (strategy $\bar{b}$). If Player 2 chooses $\bar{b}$, then the game in figure 4.6 is played. If instead Player 2 chooses b, then a different game is played, one that takes into account the implications of signing the bond.

Compare the two subgames starting at Player 1's decision nodes. The one on the right is the same as in figure 4.6. As we then saw, the equilibrium payoff for Player 2 in this game is 20. The subgame on the left-hand side is identical to the one on the right except for Player 2's payoff following (e, r). The value is now -20 instead of 20. At first, it might seem that this makes Player 2 worse off: Payoffs are the same in every case except one, and in that one case, payoff is actually lower than it was initially. However, as we will see next, Player 2 is better off playing the left-hand-side subgame than the right-hand-side subgame.

Let us solve the left-hand-side subgame backward, as before. When it comes to Player 2 to choose between r and $\bar{r}$, the optimal choice is r. In fact, this gives Player 2 a payoff of -10, whereas the alternative would yield -20 (Player 2 would have to pay for breaking the bond). Given that Player 2 chooses r, Player 1 finds it optimal to choose $\bar{e}$: It is better to receive a payoff of zero than to receive -10, the outcome of e followed by r. In summary, the subgame on the left-hand side gives Player 2 an equilibrium payoff of 50, the result of the combination of $\bar{e}$ and r.

[e] This is a very strong assumption as most contracts are renegotiable. However, for the purposes of the present argument, what is important is that Player 2 has the option of imposing on itself a cost if it does not choose r. This cost may result from breach of contract or from a different cause.

We can finally move backward one more stage and look at Player 2's optimal choice between b and $\bar{b}$. From what we saw above, Player 2's optimal choice is to choose b and eventually receive a payoff of 50. The alternative, $\bar{b}$, eventually leads to a payoff of 20 only.

This example illustrates two important points. First it shows that

> A **credible commitment** may have significant strategic value.

By signing a bond that imposes a large penalty when playing $\bar{r}$, Player 2 credibly commits to playing r when the time comes to choose between r and $\bar{r}$. In so doing, Player 2 induces Player 1 to choose $\bar{e}$, which in turn works for Player 2's benefit. Specifically, introducing this credible commitment raises Player 2's payoff from 20 to 50. The value of commitment is 30 in this example.

The second point illustrated by the example is a methodological one. If we believe that Player 2 is credibly committed to choosing r, then we should model this by changing Player 2's payoffs or by changing the order of moves. This can be done as in figure 4.7, where we model all the moves that lead to Player 2 effectively precommiting to playing r. Alternatively, this can also be done as in figure 4.8, where we model Player 2 as choosing r or $\bar{r}$ "before" Player 1 chooses its strategy. The actual choice of r or $\bar{r}$ may occur in time after Player 1 chooses e or $\bar{e}$. However, if Player 2 precommits to playing r, we can model that by assuming Player 2 moves first. In fact, by solving the game in figure 4.8 backward, we get the same solution as in figure 4.7, namely the second Nash equilibrium of the game initially considered.

To conclude this section, we should mention another instance in which the sequence of moves plays an important role. This is when the game under consideration

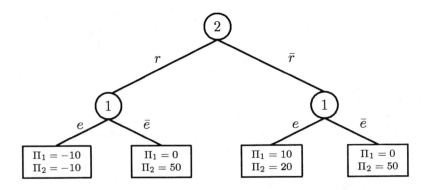

FIGURE 4.8 MODELING PLAYER 2'S CAPACITY TO PRECOMMIT.

FIGURE 4.9   A GAME WITH LONG-RUN AND SHORT-RUN STRATEGY CHOICES (TIMING OF MOVES).

depicts a long-term situation where players choose both long-run and short-run variables. For example, capacity decisions are normally a firm's long-term choice, for production capacity (buildings, machines) typically lasts for a number of years. Pricing, on the other hand, is typically a short-run variable, for firms can change it relatively frequently at a relatively low cost.

When modeling this sort of strategic interaction, we should assume that players choose the long-run variable first and the short-run variable second. Short-run variables are those that players choose *given* the value of the long-run variables. And this is precisely what we get by placing the short-run choice in the second stage.

This timing of moves is depicted in figure 4.9. This figure illustrates yet a third way of representing games: a time line of moves. This is not as complete and rigorous as the normal-form and extensive-form representations we saw before; however, it proves to be useful in analyzing a variety of games.

In a real-world situation, as time moves on, firms alternate between choosing capacity levels and choosing prices, the latter more frequently than the former. If we want to model this in a simple, two-stage game, then the right way of doing it is to place the capacity decision in the first stage and the pricing decision in the second stage. The same principle applies generally when there are long-run and short-run strategic variables. In the following chapters, we encounter examples of this in relation to capacity/pricing decisions (chapter 7), product positioning/pricing decisions (chapter 12), and entry/output decisions (chapter 15).

4.3   REPEATED GAMES

Many real-world situations of strategic behavior are repeated over an extended period of time. Sometimes, this can be modeled by an appropriate static model. For example, in the previous section, we saw how a two-stage game can be used to model competition in long-term and short-term variables.

Consider, however, the strategic phenomenon of **retaliation**, that is, the situation whereby a player changes its strategic variable in response to a rival's action. Clearly, this cannot be achieved in a static, simultaneous-move game, for in such game there is no time for a player to react to another player's actions.

Player 2

		L		C		R	
			5		6		0
	T	5		3		0	
			3		4		0
Player 1	M	6		4		0	
			0		0		1
	B	0		0		1	

FIGURE 4.10 STAGE GAME.

A useful way to model the situation whereby players react to each other's strategic moves is to consider a repeated game. Consider a simultaneous-choice game like the one in figure 4.1. Because in this game each player chooses one action only once, we refer to it as a **one-shot game**. A **repeated game** is defined by a one-shot game—also referred to as **stage game**—which is repeated a number of times. If repetition takes place a finite number of times, then we have a finitely repeated game; otherwise, we have an infinitely repeated game.

In one-shot games, strategies are easy to define. In fact, strategies are identified with actions. In repeated games, however, it is useful to distinguish between actions and strategies. Consider the one-shot game in figure 4.10. In this game, each player has three actions/strategies to choose from: T, M, B for Player 1; and L, C, R for Player 2.

Now suppose that this one-shot game is repeated twice. In each period, Player 1 still has three actions to choose from. However, the set of possible *strategies* for Player 1 is now much more complex. A strategy for Player 1 has to indicate what to choose in period 1 and what to choose in period 2 *as a function of the actions that were taken in period 1*. Generally, a **strategy** is defined as a player's complete contingent plan of action for all possible occurrences in the game. Because there are nine possible outcomes in the first period, three possible actions in the second period, and three possible actions in the first period, Player 1 has 3 times 3 to the power of 9, or 59,049, possible strategies!

Does this proliferation of strategies add anything of interest that was not present in the one-shot version of the game? In many cases, the answer is "yes." Let us start by looking at the equilibria of the one-shot game. Direct inspection reveals that this game has two Nash equilibria: (M, C) and (B, R).[f] Notice that the best payoff for both players would be (T, L), yielding each a payoff of 5, but such an outcome is not a Nash equilibrium. The best Nash equilibrium yields each player a payoff of 4.[g]

Let us now derive the equilibria of the repeated game. One first observation is that the repeated play of the equilibrium strategies of the one-shot game forms an equilibrium

[f] *Technical note*: We are referring only to equilibria in pure strategies.

[g] This game is identical to that in figure 4.1 except that we add a third strategy to each player. Although this third strategy leads to an extra Nash equilibrium, the main feature of the game in figure 4.1 is still valid—namely, the conflict between individual and joint incentives that characterizes the "prisoner's dilemma."

of the repeated game. So, for example, (M, C) in both periods is an equilibrium. The implicit strategies that lead to such equilibrium of the repeated game are, for Player 1, "choose M in period 1 and choose M in period 2 regardless of what happened in period 1"; and likewise for Player 2. That is, players choose history-independent strategies.

The interesting question is whether there are equilibria of the repeated game that do not correspond to equilibria of the one-shot game. Consider the following strategy for Player 1: play T in period 1. In period 2, play M if period 1 actions were (T, L); otherwise, play B. As for Player 2, take the following strategy: play L in period 1. In period 2, play C if period 1 actions were (T, L); otherwise, play R.

Let us now check that these strategies constitute an equilibrium of the repeated game. In period 2, assuming that the period 1 outcome was (T, L), the designated strategies call for players to choose (M, C). Because these actions form a Nash equilibrium of the one-shot game, it must be in the players' best interest to choose them in the second period of a two-period repeated game. That is, no player would be able to improve its payoff by choosing something different. Likewise, in period 2 and assuming that the period 1 outcome was different from (T, L), the designated strategies call for players to choose (B, R). Because the latter also constitute an equilibrium of the one-shot game, the same reasoning applies.

Finally, we have to check that period 1 actions are also part of a Nash equilibrium strategy. Take Player 1: Choosing the action T, as indicated by the designated strategy, yields a payoff of 5 in the first period. Because, by assumption, Player 2 is playing the designated strategy (L in period 1), Player 1's period 1 choice will lead to (M, C) in period 2, yielding Player 1 an additional payoff of 4. Total payoff is therefore 9.

Now suppose that, in period 1, Player 1 chooses M instead. Period 1 payoff would then be 6, because Player 2 chooses L. However, choosing M in period 1 would lead to the play of (B, R) in period 2, yielding Player 1 an additional payoff of only 1. Total payoff would therefore be 7, which is less than 9. A similar comparison is obtained if we consider other deviations from the designated strategies by either Player 1 or Player 2. We conclude that the designated strategies constitute a Nash equilibrium.

In words, the previously designated strategies may be described in the following way. The players agree to choose the payoff-maximizing actions in the first period: (T, L). Although this cannot be sustained in a one-shot game—both players would have an incentive to deviate—an arrangement can be made whereby (T, L) is part of an equilibrium in the two-period game. The idea is that period 2 actions are used to "punish" players in case they deviate from the designated period 1 actions. Because of this period 2 "punishment," a period 1 deviation that would be profitable in the short run (that is, in the one-shot game) is not profitable once the two periods are taken into consideration. In fact, the period 1 gain from deviation (6 minus 5) is less than the loss in period 2 payoff that results from Player 2's "retaliation" (4 minus 1).

We conclude:

> Because players can react to other players' past actions, repeated games allow for equilibrium outcomes that would not be an equilibrium in the corresponding one-shot game.

As we see in chapter 8, this idea of "agreements" between players that are enforced by mutual retaliation plays an important role in explaining the working of cartels and, more generally, the nature of collusive behavior.

SUMMARY

- A game is a model that depicts a situation of strategic behavior. A game consists of a set of players, rules, and a set of payoff functions.

- Games may be represented in normal form (matrix) or in extensive form (game tree). Normally, games with simultaneous choices are represented in the normal form, whereas games with sequential choices are represented in the extensive form.

- Simultaneous strategy choices should not be interpreted literally: When observation lags are significant, it is *as if* players were simultaneously choosing strategies.

- The equilibrium of a game indicates the strategies that one would expect players to choose. The most common equilibrium concept is that of Nash equilibrium—a situation such that no player would unilaterally find it optimal to change its strategy.

- In analyzing games, it is important not only whether players are rational. It is also important whether players believe the other players are rational.

- Sequential games should be solved backward. Such procedure excludes strategies that are not credible.

- Committing to take a future action which is ex-post suboptimal may have an ex-ante strategic value.

- Repeated games are a way of modeling repeated interaction between players. Because players can react to other players' past actions, repeated games allow for equilibrium outcomes that would not be an equilibrium in the corresponding one-shot game.

KEY CONCEPTS

- game
- normal form and extensive form
- dominant and dominated strategies
- Nash equilibrium
- backward induction
- credible commitment
- repeated game

REVIEW AND PRACTICE EXERCISES

4.1 What are the assumptions regarding player rationality implicit in solving a game by elimination of dominated strategies? Contrast this with the case of dominant strategies.

4.2 The U.K. Office of Fair Trading has recently unveiled a plan that will offer immunity from prosecution to firms who blow the whistle on their co-cartel conspirators. In the United States, this tactic has proven extremely successful: Since its introduction in 1993, the total amount of fines for anticompetitive behavior has increased twentyfold.

Show how the tactic initiated by the U.S. Department of Justice, soon to be followed by the U.K. Office of Fair Trading, changes the rules of the game played between firms in a secret cartel.

4.3 Figure 4.11 represents a series of two-player games that illustrate the rivalry between *Time* magazine and *Newsweek*. Each magazine's strategy consists of choosing a cover story: "Impeachment" and "Financial Crisis" are the two choices.[h]

The first version of the game corresponds to the case when the game is symmetric (*Time* and *Newsweek* are equally well positioned). As the payoff matrix suggests, "Impeachment" is a better story but payoffs are lower when both magazines choose the same story. The second version of the game corresponds to the assumption that *Time* is a more

[h] In each cell, the first number is the payoff for the row player (*Time*).

Newsweek

	Impeachment	Financial Crisis
Impeachment	35, 35	70, 30
Financial Crisis	30, 70	15, 15

Time (to the left of the table)

(i) *Time* and *Newsweek* are evenly matched.

Newsweek

	Impeachment	Financial Crisis
Impeachment	42, 28	70, 30
Financial Crisis	30, 70	18, 12

Time (to the left of the table)

(ii) *Time* is more popular than *Newsweek*.

Newsweek

	Impeachment	Financial Crisis
Impeachment	42, 28	70, 50
Financial Crisis	50, 70	30, 20

Time (to the left of the table)

(iii) Some readers will buy both magazines.

FIGURE 4.11   THE COVER-STORY GAME.

popular magazine (*Time's* payoff is greater than *Newsweek's* when both magazines cover the same story). Finally, the third version of the game illustrates the case in which the magazines are sufficiently different that some readers will buy both magazines even if they cover the same story.

For each of the three versions of the game,

a. Determine whether the game can be solved by dominant strategies.

b. Determine all Nash equilibria.

c. Indicate clearly which assumptions regarding rationality are required in order to reach the solutions in (a) and (b).

4.4* In the movie *E.T.*, a trail of Reese's Pieces, one of Hershey's chocolate brands, is used to lure the little alien out of the woods. As a result of the publicity created by this scene, sales of Reese's Pieces trebled, allowing Hershey to catch up with rival Mars.

Universal Studio's original plan was to use a trail of Mars' M&Ms. However, Mars turned down the offer, presumably because it thought $1 million, the price demanded by the producer of *E.T.*, was very high. The makers of *E.T.* then turned to Hershey, who accepted the deal.

Suppose that the publicity generated by having M&Ms included in the movie would increase Mars' profits by $800,000. Suppose moreover that Hershey's increase in market share cost Mars a loss of $500,000. Finally, let b be the benefit for Hershey from having its brand be the chosen one.

Describe the preceding events as a game in extensive form. Determine the equilibrium as a function of b. If the equilibrium differs from the actual events, how do you think they can be reconciled?

4.5   Hernan Cortéz, the Spanish navigator and explorer, is said to have burnt his ships upon arrival to Mexico. By so doing, he effectively eliminated the option of him and his soldiers returning to their homeland. Discuss the strategic value of this action, knowing the Spanish colonists were faced with potential resistance from the Mexican natives.

4.6   Consider the following game depicting the process of standard setting in high-definition television (HDTV).[47] The United States and Japan must simultaneously decide whether to invest a high or a low value into HDTV research. Each country's payoffs are summarized in figure 4.12.

a. Are there any dominant strategies in this game? What is the Nash equilibrium of the game? What are the rationality assumptions implicit in this equilibrium?

b. Suppose now that the United States has the option of committing to a strategy before Japan's decision is reached. How would you model this new situation? What are the Nash equilibria of this new game?

c. Comparing the answers to (a) and (b), what can you say about the value of commitment for the United States?

d. "When precommitment has a strategic value, the player that makes that commitment ends up 'regretting' its actions, in the sense that, given the rival's choices, it could achieve a higher payoff by choosing a different action." In light of your answer to (b), how would you comment on this statement?

Japan

		Low		High	
			3		4
U.S.	Low	4		2	
			2		1
	High	3		1	

FIGURE 4.12   THE HDTV GAME: EACH COUNTRY CHOOSES A HIGH OR A LOW LEVEL OF R&D ON HDTV.

4.7   Consider a one-shot game with two equilibria and suppose that this game is repeated twice. Explain in words why there may be equilibria in the two-period game that are different from the equilibria of the one-shot game.

EXTENSION EXERCISE

4.8**   Consider the game in figure 4.13.[48] Show, by backward induction, that rational players choose d at every node of the game, yielding a payoff of 2 for Player 1 and zero for Player 2. Is this equilibrium reasonable? What are the rationality assumptions implicit in it?

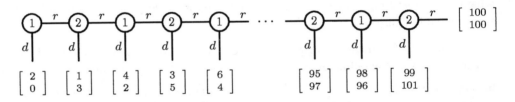

FIGURE 4.13   THE CENTIPEDE GAME.

In the payoff vectors, the top number is player 1's payoff, the bottom one player 2's.

FROM MONOPOLY TO
PERFECT COMPETITION

CHAPTER 5

MONOPOLY AND REGULATION

One of the first steps in the process of studying industrial organization is to have an idea of what types of industry structure there may be. Different authors present different classifications. Normally, there is a long list that covers various possibilities from monopoly to competition: pure monopoly, dominant firm, tight oligopoly, loose oligopoly, monopolistic competition, pure competition.[49]

Pure monopoly is the situation in which one firm holds a 100% share of the market. Examples include many electric, telephone, water, bus, and other utilities. A dominant firm may be classified as one with 50% to 100% of the market and no close rival. Campbell soup, Gillette razor blades, and Kodak film are possible examples. In this chapter, we deal with the cases where one firm dominates the entire market, or almost the entire market. In the next chapter, we address the opposite extreme, looking at the cases of perfect competition and monopolistic competition. The intermediate case—oligopoly—is the object of a series of chapters beginning with chapter 7.

5.1   MONOPOLY

The model of **monopoly** is based on the assumption that there is a well-defined market with one single supplier. The monopolist sets price p and consumers demand quantity $D(p)$; or, to put it in the reverse form: To sell a quantity q, the seller must set a price $P(q)$, where $P(\cdot)$ is the inverse function of $D(\cdot)$. By producing q, the monopolist incurs a cost $C(q)$. Finally, it is assumed that the seller chooses a price to maximize profits.

Notice that, because price and output are related by the demand function, it is the same thing to choose the optimal price or to choose the optimal output. That is, even though the monopolist is assumed to set price and consumers choose quantity as

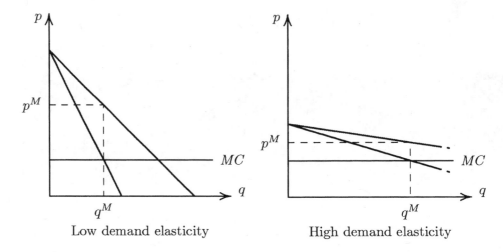

FIGURE 5.1 DEMAND ELASTICITY AND OPTIMAL MONOPOLY MARGIN.

a function of price, we can think of the monopolist as choosing the optimal quantity it wants consumers to buy and then setting the corresponding price. In what follows, we treat the monopolist's decision as that of selecting an output level. Profit maximization occurs when the firm uses the optimal rule that marginal revenue equals marginal cost. It can be shown that this implies the well-known **elasticity rule**:

$$\frac{p - MC}{p} = \frac{1}{\epsilon}, \tag{5.1}$$

where MC is marginal cost and $\epsilon \equiv -\frac{dD}{dp}\frac{p}{q}$ is the price elasticity of demand.[a] In other words:

> A monopolist should set a price-cost margin that is greater the lower is the price elasticity of demand.

This is illustrated in figure 5.1, which depicts the optimal price (and margin) for different demand functions. The graph on the left shows a low-elasticity demand curve. As predicted by equation 5.1, optimal price (and margin) are greater than for a high-elasticity demand curve (graph on the right).

DOMINANT FIRMS

Pure monopolies are fairly rare. Aside from utilities, one is hard pressed to find a good example of a firm that controls 100% of its market. It is not uncommon, however, to find industries where one of the firms commands a market share of 50% or more, and a set

[a] Alternatively, we may write the above equation as

$$p\left(1 - \frac{1}{\epsilon}\right) = MC,$$

which shows more clearly that the monopolist optimally sets a markup over marginal cost.

of small firms divide the remainder of the market among themselves. Examples include the mainframe computer industry in the 1960s and 1970s, IBM being the dominant firm; and, for several years, the market for photographic film, Kodak being the dominant firm in this case. Normally, the dominant firm holds some competitive advantage with respect to rivals, by reason of either lower costs or higher quality (or better reputation for quality).

Consider a third example, that of long-distance telecommunications in the United States in the second half of the 1980s. AT&T was a monopolist until 1984; since then, a number of relatively small competitors have entered the market. Until the early to mid 1990s, there were two important differences between AT&T and its rivals. First, most of the rivals had a smaller capacity than AT&T. Second, rivals were not subject to the same type of regulation that the former monopolist was.[b] As a result, AT&T's competitors could change prices more quickly and more easily.

For this reason, AT&T was, in some sense, a price leader. Whichever price was set, competitors typically would follow by pricing at the same level or slightly lower. Table 5.1 illustrates this point: Most price changes effected by MCI and Sprint in the period from 1987 to 1994 followed price changes by AT&T; the prices set by AT&T's rivals tended to be just below those of the former monopolist.[c]

Suppose that consumers choose the firm offering the lowest price and that the small carriers are capacity constrained, having a total capacity of K. This situation is depicted in figure 5.2. Whichever price AT&T sets (above marginal cost), the small carriers will set a slightly smaller price and sell up to capacity. In practice, this implies that AT&T

TABLE 5.1 LONG-DISTANCE TELEPHONE RATES: AT&T, MCI, AND SPRINT.[50]

AT&T		MCI		Sprint	
Date Rate Changed	New Rate	Months After	New Rate	Months After	New Rate
January 87	.298	2	.289	2	.289
January 88	.265	2	.256	2	.259
January 89	.254	0	.244	0	.250
January 90	.233	1	.223	1	.228
January 91	.228	1	.222	5	.228
July 91	.227	5	.223	1	.227
January 92	.228	0	.224	2	.228
June 92	.227	0	.225	5	.227
February 93	.228	1	.225	2	.228
August 93	.229				
September 93	.235	0	.234	1	.235
January 94	.256	0	.255	0	.256

[b] In 1996, AT&T ceased to be subject to price regulation. Moreover, the rivals' capacity and market share increased considerably. The recent proposed merger between MCI and Sprint would represent an additional important change in the market, which now more resembles a duopoly than one with a dominant firm.

[c] MCI changed its rates in the same month as AT&T in 5 out of 12 price changes. Sprint has set the exact same rates as AT&T from 1991 to 1994 (although it reacted to the latter's changes with some lag).

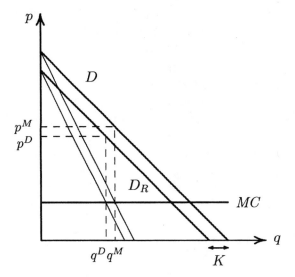

FIGURE 5.2 DOMINANT-FIRM OPTIMAL PRICE.

is faced with the **residual demand** D_R, obtained from market demand D by moving it K units to the left, where K is the total capacity of the small competitors.

Given the residual demand D_R, AT&T's optimal price is derived in the usual way, by equating marginal revenue with marginal cost (MC). This results in an optimal price p^D and output q^D. Notice that, so long as K is small, p^D is close to p^M, the monopoly price. This suggests that a dominant firm behaves in a way that is similar to that of a monopolist.

In reality, things are a bit more complicated. Long-distance telecommunications is not a homogeneous product, or at least is not perceived as such by consumers. In fact, AT&T's advantage resulted primarily from a large base of loyal consumers who perceived AT&T's service as superior. This caveat notwithstanding, the preceding model illustrates the idea that the monopoly model provides a good approximation to the behavior of dominant firms.

MONOPOLY AND MONOPOLY POWER

Are there any monopolies? In the beginning of the chapter, we suggested the example of utilities (electricity, telephone, etc.). But most of these have been deregulated (in most countries), so that it seems more and more difficult to find an example of a pure monopoly. Or is it?

Consider the case of Apple Computer. Apple is the sole manufacturer of the Apple MacIntosh line of personal computers.[d] That is, Apple is the monopoly supplier of the MacIntosh PC. But calling Apple a monopolist would be an artifact of a very contrived market definition. It would probably make more sense to talk about the market

[d] For a while, Apple allowed other firms to manufacture the MacIntosh—or "Mac clones"—but this is no longer the case.

for personal computers, in which case a host of Windows-based computers should be included, leaving Apple with a modest 10% or so market share.

Simplistic as it might be, this example illustrates the point that defining monopoly based on a market share calculation is bound to lead to problems of market definition. Different market definitions lead to potentially very different market shares. But why should we attach so much importance to market share when assessing a monopoly? Consider the two graphs in figure 5.1. In both cases, we have, by assumption, a monopoly, that is, a firm with a 100% market share. However, the degree of **monopoly power**, defined as the ability to sell at a price substantially above cost, is much lower in the right-hand-side case, the case when demand is more elastic. The general point is that:

> The degree of monopoly power is inversely related to the demand elasticity faced by the firm.

This definition of monopoly power seems more sensible than the one based on market share. For instance, suppose that the firm on the left-hand side of figure 5.1 commands a market share of 90%, whereas the one on the right-hand side is a pure monopoly (100% market share). Even though, in terms of market share, the firm on the right is more of a monopoly, in terms of monopoly power the firm on the left seems more of a monopoly.

The demand elasticity depends on many factors—some static, some dynamic. This makes it difficult to judge the extent of monopoly power in actual situations. Take for example, Microsoft in the market for operating systems. In terms of market share, there is no question that Microsoft is a near-monopolist (a dominant firm). But does it truly have monopoly power? Box 5.1 addresses this question in greater detail.

Public policy reflects, to some extent, the distinction between monopoly market share and monopoly power. In Europe, Article 86 of the Treaty of Rome states that a dominant position—presumably a reference to a large market share—is not illegal per se; that is, it is not illegal in and of itself. Rather, what violates the Treaty of Rome is the *abuse* of that dominant position—presumably a reference to monopoly power. In practice, however, things are a bit more complicated and it is not clear what "abuse of dominant position" actually means. For example, in the *Sacem* case, French discos argued that they were overcharged by Sacem, which controls music copyrights. However, the EU Court of Justice decided that, as Sacem's charges were similar to those of similar firms with similar market shares in other countries, there was no evidence of abuse of dominant position. In the United States, merger policy is moving in a direction that follows the distinction between monopoly market shares and monopoly power, as the *Staples* case illustrates. In September 1996, Staples and Office Depot announced their intention to merge their office-supplies superstore chains, a proposal that was challenged

BOX 5.1 MICROSOFT: MONOPOLY AND MONOPOLY POWER[51]

The legal battle between Microsoft and the U.S. Justice Department is an interesting instance of the concepts of monopoly and monopoly power. There is little doubt that Microsoft holds a position of near-monopoly in the market for operating systems. The Windows operating system is used in about 80% of the world's personal computers. Hewlett-Packard's operations manager claims that "absolutely there is no choice" when it comes to selecting an operating system for its Pavillon computers. The world depends on Windows.

Yet, Microsoft claims it "cannot charge a monopoly price because it faces competition from rival operating systems, potential entrants, its own installed base, and pirated software." In other words, Microsoft has a (near) monopoly market share but virtually no monopoly power, it claims. Richard Schmalensee, one of Microsoft's main witnesses in the recent antitrust case, calculates that an unchallenged-monopoly profit-maximizing price would fall in the $900 to $2000 range. Because Microsoft is a profit-maximizing concern and charges substantially less than that, the argument goes, it follows that Microsoft has no monopoly power.

Microsoft's distinction between monopoly market share and monopoly power in operating systems is based, among other things, on the idea that software is a durable good. Unlike breakfast cereals and gasoline, consumers don't need to buy a new operating system every week. If Microsoft were to set a high price for Windows 98, PC users would simply carry on with Windows 95, delaying the upgrade until prices came down to more reasonable levels. In other words, Microsoft's monopoly power is curtailed by its own installed base and its inability to commit to not setting a low price. (This issue is discussed in greater detail in chapter 10.)

However, it seems difficult to deny that Microsoft has used its monopoly power in operating systems to extend its dominant position to other areas of business. Alleged anticompetitive practices include exclusionary agreements with PC makers and online service and content providers. For example, in 1997, Microsoft forced an agreement on Intuit Inc. that prohibited the financial-software maker from promoting Netscape's browser. This sort of agreement, together with the policy of bundling Windows with Microsoft's Internet Explorer, has eroded Netscape's market share in the browser market to an extent that would probably not have been reached if Microsoft didn't control the operating systems market.

by the Federal Trade Commission (FTC). Much of the preliminary discussion seemed to mimic previous merger cases: Staples argued that the relevant market definition is that of stores that sell office supplies, in which case the combined market share of Staples and Office Depot would be very low. The FTC in turn argued that the relevant market definition is that of office-supplies superstores, in which case the combined market share of Staples and Office Depot would be greater than 70%. However, what eventually clinched the decision to block the merger was the econometric evidence that prices would be substantially greater in areas where the merger would increase the concentration of superstores ownership. Generally, there is a move toward giving greater importance to the impact of mergers on prices (market power) than to the impact of mergers on market shares.[e]

5.2   REGULATION[52]

It is well known that monopoly pricing implies allocative inefficiency. The price set by a monopolist is greater than marginal cost. Or, to put it differently, the output set by a monopolist is lower than the optimal output: An increase in output would increase social welfare, for the marginal willingness to pay (price) would be greater than the marginal cost.

Competition is a way of achieving the efficiency lost in monopoly pricing (as we will see in greater detail in the next chapters). However, if fixed costs are large—or, more generally, if scale economies are very significant—then competition may not be a viable alternative. An extreme situation is given by a **natural monopoly**, the case when the cost structure is such that costs are minimized with one supplier only. In these cases, direct **regulation** of the monopolist (or dominant firm) may be the optimal solution.

Let us start by considering the simplest case of monopoly regulation. There is a firm with a cost function given by $C = F + cq$, where F is the fixed (capital) cost and c marginal cost (for simplicity, we assume marginal cost to be constant). Absent regulation, the monopolist sets price at the monopoly level, p^M, as shown in figure 5.3. Because the social optimum would be to set price at marginal cost, monopoly price implies that output is lower than optimum and that allocative efficiency is lower than optimum by the area E. As for the monopolist, it receives a *variable* profit $\pi = q^M(p^M - c)$, so that net profit is given by $\pi - F$.

A first natural solution for a regulator is to force the monopolist to set price equal to marginal cost: $p^R = c$, where R stands for "regulated." In this case, output is given by q^R and maximum allocative efficiency is achieved (i.e., the area E is equal to zero). One problem with marginal cost pricing is that it may imply negative profits for the firm. This is certainly the case when marginal cost is constant: Variable profit, π, is zero, and total profit is therefore $-F$.

[e] Further discussion on merger policy may be found in chapter 15.

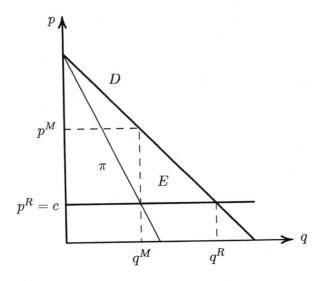

FIGURE 5.3 UNREGULATED AND REGULATED MONOPOLY.

Clearly, a firm that makes losses of F cannot survive. To solve this problem, the regulator might give the firm a subsidy of F. However, this would likely create additional problems. First, to obtain the value F, the regulator may have to raise taxes elsewhere in the economy. The efficiency loss implied by these taxes, E', may be greater than the efficiency loss that marginal cost pricing is supposed to eliminate, E. Second, the possibility of transfers from the regulator to the regulated firm gives the former more discretion, and opens the doors for the possibility of regulatory capture. By **regulatory capture,** we mean the situation whereby firms invest resources into influencing the regulator's decisions, to the point that the latter reflect the objective of profit maximization more than that of welfare maximization. In fact, even if the regulator is not actually influenced, the use of resources attempting to do so is socially wasteful.[f]

Given the problems of marginal cost pricing, an interesting alternative is that of **average cost pricing**. Under this regime, the firm is forced to set the lowest price consistent with making non-negative profits, that is, price is equal to average cost. This situation is depicted in figure 5.4, where $p^A = AC(q^A)$ and $q^A = D(p^A)$. As can be seen, this solution is intermediate between those of marginal cost pricing and unregulated monopolist. In the United States, the mechanism that in the past has mostly been used for regulating utilities is that of **rate-of-return regulation**. This is a mechanism whereby prices are set so as to allow the firm a fair rate of return on the capital it invests. Roughly speaking, this corresponds to average cost pricing.[g]

[f] See also the discussion on rent seeking presented in chapter 1.

[g] If there is only one output and capital is the only input, then this is exactly the same mechanism as average cost pricing.

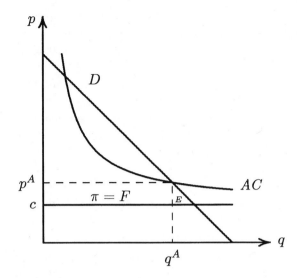

FIGURE 5.4 AVERAGE COST REGULATION.

One major problem with rate-of-return regulation is that it gives the firm very few incentives for cost reduction. In fact, lowering cost implies that the allowed price will be accordingly lowered, leaving the firm with the same rate of return. In practice, there is a gap between the time when the firm reduces its cost and the time when the new regulated prices take effect—what might be called a **regulatory lag**—and this may provide the firm with some transitory gains. But the mechanism of rate-of-return is fundamentally flawed when it comes to incentives for cost reduction.

In the terminology of regulation theory, we say that rate-of-return regulation is a **low-power incentive mechanism**: Price varies in the same exact measure as cost, a fact that minimizes the incentives for cost reduction. At the other extreme, we have the most **high-power incentive mechanism**: This is the mechanism whereby price is set beforehand and does not change at all, even if cost changes. Roughly speaking, this is the essence of the **price cap regulation** mechanism. This mechanism provides maximum incentives for cost reduction: A one-dollar saving in costs implies a one-dollar increase in profits.[53]

Or does it? Imagine that the regulator sets a price, or a price path, for a period of five years. During that period, the firm invests heavily in cost reduction. By the end of the five-year period, the firm's cost is, say, one half of what it was initially. It is difficult to imagine how the regulator can ignore the extent of this cost reduction at the time of setting the price cap for the new five-year period. In fact, the greater the cost reduction achieved by the regulated firm during the first five-year period, the lower the price cap set for the second five-year period.

Following this line of argument, a somewhat extreme appraisal of price-cap regulation is to view it as rate-of-return regulation with a long regulatory lag (five years in the preceding example). The discussion is then focused on the length of the period that the regulator commits to a price-cap (or a price path). Ten years would seem like a reasonable period, sufficient to make price cap regulation substantially different from rate-of-return regulation. But the experience of several countries—including Great Britain, where the mechanism was first implemented—suggests that revisions of the price cap normally occur at smaller intervals. This in turn casts some doubt about the effectiveness of price-cap regulation as an incentive scheme.

Another problem with price-cap regulation is that it creates few incentives for the provision of product or service quality, an aspect we have ignored until now. Unable to increase price, the regulated firm may have an incentive to reduce quality, thereby effectively increasing price "per unit of quality."

Finally, implementing price-cap regulation raises the problem of determining the price cap. A high price cap implies the allocative inefficiency of a price greater than marginal cost (in addition to a transfer from consumers to the regulated monopolist). A low price cap may not be sustainable, as the regulated firm suffers losses. More generally, a high-power incentive scheme—of which price-cap regulation is an extreme—implies a high degree of risk for the regulated firm. In this sense, rate-of-return regulation is a better mechanism: The risk for the regulated firm is minimal. In summary:

> A high-power regulation mechanism provides strong incentives for cost reduction but few incentives for quality provision. In addition, it implies a high degree of risk for the regulated firm and requires strong commitment on the regulator's part.

5.3   ESSENTIAL FACILITIES AND ACCESS PRICING

Competition is the best way of recovering the allocative inefficiency lost in monopoly pricing. Regulation, in turn, is the best alternative when, because of natural monopoly conditions, competition is not feasible. The question is then when and to what extent we are in a natural monopoly situation.

The classification of many industries as natural monopolies has come into question. Take, for example, electricity. It is generally agreed that the basic network for the transmission of electric power is a natural monopoly—the costs of having two parallel networks would be much too high. However, there is little evidence of natural monopoly at the stage of generation of electric power. Gas and railways are also examples of industries in which only one part is subject to natural monopoly (the gas transportation network and the railway track network, respectively). Still another example is given by telecommunications, where the natural monopoly would be the local network.[h]

Suppose that competition is allowed in the parts of those industries where natural monopoly is not an issue (electricity generation, long-distance telecommunications, and so on). The problem that typically arises is that these parts cannot exist independently from the part that is a natural monopoly: An electricity generator needs the distribution network to sell its power; a long-distance carrier needs to place its calls through the local network; and so forth. Specifically, what we have is a monopolist (e.g., the local telecommunications operator) selling services to firms in the competitive segment (e.g., long-distance telecommunications) who in turn sell to the final consumer. In these cases, we say that the monopolist is an upstream **bottleneck** and that the monopolist's assets or output is an **essential facility**. Seen from this perspective, the list of examples goes beyond that of public utilities (as considered in the preceding discussion). An airport, for example, is an essential input for transportation services into a certain city. Although there may be many competing airlines (downstream firms), there is frequently only one airport in each city, the owner of which is the upstream firm. In summary, essential facilties are a fairly common situation.

The regulation of essential facilities shares the same problems as those of monopoly regulation, which we addressed in the previous section. Moreover, it is frequently the case that the owner of an upstream essential facility also competes downstream. For example, France Telecom owns the essential facility (local network) and competes in the market for long-distance telecommunications. This type of situation raises a number of additional issues.

One possible concern is that the upstream firm may use its monopoly power to extend it downstream, thus creating monopoly power at the lower level as well. For one reason or another, the upstream firm may be unable to extract from the downstream competitors all of the monopoly rents in the value chain. By foreclosing its downstream competitors from the market, the upstream firm is able to recapture its maximum monopoly profits.

From a social welfare point of view, foreclosure would seem to decrease consumer welfare (and total welfare): Consumers pay a higher price and have less product variety to choose from. One way of avoiding this is to force the upstream firm to divest its interests in the downstream market. For example, AT&T was broken up in 1984, resulting in a long-distance carrier (the new AT&T) and a series of regional telecom operators (the "baby bells"). Competition was opened in the downstream markets (long-distance), while monopoly was preserved in the upstream, (local) markets.[i]

However, as we saw in chapter 3, there may be important efficiency gains from vertical integration. For example, if the U.S. government had barred the merger between GM and Fisher Body, it is likely that the industry would have become much less efficient, on account of the difficulty to contract for investments in specific assets. As in many other instances of industrial organization, we have a trade-off between efficiency and market power.

[h] The latter example is open to debate, however. Some argue that not even the local network is a natural monopoly.

[i] The 1996 Telecommunications Act allows for the possibility of local operators entering into long-distance telecommunications as well.

BOX 5.2   A TALE OF TWO MARKET DEREGULATIONS[54]

France and Germany provide an interesting contrast of the path toward telecommunications deregulation. Both countries started from a similar initial situation, with a large, state-owned operator controlling virtually all of the country's telecommunications. Both countries allowed new competitors to enter the market at about the same time. Beyond this, the differences are more significant than the similarities.

One of the most important steps in the deregulation process is the "interconnection decision," that is, determining the amount of money a competitor has to pay to use the incumbent's local network. In France, a distinction was made between new competitors that built their own networks and those that didn't: The latter were required to pay a higher access fee. No such distinction was made in Germany. This gave bare-bones resellers an advantage in Germany, at least during the first year. In fact, these firms did not have to make significant investments and nevertheless were able to access the Telekom network at the same price as other new entrants.

The treatment of new competitors in Germany is more favorable in several respects. For example, German customers wishing to try a new long-distance carrier can do so by simply dialing the access code and then the desired number. They are billed in a single Deutsche Telekom statement, and the corresponding amount is transferred to the new competitor. No such "call-by-call" option is available in France.

The most significant difference between Germany and France is, however, the *level* of the access fees. Before the interconnection decision was made in Germany, Deutsche Telekom asked for a fee of 6.5 pfennig per minute. Competitors pushed for a one-pfennig rate. The German regulator followed an unexpected route: It took the average of the access fee in 10 countries and came up with the value of 2.7 pfennigs. That this value was unexpectedly low is proved by the fact Deutsche Telekom's stock dropped by 7.7% in a single day and by a further 6% a few days later. After one year of competition, 51 new rivals entered the market to steal about one third of Deutsche Telekom's long-distance business. During the same period, France Telecom lost a mere 3% market share.

Deutsche Telekom's CEO claims his competitors are nothing but "arbitragers" who simply use the low access fees to piggyback on Telekom's network. In fact, few carriers invested in their own network during the first year after deregulation. In December 1998, the German regulator reacted to this problem by allowing Deutsche Telekom to charge higher access fees to resellers who don't build their own network, a distinction the French regulator made from the start.

Box 5.2 (CONTINUED)

The importance of the interconnection decision shows in the numbers. Whereas Deutsche Telekom's stock had its ups and downs, France Telecom's shares soared 103% during the first year of full competition. In contrast, long-distance charges in Germany have fallen by nearly 90% in one year, and local competition exists in more than one dozen cities. Rates in Germany have gone from among the highest in the world to among the lowest in the world. Rates in France have also dropped, but by much less than in Germany.

A regulatory alternative to divestiture consists of allowing the upstream firm to compete downstream but preventing it from discriminating against downstream competitors. In most European countries, this was the chosen solution in the case of telecommunications.[j] One of the central aspects of this alternative is the regulation of the **access price**, the price paid by downstream firms for access to the essential facility.

The **Efficient Component Pricing Rule** (ECPR) has been proposed as a means to achieve this end.[55] It states that the wholesale price offered to an independent downstream firm cannot be higher than the difference between p, the final price set by the integrated firm, and the marginal cost of the integrated firm at the downstream stage.

To motivate these ideas, suppose there is a telecommunications company T, which is integrated with a mobile phone provider M_1, and a second (independent) mobile phone provider, M_2. Each mobile phone company has a marginal cost c_i, $i = 1, 2$. Suppose the integrated firm sets final price p_1 (the wholesale price is irrelevant here; it would simply be a transfer price). The ECPR states that the maximum wholesale price that firm $T\&M_1$ can charge M_2 is given by $w_2 = p_1 - c_1$. The idea is that, at this wholesale price, M_2's margin is

$$p_2 - (c_2 + w_2) = (p_2 - p_1) + (c_1 - c_2).$$

(Notice that M_2's marginal cost now includes two components: the direct marginal cost c_2 and the wholesale price w_2.)

From the preceding equation, we conclude that, if M_2 were to set a competitive price with respect to the rival, say, $p_2 = p_1$, then it would receive a *positive margin if and only if $c_2 < c_1$*. This is the idea of the ECPR: It allows the independent downstream firms to survive if and only if they are competitive with respect to the vertically integrated firm. The point is that, *if the ECPR is applied, then production efficiency is maximized.*

However, it is far from clear that the ECPR will have any definite benefit. Suppose that mobile phone operators are equally efficient, that is, $c_1 = c_2$. It can be seen that $T\&M_1$'s optimal price is $p_1 = p^M$, the monopoly price. Consistent with the ECPR, the

[j] Box 5.2 looks at the cases of France and Germany.

access price would then be set at $w_2 = p^M - c_1$. At this wholesale price, the best the downstream firm can do is to sell at p^M for a margin of zero. Whichever amount M_2 sells, the manufacturer receives full monopoly profits, and consumers pay monopoly prices. In other words, although the ECPR implies productive efficiency, it has no bite with respect to price levels. In fact, prices are set at the same level as those in an unrestricted monopoly.[k]

Despite these limitations, the ECPR is popular among regulators. In March of 1999, Deutsche Telekom was barred from launching a low-cost online service unless it were also to lower its access fee. Says the president of the regulatory authority: "To prevent discrimination (in pricing), the unbundled-access charge would have to be lowered."[57] Otherwise, online service competitors such as AOL Europe would be at a disadvantage as they don't have any way of accessing customers other than through Deutsche Telekom's local loop. Broadly speaking, this decision reflects the spirit of the ECPR.

The most clear example of application of the ECPR rule is, however, given by New Zealand. The Telecom Corporation of New Zealand (TCNZ) is the main telecommunications operator. In particular, it holds the monopoly over the local network. In the early 1990s, rival operator Clear Communications challenged TCNZ in Court, arguing that the latter's access charges were predatory, that is, were unfairly forcing Clear Communications out of the industry. Clear Communications argued that Telecom ought to charge an access price in line with the actual cost of providing access. Telecom in turn wished to apply the ECPR rule, which, as seen earlier, may imply an access fee substantially higher than the cost of providing access. Ultimately, the case was decided in London, where the Lords of the Judicial Committee of the Privy Council upheld Telecom's view.[58]

SUMMARY

- The degree of monopoly power is inversely related to the demand elasticity faced by the firm.

- A high-power regulation mechanism provides strong incentives for cost reduction but few incentives for quality provision. In addition, it implies a high degree of risk for the regulated firm and requires strong commitment on the regulator's part.

[k] To avoid this problem, some authors have proposed a solution whereby the upstream firm is subject to a price-index cap. The price index includes both the final price set by the integrated firm and the access price charged to downstream competitors. This implies that, if the integrated firm wants to increase the final price, it has to decrease the access price, and vice versa.[56]

KEY CONCEPTS

- monopoly
- elasticity rule

- residual demand

- monopoly power

- natural monopoly

- regulation and regulatory capture

- low-powered and high-powered regulation mechanisms

- rate-of-return regulation and price-cap regulation

- essential facility

- access pricing

REVIEW AND PRACTICE EXERCISES

5.1   "The degree of monopoly power is limited by the elasticity of demand." Comment.

5.2   A firm sells one million units at a price of $100 each. The firm's marginal cost is constant at $40, and its average cost (at the output level of one million units) is $90. The firm estimates that its elasticity of demand is constant at 2.0. Should the firm raise price, lower price, or leave price unchanged? Explain.[59]

5.3   One study estimates the long-run demand elasticity of AT&T in the period 1988–1991 to be around 10.[60] Assuming the estimate is correct, what does this imply in terms of AT&T's market power?

5.4   Sprint offers long-distance telephone service to residential customers at a price of 8¢ per minute. At this price, Sprint sells 200 million minutes of calling per day. Sprint believes that its marginal cost per minute of calling is 5¢. So, Sprint's residential long-distance telephone service business is contributing $6 million per day toward overhead/fixed costs.

Based on a statistical study of calling patterns, Sprint estimates that it faces a constant elasticity of demand for long-distance calling by residential customers of 2.0.

a. Based on this information, should Sprint raise, lower, or leave unchanged its price?

b. How much additional contribution to overhead, if any, can Sprint obtain by optimally adjusting its price?[61]

5.5   After spending 10 years and $1.5 billion, you have finally gotten Food and Drug Administration (FDA) approval to sell your new patented wonder drug, which reduces the aches and pains associated with aging joints. You will market this drug under the brand name of Ageless. Market research indicates that the elasticity of demand for Ageless is 1.25 (at all points on the demand curve). You estimate the marginal cost of manufacturing and selling one additional dose of Ageless is $1.

a. What is the profit-maximizing price per dose of Ageless?

b. Would you expect the elasticity of demand you face for Ageless to rise or fall when your patent expires?[62]

5.6   Is the Windows operating system an essential facility? What about the Intel Pentium microprocessor? To what extent does the discussion in section 5.3 on essential facilities (vertical integration, access pricing) apply to the preceding examples?

CHAPTER 6

Perfect (and Almost Perfect) Competition

In chapter 5, we looked at the extreme cases of monopoly and dominant firm, the cases when one firm controls 100%—or nearly 100%—of the market. In this chapter, we consider the opposite case: perfect competition and near-perfect competition. Chapter 5 shows that there are very few examples of pure monopolies. Still, the monopoly model provides a useful approximation to industries that are close to monopolies. In this chapter, we find something similar: Although examples of pure competition are rare, the model of perfect competition provides a good approximation to the behavior of many real-world industries.

We begin the chapter by reviewing the assumptions and the results of the perfect competition model. In section 6.2, we present a series of stylized facts, which suggest that perfect competition may not be such a good approximation after all. This observation suggests an extension of the model into a framework of competitive selection, an extension that is presented in section 6.3. This framework assumes that different firms have different efficiency levels and that each firm gradually learns about its own efficiency. An alternative change to the model of perfect competition is to introduce product heterogeneity. This leads to the model of monopolistic competition, which is presented in section 6.4.

6.1   PERFECT COMPETITION

The model of **perfect competition** is based on five central assumptions. First, the assumption of **atomicity**, namely that there are many suppliers in the market: Each supplier is so small that its actions have no significant impact on other suppliers. Second, the assumption of **product homogeneity**, namely that the product supplied by the different firms is the same. Third, the assumption of **perfect information**, namely that all agents (firms, consumers) know the prices set by all firms. Fourth, the assumption of **equal access**, namely that all firms have access to all production technologies. Finally, the assumption of **free entry**, namely that any firm may enter or exit the market as it wishes.

Similarly to the case of monopoly, we assume that each firm's objective is to maximize profits, which implies that marginal revenue equals marginal cost. However, *in a perfectly competitive market, marginal revenue is equal to price*, so the optimal rule becomes

$$p = MC.$$

The equality $MR = p$ under perfect competition is an approximate one. If the firm sets a price above that of the other firms, then it sells nothing. If, on the other hand, the firm sets a price below the other firms', then it receives all of the market demand, which, in comparison to its capacity, is a large quantity. That is, at the price level set by the other firms, demand goes from zero to "infinity": Market demand, at the scale of each firm's capacity, is like infinity. We represent this by assuming that the demand faced by each firm is horizontal and that each firm is a **price taker**.

The model of perfect competition shows that competition is a good thing. Specifically, the equilibrium under perfect competition is *efficient*, in two senses. First, each firm sets the efficient output level, that is, the output level such that price equals marginal cost: A lower output level would be less efficient, for willingness to pay would be greater than cost; conversely, a higher output level would also be inefficient, for willingness to pay would be lower than cost. Second, the set of firms active in the long run is efficient: Because of free entry, firms produce a long-run output such that price equals the minimum average cost. A higher or a lower number of firms would imply a greater level of total cost for the same output level.

Notice that the efficiency concept that we refer to is one of static efficiency (even though we talk about a "long-run" equilibrium). In particular, perfect competition leads to maximum efficiency *given the existing technology*. However, the model is silent about the implications of competition for technical progress. This is a problem that we address in chapter 16. For now, we simply note:

> Perfect competition implies maximum efficiency in a static sense, that is, for a given set of available technologies.

Although one can find examples that come close to the model of perfect competition, no real-world industry can aptly be described as perfectly competitive. At best, the model of perfect competition provides an approximation to the behavior of those industries. In section 6.2, we present a series of stylized facts that suggest the model of perfect competition may not always be a good approximation. We then present two extensions of the basic model that account for the observed stylized facts. The model of competitive selection (section 6.3) addresses the issue of entry. The model of monopolistic competition (section 6.4) addresses the issue of product differentiation.

6.2   FROM THEORY TO STYLIZED FACTS

What does the model of perfect competition have to say about entry, exit, and firm size? The long-run equilibrium under perfect competition is a limit point that industries converge to by means of successive entry and exit. If active firms make positive profits, then new firms are attracted to the industry. If, on the contrary, active firms make losses, then some of those firms exit. Finally, in the long-run equilibrium, price equals the minimum of the long-run average cost. Because technology (i.e., the cost function) is the same for all firms (because of the equal access assumption), each firm receives zero supranormal profits and there is neither entry nor exit.

Concerning the size distribution of firms, the perfect competition model is either rather extreme or extremely scant: Assuming plant-level cost functions are U-shaped, all plants must be of the same size in the long run (i.e., there is only one output level that minimizes average cost). If the managerial costs of owning more than one plant are positive, then each firm owns one plant only and all firms are of the same size. If, on the contrary, managerial costs are zero, then there exists a virtually uncountable number of possible industry configurations, all of which are consistent with the model.[a]

The empirical evidence from various industries with "many" small firms is, however, widely at odds with the above view of industry dynamics. First, in any given period and industry, entry and exit take place simultaneously. Second, many firms earn supranormal rates of profit even in the long run. Third, the size distribution of firms displays a number of regularities and is not concentrated on a single size. In the remainder of this section, we present data on these and related stylized facts.

PROFITS IN THE LONG RUN

Empirical evidence suggests that *profit rates are persistent in the long run*, contrary to the implication of perfect competition. In particular, one author examined profit rates for a sample of 600 U.S. firms from 1950 to 1972. He classified firms in groups of 100 according to average profits in the period from 1950 to 1952 and computed average profit rates in the whole 23-year period for each of the groups. The hypothesis that profits converge to the competitive level in the long run would imply that inter group differences are insignificant on average. However, the data reject that any pair of averages is equal. In other words, average differences in profitability across the groups persist even after 23 years.[64]

[a] In fact, there may be economies of scale in multi-plant firms—for example, large-scale purchasing discounts—that counteract increased managerial costs. But this would take us back to a U-shaped cost curve and the prediction that all firms have the same number of plants.[63]

Table 6.1 Annual Gross Entry and Exit Rates (%). [65]

Country	Gross Entry	Gross Exit	Time Period	Data*
Belgium/Man	5.8	6.3	80–84	130/3/E/E
Belgium/Serv	13.0	12.2	80–84	79/3/E/E
Canada	4.0	4.8	71–79	167/4/E/S
FRG	3.8	4.6	83–85	183/4/F/S
Korea	3.3	5.7	76–81	62/4,5/F/S
Norway	8.2	8.7	80–85	80/4/F/S
Portugal	12.3	9.5	83–86	234/5/E/E
United Kingdom	6.5	5.1	74–79	114/4/F/S
United States	7.7	7.0	63–82	387/4/F/S

* Number of industries/aggregation level (no. digit industries)/Firm or Establishment level/ Employment or Sales data.

Entry and Exit Rates

The perfect competition model predicts that, in any given period, there will be either entry into an industry (active firms are earning supranormal profit rates), or exit from that industry (active firms are earning infranormal profit rates). The empirical evidence suggests that, in any given period and industry, *entry and exit take place at the same time*, with the gross entry and exit rates being much higher (typically one order of magnitude higher) than the *net* entry rate.[b]

Table 6.1 presents data from several countries. For example, in Norway in the period from 1980 to 1985, the average gross entry rate for a 4-digit industry was 8.2%, whereas the average exit rate was 8.7%.[c] The difference, $8.2 - 8.7 = -.5\%$, an approximation of the average net entry rate, is one order of magnitude lower than either the gross entry or the gross exit rate.

Size, Growth, and Survival

[b] By "one order of magnitude higher," we mean with one extra digit, that is, about ten times greater.

[c] Industries are classified in groups, subgroups, subsubgroups, and so forth. For each subdivision, one digit is added to the classification. So, a five-digit classification is more detailed than a four-digit one.

Empirical evidence suggests that the average size of entrants and exiters is much smaller than industry average size. From a sample of eight countries, one obtains values between 6.7% (U.S.) and 44.9% (U.K.) for entrants. That is, the average entrant's size in the United States is 6.7%, the average incumbent's size. For exiters, the rates vary between 6.9% (U.S.) and 61.2% (U.K.).[66]

Several empirical studies indicate that expected growth rates are decreasing in size and in age. In other words, it is mainly small, young firms that grow fast. The same occurs with respect to survival rates: It is mainly young and small firms that exit (note that the second fact is consistent with the evidence presented in the preceding paragraph).

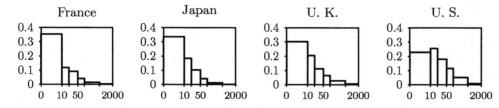

FIGURE 6.1   FIRM SIZE DISTRIBUTION, WHERE SIZE IS MEASURED BY NUMBER OF EMPLOYEES.[67]

FIRM SIZE DISTRIBUTION

The model of perfect competition implies that all firms are of the same size (assuming U-shaped cost curves) or that almost any size distribution is consistent with the model (assuming constant returns to scale). The data however exhibit significant regularities in the firm-size distribution. The histograms in figure 6.1, for example, display the distribution of manufacturing firm size for selected countries.[d] Although these countries are very different in total size, the distributions look remarkably similar. Similar results are obtained with sectoral distributions.

6.3   COMPETITIVE SELECTION[68]

To explain the stylized facts described in the previous section, we need to relax some of the assumptions of the model of perfect competition. We maintain the assumptions that (1) firms are price takers; (2) the product is homogeneous; (3) information about prices is perfect. However, in contrast with the perfect competition model, suppose that (4) firms must pay a sunk cost in order to enter; and (5) not all firms have access to the same technology.

Specifically, suppose that *different firms have different degrees of efficiency*, which in turn correspond to different cost functions: More efficient firms have a lower marginal cost schedule. These differences may result from a variety of factors. For example, some managers are more efficient in organizing resources than others (more on this later).

Suppose moreover that *each firm is uncertain about its own efficiency*. When a firm first enters an industry, it has only a vague idea of what its efficiency is. As times goes by, and based on each period's experience, the firm gradually forms a more precise estimate of its true efficiency. In each period, the firm chooses optimal output based on its current expectation of efficiency—basically, the output level such that price is equal to expected marginal cost.

Given the preceding elements, we conclude that firms that get a series of bad signals (high production costs) gradually become "pessimistic" about their efficiency level, gradually decrease their output, and, eventually, may decide to exit the industry

[d] Each bar on a histogram gives the frequency with which a given firm size occurs. For example, the first bar in the histogram for France indicates that most firms in France have fewer than 10 employees: The area of the first bar is greater than the total area of the remaining bars.

(as variable profit does not compensate for the fixed cost). By contrast, firms that receive a series of good signals (low production costs) remain active and gradually increase their output.

This model of **competitive selection** is consistent with several of the stylized facts described in the previous section. First, the model implies that *different firms earn different profit rates, even in the long run* although, arguably, this is a bit of a tautology, for we *assumed* that different firms have different cost functions. Second, the model is consistent with the stylized fact of *simultaneous entry and exit in the same industry*. Firms that accumulate a series of unfavorable productivity signals hold an unfavorable estimate of their own efficiency. As a result, their expected value from remaining active is negative, which in turn leads them to exit. New entrants have no information regarding their efficiency. Their expected efficiency is therefore much better than that of exiting firms: No news is better than bad news. This justifies that their expected value from being active is positive, in fact, greater than the entry cost. In summary, it is possible for a firm with no information about its efficiency to enter while a firm with unfavorable information about efficiency exits.

Efficient firms are firms with a low marginal cost function. Because firms equate price with (expected) marginal cost, it follows that more efficient firms sell a higher output. Together with the previous results, this implies that exiters (the active firms with lowest expected efficiency) are also the firms with lower output. By selection, the firms that remain active have an efficiency that is higher than average. In particular, it is higher than that of the average entrant. It follows that entrants' output is lower than the average output of surviving firms. In this way, the model is also consistent with the stylized fact that *firms that enter and firms that exit are smaller than average*.

Heterogeneity of, and uncertainty about, firm efficiency reconciles the competitive model with empirical observation regarding (a) simultaneous entry and exit; (b) relative size of entrants/exiters vis-à-vis incumbents.

Finally, the competitive selection model is also consistent with the empirical observation that the firm size distribution is neither single-valued nor indeterminate, as the perfect competition model would imply. In fact, a given population distribution of efficiency levels implies a particular distribution of firm sizes.

At this point, it may be worth pointing out that the competitive selection model does not depend on firms being asymmetric with respect to costs. We could alternatively assume that some firms make products that are better than others. Consider, for example, the laser industry. Most new firms in this industry are spin-offs from existing firms. Typically, a scientist/engineer from one firm leaves it to form his or her own firm. This industry is an interesting example because (1) it illustrates a source of variation across firms (scientific know how); and (2) it suggests that differences across firms need not be limited to cost differences.

However, it must be admitted that the above characterization of the firm size distribution is, to a great extent, tautological: The distribution of efficiency levels is *assumed* rather than derived; a more satisfactory model would also explain the distribution of efficiency levels.[e]

COMPETITIVE SELECTION AND EFFICIENCY

For all its differences with respect to perfect competition, competitive selection maintains one important property—efficiency. First, notice that each firm's output decision in each period is efficient: Price equal to expected marginal cost is the most efficient output decision, that is, the one that maximizes total surplus. Moreover, it can be shown that the firm's entry and exit decisions are also optimal from a social point of view. The basic idea is the same as in the model of perfect competition: A very small firm has a negligible impact on other firms and on price. It follows that it internalizes all of the costs and benefits from entering or exiting the industry: What is good for the firm is good for society.

It might seem inefficient to have firms entering and exiting the industry simultaneously. But we must remember that firms are uncertain about their efficiency. The only way to determine a firm's efficiency is to actually enter the industry. A central planner who attempted to maximize total surplus would not be able to do better than the market.

> The equilibrium under competitive selection is efficient.

6.4 MONOPOLISTIC COMPETITION

One of the criticisms frequently addressed to the model of perfect competition is that it is based on the assumption of product homogeneity, that is, the assumption that all firms produce the same identical product. There are many industries comprising a large number of firms (as in the perfect competition model) whose products are not exactly identical. Examples of this include small restaurants and shampoo. Both of these examples feature a large number of sellers: Witness, for example, the number of different shampoo brands typically displayed on a supermarket shelf. Moreover, the technology for making shampoo or serving meals is fairly well known and accessible. These observations would suggest perfect competition as the relevant model. However, different restaurants serve different types and quality of food, and likewise not all shampoos are equal. This is where the model of perfect competition fails.

[e] One possibility is to assume that firms invest in R&D and that efficiency levels result from these R&D investments.[69] A completely different approach to understanding the firm size distribution is to consider a model of dynamic stochastic growth wherein different growth rates result in a distribution of firm sizes. Suppose, for example, that there is a set of laser machine manufacturers and that, in each period, a new machine is demanded in the market. Suppose, moreover, that each of the existing firms receives each new order with equal probability. It can be shown that a process of this sort implies a distribution of firm size, in fact, one that approximates the empirically observed distribution fairly well. We return to this sort of model in chapter 14.

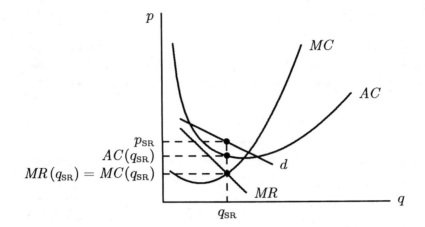

FIGURE 6.2 SHORT-RUN EQUILIBRIUM UNDER MONOPOLISTIC COMPETITION.

To account for this type of industry, E. Chamberlin proposed the model of monopolistic competition as an alternative reference point with respect to the model of perfect competition.[70]

The **monopolistic competition model** assumes that there is a large number of firms, so that the impact of each firm upon its rivals is negligible (as in the perfect competition model). However, because of product differentiation, the demand curve faced by each firm is not horizontal, that is, each firm is a price maker, not a price taker. Finally, as in perfect competition, we assume that there is free entry and free access to all available technologies. In summary, *the monopolistic competition model maintains all of the assumptions of perfect competition except that of product homogeneity*.

One of the main learning points of the monopolistic competition model is that abandoning the assumption of product homogeneity implies abandoning some of the results of the perfect competition model, while maintaining others. This is illustrated in figures 6.2 and 6.3. Let us first consider the short-run equilibrium, that is, the equilibrium when the number of firms is given. In figure 6.2, d is the demand curve for a typical firm and MR the corresponding marginal revenue curve;[f] AC is the average cost curve and MC the corresponding marginal cost curve. A profit-maximizing firm will choose an output level such that marginal revenue equals marginal cost, that is, an output of q_{SR}.

At the short-run output level in figure 6.2, the price received by each firm, p_{SR}, is greater than average cost, $AC(q_{SR})$. This is a feature of the particular short-run equilibrium we are considering, that is, there could be a different short-run equilibrium for which price would be lower than average cost; it all depends on the number of firms in the market in the short run.

Whichever is the case, so long as price is different from average cost, the short-run equilibrium is not a long-run equilibrium. If $p > AC(q_{SR})$, as in figure 6.2, then outside firms are willing to enter the market. In fact, all firms have access to the same technology,

[f] We use lowercase d to indicate that this is the demand curve faced by each firm, not the market demand curve.

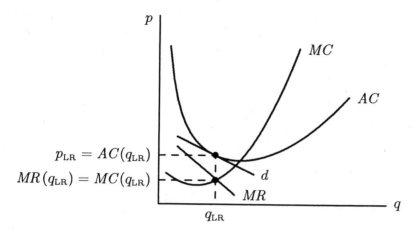

FIGURE 6.3 LONG-RUN EQUILIBRIUM UNDER MONOPOLISTIC COMPETITION.

and each firm is so small that its impact upon other firms is negligible. This implies that a potential entrant expects profits of approximately the same amount as those of the typical incumbent, that is, $\pi = \left(p_{SR} - AC(q_{SR})\right) q_{SR}$. If, on the contrary, $p < AC(q_{SR})$, then incumbent firms earn negative profits and would do better by exiting the market.

The long-run equilibrium is then the situation in which (1) firms maximize profits, so that marginal revenue equals marginal cost; and (2) firms make zero profits (that is, price equals average cost), so that no active firm wishes to become inactive or vice versa. Figure 6.3 depicts such an equilibrium.

Comparing this with the long-run equilibrium of the perfect competition model, we notice one important similarity and one important difference. Common to both models is the feature that, *because of free entry, profits are zero in the long run.* However, this zero-profit equilibrium implies that price equals the minimum average cost in the perfect competition model, whereas *under monopolistic competition, price is greater than the minimum average cost.* To put it differently, price equals marginal cost under perfect competition, whereas *price is greater than marginal cost under monopolistic competition.*

Under free entry, the propositions "price is greater than the minimum of average cost" and "price is greater than marginal cost" are equivalent (see Exercise 6.3). However, they imply two different (though related) sources of allocative inefficiency. The fact that price is greater than the minimum of average cost implies that, by reallocating production across firms, it is possible to reduce total industry cost. Specifically, each firm produces too small an output under monopolistic competition (see figure 6.3): Total costs would be lower if there were fewer firms producing a higher output. The fact that price is greater than marginal cost implies that, by increasing output, total surplus increases: At the margin, what consumers are willing to pay (price) is greater than what firms have to pay (marginal cost).

Under perfect competition, we have both zero profits (price equal to average cost) and efficiency (price equal to marginal cost). This coincidence has led many to equate zero profits with efficiency. The monopolistic competition model shows that such equivalence is, in general, unwarranted. Zero profits are the result of free entry.[8] The models of both perfect competition and monopolistic competition are based on the assumption of free entry, and therefore result in zero profits. Productive efficiency obtains when production costs are minimized. Such minimization takes place under perfect competition (because firms are price takers), but not under monopolistic competition (where firms are price makers). In summary:

> Equilibrium profits under monopolistic competition are zero, but firms do not produce at the minimum of their average cost.

It follows that *zero profits do not necessarily imply efficiency*.

The monopolistic competition model also shows that *perfect competition is best thought of as an approximation*. It is true that very few industries, if any, satisfy the extreme assumptions of the perfect competition model, in particular the assumption of product homogeneity. However, if the product is approximately homogeneous, then outcomes are approximately like those of perfect competition. In fact, as the degree of product differentiation decreases, the residual demand faced by each firm becomes flatter and flatter, and the point at which price equals average cost (long-run equilibrium) becomes closer and closer to the point where price equals marginal cost (efficiency).

Finally, notice that allocative inefficiency under monopolistic competition (price greater than marginal cost and the minimum of average cost) does not necessarily imply overall inefficiency; one must also consider the benefits from product variety. If each firm were to produce at the level q such that average cost is minimum, and if price were to equal average cost (and marginal cost), then the number of active firms would be lower than under the long-run monopolistic competition equilibrium. But, assuming that consumers value variety (which is consistent with the assumption that individual demands are downward sloping), then such a move would imply a loss of consumer utility. This loss of product variety must be weighed against the gain in terms of production costs when determining the efficiency of the long-run equilibrium. More on this in chapter 14.

[8] To be more precise, zero profits result from free entry *and* equal access to the best available technologies. The case when the first condition holds but not the second was addressed in section 6.3.

6.5 COMING NEXT

Although the models of monopoly and perfect competition correspond to two opposite extremes in the set of possible market structures, they have several things in common. In particular, strategic considerations are absent from both models: Under perfect competition (or competitive selection, or monopolistic competition), firms are, by assumption, small, so that the impact of their actions upon rivals is negligible; under monopoly, there is only one large firm, so that, again, strategic considerations are absent.

This leaves out a whole variety of intermediate market structures wherein there is more than one "large" firm. Under these circumstances, strategic considerations play an important role: When choosing its actions, a firm must account for the impact that such actions will have upon rivals, and how rivals will likely react to the firm's actions. The firm must also try to guess what its rivals' actions are going to be, for such actions will have an impact on its profits.

The next few chapters are devoted to the analysis of competition under **oligopoly**, the situation in which there are several large firms competing with each other. We begin by looking at the basic theory of oligopoly (chapter 7), which is then extended to consider dynamic elements (chapter 8), product differentiation (chapter 12), entry and exit (chapter 14), and research and development (chapter 16), among others.

Table 6.2 lists the main assumptions of oligopoly as well as those of each of the models surveyed in this and the previous chapters. In addition to the extremes of monopoly and perfect competition, we also looked at "neighboring" models to perfect competition, models that are obtained by changing one of the assumptions. One of the main points in this chapter is that changing the assumptions regarding product differentiation, free access, or competitive entry does not change significantly the performance of the perfect competition models. As the next few chapters show, strategic behavior changes things much more radically. In this sense, we can divide industry structures, and models of industry behavior, into three categories: (1) highly concentrated industries (monopolies or industries with a dominant firm); (2) oligopolies; and (3) competitive industries (with or without product differentiation; with or without free access to the best available technologies). The separation between lines in table 6.2 highlights this division.

TABLE 6.2 SUMMARY OF MAIN MODELS OF MARKET COMPETITION.

Model	Strategic Behavior	Homogeneous Product	Free Entry	Equal Access
Monopoly	No	Yes	No	No
Oligopoly	Yes	Yes/No	No/Yes	Yes/No
Competitive Selection	No	Yes	Yes	No
Monopolistic Competition	No	No	Yes	Yes
Perfect Competition	No	Yes	Yes	Yes

Equal access refers to equal access by all firms to the best available technology (i.e., symmetric cost functions). Yes/No entries result from differences between basic version and more elaborated versions of the model.

SUMMARY

- Perfect competition implies maximum efficiency in a static sense, that is, for a given set of available technologies.

- Heterogeneity of, and uncertainty about, firm efficiency reconciles the competitive model with empirical observation regarding (1) simultaneous entry and exit; and (2) relative size of entrants/exiters vis-à-vis incumbents.

- Equilibrium profits under monopolistic competition are zero, but firms do not produce at the minimum of average cost.

KEY CONCEPTS

- perfect competition

- atomicity

- product homogeneity

- perfect information

- equal access

- free entry

- price-taking behavior

- competitive selection

- monopolistic competition

REVIEW AND PRACTICE EXERCISES

6.1   The technology of book publishing is characterized by a high fixed cost (type-setting the book) and a very low marginal cost (printing). Prices are set at much higher levels than marginal cost. However, book publishing yields a normal rate of return. Are these facts consistent with profit maximizing behavior by publishers? Which model do you think best describes this industry?

6.2 The market for laundry detergent is monopolistically competitive. Each firm owns one brand, and each brand has effectively differentiated itself so that is has some market power (i.e., faces a downward sloping demand curve). Still, no brand earns economic profits because entry causes the demand for each brand to shift in until the seller can just break even. All firms have identical cost functions, which are U-shaped.

Suppose that the government does a study on detergents and finds out they are all alike. The public is notified of these findings and suddenly drops allegiance to any brand. What happens to price when this product that was brand-differentiated becomes a commodity? What happens to total sales? What happens to the number of firms in the market?[71]

6.3** Show that, in a long-run equilibrium with free entry and equal access to the best available technologies, the comparison of price to the minimum of average cost and the comparison of price to marginal cost are equivalent tests of allocative efficiency. In other words, price is greater than the minimum of average costs if and only if price is greater than marginal cost.

Show, by example, that the same is not true in general.

PART THREE

OLIGOPOLY

CHAPTER 7

OLIGOPOLY COMPETITION

In part two of this book, we have looked at the extreme market structures of monopoly and perfect competition. Although these are useful points of reference, empirical observation suggests that most real-world markets are somewhere between the extremes. Normally, we find industries with a few (more than one) firms, but less than the "very large number" usually assumed by the model of perfect competition. The situation in which there are a few competitors is designated by **oligopoly** (**duopoly** if the number is two).

One thing the extremes of monopoly and perfect competition have in common is that each firm does not have to worry about its rivals' reactions. In the case of monopoly, this is trivial as there are no rivals. In the case of perfect competition, the idea is that each firm is so small that its actions have no significant impact on rivals. Not so in the case of oligopoly. Consider the following news article excerpt:

In a strategic shift in the United States and Canada, Coca-Cola Co. is . . . gearing up to raise the prices it charges its customers for soft drinks by about 5% . . . The price changes could help boost Coke's profit . . .

 Important to the success of Coke and its bottlers is how Pepsi-Cola . . . responds. The No. 2 soft-drink company could well sacrifice some margins to pick up market share on Coke, some analysts said.[72]

As this example suggests, by contrast with the extremes of monopoly and perfect competition, an important characteristic of oligopolies is the strategic interdependence between competitors: An action by Firm 1, say, Coke, is likely to influence Firm 2's profits, say, Pepsi, and vice versa. For this reason, Coke's decision process should take into account what it expects Pepsi to do, specifically, how Coke expects its decisions to impact on Pepsi's profits and, consequently, how it expects Pepsi to react. Part three of this book is dedicated to the formal analysis of oligopoly competition. We begin in this chapter with some simple models that characterize the process of interdependent strategic decision making under oligopoly: the Bertrand model and the Cournot model.

7.1   THE BERTRAND MODEL

Pricing is probably the most basic strategy that firms must decide on. The demand received by each firm depends on the price it sets. Moreover, when the number of firms is small, demand also depends on the prices set by rival firms. It is precisely this interdependence between rivals' decisions that differentiates duopoly competition (and more generally oligopoly competition) from the extremes of monopoly and perfect competition. When Compaq, for example, decides which prices to set for its PCs, the company has to make some conjecture regarding the prices set by rival Dell. Based on this conjecture it must determine the optimal price, taking into account how demand for the Compaq PC depends on both the Compaq price and the Dell price.[a]

To analyze the interdependence of pricing decisions, we begin with the simplest model of duopoly competition, the Bertrand model.[73] The model consists of two firms in a market for a homogeneous product and the assumption that firms simultaneously set their prices. We will also assume that both firms have the same marginal cost, MC, that marginal cost is constant, and that the demand is linear.[b]

Because the duopolists' products are perfect substitutes (the product is homogeneous), whichever firm sets the lowest price gets all of the demand. Specifically, if p_i, the price set by firm i, is lower than p_j, the price set by firm j, then firm i's demand is given by $D(p_i)$ (the market demand), whereas firm j's demand is zero. If both firms set the same price, $p_i = p_j = p$, then each firm receives one half of the market demand, $\frac{1}{2}D(p)$.

What is each firm's best strategy in this context? As suggested previously, Firm 1's optimal price depends on what it conjectures Firm 2 will choose, and vice versa. Suppose that Firm 1 expects Firm 2 to price above monopoly price. Then Firm 1's optimal strategy is to price at the monopoly level. In fact, by doing so, Firm 1 gets all of the demand and receives monopoly profits (the maximum possible profits). If Firm 1 expects Firm 2 to price below monopoly price but above marginal cost, then Firm 1's optimal strategy is to set a price just below that of Firm 2.[c] Pricing above would lead to zero demand and zero profits. Pricing below gives firm i all of the market demand, but with lower profits, the lower the price is. Finally, if Firm 1 expects Firm 2 to price below marginal cost, then Firm 1's optimal choice is to price higher than Firm 2, say, at marginal cost level.

The preceding set of optimal prices defines Firm 1's best response with respect to Firm 2's choice. More generally, firm i's **best response** (also known as **reaction function**) is a function $p_i^*(p_j)$ that gives, for each price by firm j, firm i's optimal price.

[a] Moreover, in a dynamic setting, Compaq must also take into account that current price choices will likely influence the rival's future price choices. This we will see in chapter 8.

[b] The Bertrand model is more general than the simplified version presented here, but the main ideas are the same.

[c] What does "just below" mean? If p_1 could be any real number, then "just below" would not be well defined: There exists no real number "just below" another real number. In practice, prices have to be set on a finite grid (in cents of the dollar, for example), in which case "just below" would mean one cent less. This points to an important assumption of the Bertrand model: Firm 1 will steal all of Firm 2's demand even if its price is only one cent lower than the rival's.

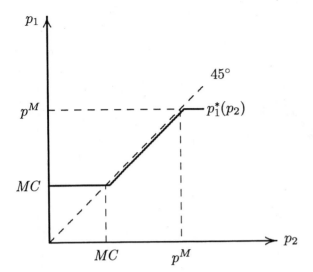

FIGURE 7.1 BERTRAND MODEL: FIRM 1'S REACTION CURVE.

Figure 7.1 depicts Firm 1's reaction curve, $p_1^*(p_2)$, in a graph with each firm's strategy on each axis. Consistent with the above derivation, for values of p_2 less than MC, Firm 1 chooses $p_1 = MC$. For values of p_2 greater than MC but lower than p^M, Firm 1 chooses p_1 just below p_2. Finally, for values of p_2 greater than monopoly price, p^M, Firm 1 chooses $p_1 = p^M$.

Because Firm 2 has the same marginal cost as Firm 1, its reaction curve is identical to that of Firm 1, that is, symmetrical with respect to the 45° line. Figure 7.2 depicts Firm 2's reaction curve, $p_2^*(p_1)$, in addition to that of Firm 1.

A Nash equilibrium is a pair of strategies—a pair of prices, in this case—such that no firm can increase profits by unilaterally changing price. In terms of figure 7.2, this is given by the *intersection of the reaction curves*, point N. In fact, this is the point at which $p_1 = p_1^*(p_2)$ (because the point is on Firm 1's reaction curve) and $p_2 = p_2^*(p_1)$ (because the point is on Firm 2's reaction curve). As can be seen from figure 7.2, point N corresponds to both firms setting a price equal to marginal cost, MC.

Another way of deriving the same conclusion is to think about a possible equilibrium price p' greater than marginal cost. If both firms were to set that price, each would earn $\frac{1}{2}D(p')(p' - MC)$. However, by setting a slightly smaller price, one of the firms would be able to almost double its profits to $D(p' - \epsilon)(p' - \epsilon - MC)$, where ϵ is a small number. This argument holds for any possible candidate equilibrium price p' greater than

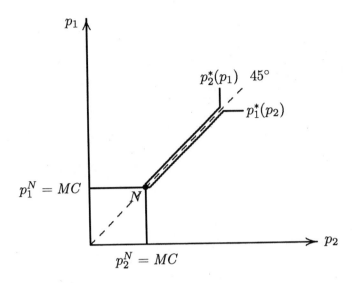

FIGURE 7.2 BERTRAND MODEL: EQUILIBRIUM.

marginal cost. We thus conclude that the only possible equilibrium price is $p = MC$. In summary:

> Under price competition with homogeneous product and constant, symmetric marginal cost (Bertrand competition), firms price at the level of marginal cost.

Notice that this result is valid even with only two competitors (as we have considered earlier). This is a fairly drastic result. As the number of competitors goes from one to two, equilibrium price goes from monopoly price to perfect competition price. Two competitors are sufficient to guarantee perfect competition.

7.2   PRICING WITH CAPACITY CONSTRAINTS

The prediction of the Bertrand model does not seem very realistic. In real-world markets, an increase in the number of firms (beyond 2) normally implies a decrease in equilibrium price, whereas the Bertrand model would predict no change in price. Moreover, most industries with only two competitors seem to make more than zero profits.

In deriving the Bertrand equilibrium, we have seen that a price above marginal cost cannot be an equilibrium price. At that price, at least one firm would have an incentive to undercut the rival and thus capture all of the demand. This is certainly consistent with the assumptions of the Bertrand model; but is it realistic? A close examination of the assumptions that underline this feature of the Bertrand model suggests some solutions, or explanations, for the apparent paradox of the Bertrand model.

1. **Product differentiation.** The Bertrand model assumes that both firms sell the same product. If, however, firms sell differentiated products, then duopoly price competition does not necessarily drive prices down to marginal cost, as in the Bertrand model. In fact, undercutting the rival does not guarantee a firm total market demand as in the Bertrand model. The case of product differentiation is developed in chapter 12.

2. **Dynamic competition.** The Bertrand model assumes that firms compete in one period only, that is, price is chosen once and for all. One of the likely consequences of undercutting a rival's price is that the latter will retaliate by lowering its price too, possibly initiating a price war. In that case, undercutting does not guarantee a firm total market demand, except perhaps in the short run. The possibility of retaliation is not considered in the Bertrand model because of its static nature. In the next chapter, we will consider dynamic games and will show that, even when firms set prices and the product is homogeneous, there exist equilibria wherein price is strictly greater than marginal cost.

3. **Capacity constraints.** By undercutting the rival, a Bertrand duopolist receives all of the market demand. But what good is this if the firm does not have sufficient capacity to satisfy all of this demand? In other words, one important assumption of the Bertrand model is that firms have no capacity constraints. In what follows, we show how capacity constraints can also solve the Bertrand "paradox."

We maintain the same assumptions as in the previous section: Firms simultaneously set prices, marginal cost is constant (zero, for simplicity), and the product is homogeneous. However, we now additionally assume that each firm is constrained by its capacity, k_i. That is, firm i cannot sell more than k_i; if its demand turns out to be greater than k_i, then its sales will be only k_i.

Under Bertrand competition, if Firm 2 were to set a price greater than that of Firm 1, its demand would be zero. The same is not necessarily true if Firm 1 is capacity-constrained, however. Suppose that $p_2 > p_1$ and that $D(p_1) > k_1$, that is, Firm 1 is capacity-constrained. Firm 1's sales will be given by k_1: it will sell as much as it can. Firm 2's demand, in turn, will be given by $D(p_2) - k_1$ (or zero, if this expression is negative). $D(p_2)$ would be Firm 2's demand if it had no competition. Having a rival price below, some of that demand will be stolen, specifically, k_1. However, if k_1 is small enough, a positive residual demand will remain.[d]

[d] This expression for firm i's residual demand, $D(p_i) - k_j$, is valid only under the assumption that the customers served by firm j are the ones with the greatest willingness to pay.[74]

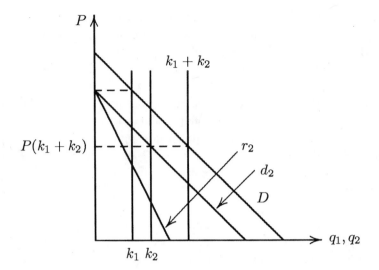

FIGURE 7.3 FIRM 2'S OPTIMUM.

The situation of price competition (Bertrand competition) with capacity constraints is illustrated in figure 7.3. $D(p)$ is the demand curve. Two vertical lines represent each firm's capacity. In this example, Firm 2 is the one with greater capacity: $k_2 > k_1$. The third vertical line, $k_1 + k_2$, represents total industry capacity.

Let $P(Q)$ be the inverse demand curve, that is, the inverse of $D(p)$.[e] Moreover, let $P(k_1 + k_2)$ be the price level such that, if both firms were to set $p = P(k_1 + k_2)$, total demand would be exactly equal to total capacity. This price level is simply derived from the intersection of the demand curve with the total capacity curve. We will now argue that the equilibrium of the price-setting game consists of both firms setting $p_i = P(k_1 + k_2)$. In other words, firms set prices such that total demand equals industry capacity.

Let us consider Firm 2's optimization problem assuming that Firm 1 sets $p_1 = P(k_1 + k_2)$. Can Firm 2 do better than setting $p_2 = p_1 = P(k_1 + k_2)$? One alternative strategy is to set $p_2 < P(k_1 + k_2)$. By undercutting its rival, Firm 2 receives all of the market demand. However, because Firm 2 is already capacity-constrained when it sets $p_2 = P(k_1 + k_2)$, setting a lower price does not help: On the contrary, Firm 2 receives lower profits by setting a lower price (same output sold at a lower price).

What about setting a price higher than $P(k_1 + k_2)$? The idea is that, because Firm 1 is capacity-constrained when $p_1 = P(k_1 + k_2)$, Firm 2 will receive positive demand even if it prices above Firm 1. Figure 7.3 depicts Firm 2's residual demand, d_2, under the assumption that $p_2 > p_1$ and $p_1 = P(k_1 + k_2)$: Firm 2 gets $D(p_2)$ minus Firm 1's output, k_1, so d_2 is parallel to D, the difference being k_1. The figure also depicts Firm 2's marginal revenue curve, r_2. As can be seen, marginal revenue is greater than marginal cost (zero) for every value of output less than Firm 2's capacity. This implies that setting a higher

[e] $D(p)$, the direct demand curve (or simply demand curve), corresponds to taking price as the independent variable, that is, quantity as a function of price; $P(Q)$, the inverse demand curve, corresponds to taking quantity as the independent variable, that is, price as a function of quantity.

price than $P(k_1 + k_2)$, which is the same as selling a lower output than $q_2 = k_2$, would imply a lower profit: The revenue loss (the positive marginal revenue) is greater than the cost saving (the value of marginal cost, which is zero).

A similar argument would hold for Firm 1 as well: Given that $p_2 = P(k_1 + k_2)$, Firm 1's optimal strategy is to set $p_1 = P(k_1 + k_2)$. We thus conclude that $p_1 = p_2 = P(k_1 + k_2)$ is indeed an equilibrium. Notice that, if capacity levels were high, then the previous argument would not hold; that is, it might be optimal for a firm to undercut its rival's price. However, if capacities are relatively small, then the result obtains that *equilibrium prices are such that total demand equals total capacity*.[f] In summary:

If total industry capacity is low in relation to market demand, then equilibrium prices are greater than marginal cost.

To conclude, notice that the same analysis applies to the case when firms must decide beforehand how much to produce and then set prices. In this case, each firm's sales are equal to the minimum of that firm's demand and its output. As a result, if total quantity produced is low relative to total demand, then in equilibrium, firms set prices such that total demand just clears the total output previously produced. That is, for each pair of output choices (q_1, q_2), equilibrium prices are given by $p_1 = p_2 = P(q_1 + q_2)$.

7.3   THE COURNOT MODEL

In the previous section we concluded that, if firms' sales are limited by the output they produced beforehand, then in equilibrium, firms set prices such that total demand just clears total output.[g] This analysis can be taken one step back: What output levels should firms choose in the first place? Suppose that output decisions are made simultaneously before prices are chosen. Based on this analysis, firms know that, for each pair of output choices (q_1, q_2), equilibrium prices will be $p_1 = p_2 = P(q_1 + q_2)$. This implies that firm i's profit is given by $\pi_i = q_i (P(q_1 + q_2) - c)$, assuming, as before, constant marginal cost, c. The game wherein firms simultaneously choose output levels is known as the Cournot model.[76] Specifically, suppose there are two firms in a market for a homogeneous product. Firms choose simultaneously the quantity they want to produce. The market price is then set at the level such that demand equals the total quantity produced by both firms.

As in section 7.1, our goal is to derive the equilibrium of the model, that is, the equilibrium of the game played between the two firms. Also as in section 7.1, we do so in two steps. First, we derive each firm's optimal choice given its conjecture of what the

[f] If capacity costs are sufficiently high, then firms' capacity levels will surely be sufficiently low such that the previous result holds. However, it can be shown that, even if capacity costs were low, the same would be true.[75]

[g] The same applies for the choice of production capacity. However, for the purpose of this section, we focus on the case when firms choose output level in the first place.

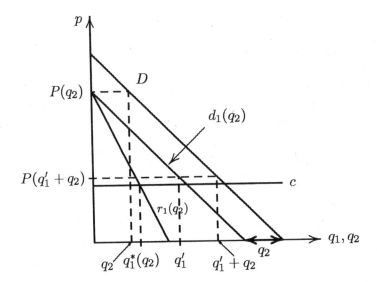

FIGURE 7.4   FIRM 1'S OPTIMUM.

rival does, that is, the firm's reaction curve. Second, we put the reaction curves together and find a mutually consistent combination of actions and conjectures.

Suppose that Firm 1 believes Firm 2 is producing a quantity q_2. What is Firm 1's optimal quantity? The answer is provided by figure 7.4. If Firm 1 decides not to produce anything, then price is given by $P(0 + q_2) = P(q_2)$. If Firm 1 instead produces, say, q_1', then price is given by $P(q_1' + q_2)$. More generally, for each quantity that Firm 1 might decide to set, price is given by the curve $d_1(q_2)$. The curve $d_1(q_2)$ is called Firm 1's **residual demand**: It gives all possible combinations of Firm 1's quantity and price *for a given a value of q_2*.

Having derived Firm 1's residual demand, the task of finding Firm 1's optimum is now similar to finding the optimum under monopoly, which we have already done in chapter 5. Basically, we must determine the point at which marginal revenue equals marginal cost. Marginal cost is constant by assumption and equal to c. Marginal revenue is a curve with twice the slope of $d_1(q_2)$ and with the same vertical intercept.[h] The point at which the two curves intersect corresponds to quantity $q_1^*(q_2)$.

Notice that Firm 1's optimum, $q_1^*(q_2)$, depends on its belief about what Firm 2 is doing. To find an equilibrium, we are interested in deriving Firm 1's optimum for other possible values of q_2. Figure 7.5 considers two other possible values of q_2. If $q_2 = 0$, then Firm 1's residual demand is effectively the market demand: $d_1(0) \equiv D$. The optimal solution, not surprisingly, is for Firm 1 to choose the monopoly quantity; $q_1^*(0) = q^M$, where q^M is the monopoly quantity. If Firm 2 were to choose the quantity corresponding to perfect competition, that is $q_2 = q^C$, where q^C is such that $P(q^C) = c$, then Firm 1's

[h] This results from our assumption that demand is linear. In general, the marginal revenue curve has the same intercept as the demand curve and a higher slope (in absolute value), not necessarily twice the slope of the demand curve.

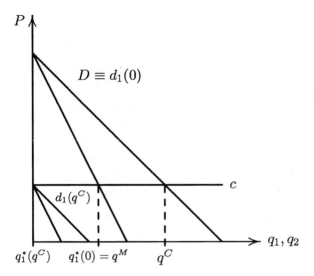

FIGURE 7.5 TWO EXTREME CASES.

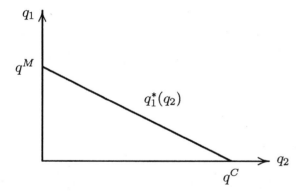

FIGURE 7.6 FIRM 1'S REACTION FUNCTION.

optimum would be to produce nil: $q_1^*(q^C) = 0$. In fact, this is the point at which marginal cost intercepts the marginal revenue corresponding to $d_1(q^C)$.

It can be shown that, given a linear demand and constant marginal cost, the function $q_1^*(q_2)$ is also linear. Because we have two points, we can draw the entire function $q_1^*(q_2)$, as illustrated in figure 7.6. Notice that the axes are now different from the previous figures. On the horizontal axis, we continue measuring quantities, specifically, Firm 2's quantity, q_2. On the vertical axis, we now measure Firm 1's quantity, q_1, not price. The function $q_1^*(q_2)$ is called Firm 1's reaction function. It gives Firm 1's optimal choice for each possible choice by Firm 2. Or, to look at it from a different perspective: It gives Firm 1's choice given what it believes Firm 2 is choosing.

Throughout this chapter, in parallel with the graphical derivation of equilibria, we present the correponding algebraic derivation. Except for some results in the next section, algebra is not necessary for the derivation of the main results; but it may help, especially if the reader is familiar with basic algebra and calculus. Let us start with the algebraic derivation of Firm 1's reaction function. Suppose that (inverse) demand is given by $P(Q) = a - bQ$, whereas cost is given by $C(q) = cq$, where q is the firm's output and $Q = q_1 + q_2$ is total output.

Firm 1's profit is

$$\pi_1 = Pq_1 - C(q_1) = (a - b(q_1 + q_2)) q_1 - cq_1.$$

The first-order condition for the maximization of π_1 with respect to q_1, $\partial \pi_1 / \partial q_1 = 0$, is

$$-bq_1 + a - b(q_1 + q_2) - c = 0,$$

or simply

$$q_1 = \frac{a - c}{2b} - \frac{q_2}{2}.$$

Because this gives the optimum q_1 for each value of q_2, we have just derived the Firm 1's reaction function, $q_1^*(q_2)$:

$$q_1^*(q_2) = \frac{a - c}{2b} - \frac{q_2}{2}. \tag{7.1}$$

We are now ready for the last step in our analysis, that of finding the equilibrium. An equilibrium is a point at which firms choose optimal quantities given what they conjecture the other firm is doing; and those conjectures are correct. Specifically, an equilibrium correspond to a pair of values (q_1, q_2) such that q_1 is Firm 1's optimal response given q_2 and, likewise, q_2 is Firm 2's optimal response given q_1. We have not derived Firm 2's reaction function. However, given our assumption that both firms have the same cost function, we conclude that Firm 2's reaction function, $q_2^*(q_1)$, is the symmetric of Firm 1's. We can thus proceed to plot the two reaction functions on the same graph, as in figure 7.7.

The equilibrium point in the Cournot model is then given by the *intersection of the reaction curves*, point N. In fact, this is the point at which $q_1 = q_1^*(q_2)$ (because the point is on Firm 1's reaction curve) and $q_2 = q_2^*(q_1)$ (because the point is on Firm 2's reaction curve).[i]

[i] The equilibrium concept we are using here is that of Nash equilibrium, or Nash–Cournot equilibrium, thus the notation N. In general, more than one equilibrium can exist. However, when the demand curve is linear and marginal cost is constant, there exists only one equilibrium.

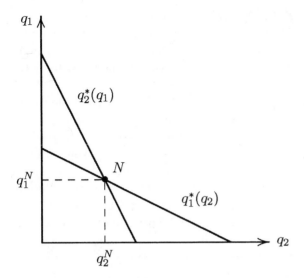

FIGURE 7.7 COURNOT EQUILIBRIUM.

We now proceed with our algebraic derivation. In equilibrium, it must be that Firm 1 chooses an output that is optimal given what it expects Firm 2's output to be. If Firm 1 expects Firm 2 to produce q_2^e, then it must be $q_1^N = q_1^*(q_2^e)$. Moreover, in equilibrium Firm 1's conjecture regarding Firm 2's choice should be correct: $q_2^e = q_2^N$. Together, these conditions imply that $q_1^N = q_1^*(q_2^N)$. The same conditions apply for Firm 2, that is, in equilibrium it must also be the case that $q_2^N = q_2^*(q_1^N)$. An equilibrium is thus defined by the system of equations

$$q_1^N = q_1^*(q_2^N)$$
$$q_2^N = q_2^*(q_1^N).$$

Equation (7.1) gives Firm 1's reaction function. We can thus write the first equation of the preceding system as

$$q_1^N = \frac{a-c}{2b} - \frac{q_2^N}{2}.$$

Because the two firms are identical (same cost function), the equilibrium will also be symmetric, that is, $q_1^N = q_2^N = q^N$. We thus have

$$q^N = \frac{a-c}{2b} - \frac{q^N}{2}.$$

Solving for q^N, this yields

$$q^N = \frac{a-c}{3b}.$$

MONOPOLY, DUOPOLY, AND PERFECT COMPETITION

Duopoly is an intermediate market structure, between monopoly (maximum concentration of market shares) and perfect competition (minimum concentration of market shares). One would expect equilibrium price and output under duopoly also to lie between the extremes of monopoly and perfect competition.

This fact can be checked in figure 7.8, which is based on figure 7.7 with a few lines added. Recall that each firm's reaction curve intercepts the axes at the values q^M and q^C. Therefore, a line with slope -1 intersecting the axes at the farther extremes of the reaction curves unites all points such that $q_1 + q_2 = q^C$ (see figure 7.8). Likewise, a line with slope -1 intersecting the axes at the closer extremes of the reaction curves unites all points such that $q_1 + q_2 = q^M$ (see figure 7.8). We can see that the Cournot equilibrium point, N, lies between these two lines. This implies that total output under Cournot is greater than that under monopoly and lower than that under perfect competition.

To summarize, according to the Cournot model:

> Duopoly output is greater than monopoly output and lower than perfect competition output. Likewise, duopoly price is lower than monopoly price and greater than price under perfect competition.

In chapter 9, we present a generalization of this principle: In an oligopoly with n firms, equilibrium price is closer to perfect competition the greater n is.

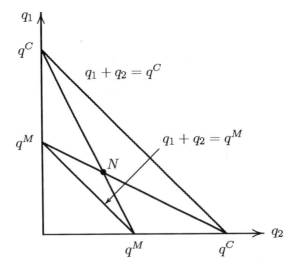

FIGURE 7.8 COMPARING THE COURNOT EQUILIBRIUM WITH MONOPOLY AND PERFECT COMPETITION.

7.4 BERTRAND VERSUS COURNOT

The two models of duopoly competition presented in the previous sections, though similar in assumptions, are in stark contrast when it comes to predicted behavior. The Cournot model predicts that price under duopoly is lower than monopoly price but greater than that under perfect competition. The Bertrand model, by contrast, predicts that duopoly competition is sufficient to drive prices down to marginal cost level, that is, two firms are enough to achieve the perfect competition price level.

This contrast suggests two questions: Which model is more realistic? Why should we consider more than one model instead of just choosing the "best" one? The answer to both questions is that industries differ. Some industries are more realistically described by the Cournot model, some by the Bertrand model.

Specifically, suppose that firms must make capacity (or output) decisions in addition to pricing decisions. In this context the relative timing of each decision (output/capacity and pricing) is the crucial aspect that selects Cournot or Bertrand as the right model. As we saw in chapter 4, games with two strategic decisions are best modeled as two-stage games, with the long-run decisions taken in the first stage and the short-run decisions in the second one. The idea is that the short-run decisions (second stage) are taken *given* the values of the long-run decisions (first stage).

Suppose that capacity or output is a long-run decision with respect to prices. In other words, suppose that it is more difficult to adjust capacity/output than it is to adjust prices. Then, the "right" model is one wherein firms first set capacity/output and then prices. From the analysis of the previous sections, we know this corresponds to the Cournot model.

Suppose, by contrast, that output is a short-run decision with respect to prices, that is, it is easier to adjust output levels than it is to adjust prices. Then, the "right" model is one whereby firms set prices first and then output levels. Although we have not presented the Bertrand model as such, this is essentially what it corresponds to. In the Bertrand model, firms simultaneously set prices and receive demand based on those prices. Implicitly assumed in the model is that firms produce an output exactly equal to the quantity demanded, that is, output is perfectly adjusted to the quantity demanded at the prices (initially) set by firms.

To summarize:

> If capacity and output can be easily adjusted, then the Bertrand model is a better approximation of duopoly competition. If, by contrast, output and capacity are difficult to adjust, then the Cournot model is a good approximation of duopoly competition.

Most real-world industries seem closer to the case when capacity is difficult to adjust. In other words, capacity or output decisions are normally the long-run variable, prices being set in the short run. Examples include wheat, cement, steel, cars, and computers. Consider, for instance, the video-game industry. In August 1999, Sony cut the price of its system from $129 to $99. *One hour* after Sony's price-change notice, Nintendo sent out a news release announcing its price cut to match Sony's.[77] Aggressive pricing by Sony and Nintendo boosted demand for their products. In fact, Nintendo suffered severe shortages during the 1999 holiday season. These events suggest that, in the context of video-game systems, prices are easier to adjust than quantities. The Cournot model would then seem a better approximation to the behavior of the industry.

There are, however, situations where capacities—or at least output levels—are adjusted more rapidly than prices. Examples include software, insurance, and banking. A software company, for example, can easily produce additional copies of its software almost on demand; sometimes, in fact, it will simply ship a copy electronically. In this sense, the Bertrand model would provide a better approximation than the Cournot model.[j] A specific example is provided by encyclopedias.[78] *Encyclopedia Britannica* has been, for more than two centuries, a standard reference work. Until recently, the thirty-two-volume hardback set sold for $1600. In the early 1990s, Microsoft entered the market with *Encarta*, which it sold on CD for less than $100. *Britannica* responded by issuing its own CD version as well. Recently, both *Britannica* and *Encarta* were selling for $89.99. Although this is still far from the Bertrand equilibrium (price equal to the cost of the CDs), it is certainly closer to Bertrand than the initial, monopoly-like price of $1600.

7.5 THE MODELS AT WORK: COMPARATIVE STATICS

What is the use of solving models and deriving equilibria? Models are simplified descriptions of reality, a way of understanding a particular situation. Once we understand how a given market works, we can use the model to predict how the market will change as a function of changes in various exogenous conditions, for example, the price of an input or of a substitute product. This exercise is known in economics as **comparative statics**: The meaning of the expression is that we compare two equilibria, with two sets of exogenous conditions, and predict how a shift in one variable will influence the other variables. The word "statics" implies that we are not predicting the dynamic path that takes us from one equilibrium to the other, but rather answering the question, "Once all of the adjustments have taken place and we are back in equilibrium, what will things look like?" In this section, we look at some examples of how the Cournot and Bertrand models can be used to perform comparative statics.

[j] There are, however, other aspects to be taken into account in an industry like software: product differentiation (see chapter 12) and network externalities (see chapter 17). The same qualification applies to the video-game industry.

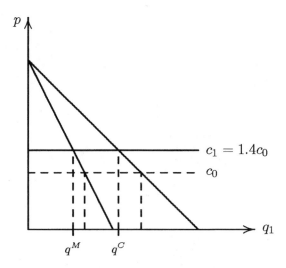

FIGURE 7.9 OPTIMAL SOLUTION AFTER INCREASE IN MARGINAL COST: TWO EXTREME CASES.

INPUT COSTS AND OUTPUT PRICE

Suppose the market for transatlantic flights between London and New York is served by two firms, American Airlines (AA) and British Airways (BA). Both firms have the same marginal cost, which can be divided into labor costs (50%) and fuel costs (50%). Suppose the oil price goes up by $10 a barrel, which in turn shoots up fuel prices by 80%. What will happen to transatlantic airfares between London and New York?

Suppose AA and BA compete *à la* Cournot. This assumption might be justified, in line with the discussion in the previous section, by the fact that firms must decide beforehand how much capacity (aircraft) to allocate to the market.

An 80% increase in fuel costs implies an 80%×50%=40% increase in marginal cost because fuel prices are 50% of marginal cost. This increase in marginal cost is experienced by both firms. What will it imply in terms of equilibrium output prices (i.e., fares)?

In reviewing the graphical derivation of the Cournot equilibrium, we see that each firm's reaction function depends on its marginal cost.[k] We should thus compute a new reaction curve based on the higher value of marginal cost. In figure 7.9, we compute the new $q_1^*(0)$ (that is, q^M), and the new value q^C such that $q_1^*(q^C) = 0$, the two extreme points of the reaction curve. Based on these extreme points, we can draw the new reaction curve. This is shown in figure 7.10.

An increase in marginal cost implies a downward shift of the reaction curve.

---

[k] Firm 1's reaction function depends on the rival's output but not on the rival's marginal cost. *In equilibrium*, the rival's output will depend on its marginal cost, so that, *indirectly*, Firm 1's output will depend on Firm 2's marginal cost. However, when we talk about the reaction function, what is important is whether Firm 1's output depends *directly* on Firm 2's marginal cost, which is not the case.

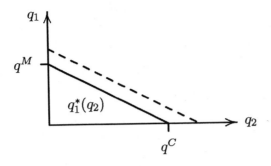

FIGURE 7.10 **SHIFT IN THE FIRM 1 REACTION CURVE.**

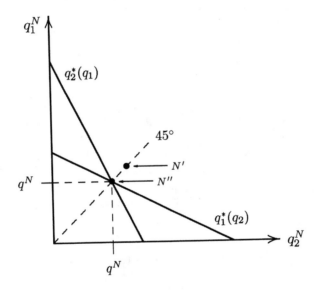

FIGURE 7.11 **COURNOT EQUILIBRIUM AFTER INCREASE IN MARGINAL COST (N'').**

This is an important fact which will reappear in different applications. By symmetry, we know that both firms will experience the same shift in their reaction curve. We thus have everything that is needed to determine the new equilibrium, which is depicted in figure 7.11. The new equilibrium point is denoted by N''. For comparison, the previous equilibrium, N', is also shown. As expected, each firm's output as well as total output are lower in the new equilibrium; it follows that price is greater.

Let us now solve the problem algebraically. As we saw in section 7.3, the equilibrium output in a (symmetric) Cournot equilibrium is given by

$$q^N = \frac{a-c}{3b}.$$

Total output is therefore

$$Q^N = 2\frac{a-c}{3b}.$$

Substituting in the demand function, we obtain equilibrium price:

$$p^N = a - bQ^N$$
$$= a - b2\frac{a-c}{3b}$$
$$= \frac{a+2c}{3}.$$

(7.2)

We thus have

$$\frac{d\,p^N}{d\,c} = \frac{2}{3}.$$

Therefore, if marginal cost (c) increases by 40%, p will increase by $\frac{2}{3}40\% = 26.6\%$.

EXCHANGE RATE FLUCTUATIONS AND MARKET SHARES

Consider a duopoly with two different firms from two different countries—for example, two producers of microchips, one in Japan (Firm 1) and one in the United States (Firm 2). The market for microchips is in U.S.$ (i.e., all sales are made in U.S.$). However, the costs of the Japanese firm are paid in Japanese yen. (The American firm's costs are in U.S.$.)

Suppose that firms compete *à la* Cournot. In fact, this is one case where the reduced-form interpretation of the Cournot model seems appropriate: Microchip manufacturers set production capacities and then set prices (given capacities), the result of the two-stage game being identical to Cournot competition.

In an initial equilibrium, both firms have the same cost, and the market is divided equally between the two. One question that comparative statics might help to answer is: What is the impact on market shares of a 50% devaluation of the yen? Because the market is in U.S.$, a shift in the exchange rate will change the Japanese firm's marginal cost *in dollars*, while keeping the U.S. firm's marginal cost constant. Specifically, suppose that both firms start with marginal cost c. Then the Japanese firm's marginal cost will change to c/e as a result of the devaluation, where e is the exchange rate in yen/$.

For example, suppose marginal cost was initially $10 for the U.S. firm and Y1000 for the Japanese firm and that the initial exchange rate was 100 Y/$. This implies that the Japanese firm's marginal cost *in U.S.$* was 1000/100=$10. A 50% devaluation of the yen means that $1 is now worth Y150. The Japanese firm's marginal cost *in U.S.$* is now

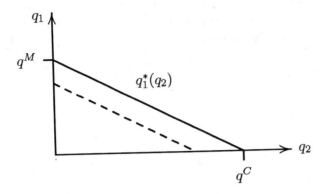

Figure 7.12   Shift in the Japanese Firm's Reaction Curve.

1,000/150 = \$6.6. We thus have to compute the new equilibrium wherein one of the firm's marginal costs is lower.

In the previous application, we saw that an increase in marginal cost implies a downward shift in the reaction curve. By analogy, we now deduce that the Japanese firm's reaction curve will shift upward as a result of the reduction in its marginal cost (in U.S.\$). Figure 7.12 depicts the new reaction curve (*solid line*) as well as the initial one (*dashed line*).

Because only the Japanese firm's reaction curve has changed, we are now ready to determine the shift in the equilibrium. This is shown in figure 7.13, where the Japanese

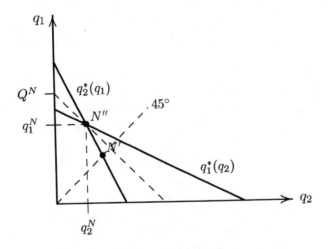

Figure 7.13   Cournot Equilibrium after Exchange Rate Devaluation.

firm's output is measured on the vertical axis and that of the American firm is given on the horizontal one. As can be seen, the new equilibrium point N'' is above the 45° line, that is, the Japanese firm's output is now greater than that of the American firm. This is not surprising, as the Japanese firm has decreased its cost (in U.S.$), whereas the U.S. firm's cost has remained unchanged.

Total output, Q^N, can be measured in the vertical axis by drawing a line with slope -1 through the equilibrium point. As can be seen, total output is greater in the new equilibrium, N'', than in the initial equilibrium, N'.

The graphical analysis has the limitation that it is difficult to determine the precise value of market shares. The best strategy is then to solve the model algebraically, which we do now. The first thing we must do is to determine the Cournot equilibrium for the asymmetric case. From section 7.3, we have seen that a firm's reaction function is given by

$$q_1^*(q_2) = \frac{a - c}{2b} - \frac{q_2}{2},$$

where c is marginal cost. Let marginal costs of Firms 1 and 2 now be given by c_1 and c_2, respectively. The two reaction functions are then given by

$$q_1^*(q_2) = \frac{a - c_1}{2b} - \frac{q_2}{2}$$
$$q_2^*(q_1) = \frac{a - c_2}{2b} - \frac{q_1}{2}.$$

Substituting the first equation for q_1 in the second and imposing the equilibrium condition $q_2 = q_2^*(q_1)$, we get

$$q_2 = \frac{a - c_2}{2b} - \frac{\frac{a - c_1}{2b} - \frac{q_2}{2}}{2}.$$

Solving for q_2, we get

$$q_2^N = \frac{a + c_1 - 2c_2}{3b}.$$

Likewise,

$$q_1^N = \frac{a - 2c_1 + c_2}{3b}. \tag{7.3}$$

(The latter expression is obtained by symmetry; all we have to do is to interchange the subscripts 1 and 2.) Total quantity is given by

$$Q^N = q_1^N + q_2^N = \frac{2a - c_1 - c_2}{3b}, \tag{7.4}$$

Finally, Firm 1's market share, s_1, is given by

$$s_1 = \frac{q_1}{q_1 + q_2} = \frac{a - 2c_1 + c_2}{2a - c_1 - c_2}. \tag{7.5}$$

Calibration

Regarding the right-hand side of this equation, all we know is that, initially, $c_1 = c_2$, whereas, after the devaluation, $c_1 = c_2/e = c_2/1.5$. To derive the numerical value of s_1, we would have to obtain additional information regarding the initial equilibrium; based on that information, we must determine the values of a and c. The process of obtaining values for the model parameters based on information about the equilibrium is known as **calibration**.

Suppose, for example, that before devaluation, output price was 13.33 and marginal cost 10. From the previous application, we know that, in equilibrium,

$$p = \frac{a + 2c}{3}.$$

where c is the initial value of marginal cost. Solving with respect to a, we get

$$a = 3p - 2c = 3(16.66) - 2(10) = 20.$$

Because $c = 10$ is the initial value of marginal cost, after devaluation we have $c_2 = 10$ and $c_1 = 10/1.5 = 6.66$. Substituting these values in (7.5), we get

$$s_1 = \frac{20 - 2 \times 10/1.5 + 10}{2 \times 20 - 10/1.5 - 10} \approx 71\%.$$

In summary, a 50% devaluation of the yen increases the Japanese firm's market share to 71% from an initial 50%.

NEW TECHNOLOGY AND PROFITS

Consider the industry for some chemical product, a commodity that is supplied by two firms. Firm 1 uses an old technology and pays a marginal cost of $15. Firm 2 uses a modern technology and pays a marginal cost of $10. In the current equilibrium, price is at $16.66 and output at 8.33. How much would Firm 1 be willing to pay for the modern technology?

Quite simply, the amount that Firm 1 should be willing to pay for the technology is the difference between its profits with lower marginal cost and its current profits. We thus have to determine Firm 1's equilibrium profits in two possible equilibria and compute the difference. In a way, this problem is the reverse of the one examined before. In the case of exchange-rate devaluation, we started from a symmetric duopoly and moved to an asymmetric one. Now, we start from an asymmetric duopoly (Firm 2 has lower marginal cost) and want to examine the shift to a symmetric duopoly, whereby Firm 1 achieves the same marginal cost as its rival.

From (7.4), we know that total output is given by

$$Q^N = q_1^N + q_2^N = \frac{2a - c_1 - c_2}{3b}.$$

Substituting in the demand function, we get

$$p^N = a - bQ^N = \frac{a + c_1 + c_2}{3}. \tag{7.6}$$

(Notice that, in the particular case when $c_1 = c_2 = c$, we get (7.2), the equilibrium price in the symmetric duopoly case.)

Given the expressions for Firm 1's output (7.3) and for equilibrium price (7.6), we can now compute Firm 1's equilibrium profits:

$$\pi_1 = pq_1 - c_1 q_1$$
$$= \frac{a + c_1 + c_2}{3} q_1 - c_1 q_1$$
$$= \left(\frac{a + c_1 + c_2}{3} - c \right) q_1$$
$$= \left(\frac{a + c_1 + c_2}{3} - c \right) \frac{a + c_2 - 2c_1}{3b}.$$
$$= \frac{a + c_2 - 2c_1}{3} \cdot \frac{a + c_2 - 2c_1}{3b}.$$
$$= \frac{1}{b} \left(\frac{a + c_2 - 2c_1}{3} \right)^2.$$

Finally, the value that Firm 1 would be willing to pay for the improved technology would be the difference in the value of the preceding expression with $c_1 = 15$ and $c_1 = 10$. To determine the precise value, we need, once again, to calibrate the model.

By analogy with what was done in the previous application, we can invert the price equation (7.6) to obtain

$$a = 3p - c_1 - c_2.$$

Because $p = 16.66$, $c_1 = 15$, $c_2 = 10$, this implies that $a = 3 \times 16.66 - 15 - 10 = 25$. Moreover, (7.4) can be inverted to obtain

$$b = \frac{2a - c_1 - c_2}{3Q}.$$

Because $Q = 8.33$, it follows that $b = (2 \times 25 - 15 - 10)/(3 \times 8.33) = 1$.

Therefore, in the initial equilibrium, Firm 1's profits are given by

$$\pi_1 = \left(\frac{25 + 10 - 2 \times 15}{3} \right)^2 = \left(\frac{5}{3} \right)^2,$$

whereas, with the new technology, profits will be given by

$$\pi_1 = \left(\frac{25 + 10 - 2 \times 10}{3}\right)^2 = \left(\frac{15}{3}\right)^2 .$$

We conclude that Firm 1 should be willing to pay

$$\left(\frac{15}{3}\right)^2 - \left(\frac{5}{3}\right)^2 \approx 22.22$$

for the new technology.

Let us return to the issues from the beginning of this section. Why is it useful to perform comparative statics? Take, for example, the last application considered earlier. The question we posed was: How much would Firm 1 (the inefficient firm) be willing to pay for an innovation that reduces marginal cost to 10 (the efficient firm's cost level)? Our analysis produced an answer to this question: Firm 1 would gain 22.22 from adopting the more efficient technology.

Is it worth going through all the algebraic trouble to get this answer? A simpler estimate for the gain might be the following: Take Firm 1's initial output as given and compute the gain from reducing marginal cost. Because initial output is 1.66, this calculation would yield the number $1.66(15 - 10) = 8.3$. This number greatly underestimates the true gain. Why? The main reason is that, upon reducing marginal cost, Firm 1 becomes much more competitive: Not only does it increase its margin, it also increases its output.

Let us then consider an alternative simple calculation. Because Firm 1 will have a marginal cost identical to that of Firm 2, we can estimate the gain by the difference between Firm 2's and Firm 1's initial profits. Firm 2's output (in the initial equilibrium) is 6.66, whereas price is given by 16.66; its profit is thus $6.66(16.66 - 10)$. Firm 1, in turn, is starting from a profit of $1.66(16.66 - 15)$. We would thus estimate a gain of $6.66(16.66 - 10)$ minus $1.66(16.66 - 15)$, which is approximately 41.6. This time we are grossly overestimating the true value. Why? The main reason is that, when Firm 1 becomes more aggressive (with a lower marginal cost), Firm 2 reduces its output. In other words, the main reason why Firm 2 has such a high output (and profit) in the initial equilibrium is that it faces an inefficient competitor. Moreover, when Firm 1 reduces its marginal cost, the market becomes more competitive, that is, price goes down, which increases the estimate error from using the initial equilibrium levels.

The advantage of the equilibrium analysis, that is, comparative statics, is that it takes into account all of the effects that follow from an exogenous change, such as a reduction in one firm's marginal cost. Taking the initial equilibrium values as constant may lead to gross misestimation of the impact of an exogenous change, especially if the change is significant in magnitude (as in the example we have considered).

Naturally, this defense of comparative statics is based on the presumption that the equilibrium solution is sensible. This section concludes with an additional argument in favor of the methodology we have been using.

A "DYNAMIC" INTERPRETATION OF THE COURNOT EQUILIBRIUM

It is easy to understand why the Cournot equilibrium is a stable solution: No firm would have an incentive to choose a different output. In other words, each firm is choosing an optimal strategy given the strategy chosen by its rival. But, is the Cournot equilibrium a realistic prediction of what will happen in reality?

The equilibrium concept we have used is that of Nash equilibrium, first introduced in chapter 4. There, we presented possible justifications for the concept of Nash equilibrium. Here, we present an argument, first proposed by Cournot himself, which is similar to the idea of solution by elimination of dominated strategies.

Although the Cournot model is a static game, let us consider the following dynamic interpretation. At time one, Firm 1 chooses some output level. Then, at time 2, Firm 2 chooses the optimal output level given Firm 1's output choice. At time 3, it's again Firm 1's turn to choose an optimal output given Firm 2's current output, and so on. Firm 1 chooses output at odd time periods, and Firm 2 at even time periods.

Figure 7.14 gives an idea of what this dynamic process might look like. We start from a point in the horizontal axis (Firm 2's output at time zero). At time 1, we move vertically toward Firm 1's reaction curve (Firm 1 is optimizing). At time 2, we move horizontally to Firm 2's reaction curve (Firm 2 is optimizing). At time 3, we move again vertically toward Firm 1's reaction curve. And so on. As can be seen from the figure, the

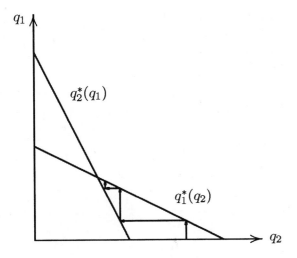

FIGURE 7.14 CONVERGENCE TO COURNOT EQUILIBRIUM.

dynamic process converges to the Cournot equilibrium. In fact, *no matter what the initial situation, we always converge to the Nash equilibrium.*

This is reassuring insofar as it provides an additional motivation for the idea of Cournot equilibrium.[1] Moreover, it reinforces the idea that static models (like Cournot) are useful for comparative statics only. They do not describe the dynamic process that leads from one equilibrium to another one. Static models give an idea of where the "system" will converge after all of the interim adjustments have taken place.[m]

SUMMARY

- Under price competition with homogeneous product and constant, symmetric marginal cost (Bertrand model), firms price at the level of marginal cost.

- If firms set output or capacity levels (Cournot model), then duopoly output is greater than monopoly output and lower than perfect competition output. Likewise, duopoly price is lower than monopoly price and greater than price under perfect competition.

- If capacity and output can be easily adjusted, then the Bertrand model is a better approximation of duopoly competition. If, by contrast, output and capacity are difficult to adjust, then the Cournot model is a good approximation of duopoly competition.

[l] In fact, the point we are making here is more generally applicable to the justification of Nash equilibria in a certain class of games. The argument we are using is similar to elimination of dominated strategies, a topic we dealt with in chapter 4.

[m] In fact, the dynamic process we consider earlier is not very realistic: At each moment in time, one of the firms is choosing an optimal output, assuming that the rival's output remains constant, which in fact does not occur except in the Nash equilibrium.

KEY CONCEPTS

- oligopoly

- duopoly

- best response

- reaction function

- residual demand

- comparative statics

- calibration

REVIEW AND PRACTICE EXERCISES

7.1 According to Bertrand's theory, price competition drives firms' profits down to zero even if there are only two competitors in the market. Why don't we observe this in practice very often?

7.2 Three criticisms are frequently raised against the use of the Cournot oligopoly model: (1) firms normally choose prices, not quantities; (2) firms don't normally make their decisions simultaneously; (3) firms are frequently ignorant of their rivals' costs; in fact, they do not use the notion of the Nash equilibrium when making their strategic decisions.

   How would you respond to these criticisms? (*Hint:* in addition to this chapter, you may want to refer to chapter 4.)

7.3 Which model (Cournot, Bertrand) would you think provides a better approximation to each of the following industries: oil refining, internet access, insurance. Why?

7.4* Two firms, CS Corporation and jl & Associates, make identical goods, GPX units, and sell them in the same market. The demand in the market is $Q = 1200 - p$. Once a firm has built capacity, it can produce up to its capacity each period with a marginal cost of $MC = 0$. Building a unit of capacity costs 2400 (for either CS or jl) and a unit of capacity lasts four years. The interest rate is zero. Once production occurs each period, the price in the market adjusts to the level at which all production is sold. (In other words, these firms engage in quantity competition, not price competition.)

a. If CS knew that jl were going to build 100 units of capacity, how much would CS want to build? If CS knew that jl were going to build x units of capacity, how much would CS want to build (that is, what is CS's best response function in capacity)?

b. If CS and jl each had to decide how much capacity to build without knowing the other's capacity decision, what would the one-shot Nash equilibrium be in the amount of capacity built?[79]

7.5** Consider a market for a homogeneous product with demand given by $Q = 37.5 - p/4$. There are two firms, each with constant marginal cost equal to 40.

a. Determine output and price under a Cournot equilibrium.

b. Compute the efficiency loss as a percentage of the efficiency loss under monopoly.

7.6** Show analytically that equilibrium price under Cournot is greater than price under perfect competition but lower than monopoly price.

EXTENSION EXERCISE

7.6** Consider a duopoly for a homogenous product with demand $Q = 10 - p/2$. Each firm's cost function is given by $C = 10 + q(q + 1)$. Determine the values of the Cournot equilibrium.

CHAPTER 8

COLLUSION

In any of the oligopoly structures we have considered so far, total profits, in equilibrium, are lower than monopoly profits. This decrease in total profits results from the **externality** inherent to the process of imperfect competition: When, for example, a firm chooses quantity under Cournot competition, it maximizes its own profit, not taking into account the fact that part of the increase in profits is obtained at the expense of the rival firm's profits. It is therefore natural that firms attempt to establish agreements between themselves with a view toward increasing their **market power**. In fact, it is, in general, possible to find alternative solutions such that all firms are better off (normally at the expense of consumers). This type of behavior is generically designated by **collusion**.

Cartel agreements, in particular, are an institutional form of collusion. The increase in oil prices in October 1973, decreed by the OPEC (the oil cartel), is a classic example of cartel behavior. However, collusive behavior does not need to be based on public and institutional agreements. Frequently, collusion results from **secret agreements**, not least because they are illegal (in Europe, by Article 85 of the Treaty of Rome; in the United States, by the Sherman Act). A classic example of collusion by secret agreements is the U.S. electrical goods industry in the 1950s, especially with respect to goods, such as turbine generators, that were sold through "competitive" bidding. As a result of a criminal investigation, a number of details of the agreement became known: There was an elaborate process to determine which firm should be the winner of each tender and at which price, the prices that the designated bidding losers should set, and so on.[80]

Finally, collusion may simply result from **tacit agreements** that are attained for some historical reason or simply because they are natural focal points. For example, in the United Kingdom, as of December 1996, a particular Sony TV set model was being sold for £499.99 by most sellers around Oxford Street (one of them, Harrods, was selling for £500). This price is significantly higher than marginal cost (as evidenced by the price set by some discount sellers). The price of £499.99 may have been reached by agreement between retailers (possibly with Sony acting as a coordinator between retailers), or simply because £499.99 is a "natural" discount on a natural "round" number—a focal point.

For the most part of this chapter, we will consider agreements with the objective of restricting supply (or increasing price). However, collusion may also refer to other decisions—restricting advertising expenditures, setting the level of service quality (cf European airlines until recently), or limiting each firm's territory. A good example of the latter is the chemical industry cartel in the twenties. According to the agreement—which was declared illegal around 1930—ICI would concentrate on the United Kingdom and the Commonwealth countries, German firms in Europe, and DuPont in America.

8.1 REPEATED INTERACTION AND THE STABILITY OF COLLUSIVE AGREEMENTS

Consider a homogeneous-product duopoly where firms simultaneously set prices and marginal cost is constant (i.e., no capacity constraints). If firms were to set prices once and for all, then this industry would correspond to the Bertrand model. From the previous chapter, we know that the equilibrium in such industry would consist of both firms setting price equal to marginal cost.

A more realistic model should consider the possibility of firms changing their prices over time. Specifically, suppose that time is divided into a series of periods $t = 1, 2, \ldots$, and that, in each period, firms simultaneously set prices. In other words, suppose that firms play a Bertrand game in each of an infinite series of periods. In the jargon of game theory, we say that firms play a **repeated game**. What is the equilibrium of such a dynamic game? Clearly, one possible equilibrium consists of firms playing according to the Nash–Bertrand equilibrium in each period, ignoring at each stage what the previous history of the industry was. In fact, if Firm 1 knows that Firm 2 will set price equal to marginal cost in every period, regardless of what Firm 1 does, then the optimal response is to set price equal to marginal cost as well.

There can be other equilibria, however. Suppose that firms play the following **grim strategies**.[81] In the first period, both firms set price at the monopoly level, p^M, and share monopoly profits equally ($\frac{1}{2}\pi^M$). In each subsequent period, firms observe the price history before setting their own prices. If historical prices have all been at the monopoly level, that is, if both firms have "respected" the collusive agreement, then each firm sets p^M in the current period. Otherwise, they set price at the level of marginal cost. To put it differently: Firm 1 will set $p = p^M$ so long as Firm 2 sets $p = p^M$ as well. The moment Firm 1 observes its rival setting a different price, it "punishes" the deviation by reverting (forever) to price at the marginal cost level.[a]

To determine whether such strategies form an equilibrium, we must check whether the firms' **no-deviation constraints** are satisfied. If both firms stick to their equilibrium

[a] Note that, because Firm 2 knows that its deviation implies that Firm 1 reverts to pricing at marginal cost, Firm 2 also will set price at marginal cost level following a deviation by itself. Thus the designated strategy calls for firms to revert to pricing at marginal cost whenever *some* firm sets price different from monopoly price in the past.

strategy, then Firm 1's expected discounted payoff is given by

$$\frac{1}{2}\pi^M + \delta\frac{1}{2}\pi^M + \delta^2\frac{1}{2}\pi^M + \cdots \tag{8.1}$$

where δ is the **discount factor**, that is, the value of $1 one period into the future compared to $1 now. Simplifying (8.1), we get

$$V = \frac{1}{2}\pi^M\frac{1}{1-\delta}, \tag{8.2}$$

where V denotes discounted equilibrium payoff or value.

If Firm 1 deviates by setting $p_1 \neq p^M$ in some period t, then its future payoff is zero because, by assumption, both firms revert thereafter to pricing at marginal cost. Because future payoffs are not a function of *what* the deviation was, but only *whether* there was a deviation at all, it follows that the best deviation for Firm 1 is the one that maximizes short-run profits. The price that maximizes Firm 1's short-run profits is $p^M - \epsilon$, where ϵ is a low number. By slightly undercutting Firm 2's price, Firm 1 gets all of the demand and a total profit of approximately π^M.[b] It thus follows that the payoff from the optimal deviation is

$$V' = \pi^M. \tag{8.3}$$

(Short-run profits plus zero future profits.) The condition that the proposed strategies form an equilibrium is that $V \geq V'$. Pulling (8.2) and (8.3) together, we get

$$\frac{1}{2}\pi^M\frac{1}{1-\delta} \geq \pi^M,$$

or simply

$$\delta > \frac{1}{2}. \tag{8.4}$$

As was mentioned before, the discount factor measures how much $1 one period into the future is worth compared with $1 now. Normally, $0 < \delta < 1$. There are several reasons why $\delta < 1$. One is the opportunity cost of time: Given one period of time, an investor might use $1 to gain $(1 + r)$ next period, where r is the interest rate per period. In this sense, we would compute δ as

$$\delta = \frac{1}{1+r}.$$

In the preceding equation, the relevant rate is the rate corresponding to the period between successive decisions. Specifically, suppose that r is the annual rate and that the frequency with which firms change their prices is given by f (times per year). Then, we would have

$$\delta = \frac{1}{1+r/f}.$$

[b] The exact value of Firm 1's payoff would be smaller than π^M, as it needs to undercut its rival. But because ϵ can be arbitrarily small, we assume that the profit from deviation is equal to π^M.

Another important factor to take into account in the computation of δ is the probability that the payoff in the next period will be received at all. For example, if two pharmaceutical firms were to collude, they would have to consider the (likely) possibility that, before the next period, a third firm would discover a superior drug that would essentially eliminate the market for the two first firms. In other industries (cement, for example), this probability would be rather low. Specifically, let h be the probability that the industry will still "exist" one period later. Then, we compute the discount factor as

$$\delta = \frac{1}{1 + r/f} \, h.$$

The opposite effect of an industry disappearing is for that industry to grow. Suppose that demand is growing at a rate g. This implies that, everything else constant, profits are greater in period $t + 1$ than in period t by a factor $1 + g$. One way to represent this formally is to assume a "constant" profit function but a discount factor such that $1 a period in the future is worth *more* than $1 in the current period, by a factor $1 + g$, on account of industry growth. The discount factor would then be

$$\delta = \frac{1}{1 + r/f} \, h \, (1 + g). \tag{8.5}$$

Notice that δ is increasing in f, h, and g.

Given this derivation of the value of δ, condition (8.4) can be interpreted as follows:

> Collusive pricing is more likely to be an equilibrium the greater the frequency with which firms interact and the greater the probability of continuation and growth of the industry.

So, for example, regarding the value of f: Collusion between two service stations that set gas prices on a daily basis is likely to be easier than collusion between two summer holiday resorts where rates are set on an annual basis. Regarding the value of h: Collusion between two pharmaceutical firms in a given therapeutical market where products become obsolete at a fast rate is likely to be more difficult than collusion in the cement industry, where most likely the market will remain unchanged in the next period.

WHY DON'T FIRMS COLLUDE MORE OFTEN?

In chapter 7, we saw that, under the assumptions of Bertrand competition, two firms are enough for equilibrium prices to be at marginal cost level—the Bertrand paradox. In this section, we see that, under repeated interaction and for a low enough interest rate (and no capacity constraints), it may be possible to sustain monopoly prices even if firms simultaneously set prices.

In other words, if without repetition we were led to a puzzle (competitive prices even with only two firms), we now have the opposite puzzle, as it were: The model predicts that firms can almost always collude to set monopoly prices. Why don't firms collude more often in practice? As the preceding analysis suggests, such strategy would be an equilibrium and would increase firms' profits. In fact, suppose that the annual interest rate is 10%, and suppose that firms set prices on a monthly basis. Then it can be shown that, even if there are *hundreds* of symmetric Bertrand oligopolists, there exists an equilibrium such that all firms set monopoly prices in every period! Why doesn't this happen more often?

One possible explanation is that antitrust policy is a binding constraint on the firms' actions. For one, explicit cartel agreements are illegal. But even tacit collusion agreements may run into problems with antitrust authorities, as we will see in section 8.4.

A second explanation is suggested by the preceding analysis. The discount factor that should be used for the purpose of determining the equilibrium conditions includes, in addition to the value of time, the probability of continuation. Consider an industry with a high turnover, that is, a high rate of entry and exit. In this context, the probability that a given firm exits the market in each period is high, and accordingly, its discount factor is small. This in turn implies that only for unreasonably low values of the interest rate is it an equilibrium for firms to set monopoly prices. In other words, if a firm expects to exit the industry with a high probability, its incentives to deviate from a collusive agreement are also high, for there is little to lose, in terms of expected future profits, from cheating today.

A third explanation why collusive agreements of the sort presented earlier are not more common is that they really are not an equilibrium. To be sure, they form a Nash equilibrium. The point, however, is that such equilibrium is unreasonable and unrealistic. Suppose that cheating from the monopoly pricing agreement is punished with an infinite price war, as assumed in the preceding discussion. Suppose that one of the firms actually cheats and reversion to a price war takes place. One can imagine the deviating firm would have an incentive to approach its rival and try to convince it that there are mutual gains from abandoning the price war and reverting to collusive pricing. But if firms were to agree on this—and it seems reasonable they would—then the threat of engaging in a price war in the first place would no longer be credible. And cheating from monopoly pricing might after all be profitable, thus breaking the monopoly pricing equilibrium.

A fourth reason why collusion may in practice be more difficult than the preceding model would predict is that not all prices are observed with precision. In a world of imperfect observability, the possibility of secret price cuts must be taken into account. And, as we will see in the next section, this possibility makes collusive agreements more difficult to sustain.

To summarize, few real-world collusive agreements work in exactly the same way as the model presented earlier. However, the main intuition, namely that each firm's decision involves a trade-off between short-run gains and medium- to long-term losses, is the essence of the problem of cartel stability. Box 8.1 presents the example of the diamond

Box 8.1 The Diamond Cartel

DeBeers Consolidated Mines Ltd. was established in the 1870s. Since then, the firm, owned by the Oppenheimer family, has maintained a remarkable control over the world diamond industry. DeBeers owns all of the diamond mines in South Africa and has interests in other countries as well. However, in terms of mining, its share of the world market is relatively small, especially since the discovery of the Russian mines. The key to DeBeers's control of the market is the Central Selling Organization (CSO), its London-based marketing arm.

The CSO serves as an intermediary between the mines and the diamond cutters and polishers. More than 80% of the world's diamonds are processed by the CSO, although only a fraction of these originate from DeBeers mines. CSO staff classify the diamonds by category (there are literally thousands of types of diamonds). This is a highly skill-intensive task in which DeBeers has unmatched expertise. The CSO also regulates the market to achieve price stability, building up its stocks during periods of low demand and releasing those same stocks during periods of high demand.

The high margins earned by DeBeers are a constant temptation for mining companies, who figure the same margins might be earned by selling directly to the diamond cutters. What stops them from doing so? First, many of the diamond producers see the current cartel structure as a benefit to the whole industry. In addition to stabilizing prices, DeBeers plays the crucial role of advertising diamonds. Both price stabilization and advertising are "public goods" at the industry level: Every producer benefits, although only DeBeers pays for it.

A second reason for compliance with DeBeers's dominance is the fear of retaliation if they defect from the cartel. In 1981, President Mobutu announced that Zaire, the world's largest supplier of industrial diamonds, would no longer sell diamonds through the CSO. At the same time, contacts were set up with two Antwerp brokers and one British broker. Two months later, about one million carats of industrial diamonds flooded the market, and the price fell from $3 to less than $1.80 per carat. Although the source of this supply surplus is unknown, many believe the move was DeBeers's way of showing who's in control.

For DeBeers, this was a costly operation, but it was a case of "it's not the money, it's the principle." And the point was made: In 1983, Zaire requested the renewal of its old contract with DeBeers. In fact, the contract it ended up with was less favorable than the original one.

industry. Although this is, in many respects, a peculiar industry, it does illustrate the main points developed in this section.

8.2 PRICE WARS

By comparison with the models in the previous chapter (Cournot and Bertrand), adding dynamics brings a fair amount of realism to the analysis of duopoly competition. For example, zero margins are not the only outcome when there are two price-setting competitors. Even so, the model presented in the previous section is too stylized to explain observed patterns of several industries. In particular, one common observation is that industry prices oscillate between high levels (close to the collusive price level described in the previous section) and low levels (close to the competitive price level described in the previous chapter). For example, the market for rail shipping, discussed in box 8.2, seems to exhibit this pattern, as can be seen from the figure inserted within the box. However, although the model presented in the previous section features the possibility of a shift in price levels, it predicts that, in equilibrium, prices are always at the monopoly level. In this section, we consider extensions of that model in an attempt to explain the observed patterns.

SECRET PRICE CUTS[82]

Ready-mixed concrete and ocean shipping are examples of **customer markets**. These are industries where each customer is sufficiently large that prices are negotiated on a case-by-case basis. For this reason, collusive agreements are difficult to monitor: Although firms may agree on what prices to set, the temptation to secretly cut prices for a particular customer is large. In fact, what deters firms from cheating on a collusive agreement is the threat of reversion to a "bad" equilibrium. But if deviations from the prescribed equilibrium cannot be directly observed, then the deterrence effect is greatly decreased.

Suppose that demand fluctuates and that these fluctuations cannot be perfectly observed. All that each firm can observe is the price it sets and the demand it receives. If a firm receives unexpectedly low demand, it is faced with a guessing problem: Its low demand may result from low overall demand, or it may result from some rival having undercut prices with respect to the agreement. Should the firm punish its rival when it receives low demand? Could it not be punishing an innocent firm?

Suppose firm i decides not to punish firm j, on the assumption that its low demand resulted from a market downturn, not firm j's cheating. Can this be an equilibrium? Clearly not. If that were firm i's strategy, firm j would be better off by secretly cutting prices and blaming firm i's low demand on market conditions. Suppose instead that each time firm i receives low demand it reverts to an infinite price war, on the assumption that low demand resulted from firm j's cheating. Such harsh punishment would most likely suffice to keep firm j from offering secret price cuts. But that is little consolation,

Box 8.2 Collusion and Price Wars: The Joint Executive Committee, 1880–1886[83]

"The Joint Executive Committee (JEC) was a cartel that controlled eastbound freight shipments from Chicago to the Atlantic seaboard in the 1880s. It was formed in April 1879 by an agreement of the railroads involved in the market. The firms involved publicly acknowledged this agreement, as it preceded the passage of the Sherman Act (1890) and the formation of the Interstate Commerce Commission (1887)," both of which formally prohibited this kind of agreement (see section 8.4). "A separate agreement was reached for westbound shipments on the same railroad lines, primarily because of the essential physical differences of the products being transported."

The internal enforcement mechanism adopted by the JEC was a variant of the trigger price strategy discussed in the first part of section 8.2. "There were several instances in which the cartel thought that cheating had occurred, cut prices for a time, and then returned to the collusive price." The following figure shows the evolution of price in the period from 1880 to 1886.

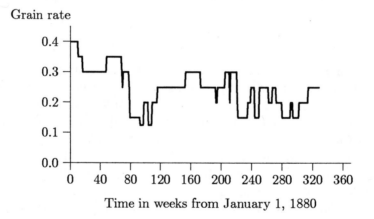

"The assumption that a homogeneous good was sold seems to have been approximately satisfied. . . . Lake steamers and sail ships were the principal source of competition for the railroads, but at no point did they enter into an agreement with the JEC. The predictable fluctuations in demand that resulted from the annual opening and closing of the Great Lakes to shipping did not disrupt industry conduct. Rather, rates adjusted systematically with the lake navigation season."

Therefore, the conduct of the JEC from 1880 to 1886 is largely consistent with the model of collusive equilibrium described in the first part of section 8.2, "as price wars were caused by unpredictable disturbances, rather than by entry or predictable fluctuations in demand."

for, sooner or later, a market downturn would imply low demand for firm i regardless of firm j's behavior. The industry would revert into an indefinite price war even if no cheating on the agreement had occurred.

Finally, consider an intermediate solution: Each time firm i or firm j receives low demand, both firms move into a price war for T periods, upon which they revert back to pricing at the collusive level. Let T be sufficiently large such that no firm has an incentive to undercut the rival. In fact, if the future is sufficiently important for each firm (i.e., if the interest rate is sufficiently low), then such T will indeed exist. We thus have an equilibrium with collusion phases alternating with price war phases, just as empirical observation suggests. Notice that, *although price wars occur in equilibrium, no firm cheats in equilibrium.* That is, price wars are a necessary evil of equilibrium collusion: If firms never engaged in price wars, the incentives for cheating would be too great for the collusive agreement to be stable.

> If price cuts are difficult to observe, then occasional price wars may be necessary to discipline collusive agreements.

DEMAND FLUCTUATIONS

The previous model is based on the somewhat extreme assumption that demand fluctuations are not observable (nor is the demand received by rival firms). Suppose instead that demand fluctuates over time but that, during each period, the state of demand is observed by all firms. If firms collude with each other, how will prices fluctuate with demand? A collusive equilibrium, as we have seen before, must be such that firms have no incentive to undercut their rivals' price. In other words, the difference between future collusive profits and future profits in case of a price war must be sufficiently large so as to deter a firm from pursuing the short-term gains of cheating on the collusive agreement.

Suppose that demand shocks are independent across periods. This implies that, in terms of future demand levels, the future looks the same in every period, regardless of the current state of demand. Consequently, expected future profits from collusion (or punishment) are the same regardless of the current state of demand. *Current profits,* however, do depend on the current state of demand. In particular, the gains from cheating on the cartel agreement are greater when demand is higher.[c] This implies that the constraint that no firm wants to cheat on the collusive agreement is more serious when demand is high. To achieve an equilibrium, it may be necessary to reduce price during the periods of high demand. In fact, if price is lower, the gains from cheating are also lower.[d] In a number of settings, this may result in an equilibrium where *prices are lower in periods when demand is higher* (price wars during booms). In other words, the preceding model implies that prices move counter-cyclically. This contrasts with the prediction of

[c] Recall that, under duopoly competition with a homogeneous product and constant marginal cost, a firm that undercuts its rival doubles its profit. If demand is higher, then this gain is also higher.

[d] The argument is similar to the one in footnote (c).

the first model presented in this section, wherein firms enter into a price war following a period of low demand.

The stark contrast between the predictions of the two models shows how important different assumptions can be. In the first model, we assume that demand shocks are not observable, whereas in the second one we assume that, before choosing prices in each period, firms observe that period's demand shock.

Empirical evidence suggests that both sets of assumptions are realistic approximations to different industries, and that different industries evidence patterns of pro- or counter-cyclical price movements. Based on yearly data from 1947 to 1981, it can be shown that the price of cement varies counter-cyclically: A 1% increase in GNP is associated with a decrease in the relative price of cement between .5 and 1%.[84] This evidence is consistent with the second model. On the other hand, the market for eastbound freight shipments from Chicago to the Atlantic seaboard, during the period from 1880 to 1886, provides a good example of the first model and of its empirical prediction.[85]

ASYMMETRIC SHOCKS

The two models presented previously, for all of their differences, have one thing in common: Price wars are an equilibrium phenomenon. In other words, price wars are necessary to maintain long-term collusion in the industry. However, many price wars observed in practice fail to fit into this behavior category. Consider, for example, the airline industry. Industry analysts suggest that the main cause for price wars is the financial trouble of individual carriers: "Fares are dictated not by the strongest, but by the financially troubled," claims the CEO of Alaska Airlines.[86]

A simple model that would explain behavior of this type must be based on some form of asymmetry between firms. Suppose, for example, that each firm's discount factor starts up by being $\bar{\delta}$. However, with some probability, a firm's discount factor may switch to a lower value, say, $\underline{\delta}$. A lower value of δ means that the future is less important for the firm. As was seen in the first section of this chapter, one of the elements that goes into a firm's discount factor is the probability that the future will exist. A firm that is in a difficult situation (financially or otherwise) has a lower discount factor than a firm in a solid situation. The former attributes a higher probability to exiting the industry.

If the difference between $\bar{\delta}$ and $\underline{\delta}$ is sufficiently high, it may be true that collusion is possible among "patient" firms ($\delta = \bar{\delta}$) but not among "impatient" firms ($\delta = \underline{\delta}$). Notice that, in equilibrium, no firm can have an incentive to deviate if a high price is to be maintained: All firms must therefore have $\delta = \bar{\delta}$. As soon as a firm sees its δ turn from $\bar{\delta}$ to $\underline{\delta}$, that firm will deviate and initiate a price war: Although the short-run gains from deviation remain the same, the long-run (expected) gains from sticking to the collusion agreement are now much lower.

Price wars need not necessarily be initiated by the weaker firms, however. Consider the case of the British newspaper industry. In July 1993, Rupert Murdoch reduced the price of the *Times* from 45p to 30p. Ten months later, the price was further dropped to 20p, less than one half the starting level. This aggressive strategy launched the entire newspaper quality market into a price war that lasted for longer than 18 months. Although most newspapers increased circulation (especially the *Times*), the price war had a marked negative impact on average industry profitability.

The most likely reason why Murdoch cut the price of the *Times* in 1993 is that circulation was deteriorating rapidly, falling below 360,000. By May 1995, circulation was well above 650,000. At that point, Murdoch sent the signal for putting an end to the price war. At a press conference, he stated that prices "will probably have to be corrected" in response to a 30% to 40% increase in newsprint costs, which has "changed the economics of the industry."[87] Was it the increase in costs, or was it the fact that the *Times* had recaptured a more comfortable market share after two years of reduced prices?

Even if this price war reflected the *Times's* weak market share in 1993, Murdoch might not have taken the initiative if his financial position was not as strong as it was. In fact, an alternative explanation for his strategy is that, by cutting prices, he was simply attempting to drive rivals out of the market.[e] In other words, although the airline and the newspaper examples share the feature that price wars are unilaterally initiated by one firm, in the former case it was the weaker firm that got the price war started, and in the latter, it was the stronger player that cut prices first.

8.3   FACTORS THAT FACILITATE COLLUSION

In section 8.1, we derived some of the conditions that make an industry more prone to collusive agreements. In particular, we mentioned frequency of interaction and market growth. Moreover, some of the cases considered—the diamond industry, for example—suggest that the severity and credibility of punishments also play an important role. Section 8.2 introduced another important factor, namely the probability of detection of a deviation from collusive agreements. In this section, we continue the discussion of factors that may facilitate the formation and maintenance of collusive agreements.

MARKET STRUCTURE AND COLLUSION

In the previous sections, we maintained (for simplicity) the assumption of a symmetric duopoly. This assumption is unlikely to be satisfied by most real-world examples. Normally, there are more than two firms with asymmetrically distributed market shares. How do the number of firms and the distribution of market shares influence the likelihood of collusive behavior?

One idea is that collusion is more likely in concentrated industries than in fragmented ones. First, it is easier to *establish* a collusive agreement when there are few competitors than when there are many competitors. In fact, both bargaining theory and anecdotal evidence suggest that agreements are more difficult to reach the greater the number of interested parties. Moreover, it is easier to *maintain* a collusive agreement

[e] This type of strategy is examined in chapter 15.

with few competitors. Consider the case of repeated price competition, presented in section 8.1 for the case of two firms. If there were $n > 2$ competitors, profit per firm would be smaller. However, the profit that a price cutter would gain would still be the same. Consequently, the temptation to cut prices is relatively greater when there are more competitors, and collusion is more difficult to sustain. This point is further developed in exercise 8.14.

A second aspect relating to market structure is symmetry between firms. It is normally easier to maintain collusion among similar firms than among asymmetric ones.[f] To understand the reason for this, consider a price-setting duopoly where one firm has a cost advantage over the other one. For example, Firm 1's constant marginal cost is $\underline{c}$, whereas Firm 2's is given by $\overline{c}$, which is greater than $\underline{c}$ but lower than the low-cost firm's monopoly price. The efficient collusive agreement is for Firm 1 to set its monopoly price and for Firm 2 to set a higher price and sell zero. In fact, this is the price and market share allocation that maximize joint profits. However, such an agreement is clearly not stable, for Firm 2 would have an incentive to undercut Firm 1 and make some positive profit in the short run. Note that this is true regardless of the value of the discount factor, for in the efficient solution, Firm 2 makes zero profits. It follows that *no punishment can detain Firm 2 from deviating,* as it has nothing to lose.

An alternative solution might be for both firms to price at the same (high) level. This would alleviate the problem of Firm 2 wanting to deviate, but it might create a new problem, namely that Firm 1 may now want to deviate. First, Firm 1's gains from deviation are large, for it sells at a large margin. Second, the punishment Firm 2 might be able to impose on Firm 1 is likely to be smaller: Even if Firm 2 sets price at marginal cost, Firm 1 can still make positive profits.[g]

The bromide industry during the turn of the century provides an interesting illustration of this point. Between 1885 and 1914, a period when the industry was dominated by a cartel, six price wars occurred. Two of these wars took place right after publicly announced violations of the cartel agreement. Clearly, these were not equilibrium price wars in the sense explained in the previous section. Rather, they resulted from disagreement among cartel members regarding the distribution of profits. If all firms were symmetric, then profit distribution would be a simple issue: The natural solution then is for profits to be equally distributed. If firms are asymmetric, however, then the cartel is subject to an additional strain, namely agreement on profit distribution.[88]

> Collusion is normally easier to maintain among few and similar firms.

MULTIMARKET CONTACT[89]

Theoretical analysis and empirical evidence suggest that firms that compete with each other in several markets have a greater propensity to collude, and/or collude to a greater

[f] The diamond industry is an important exception to this rule. Given the peculiar nature of the product (diamonds), the leadership of one of the firms (DeBeers) has played an essential role in maintaining high prices, basically by maintaining—through advertising and stock management—the perception that diamonds are scarce (though they are not).

[g] Strictly speaking, Firm 2 can impose an equally severe punishment on Firm 1: By setting $p_2 = \underline{c}$, Firm 2 forces Firm 1 to zero profits. The problem is that in the process, Firm 2 makes losses, which in many real-world settings may be difficult to sustain.

BOX 8.3 MULTIMARKET CONTACT BETWEEN U.S. AIRLINES[90]

In air travel, a market might be defined as the flight connection between two different cities. In this sense, airlines compete in several markets, and competing airlines overlap in the markets that they cover. Consider, for example, the top 1000 routes in the United States. Define average contact in each market as the average number of other markets in which the competing airlines face each other. For example, consider a particular route, which in 1988, was serviced by American, Delta, and Northwest. During that year, American and Delta appeared jointly in 527 of the top 1000 routes; American and Northwest were present in 357 routes, and Delta and Northwest in 323 routes. Average route contact would then be (527+357+323)/3=402.3.

Econometric evidence shows that this variable, when controlled for a host of other factors, has a significant positive impact on airfares. This in turn suggests that airlines use competition in other routes as a means to collude in a given route. Price cutting in a particular route might lead to a profit increase in the short run. However, not only would this lead to a price war in that route, it would also lead to more severe price competition in other routes.

extent. For example, it has been estimated that multimarket contact has a significant positive impact on airfares (box 8.3).

Why would multimarket contact increase the chances of collusion? Perhaps the best way to begin addressing this question is to see why multimarket contact might *not* improve the chances of collusion. Consider a price-setting homogeneous-product duopoly where marginal cost is constant and the same for both firms. If firms set prices at the monopoly level, p^M, then each receives $\frac{1}{2}\pi^M$, where π^M is monopoly profits. If one of the firms were to set a slightly lower price, then it would receive all of the monopoly profits, that is, twice as much. The worst price war to punish such deviation would consist of setting price at marginal cost forever, that is, zero profits. Collusion is therefore possible if and only if

$$\frac{1}{2}\pi^M + \frac{\delta}{1-\delta}\frac{1}{2}\pi^M \geq \pi^M,$$

or simply $\delta \geq \frac{1}{2}$.

Consider now a case in which firms compete in two identical markets, each of which is described as in the previous paragraph. What is now the lowest value of the discount factor such that collusion is stable? The future cost of a deviation is now greater—a price war in both markets. But the benefits from deviation are also greater—increased profits in both markets. In fact, the new stability condition is

$$\left(\frac{1}{2}\pi^M + \frac{1}{2}\pi^M\right) + \left(\frac{\delta}{1-\delta}\frac{1}{2}\pi^M + \frac{\delta}{1-\delta}\frac{1}{2}\pi^M\right) \geq \left(\pi^M + \pi^M\right),$$

which again implies $\delta \geq \frac{1}{2}$. In words, if the different markets are simply a replication of each other, then multimarket contact seems to have little effect: The potential punishment from a deviation increases, but so does the benefit, in fact in the exact same proportion.

Now suppose that each firm has a cost advantage in one of the markets. For example, Firm 1's cost in market 1 is $\underline{c}$, whereas Firm 2 has a cost of $\overline{c} > \underline{c}$; in Market 2, Firm 2's cost is $\underline{c}$, whereas Firm 1's is $\overline{c}$. One possible interpretation would be that each firm is located in a different country and $\overline{c} = \underline{c} + t$, where t is the transportation cost across the countries.

As was seen in the previous subsection, the efficient collusive agreement in Market 1 is for Firm 1 to set its monopoly price and for Firm 2 to set a higher price and sell zero. The reverse is true in Market 2. Taken in isolation, such agreements are clearly not stable. However, if we consider the two markets together, then the situation is quite different. Firm 1 might be able to convince Firm 2 not to undercut its monopoly price in Market 1 with the threat that it would undercut Firm 2 in its "own" market if that were to happen. In fact, suppose that the punishment from deviation would be for firms to engage in a price war whereby price equals the high marginal cost, $\overline{c}$.[h] One can easily show that if the discount factor is sufficiently high, then firms will be able to collude and set prices at the monopoly level (see exercise 8.15). Multimarket contact matters.

> Collusion is normally easier to maintain when firms compete in more than one market.

One example that illustrates this kind of reasoning is that of the chemical industry in the 1920s (discussed in the introduction). According to the collusive agreement—which was declared illegal around 1930—ICI would concentrate on the United Kingdom, and the Commonwealth countries, German firms in Europe, and DuPont in America. A more recent example, discussed in box 8.4, is that of the dog food industry, in which two segments—dry and moist dog food—were dominated by two different firms.

INSTITUTIONAL FACTORS

In addition to structural factors such as the number of firms and the number of markets in which firms interact, there are a number of institutional factors that may particularly facilitate collusion.[i] By institutional factors, we mean rules or regulations imposed either

[h] It can be shown that this constitutes an equilibrium of the static price game.

[i] These measures are also known as **facilitating practices**.

Box 8.4 Multimarket Contact in the Dog Food Industry[91]

With dozens of millions of dogs to feed, the pet food industry represents an important dollar value. In the United States alone, dog food sales exceed $3 billion a year. There are essentially five segments in the dog food market: dry, moist, snack, canned, and soft–dry dog food.

In 1986, Quaker Oats, a dominant player in the moist segment, acquired the financially stressed Anderson Clayton. This was not an entirely peaceful acquisition. In fact, Quaker's move preempted a bid by Ralston Purina, a competitor of Quaker's and a dominant player in the dry dog food segment (49.7% market share).

Quaker sold all of Anderson Clayton's divisions except Gaines, owner of a number of brands in different segments. This acquisition strengthened Quaker's position in the moist segment, thereby increasing its total market share from 27.9% to 80.7%. It also increased Quaker's presence in the dry segment, bringing total market share to 19.8%.

Responding to Quaker's move, Ralston Purina acquired Benco Pet Food Inc., Quaker's main rival in the moist market. One industry analyst commented that this move "was to put Quaker on notice a little bit, to say 'Hey, we can come at you in your strong area if you come after us in our strong area'." Quaker responded by launching a semi-moist product named *Moist 'n Beefy*, a clear attack at Ralston's (ex Benco's) *Moist & Meaty* brand. Ralston Purina, in turn, introduced a dry dog food called *Grrravy*, a clear attack on Quaker's *Gravy Train* brand.

by the firms or by the government. An important instance of such regulations is given by **most-favored-customer clauses.** These clauses bind firms not to offer a discount to a particular customer without offering the same discount to every other customer within a specified time. At face value, this seems like a clause that should protect the customer; in particular, it should protect the customer against paying a higher price than other customers. However, an important effect of the clause is that it significantly lowers the incentive for a firm to price aggressively: Although a price cut may allow the firm to capture market share from its rival, a price cut implies the penalty of refunding previous customers who were charged a higher price. Finally, because firms have a lower incentive to cut prices, collusive pricing arrangements are more stable than if no clause is imposed. In other words, a regulation that at first could be thought of as a protection against high prices ends up possibly causing high prices. The market for large turbine generators in the 1960s and 1970s provides an interesting example of this idea (box 8.5).

More recently, the Danish government ordered that all transaction prices for ready-mixed concrete be made public (box 8.6). Normally, contracts between buyers and sellers

BOX 8.5   THE MARKET FOR LARGE TURBINE GENERATORS[92]

Turbine generators are complicated pieces of machinery used to convert steam into electrical power. Typical buyers are electrical utilities; the main sellers are General Electric (GE) and Westinghouse. Large turbine generators are produced to order. Sellers are chosen either by direct negotiation (typical of investor-owned utilities) or as the result of sealed bids (typical of government-owned utilities).

As was mentioned earlier, a secret collusive agreement between the main competitors in the electrical goods industry (including turbine generators) was discovered and dismantled in the 1950s. As a result of the cartel breakdown, prices for large turbine generators declined by 50% between 1958 and 1963.

In May 1963, GE announced a new pricing policy for turbine generators. The policy was based on a *price book,* which contained objective rules for determining the price of each turbine generator. GE announced that, from then on, it would sell at the published prices *without exception.* Moreover, it instituted a *most-favored customer clause*: In the event that GE were to sell for a price lower than the book price, every customer from the previous six months would be entitled to the same discount. The credibility of GE's new policy was strengthened by its decision to hire an accounting firm to monitor compliance with the pricing rules. Within less than a year, Westinghouse followed GE's policy of publishing a price book and offering a price protection clause. Except for a brief episode of price cutting in 1964, the prices charged by both companies remained stable and identical until 1975. At this time, the U.S. Department of Justice decided that the policies followed by GE and Westinghouse tended to stabilize prices and were thus in violation of antitrust laws (the Sherman Act, in particular). As a result, it proposed to GE and Westinghouse a consent decree whereby the latter would abstain from such practices as "offering a price protection policy" or "revealing to any person . . . a price book or price list relating to large turbine-generators."

are kept secret. At first, this regulation seems like a way of protecting the consumer, as it makes the market more transparent: No secret price arrangements are allowed. However, as the experience of Denmark showed, market transparency may come at the cost of higher prices. The idea is that, if prices are made public, then monitoring a collusive agreement is much easier than when prices are private information. This is consistent with the analysis in the previous section, wherein we examined a model of collusion with secret price cuts.

BOX 8.6 COLLUSION IN THE DANISH READY-MIXED CONCRETE MARKET[93]

The structure of the ready-mixed concrete industry in Denmark can roughly be described as a collection of fairly tight regional oligopolies with a few firms active in most submarkets and most firms active in only one or two submarkets. Until 1993, list prices were frequently subject to individual, confidential discounts of considerable amount. This situation led industry observers and competition policy authorities to suggest that pricing behavior in the industry was far from the perfectly competitive ideal.

In response, the Danish Competition Council decided, in October 1993, to gather and regularly publish actual transaction prices set by individual firms in three regional markets for two particular grades of ready-mixed concrete. Presumably, the purpose of such publications was to improve information on the buyer side (i.e., among building contractors), whereby seller competition would be stimulated and average transaction prices would fall.

The result of the change in regulation was, however, different from what was intended. In the Aarhus market, for example, prices evolved as shown in the following figure. First, price dispersion between firms decreased dramatically (compare January '94 with November '95). Second, the average price level increased significantly. The data suggest that making all prices public information helped firms coordinate on a collusive equilibrium. The requirement to publish prices ceased soon after the period reported following.

Average 10-MPa Concrete Prices in Århus.

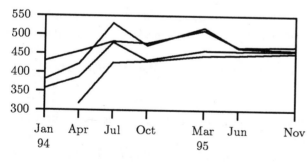

8.4   PUBLIC POLICY

Adam Smith, the founder of Classical Economics, remarked that "People of the same trade seldom meet together, even for merriment and diversion, but the conversation ends in a conspiracy against the public, or in some contrivance to raise prices."[94] In most countries, most of the industry-related public policy (antitrust, competition policy) is directed precisely toward fighting this tendency for sellers to "conspire" against the consumer.

The reasons why price fixing should be (and is) illegal are relatively obvious. From an allocative efficiency point of view, the optimal solution is for firms to set prices at marginal cost level. Any deviation from this solution implies a loss of total welfare, a loss that grows at an increasing rate with the difference between price and marginal cost.[j]

Moreover, even if the allocative efficiency loss were not significant, an increase in price above marginal cost would imply a transfer from buyer to seller, from consumers to firms as the case might be. In fact, it's fair to say that this has been the primary motivation behind public policy against price fixing. Although economists have a tendency to stress allocative efficiency considerations, with little regard for distributional issues, policymakers in turn seem more concerned with consumer welfare than with total welfare; or, at least, they seem to put a greater weight on consumer welfare than on total welfare. In the case of price fixing, the difference in motivation does not matter a great deal, for both lead to the same conclusion. The same is not true, however, in other areas of public policy (see chapter 15).

Price fixing is now illegal in most countries of the world. In Europe, for example, the prohibition follows from Article 85 of the **Treaty of Rome**, which states that

The following shall be prohibited . . . : (a) directly or indirectly fix purchase or selling prices . . . (b) limit or control production . . . (c) share markets or sources of supply . . .

In the United States, price fixing is illegal by virtue of the **Sherman Act**, which was passed in 1890:

Section 1. Every contract, combination in the form of trust or otherwise, in restraint of trade or commerce . . . is declared to be illegal.
Section 2. Every person who shall monopolize, or attempt to monopolize, or combine or conspire with any other person or persons, to monopolize any part of the trade or commerce . . . shall be deemed guilty of a felony . . .

In most other countries, similar forms of legislation are in place.

From looking at antitrust legislation in different countries, we conclude there is a consensus that collusion is illegal. In practice, however, things are quite different. First, the intensity with which the legislation is enforced varies across countries. Traditionally, antitrust enforcement has been stricter in the United States than in most other countries.

[j] If demand is linear and marginal cost constant, the efficiency loss is a quadratic function of the difference between price and marginal cost.

Second, the interpretation of what constitutes illegal collusion also differs across countries. Some examples of the difficulties in interpreting the law follow.

Many agreements and interchanges that firms establish among themselves may not necessarily amount to conspiracies against consumers. In fact, they may result in the benefit of the consumer. For example, suppose that the main semiconductor manufacturers gather for the development of a new microchip. This may be a worthwhile endeavor, one that consumers would eventually benefit from, especially if the development of a new microchip is so expensive that no single firm would take up the task by itself. The problem is that the agreement creates a much improved set of circumstances for firms to collude in fixing prices for their current microchip offerings.[k]

Another example is given by industry associations in which firms exchange information regarding costs, demand, or even prices. Information exchange per se does not violate any of the laws against price fixing. But, as the example in box 8.6 suggests, information exchange may facilitate price fixing, or at least implicit collusion. Ocean shipping is a good instance of this. The U.S. Senate is considering disallowing Pacific Ocean shipping companies from sharing information about the rates they charge. This information is currently centralized by the U.S. Federal Maritime Commission (for shipping to and from the United States). The argument is that, if information on contracts remains secret, then cartel agreements are difficult to sustain.[l]

SUMMARY

- Collusive pricing is more likely to be observed when (1) firms interact frequently, (2) the market is growing, (3) competitors are few in number and similar in size, (4) firms compete in more than one market.

- If price cuts are difficult to observe, then occasional price wars may be necessary to discipline collusive agreements.

KEY CONCEPTS

- market power

- collusion

- secret and tacit agreements

- repeated interaction and grim strategies

- price wars

[k] The particular case of R&D agreements is addressed in greater detail in chapter 16.

[l] See exercise 8.12. This is the same argument as was discussed in the case in box 8.6, except here the government is taking the opposite approach.

- multimarket contact

- facilitating practices

- most-favored-customer clause

REVIEW AND PRACTICE EXERCISES

8.1   Explain why collusive pricing is difficult in one-period competition and easier when firms interact over a number of periods.

8.2   After several years of severe price competition that damaged Boeing's and Airbus's profits, the two companies have recently pledged that they will not sink into another price war. However, in June 1999, Boeing made an unusual offer to sell 100 small aircraft to a leasing corporation at special discount prices. (Although customers never pay list prices, it was felt that this deal was particularly attractive.) Boeing's move follows a similar one by Airbus.[95]

Based on the analysis of section 8.1, why do you think it is so difficult for aircraft manufacturers to collude and avoid price wars?

8.3*   In a market with annual demand $Q = 100 - p$, there are two firms, A and B, that make identical products. Because their products are identical, if one charges a lower price than the other, all consumers will want to buy from the lower-priced firm. If they charge the same price, consumers are indifferent and end up splitting their purchases about evenly between the firms. Marginal cost is constant and there are no capacity constraints.

a. What are the single-period Nash equilibrium prices, p_A and p_B?

b. What prices would maximize the two firms' joint profits?

Assume that one firm cannot observe the other's price until after it has set its own price for the year. Assume further that both firms know that if one undercuts the other, they will revert forever to the noncooperative behavior you described in (a).

c. If the interest rate is 10%, is one repeated-game Nash equilibrium for both firms to charge the price you found in part (b)? What if the interest rate is 110%? What is the highest interest rate at which the joint profit-maximizing price is sustainable?

d. Describe qualitatively how your answer to (c) would change if neither firm was certain that it would be able to detect changes in its rival's price. In particular, what if a price change is detected with a probability of 0.7 each period after it occurs? (*Note:* Do not try to calculate the new equilibria.)

Return to the situation in part (c), with an interest rate of 10%. But now suppose that the market for this good is declining. The demand is $Q = A - p$ with $A = 100$ in the current period, but the value of A is expected to decline by 10% each year (i.e., to 90 next year, then 81 the following year, etc.).

e. Now, is it a repeated-game Nash equilibrium for both firms to charge the monopoly price from part (b)?

8.4* You compete against three major rivals in a market where the products are only slightly differentiated. The "Big Four" have historically controlled about 80% of the market, with a fringe of smaller firms accounting for the rest. Prices have been rather stable, but your market share has been eroding slowly, from 25% just a few years ago to just over 15% now. You are considering adopting an aggressive discounting strategy to gain back market share. Discuss how each of the following factors would enter into your decision.

a. You have strong brand identity and attribute your declining share to discounting by your rivals among the Big Four.

b. The Big Four have all been losing share gradually to the fringe, as the product category becomes more well known and customers become more and more willing to turn to smaller suppliers to meet their needs.

c. You believe your rivals are producing at close to their capacity, and capacity takes a year or two to expand.

d. You can offer discounts selectively, in which case it will take one or two quarters before your rivals are likely to figure out that you have become more aggressive in pricing.

e. Your industry involves high fixed costs and low marginal costs, as applies for most information goods.

f. The entire market is in rapid decline because of technological shifts unfavorable to this product.[96]

8.5 "Price wars imply losses for all of the firms involved. The empirical observation of price wars is therefore a proof that firms do not behave rationally." True or false?

8.6 Empirical evidence from the U.S. airline industry suggests that fare wars are more likely when carriers have excess capacity, caused by GDP growth falling short of its predicted trend. Fare wars are also more likely during the spring and summer quarters, when more discretionary travel takes place.[97] Explain how these two observations are consistent with the theories presented in section 8.2.

8.7   A 1998 news article reported that

Delta Air Lines and American Airlines tried to raise leisure air fares 4% in most domestic markets, but the move failed Monday when lone-holdout Northwest Airlines refused to match the higher prices. The aborted price boost illustrates the impact Northwest's woes already are having on the industry. Months of labor unrest . . . are prompting passengers to book away from the fourth largest carrier.[98]

What does this say about the nature of price dynamics in the airline industry?

8.8   In the third quarter of 1999, most North American paper and forest-products companies experienced an improvement in their profits. The industry, analysts said, was in a cyclical upswing: Not only was demand increasing at a moderate pace; more importantly, the industry practiced restraint in keeping low production levels, thus providing support for higher prices.[99]

How do you interpret these events in light of the models presented in section 8.2?

8.9   In 1918, the U.S. Congress passed a law allowing American firms to form export cartels. Empirical evidence suggests that cartels were more likely to be formed in industries where American exporters had a large market share, in capital-intensive industries, in industries selling standardized goods, and in industries that enjoyed strong export growth.[100] Discuss.

8.10   The endowments of the Ivy League universities have increased significantly. Princeton, the richest of all, boosted its endowment from $400,000 per student in 1990 to more than $750,000 in 1997. In the same period, both Harvard and Yale more than doubled their endowments.

Notwithstanding these riches, the universities have restrained from using financial incentives as a means to compete for students. For many years, the manual of the council of Ivy League Presidents stated that the schools should "neutralize the effect of financial aid so that a student may choose among Ivy Group institutions for non-financial reasons." In 1991, the Justice Department argued that this amounted to price collusion and forced the agreement to end. However, no significant price competition took place until 1998, when Princeton University started offering full scholarships for students with incomes below $40,000. Stanford, MIT, Dartmouth, and Cornell followed suit. Allegedly, Harvard sent a letter to accepted 1998 applicants stating that "we expect that some of our students will have particularly attractive offers from the institutions with new aid programs, and those students should not assume that we will not respond."[101]

How do you interpret these events in light of the theories discussed in this chapter?

8.11 Based on data from the Spanish hotel industry, it was estimated that the rate set by hotel i in market k is positively influenced by a variable that measures the intensity of multimarket competition between hotel i and its competitors in market k: The more markets $m \neq k$ in which firm i and its competitors meet, the greater the measure of multimarket contact. It was also observed that the measure of multimarket contact is highly correlated with hotel chain size, that is, the larger hotel i's chain, the greater the measure of multimarket contact for firm i.[102]

Provide two interpretations for the positive coefficient of multimarket contact on hotel rates, one based on collusion, one based on a different effect.

8.12 Comment on the following excerpt from a 1998 news item.[103]

LONG-STALLED SHIPPING REFORM BILL TAKEN UP BY SENATE. Washington—The Senate has formally begun consideration of a shipping reform bill that, if passed, would create changes for all countries shipping manufactured goods to and from the United States . . .

Until now, U.S. shipping law has been founded on the principle of common carriage—"Everybody pays the same tariff (rate) to go from Oakland to Yokohama," said the Department of Transportation (DOT) official, who asked not to be identified. Under this system, groups of liners called conferences—legal cartels with immunity from antitrust law—set the rates for their members and make those rates public through registration with the federal government. If the shipping bill passes, however, liners could make private, confidential deals with exporters-importers outside of conferences at market-set rates.

"This is going to bring marketplace economics into ocean shipping like we've never seen before," the official said. "It's going to really change the influence of ocean shipping conferences in the marketplace." . . .

The Transportation Department official said the Clinton administration has generally supported legislation for shipping reform in line with its promotion of deregulation in airlines and trucking, but has stated concerns about specific provisions of the Senate bill. Probably, the Administration's biggest concern is a provision of the bill allowing conferences also to engage in confidential contracting, he said. "In the Administration view, that conveys too much market power to the conferences," the official said.

8.13 In 1986, the U.S. Congress enacted a regulation (PL99-509) requiring railroads to disclose contractual terms with grain shippers. Following the passing of the legislation, rates increased on corridors with no direct competition from barge traffic, while rates decreased on corridors with substantial direct competition.[104] How do you interpret these events?

EXTENSION EXERCISES

8.14* Consider an n firm homogeneous-good oligopoly with constant marginal cost, the same for all firms. Let $\bar{\delta}$ be the minimum value of the discount factor such that it is possible to sustain monopoly prices in a collusive agreement. Show that $\bar{\delta}$ is increasing in n. Interpret the result.

8.15** Consider the model of multimarket contact presented in section 8.3. Determine the minimum value of the discount factor such that the optimal collusive solution is stable.

CHAPTER 9

MARKET STRUCTURE AND MARKET POWER

In chapters 7 and 8, we have observed how market performance under oligopoly lies between the extremes of perfect competition and monopoly. This is not entirely surprising, for market structure under oligopoly is itself between the extremes of perfect competition (minimum concentration) and monopoly (maximum concentration). A tantalizing possibility is that the closer market structure is to minimum concentration (respectively, maximum concentration), the closer performance is to perfect competition (respectively, monopoly). In other words, the greater market concentration is, the greater is the degree of market power.

In the first two sections of this chapter, we investigate this hypothesis, both theoretically and empirically. As part of the critique of the empirical analysis, we discuss the need to consider behavior, in addition to market structure, as a determinant of market power. The issue of estimating firm behavior is therefore treated in the third section.

9.1   CONCENTRATION AND MARKET POWER: THEORY

In our treatment of the Cournot model, we considered the simple case of duopoly. What happens when there are more than two firms? One way of addressing the general oligopoly case is to repeat the graphical analysis of chapter 7 but to consider more than two firms.

First, recall that Firm 1's profit is given by $\pi_1 = P(Q)q_1 - C(q_1)$, where Q is total output. This implies that, from Firm 1's perspective, all that matters is the total output produced by other firms, independent of how many other firms there are, or what the

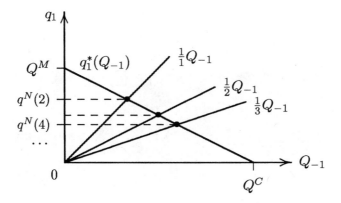

FIGURE 9.1 *N*-FIRM COURNOT EQUILIBRIUM.

output level of each is. That is, Firm 1's profit is a function of Q but not n or the value of each particular q_i ($i \neq 1$). This in turn implies that our derivation of the reaction curve is valid for the n-firm case, so long as we replace q_2 by $Q_{-1} \equiv \sum_{i=2}^{n} q_i$, the total output of all firms but Firm 1. (Notice that, in the particular case when $n = 2$, $Q_{-1} = q_2$.)

Because we are still dealing with a symmetric oligopoly, all firms will produce the same output in equilibrium, that is, $q_i^N = q^N$. We can then find q^N in the following way. In figure 9.1, we draw Firm 1's reaction curve, $q_1^*(Q_{-1})$. We also draw the line starting from the origin and with slope $1/(n-1)$, that is, the line $q_1 = Q_{-1}/(n-1)$. An equilibrium must be a point such that (1) Firm 1 chooses optimum output given what rivals choose; and (2) (by symmetry) other firms choose the same output as Firm 1, that is, $q_i = q_1$, for all i. If all firms choose the same output level as Firm 1, it must be $Q_{-1} = (n-1)q_1$, because there are $n-1$ firms other than Firm 1. The equilibrium is thus determined by the intersection of the reaction curve and the curve $q_1 = Q_{-1}/(n-1)$.

Figure 9.1 depicts the equilibrium value $q^N(n)$ for various values of n, the number of firms: $n = 2, 3, 4$. As can be seen, the equilibrium output per firm declines as the number of firms increases. In fact, as n becomes very large, the slope of the line $q_1 = Q_{-1}/(n-1)$ becomes very small, and the value of q^N becomes very small, too.

We are also interested in the evolution of *total* output as the number of firms increases. The axes in figure 9.1 give the value of Q_{-1} and q_1. Now, total output is, by construction, the sum of $Q_{-1} + q_1$ (recall that Q_{-1} is the output of all firms other than Firm 1). Therefore, lines of slope $-45°$ represent points with the same total output, that is, iso-output lines.

Figure 9.2 depicts iso-output lines crossing through the different equilibria derived in figure 9.1. There are also iso-output lines through points $(0, Q^M)$ and $(Q^C, 0)$. Iso-output lines farther away from the origin correspond to higher values of output. It can be

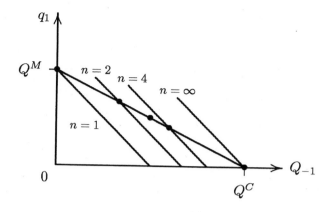

FIGURE 9.2 EQUILIBRIA UNDER MONOPOLY, COURNOT, AND PERFECT COMPETITION.

seen from figure 9.2 that: *Total output under Cournot equilibrium is greater than under monopoly but lower than under perfect competition.* (This result was proven in chapter 7 for the case of duopoly. Figure 9.2 generalizes it to the case of an *n*-firm oligopoly.) Moreover, *as the number of firms increases, total output increases.* Finally, *as the number of Cournot competitors goes to infinity, total output converges to the value under perfect competition.*[105]

How Many Is Many?

We have just seen that the performance of the Cournot model converges to perfect competition as the number of firms goes to infinity. This is an important result as it justifies the motivation of perfect competition as a reference point: *The model of perfect competition is a good approximation for markets in which there are many firms.*

This raises the following question: How many is many? Does it take 5, 50, or 500 firms for oligopoly competition to be approximately like perfect competition? Policymakers are frequently interested in the allocative inefficiency created by oligopoly prices above marginal cost. Under perfect competition, allocative efficiency is maximum, or, conversely, allocative inefficiency is nil. The above question can thus be restated as: How many firms does it take for allocative inefficiency to be close to zero (the value under perfect competition)?

Maintaining our assumption that firms behave according to the Cournot assumption, we obtain the values in table 9.1. The table presents the allocative inefficiency in the Cournot equilibrium as a percentage of the allocative inefficiency under monopoly (for comparison purposes). As can be seen, with seven identical firms, the performance of Cournot is much closer to perfect competition than to monopoly (6 is closer to zero

TABLE 9.1 ALLOCATIVE INEFFICIENCY IN COURNOT EQUILIBRIUM AS A PERCENTAGE OF ALLOCATIVE INEFFICIENCY UNDER MONOPOLY.

n	Inefficiency (%)
1	1
2	4/9
3	1/4
4	4/25
$\vdots$	$\vdots$
7	$4/64 \approx 6\%$
$\vdots$	$\vdots$
15	$4/256 \approx 1.5\%$

than to 100). With 15 identical firms, the efficiency loss is very close to zero. In other words,

> It does not take a large number of identical firms for the performance of the Cournot model to be very close to that of perfect competition.

MEASURING MARKET POWER AND MARKET CONCENTRATION

So far, we have considered symmetric oligopoly models. We have measured market power by the price cost margin ($p - MC$, or $(p - MC)/p$), whereas market concentration was (inversely) measured by the number of firms.

When firms have different cost functions, their output and marginal cost in equilibrium are different. This asymmetry calls for more general measures of market power and market concentration than the ones considered so far. Even if price is the same for all firms (as will be the case when the product is homogeneous), different marginal costs imply different margins for different firms. What then is the market power in the industry as a whole? Moreover, if firms are of different sizes, then the number of firms alone is not a good measure of concentration. Having three firms of the same size is not the same as having one with 98% of the market and the remaining two with 1% each.

Regarding market power, the measure we will use is the natural generalization of what we've considered so far. We will measure market power by the **Lerner index**, defined as the weighted average of each firm's margin, with weights given by the firms' market shares.

$$L \equiv \sum_{i=1}^{n} s_i \frac{p - MC_i}{p}.$$

where s_i is firm i's market share. Obviously, if all firms have the same marginal cost, then the Lerner index is simply the (common) margin set by all firms, as considered before.

As for concentration, there are various possible measures. The most commonly used are the coefficient C_m, the sum of the market shares of the largest m firms. For example,

$$C_4 \equiv \sum_{i=1}^{4} s_i,$$

where firms are ordered by market shares (Firm 1 is the largest firm, and so on). The value of C_4 varies between zero (minimum concentration) and one (maximum concentration).

An alternative measure of market concentration is the **Herfindahl index**, given by

$$H \equiv \sum_{i=1}^{n} s_i^2.$$

The value of H varies between zero (minimum concentration) and one (maximum concentration, i.e., monopoly). Frequently, the value of H is multiplied by 10,000, so that it varies between zero and 10,000.

The Herfindahl index provides a better measure of market concentration, as we will see below and in exercise 9.4. However, it is more difficult to compute: It requires knowledge of the market share of all firms in the industry, whereas C_4, for example, requires only knowledge of the market shares of the four largest firms.[a]

MARKET CONCENTRATION AND MARKET POWER

Consider a general Cournot model with n firms, each with a cost function $C_i(q_i)$. It can be shown that

$$L = \frac{H}{\epsilon} \tag{9.1}$$

where ϵ is the price elasticity of demand and L and H are as previously defined. This result is important as it generalizes the idea that the greater concentration is (H), the greater the degree of market power (L). It allows us to answer questions such as the following:

Consider two markets with identical demands. In one market, there are two firms with identical market shares. In the other market, there is one firm with a 70% market share and two small firms with 15% each. Assuming that both markets are in a Cournot equilibrium, where is market power the greatest?

[a] However, even if we lack information on the market shares for some of the firms, we can still find a lower and an upper bound for the value of H. See exercise 9.5.

The answer is, from (9.1), whichever market has the greatest concentration, as measured by the Herfindahl index. In this particular example, we have, in the first market, $H = 10,000(.5^2 + .5^2) = 5000$, whereas in the second market, $H = 10,000(.7^2 + .15^2 + .15^2) = 5350$. In words, market power is greater in the second market (even though n is greater); the difference, however, is small.

9.2 CONCENTRATION AND MARKET POWER: EMPIRICAL ESTIMATION

Mainstream industrial organization has been founded on the so-called **structure-conduct-performance paradigm** (SCP). The SCP paradigm provides a system for the analysis of a given industry. The industry is characterized by its structure (e.g., how concentrated it is), conduct (i.e., the behavior of its firms), and performance (market power, allocative efficiency, and so forth). Moreover, the SCP paradigm propounds that there is a causal relationship between structure, conduct, and performance: Structure influences conduct; both structure and conduct influence performance.

1. Several reasons why structure may influence conduct were proposed in the previous chapters. For example, we argued that collusion is easier among a small number of firms; likewise, it is easier to reach a price-fixing agreement when firms are similar to each other, and so on.

2. The relation between conduct and performance should be clear: The more competitively firms behave, the lower the degree of market power and the greater allocative efficiency. Compare, for example, the Bertrand solution to collusive price setting.

3. The argument that structure influences performance was developed in the previous section. Specifically, we argued that, when fixing behavior (Cournot), the more concentrated an industry is, the greater the degree of market power.

For a long time, empirical industrial economists have been concerned with the empirical implications of the preceding paradigm. Specifically, if performance is a function of structure and conduct; and conduct, in turn, is a function of structure; then we can simplify the previous three points into a relation between performance (say, market power) and structure (say, concentration).

The direct relation between concentration and market power is positive, as was derived in the previous section (equation 9.1). The relation between concentration and noncompetitive behavior is positive, as was argued in the previous chapter. Finally, by definition, the relation between noncompetitive behavior and market power is also positive. When all of these are put together, there should be a positive relationship between concentration and market power.

We thus have a testable implication, which we may call the **structure-performance hypothesis**, namely a positive relation between concentration and market power. To test this hypothesis, we need data on concentration and on market power. The former is normally easy to obtain (e.g., market shares based on sales data). Measuring the Lerner index, the index of market power we have been considering, is more difficult; in fact, it is normally impossible. However, if fixed costs are zero and marginal cost is constant and equal to c_i, then firm i's profit rate, r_i, is equal to firm i's margin, m_i:

$$r_i \equiv \frac{R_i - C_i}{R_i} = \frac{pq_i - c_i q_i}{pq_i} = \frac{p - c_i}{p} = m_i.$$

Consequently, as an approximation, the Lerner index (the average of every firm's m_i) can be measured by the average profit rate.

Accordingly, many economists have gathered data on concentration and profit rates for a number of industries and have estimated the econometric relation between those variables.[106] That is, suppose we have data on the average profit rate in industry i as well as on concentration in that industry. Then we would expect industries with higher concentration to exhibit higher average profit rates, that is, a positive coefficient in the regression of profit rate on concentration.

Alas, the result of this econometric effort is not very encouraging.[107] Most studies find a weak statistical link between structure and performance. However, before dismissing the theoretical analysis that has brought us to the structure-performance hypothesis, we must say that there are important data measurement problems that may, at least partially, explain the poor results. Lacking data on price-cost margins, most studies use as a proxy accounting profit rates, which are frequently a poor proxy. For example, book depreciation rates are normally different from economic depreciation rates. Moreover, many firms operate in many different industries, thus requiring the division of data among the different industries they belong to—an operation that is not straightforward.

THE SIMULTANEITY PROBLEM

In terms of methodology, the test of the structure-performance hypothesis suffers from an additional important limitation. Basically, it ignores the possibility of reverse causal links in the relation between structure, conduct, and performance. For example, if British Airways prices aggressively low in the London–New York route, it may succeed in reducing Virgin Atlantic's profits to such an extent as to induce the latter to leave the market or even the industry. Here, we have an instance of how conduct may have an effect on structure—a "reverse" link with respect to the ones we have considered so far.

Why is this important? To illustrate the problem, suppose that all of the industries in the sample have the same demand and cost functions, differing only in one respect: For some *exogenous* reason, the degree of collusion is higher in some industries than in others. This may result, for example, from different values of the discount factor.[b] Suppose, moreover, that any firm may enter any industry by incurring an entry cost F.

In each industry, total industry profits are $\Pi(p)$, where p is the industry equilibrium price—high in collusive industries, low in competitive ones. Because there is free entry into every industry, firms will decide to enter as long as prospective profits are positive. Profit per firm, net of entry cost, becomes zero whenever the number of firms is such that $\Pi(p)/n - F = 0$, or

$$n = \Pi(p)/F. \tag{9.2}$$

Recall that the Lerner index is given by

$$L = \frac{p - MC}{p}. \tag{9.3}$$

We then get an apparently paradoxical result: If we increase p, then $\Pi(p)$ increases as well (this assumes we start from a price level below the monopoly price). From (9.2), we see that the equilibrium number of firms increases, that is, concentration decreases. Moreover, from (9.3), we see that the degree of market power increases along with p. Putting both facts together, we conclude that, as price is increased and the number of firms adjusts, *concentration decreases as market power increases*.

The result of this alternative model implies the opposite prediction from what we considered in the previous section.[c] Before, we had a positive relation between concentration and market power. Now, we have a negative relation. The critical difference between the two models is that, before, we took market structure as given (i.e., as an exogenous variable), whereas the degree of competition was taken as an endogenous variable. In the model just presented, the degree of competition is the exogenous variable (maximum collusion attainable), whereas market structure (the number of firms) is assumed to be endogenous. In other words, before we had concentration causing market power; now, we have market power causing concentration.

In practice, it is likely that both the direct and the reverse effects in the SCP paradigm are important. This may explain why the statistical relation between concentration and profitability is not significant: It may be simply the sum of two effects with opposite signs.[d]

INTERPRETATION

Suppose that the feedback effect of performance on structure is not very important. Suppose, moreover, that statistical estimation yields a positive effect of structure on performance (as some studies have indeed found). We still have a problem of interpretation to solve, as we will see presently.

The **collusion hypothesis** is that concentration implies market power through increased collusion between firms. If this is the case, then policymakers should be concerned with anything that increases industry concentration—a merger, for example. In fact, as we will see in chapter 15, concentration indices play an important role

[b] For example, in some industries, prices are set on a daily basis, whereas in others, the frequency is weekly. As seen in section 8.1, this and other aspects imply different values of the discount factor.

[c] The issue of endogenous entry into an oligopoly is treated in greater detail in chapter 14. Exercise 14.4 is particularly relevant for the present discussion.

[d] There are statistical ways to distinguish between the two effects, and attempts at doing so have been made. Even then, the empirical results are not very encouraging, that is, they do not provide any clear support for either effect.

in the policy analysis of mergers (by the Department of Justice [DOJ] and the Federal Trade Commission [FTC] in the United States, by the European Commission in Europe). Roughly speaking, a merger that increases concentration significantly is not allowed, on the basis that it would increase market power to the detriment of consumers.

An alternative interpretation for the positive relation between structure and performance is the **efficiency hypothesis**, normally associated with the Chicago school.[108] Consider a symmetric oligopoly (all firms with identical marginal cost), and suppose that one of the firms improves its productive efficiency, thus reducing its marginal cost. A lower marginal cost by one of the firms implies a redistribution of market shares, whereby both concentration and market power increase, just as in the collusion hypothesis. However, while under the collusion hypothesis, the increase in market power is associated mainly with a decrease in allocative efficiency; under the efficiency hypothesis the increase in market power is associated mainly with an increase in productive efficiency (the transfer of market share from relatively inefficient firms to a more efficient one). It is quite possible that society is better off in the new situation, even though both concentration and market power are greater. The policy implications of this alternative hypothesis are nearly the opposite of the collusion hypothesis.

Some empirical studies have used firm-level data (as opposed to industry-level data). In these regressions, the coefficient on concentration is lower than in regressions with industry-level data. Moreover, firm market share has a positive impact on profit rate. This evidence provides some support for the efficiency hypothesis. In fact, if all firms were equally efficient (same marginal cost), then market shares would have no explanatory power with respect to profit rates.

9.3 CONDUCT AND MARKET POWER: EMPIRICAL ESTIMATION

In the previous section, we considered the empirical test of the relation between structure and performance, specifically, the relation between concentration and market power. As we have seen, there are a number of theoretical and conceptual problems with the approach taken to test the structure-performance hypothesis (i.e., the hypothesis of a positive relation between concentration and market power). In particular, by limiting ourselves to measuring only structure and performance, we are putting several different effects into the same bag—the direct effect of concentration on performance, the effect through firm conduct, and the feedback effects of conduct and performance on market structure. An additional limitation of the traditional approach is the use of profit rates as proxies for the price-cost margin.

To avoid these limitations, recent studies have attempted to directly model and estimate firm behavior. To escape some of the statistical and conceptual problems of using aggregate, intersectoral data, these recent studies tend to focus on firm-level data for one particular industry. Moreover, instead of assuming that the profit rate provides a good proxy for the price-cost margin, marginal cost is *estimated* as part of the overall statistical effort. The conceptual framework for this new approach, often referred to as the **New Empirical Industrial Organization** (NEIO), can be explained based on a generalization of equation 9.1:

$$L = \theta \frac{H}{\epsilon}. \tag{9.4}$$

The difference with respect to (9.1) is that the ratio H/ϵ is now multiplied by θ. Recall that the equality $L = H/\epsilon$ was derived on the assumption that firms compete as in the Cournot model. Therefore, if $\theta = 1$, (9.4) reduces to (9.1). Under Bertrand competition, price equals marginal cost, so $L = (p - MC)/p = 0$. In terms of equation 9.4, this corresponds to $\theta = 0$. Under monopoly or perfect collusion, we have $L = 1/\epsilon$, as was shown in chapter 5; this corresponds to $\theta = 1/H$ in Equation 9.4. More generally, under partial collusion, the Lerner index takes some value between zero and $1/\epsilon$, which is the case of perfect collusion. Each value of L then corresponds to a value of θ.[e]

Equation 9.4 provides a useful generalization of equation 9.1. The latter is derived based on a particular assumption regarding oligopoly behavior (Cournot) and shows how demand elasticity and concentration influence market power. The former, in turn, allows for any level of collusive behavior. In summary, equation 9.4 states:

> The degree of market power depends on three factors (1) demand elasticity, (2) market concentration, and (3) collusive behavior.

So, for example, given a level of concentration and a value of the demand elasticity, the more firms collude, the greater the degree of market power. However, even if firms collude perfectly, if demand is elastic, the degree of market power is small. Finally, as we saw in section 9.1, for a given level of conduct (e.g., Cournot), the more concentrated the industry is, the greater the degree of market power.[f] Of the different terms in the right-hand side of equation 9.4, concentration is perhaps the easiest to obtain: All we need are data on each firm's sales. Determining the elasticity of demand is a little more difficult: It requires data and some statistical work of estimation. The necessary data are essentially price and quantity demanded, in addition to variables that influence the cost function.[g]

What about the value of θ, which summarizes the nature of firm conduct? If we had data on marginal cost, then the solution would be easy: From price and marginal cost, determine L. Having computed H and estimated ϵ, simply obtain θ by solving (9.4): $\theta = L\epsilon/H$.

[e] The "model" underlying Equation 9.4 is frequently known as the **conjectural variations** model, the value of θ reflecting "conjectural variations." However, it is best thought of not as a model but as a device for estimating the degree of collusive power.

[f] Equation 9.4 suggests a comparison between the structure-conduct-performance paradigm framework and the more recent **five-forces framework**.[109] The five-forces framework is centered on the rivalry within the industry but also takes into account supplier power, buyer power, the threat of entry, and the threat of substitute products. In terms of equation 9.4, rivalry within the industry would correspond to the value of θ. Entry impacts on profitability through changes in the value of H (and indirectly through changes in the value of θ). Substitute products and buyer power are reflected in the value of ϵ. Finally, supplier power is one of the determinants of the value of marginal cost, which in turn determines the value of L.

[g] The problem of estimating the demand function (and the demand elasticity) is best understood by considering a competitive market. In each period, price and quantity are determined by the intersection of supply and demand. To estimate the demand function, we need data on variables that shift the supply curve and trace out the demand curve in successive equilibrium points.

Unfortunately, data on marginal cost are seldom available. In fact, even the firms themselves may have some difficulty in estimating it. We can then take the reverse path: Estimate θ and, together with H and ϵ, determine L, as given by equation 9.4.

The statistical estimation of θ based on price and quantity data can be a fairly complex problem. We will deal here with one particular case that (1) is relatively simple, and (2) illustrates the general idea. Suppose that, although we have no way of directly measuring marginal cost, data exist on a variable that is highly correlated with marginal cost. For example, the total marginal cost for a cigarette manufacturer is given by $MC = c + t$. c is the production marginal cost, which we cannot observe. t is the sales tax, which we can easily observe. In particular, we know that a $1 variation in t implies a $1 variation in marginal cost.

Given that total marginal cost is perfectly correlated with sales tax (in fact, the latter is a component of the former), the change in price in response to a change in sales tax is the same as the change in price in response to a change in marginal cost. In other words, price would change in the same way if c were to change by $1, or if t were to change by $1.

Why is this useful? Because knowing the value of the derivative of price with respect to marginal cost allows for the (indirect) estimation of θ. Table 9.2 gives the derivative of price with respect to marginal cost, ξ, assuming linear demand and constant marginal cost, under three possible conduct situations: (1) perfect collusion, (2) Cournot, and (3) Bertrand. By solving

$$\theta = \frac{1 - \xi}{\xi} \frac{1}{H},$$

we obtain the conduct parameter θ introduced earlier (equation 9.4).

An alternative to estimating the derivative of price with respect to marginal cost is to examine how price changes in response to shifts in the demand curve. For example, suppose that demand is given by $p = a + s - Q$, where s is a period-to-period shift in the demand intercept. One example might be seasonal variations in the demand for beer,

TABLE 9.2 **DERIVATIVE OF PRICE WITH RESPECT TO:**

Marginal Cost (ξ), Demand Intercept (χ), and Conduct Parameter (θ)

Equilibrium	Eq. price	$\xi \equiv \partial P / \partial MC$	$\chi \equiv \partial P / \partial a$	θ^*
Perfect collusion	$\frac{1}{2}a + \frac{1}{2}c$	$1/2$	$1/2$	$\frac{1}{H}$
Cournot	$\frac{1}{n+1}a + \frac{n}{n+1}c$	$\frac{n}{n+1} = \frac{1}{1+H}$	$\frac{H}{1+H}$	1
Bertrand	c	1	0	0

* See Eq. 9.4.

where s would be greater in the summer than in the winter. As before, table 9.2 gives the derivative, now denoted χ, of price with respect to the demand intercept a under the same three possible conduct situations: perfect collusion, Cournot, and Bertrand. By solving

$$\theta = \frac{\chi}{1 - \chi} \frac{1}{H},$$

we obtain the conduct parameter θ introduced earlier (equation 9.4).

Both of these examples are simplistic in that they assume linear demand. Although linear demand curves are useful for the purpose of theoretical illustration, most empirical applications tend to reject the assumption of linearity. If the demand curve is not linear, then the values on table 9.2 are no longer valid. It is possible, for example, that the derivative of price with respect to marginal cost may be equal to 1 under monopoly conditions, whereas a linear demand would indicate perfect competition. Despite these limitations, the preceding analysis illustrates the spirit of the exercise—to uncover the parameters that describe the firms' behavior based on limited sets of data (prices, quantities, and variables that influence the demand and cost functions).[110]

Linearity is not the only limiting assumption of the preceding analysis. As we saw in chapter 8, collusive agreements frequently imply an irregular pattern of prices, with periods of high prices alternating with periods of low prices (price wars). Equation 9.4, however, implicitly assumes that prices are constant over time.[111] By contrast, other collusive agreements show remarkably stable prices in spite of variations in marginal cost. This may result from the fact that it is costly to change prices (e.g., changing the price may require that the firms meet together). However, as we have seen, under monopoly, each \$1 change in marginal cost should imply a \$.50 change in price (under the assumption of linear demand). All of this leads us to conclude that estimating conduct, in particular, estimating the degree of collusion between firms, is a complicated process for which there is no hard and fast solution. Normally, the best strategy is to combine statistical studies with nonquantitative evidence, in particular, internal memos or related documents that provide evidence of collusive behavior.

SUMMARY

- As the number of Cournot competitors goes to infinity, total output converges to the value under perfect competition. In fact, it does not take a large number of identical firms for the performance of the Cournot model to be close to that of perfect competition.

- The degree of market power depends on three factors: demand elasticity, market concentration, and extent of collusive behavior.

KEY CONCEPTS

- Lerner index

- Herfindahl index

- structure-conduct-performance paradigm

- collusion hypothesis and efficiency hypothesis

REVIEW AND PRACTICE EXERCISES

9.1   Consider the following goods: cement, mineral water, automobiles, and retail banking. In each case, determine the relevant market boundaries, and present an estimate of the degree of concentration.

9.2   Based on data from local cement markets in the United States, a series of regressions were estimated for seven years in the period between 1948 and 1980. Each regression has the form price $= \beta \cdot C_4 +$ (other variables). The coefficient β was estimated to be positive in five of the seven years considered, negative in the remaining two. How can these results be explained?

9.3**   Based on monthly data for Portuguese commercial banks, the following relation was estimated:

$$r_t = 0.098 + 0.814 \, m_t,$$

where r_t is the interest rate charged by commercial banks and m_t is the money market rate, that is, the interest rate that banks must pay to borrow in the short term. The standard deviation of the second coefficient estimate is .0878. Knowing that the money market interest rate is highly correlated with the marginal cost of giving out loans, and knowing that H is approximately .125, what can you say about market power in this sector?

EXTENSION EXERCISES

9.4**   Consider the following criteria for a good measure of market concentration:

a. Nonambiguity: Given any two different industries, it must be possible to rank concentration between the two.

b. **Invariance to scale:** A concentration measure ought not to depend on measurement units.

c. **Transfers:** Concentration should increase when a large firm's market share increases at the expense of a small firm's market share.

d. **Monotonicity:** Given n identical firms, concentration should be decreasing in n.

e. **Cardinality:** If we divide each firm into k smaller firms of the same size, then concentration should decrease in the same proportion.

Verify whether the indices C_n and H satisfy these requirements.

9.5** Suppose you know only the value of the market shares for the largest m firms in a given industry. Although you do not possess sufficient information to compute the Herfindahl index, you can find a lower and an upper bound for its values. How?

PRICE AND NONPRICE STRATEGIES

CHAPTER 10

PRICE DISCRIMINATION

Consider two passengers traveling on the same flight between London and New York, both in economy class. Unless they booked their tickets together and at the same time, it is likely that they will have paid different fares for the same flight. Strictly speaking, what each passenger purchased was not *exactly* the same good. For example, one will have bought a ticket with no restrictions, while the other's ticket can be changed only upon the payment of some penalty. However, the very high differences in price (sometimes a factor of three) hardly seem to be justified by the small differences in the terms of sale.

Airline pricing is one of many examples in which firms set different prices of the same good (or approximately the same good). Other examples include toothpaste, computer software, and electricity, to name just a few. The practice of *setting different prices for the same good*, whereby the relevant price in each case depends on the quantity purchased, on the buyer's characteristics, or on various sale clauses, is known as **price discrimination**.

In most chapters in this book, we maintain the assumption that firms set one price only for each product. In this chapter, we consider the case when the opposite is true, that is, the case when a firm—a monopolist or an oligopolist—is able to discriminate between consumers and set different prices directed at different market segments. We begin by addressing the question of under what conditions a firm might be able to set different prices for the same good.

RESALE AND PRICE DISCRIMINATION

In a perfectly competitive market, the **law of one price** must prevail, that is, there cannot be two different prices for the same product. If there were two different prices, then an agent could earn a profit by buying at the low price and selling at the high price. In the real world, by contrast, it is common to observe more than one price set for what is apparently the same product, while little or no arbitrage occurs.[a]

For more than one price to prevail in equilibrium, it must be either that agents are imperfectly informed about the different prices (see chapter 12); or, more commonly, that the transaction costs of buying and selling are so high that resale is not profitable. For example, suppose that a supermarket sells three tubes of toothpaste for the price of two. This is an example of price discrimination, for a consumer who buys one tube pays a different price (per tube) than a consumer who buys three tubes (for the price of two). Suppose that a certain consumer is interested in buying only one tube. Then, such a consumer could buy three tubes (for the price of two) and sell two of those to other customers at the regular price, thus saving himself or herself some money (in fact, getting one tube for free). However, the costs of doing this would be so high (in terms of wasted time and so forth) so as not to compensate the effort.

In some cases, resale is illegal. In many countries, for example, one cannot—by law—resell electricity bought from a public utility.[b] In other cases, resale is physically impossible. For example, it would be very difficult to resell the services of a haircut! In fact, price discrimination is more common in the sale of services than in the sale of products for precisely this reason.

In summary:

Price discrimination requires the absence of **resale**.

COST DIFFERENCES AND PRICE DISCRIMINATION

In the definition of price discrimination we stated "different prices for the same product." But then, is a BMW in the United States the same product as a BMW in Germany? Even if it is, from a consumer's perspective, it certainly is not from a producer's perspective, for it costs more to sell a German car in the United States than to sell it in Germany, on account of transportation costs and import tariffs. For this reason, the fact that the price of a BMW is higher in the United States than in Germany would not constitute sufficient evidence of price discrimination.

An alternative test for price discrimination is that *the ratio of prices across markets is different from the ratio of marginal costs*. For example, if a hardcover book sells for $15 and the corresponding paperback sells for $5, then we have a case of price discrimination, for the $10 difference can hardly be accounted for by the cost of a hardcover.[112] Although a hard cover and a paperback version of the same book are not *exactly* the same product, they are sufficiently *similar* that the ratio test should be considered a sufficient indicator of price discrimination.

[a] **Arbitrage** refers to the practice of buying and selling to profit from a price difference; an arbitrageur is an agent that engages in such practice.

[b] We will return to the legal aspects of reselling in section 10.5.

10.1   TYPES OF PRICE DISCRIMINATION

There are multiple possibilities for price discrimination; it is thus useful to classify them in some way. The most important classification considers the information that firms have about buyers. Sometimes, firms possess information about their customers, in particular, information that is related to the customers' willingness to pay. If buyer characteristics are observable, then the seller can establish different prices as a function of the buyer's characteristics. Examples of this include country-specific prices, membership discounts, special "academic" prices for software, student discounts on magazine subscriptions, and reduced train fares for the elderly. This type of price discrimination can be referred to as **selection by indicators** or **third-degree price discrimination**.

In other instances, the seller has some information about the heterogeneity of the buyers' preferences but cannot observe the characteristics of each buyer in particular. Even so, it is possible to discriminate between different buyers by means of offering a menu of selling contracts that include various clauses in addition to price. Consider, for example, Pex or Apex fares. These are reduced airfares that require the buyer to stay over the weekend in the place of destination. Because business trips normally take place during the week, Pex fares allow the seller to discriminate indirectly between business travelers and leisure travelers. In this case, we say that there is **self-selection** on the part of the buyers. This type of discrimination is also known as **second-degree price discrimination**.

> Sellers can price-discriminate either based on observable buyer characteristics or by inducing buyers to self-select among different product offerings.

A Note on Semantics

The definition of second- and third-degree price discrimination is not universally agreed upon. As previously defined, the difference depends on whether the seller can distinguish buyers directly or only indirectly, that is, whether there is selection by indicators (third-degree) or, rather, self-selection (second-degree).[113]

An alternative definition of second-degree price discrimination is that unit price depends on quantity purchased (but not on the identity of the consumer).[114] Typical examples of this type of discrimination are the pricing of public utilities such as water, electricity, or telephone services. For example, a telephone bill normally is made up of a monthly rental (fixed fee) and call charges (variable fee). Because there is a fixed fee, unit price (price per call minute) is decreasing with the number of calls. This type of price discrimination is also known as **nonlinear pricing**. The crucial characteristic of second-degree price discrimination, under this alternative definition, is that prices *do not depend on the identity of the consumer*, but rather on the quantity consumed. In this sense, the two definitions agree. But quantity is one of several aspects that define the package bought by the consumer (quality, for example, being another one). In other words, there is nothing special about price depending on quantity, as opposed to other dimensions of the selling package. Both definitions would classify nonlinear pricing as second-degree price discrimination. The first definition, however, would extend this classification to every circumstance in which prices cannot depend on the consumers' identity, so that it is the consumers themselves who self-select between different offerings.

FIRST-DEGREE PRICE DISCRIMINATION

We have mentioned third- and second-degree price discrimination. Another form of price discrimination is given by first-degree price discrimination. This is the situation in which the seller sets different prices for each buyer and for each unit purchased by each buyer, thus extracting all of the consumer's surplus. A classic example is that of a small-town doctor who has good knowledge of the town's inhabitants, including information on their financial status. Based on this knowledge, the doctor evaluates the patient's willingness to pay before each visit and sets the fee accordingly. Another example is given by aircraft: Although manufacturers post list prices for each aircraft, in practice each airline pays a different price for each aircraft.

The practice of first-degree price discrimination, also known as **perfect discrimination**, is relatively infrequent. However, the study of this extreme situation provides a useful reference point for the purpose of welfare analysis. We will return to it in section 10.5.

10.2   THIRD-DEGREE PRICE DISCRIMINATION

This is arguably the most common form of price discrimination. As discussed previously, it corresponds to the situation in which the seller divides buyers into groups, setting a different price for each group—a practice also known as **market segmentation**. One form of market segmentation is based on geographical location. For example, the *Wall Street Journal Europe* sells for 260 escudos in Portugal and, in Spain, for 275 pesetas, a much higher price (one peseta is worth approximately 1.2 escudos). Pricing of the the *Wall Street Journal Europe* is an example of *spatial price discrimination*, a form of third-degree price discrimination. Another example is pricing of cars in Europe (box 10.1). However, market segmentation does not have to be based on geographical location. For example, many products and services are sold at special prices for students or the elderly. Still another example, subscriptions to the *American Economic Review* vary according to the subscriber's annual income.

The simplest model of third-degree price discrimination consists of a monopolist selling to two separate markets. The profit function is then given by

Box 10.1 Price Discrimination in the European Car Market[115]

A series of studies by the European Bureau of Consumers Unions shows that pretax prices for identical car models may vary by over 90% across countries. The following table presents estimates for the margins of a few models in a few countries.

RELATIVE MARKUPS[c] OF SELECTED CARS IN SELECTED EUROPEAN COUNTRIES (IN %)

Model	Belgium	France	Germany	Italy	United Kingdom
Fiat Uno	7.6	8.7	9.8	21.7	8.7
Nissan Micra	8.1	23.1	8.9	36.1	12.5
Ford Escort	8.5	9.5	8.9	8.9	11.5
Peugeot 405	9.9	13.4	10.2	9.9	11.6
Mercedes 190	14.3	14.4	17.2	15.6	12.3

These differences can be interpreted in different ways. For example, it may be that the level of collusion is greater in some countries than in others. Alternatively, import quotas can be the reason for high prices in some countries. Finally, spatial price discrimination may also explain the observed patterns. Econometric evidence suggests that price discrimination is indeed quite important. Demand elasticities are different in different countries, and manufacturers set different prices accordingly.

One pattern that is noticeable from the numbers above is that markups are higher in the country in which each car is produced (e.g., Fiat in Italy). This may correspond to a national bias that is reflected in a lower demand elasticity (e.g., Italian buyers are so keen on Fiat cars that their demand is inelastic).

By contrast, the disparity of markups for Japanese cars (e.g., the Nissan Micra) can be explained by the restrictive import quotas in France and Italy.

$$\Pi(p_1, p_2) = p_1 D_1(p_1) + p_2 D_2(p_2) - C\left(D_1(p_1) + D_2(p_2)\right),$$

where p_i is price in market i. Profit maximization implies that $MR_1 = MR_2 = MC$, where MR_i is marginal revenue in market i and MC is marginal cost. This in turn implies the well-known **elasticity rule**:

$$p_1\left(1 - \frac{1}{\epsilon_1}\right) = p_2\left(1 - \frac{1}{\epsilon_2}\right) = MC,$$

where $\epsilon_i \equiv -\frac{\partial q_i}{\partial p_i}\frac{p_i}{q_i}$ is the price elasticity of demand.

[c] Markup is the difference between price and unit cost divided by unit cost.

It follows that:

> Under third-degree price discrimination, a seller should charge a lower price in those market segments with greater price elasticity.

A model like this explains, among other things, why the export price may be lower than the price set for the domestic market. This would be optimal when the demand elasticity in the export market is sufficiently greater than the elasticity in the domestic market to the point of compensating the greater transportation cost to the export market.

10.3   NONLINEAR PRICING

There are a number of products and services for which consumers must decide not only whether to buy but also how much to buy. Examples range from utilities (electricity, water, telephone services, etc.) to the size of a cup of soda or the number of scoops in an ice cream cone. A tantalizing possibility then is for the seller to charge different prices according to the quantity consumed. As we saw in the previous section, this corresponds to nonlinear pricing, a form of second-degree price discrimination.

The simplest case of nonlinear pricing, the one we will focus on for most of this section, is a **two-part tariff**: a fixed part f, which each consumer must pay regardless of quantity purchased, and a variable part p, proportional to the quantity purchased.[d] Would a monopolist seller, say a telephone operator, gain from setting a two-part tariff? If so, what would the optimal values of f and p be? To begin with the simplest case, suppose that all consumers have the same demand curve $D(p)$ and that the monopolist has a linear cost function (constant marginal cost c), as in figure 10.1. If the seller were to set a uniform price, that is, independent of quantity, then the optimal value would be p^M. This is the monopoly price derived in chapter 5, the point where marginal revenue equals marginal cost. Under this solution, profits are given by A.

Now, suppose that the monopolist sets a two-part tariff. Whatever the value of p is, the seller should set f at the maximum value such that consumers are still willing to buy. This maximum is given by consumer's surplus, $CS(p)$, the area under the demand curve and above price. For example, for $p = p^M$, consumer surplus is given by area B, that is, $CS(p^M) = B$. If, instead, price is equal to marginal cost c, then $CS(c) = A + B + C$.

Let $\pi(p)$ be the monopolist's variable profit as a function of the price it sets, that is, $\pi(p) = (p - c)D(p)$. If the seller sets the highest fixed fee that consumers are willing to pay, then its total profits are given by

[d] Strictly speaking, the amount paid, $f + pq$, is a linear function of the quantity bought. The key point is that price per unit, $p + f/q$, is not constant.

$$\Pi(p) = \pi(p) + f = \pi(p) + CS(p).$$

But this is exactly the total surplus $W(p)$, that is, $\Pi(p) = W(p)$. This implies one first important result: *If the seller can set a two-part tariff and all consumers have identical demands, then the (variable) price that maximizes total profits is the same that maximizes total surplus, that is, the efficient price.*

As we know, efficiency (total surplus maximization) implies that price equals marginal cost, and so the optimal two-part tariff has $p = c$. The optimal fixed part would then be the consumer surplus corresponding to $p = c$, that is, $f = CS(p) = CS(c) = A + B + C$. Notice that the introduction of a two-part tariff (1) increases profits from A to $A + B + C$ (the seller makes no money at the margin but receives a huge fixed fee); (2) increases total surplus from $A + B$ to $A + B + C$ (a larger quantity is sold, as efficiency would dictate); and (3) increases gross consumer surplus from B to $A + B + C$ (the marginal price drops from monopoly price, p^M, to marginal cost; but (4) decreases net consumer surplus (net of the fixed fee) from B to zero (all of the gross consumer surplus is captured by the monopolist through the fixed fee). In other words, total efficiency increases but consumer welfare decreases as a result of a nonlinear pricing. In section 10.5, when we examine the public policy issues created by price discrimination, we will see that the trade-off between social efficiency and consumer welfare is one of the main issues to be considered.

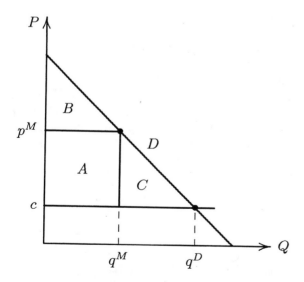

FIGURE 10.1 PRICE DISCRIMINATION.

Although the preceding result was derived for a particular set of assumptions (all consumers are identical), one can make the general point that:

A monopolist's optimal two-part tariff consists of a positive fixed fee and a variable fee that is lower than monopoly price. Total surplus is therefore greater than under uniform pricing.

MULTIPLE CONSUMER TYPES AND MULTIPLE TWO-PART TARIFFS

Suppose now that there are multiple (two, for example) types of consumer. Suppose, moreover, that type 2 users are "heavy" users, so that $CS_2(p) > CS_1(p)$ for every p, where $CS_i(p)$ is consumer surplus for type i. Given that there are different types of consumers, it is natural to assume that the seller sets different two-part tariffs. If the seller could determine directly each consumer's type, then the solution would be quite simple: The seller would set $p = c$ and $f = CS_i(c)$. The problem is that in most real-world cases, the seller cannot directly observe the consumer type; even if that were possible, price discrimination of this type (imposing different two-part tariffs on different consumers) would most likely be considered illegal.

But suppose the seller offers consumers the *choice* of different two-part tariffs. Continuing with the example of a telecom operator, this would correspond to offering

---

BOX 10.2   NONLINEAR PRICING OF MOBILE PHONE CALLS

There are four mobile-phone operators in the United Kingdom: Vodaphone, Cellnet, Orange, and One2One. In 1996, One2One announced a series of "service packages" to take effect on October 1, 1996. Essentially, a service package is a set of options and rates, including more than 15 different items. The following table shows some of the rates for two of the plans offered by One2One (four packages are available, including, in addition to the ones listed, "One2One Diamond" and "One2One Silver").

	One2One Bronze	One2One Gold
Monthly Rental	£17.50	£36.00
Weekday Daytime Rate	29p	18p

These numbers illustrate the idea of price discrimination based on sorting consumers by different combinations of fixed fee and variable fee.

different optional **calling plans**, a common practice (box 10.2). Could this improve the seller's profit? Consider the set of two-part tariffs suggested earlier: one calling plan with $p = c$ and $f = CS_1(c)$, intended to be chosen by type 1 consumers; and another calling plan with $p = c$ and $f = CS_2(c)$, intended to be chosen by type 2 consumers. This menu of calling plans would not work: Both types of consumers would strictly prefer to adopt the first calling plan: The marginal price is the same and the fixed fee is smaller for the first plan.

If the seller wants consumers to sort between calling plans, then it must make sure that type 2 consumers have no incentive to adopt the first calling plan. Moreover, the seller must make sure that each type of consumer prefers to pay the fixed fee and consume its optimal quantity rather than not consuming at all. In economics jargon, the seller must take into account (1) the **incentive-compatibility constraint** (type i prefers plan i to plan j); and (2) the **participation constraint** (each consumer prefers to consume relatively to not consuming at all).

It can be shown that the optimal menu of calling plans consists of $f_1 = CS_1(p_1)$, $p_1 > c$; and $f_1 < f_2 < CS_2(p_1)$, $p_2 = c$. In words, the high-consumption types pay a relatively high fixed fee, $f_2 > f_1$, but a low marginal fee, $p_2 = c$. The low-consumption types, in turn, pay a lower fixed fee, $f_1 = CS_1(p_1)$, but a higher marginal fee, $p_1 > c$.

It is important to understand that consumers of type i choose the calling plan (f_i, p_i) because they want to. That is, given the menu of calling plans (f_1, p_1), (f_2, p_2), type 1 consumers prefer plan 1 and type 2 consumers prefer plan 2. For this reason, the seller does not need to identify the group each consumer belongs to: Consumers are sorted out by self-selection.

By comparison with the one-type case, this solution differs in two ways. First, low types pay a price that is greater than marginal cost ($p_1 > c$), which implies that the solution is not efficient. Second, high-consumption buyers pay a fixed fee that is less than their willingness to pay, that is, $f_2 < CS_2(p_2)$, where $CS_2(p_2)$ is the willingness to pay. As a result, the seller's profit is lower than it would be were it able to differentiate consumers directly. The loss of profits is the price the seller must pay to sort buyers by means of self-selection.

10.4 VERSIONING, BUNDLING, AND OTHER FORMS OF CONSUMER SORTING

In section 10.1, we defined third-degree price discrimination as the case when different prices are charged to different groups of consumers. Several examples were presented, including student prices and pricing of cars in different European countries. These examples have one thing in common: the seller can identify the group to which each consumer belongs (in which country he or she lives, whether or not he or she is a student, and so forth) based on some observable external characteristic.

There are many examples, however, in which the seller knows that the population of potential consumers is divided into groups, but cannot identify which group each consumer belongs to. For example, airlines know that people fly for business or for leisure, and that the willingness to pay is higher among business travelers. However, it would be difficult to identify business travelers directly, especially if the fare they are charged is higher than the fare paid by leisure travelers.

Even if direct identification of each consumer's group is impossible, the seller can still attempt to *indirectly* sort consumers by group. The idea is to offer different "deals" (e.g., different combinations of price and quality) such that consumers self-select according to the group they belong to. Pex and Apex airfares are an example of this. Because these fares imply a number of restrictions—for example, a Saturday night stay in the place of destination—business travelers are unlikely to purchase such fares. Airlines are thus able to sort out low-valuation leisure travelers (and most academics), who will change their schedule to take advantage of the discount fares.

VERSIONING[116]

Dupuit, a nineteenth century French engineer and economist, remarks on the practice of the three-class rail system:

It is not because of the few thousand francs which would have to be spent to put a roof over the third-class carriages or to upholster the third-class seats that some company or other has open carriages with wooden benches. . . . What the company is trying to do is prevent the passengers who can pay the second-class fare from traveling third-class; it hits the poor, not because it wants to hurt them, but to frighten the rich. . . . And it is again for the same reason that the companies, having proved almost cruel to third-class passengers and mean to second-class ones, become lavish in dealing with first-class passengers. Having refused the poor what is necessary, they give the rich what is superfluous.[117]

This is a classical example of price discrimination: By offering a number of "packages" of price and quality level, the seller is able to sort consumers according to their willingness to pay. Examples of this practice, which we may refer to as **versioning**, are common: paperback books, business and first classes in aircraft, "gold" credit cards, and so forth.

One extreme form of versioning occurs when firms reduce the quality of some of their existing products in order to price-discriminate, that is, firms produce **damaged goods**. For example, Pex and Apex airfares are normal economy fares with additional restrictions, such as the requirement of a Saturday night stay. These restrictions create no particular benefit for the airlines; they are simply a means of reducing the quality of the service provided. Another example is provided by student versions of software packages: Mathematica's student version consists of the standard software together with a special flag that prevents the use of a math coprocessor (even if the computer has one).

As of 1993, the student version was selling for $180, less than a quarter of the normal price.

Discount airfares and student versions are examples in which production cost is the same for the high-quality and low-quality products. However, there are examples in which the firm must actually incur an extra cost to produce a low-quality product. Box 10.3 contains a number of examples of costly damaged goods. These examples are interesting for two reasons. First, they provide an unequivocal instance of price discrimination by quality differentiation, or versioning. In general, an argument can be made that price differences are the result of cost differences. For example, an airline

Box 10.3   Intel, IBM and Sony Damage Their Products[118]

The practice of selling lower quality, in fact, "damaged," goods as a means to price-discriminate between high-valuation and low-valuation consumers is common among several high-tech firms.

- Intel's 486 generation of microprocessors came under two versions: the 486DX and the 486SX. Although there were significant differences in performance, "the 486SX is an exact duplicate of the 486DX, with one important difference—its internal math coprocessor is disabled. . . . [The 486SX] sold in 1991 for $333 as opposed to $588 for the 486DX."

- "In May 1990, IBM announced the introduction of the LaserPrinter E, a lower-cost alternative to its popular LaserPrinter. The LaserPrinter E was virtually identical to the original LaserPrinter, except that the E model printed text at 5 pages per minute (ppm), as opposed to 10 ppm for the LaserPrinter. . . . The LaserPrinter uses the same "engine" and virtually identical parts, with one exception: . . . [it includes] firmware [which] in effect inserts wait states to slow print speed."

- "Sony recently introduced a new digital recording-playback format intended to replace the analog audio cassette, but offering greater convenience and dura-bility: [the MiniDisc]. Minidiscs are similar in appearance to 3.5-in computer diskettes, and they come in two varieties: prerecorded and recordable. The lat-ter, in turn, "come in two varieties: 60-minute discs and 74-minute discs. The list prices for these discs are currently $13.99 and $16.99. Despite the difference in price and recording length, the two formats are physically identical. . . . A code in the table of contents identifies a 60-minute disc and prevents recording beyond this length, even though there's room on the media."

might argue that business class fares are higher than economy fares because the marginal cost of a business class seat is higher. (Still, as Dupuit would argue, the cost difference can hardly justify the observed price difference.) But in the case of damaged goods, such argument would not hold: Price differences can be justified only by price discrimination. If it were only a matter of cost, then the low-quality product should be, if anything, more expensive than the high-quality product.

Second, the examples suggest that price discrimination may actually be good news for everyone, that is, it may lead to a strict Pareto improvement in which the firm, the high-valuation consumers, and the low-valuation consumers are all made better off.[e] The firm is clearly better off, or else it wouldn't price-discriminate. Low-valuation consumers are better off because, absent damaged goods, they wouldn't buy at all: It is better to buy at a low price a good that is damaged (a restricted fare, a crippled piece of software) than to not buy at all. Finally, high-valuation consumers are likely to be better off because the firm may have to reduce the price for the high-quality version. This is because a large price gap may induce some of the high-valuation consumers to switch to the low-quality version.

BUNDLING

Movie distributors frequently force theaters to acquire "bad" movies if they want to show "good" movies from the same distributor. Photocopier manufacturers offer bundles that include the copier itself as well as maintenance; they also offer the alternative of buying the copier and servicing separately. These are examples of **tie-in sales**, or **bundling**, an alternative strategy for sorting consumers and price-discriminating between them. A distinction can be made between **pure bundling**, whereby buyers must purchase the bundle or nothing (as in the case of movie distributors) and **mixed bundling**, whereby buyers are offered the choice between purchasing the bundle or one of the separate parts (as in the case of the photocopier and after-sales service).

As a motivating example for the analysis that follows, consider the pricing of Microsoft Office. This is a software "suite" that comprises a series of different applications: Excel, Word, Powerpoint, Access, and Microsoft Mail. The individual prices for each of these applications were, in 1993, $80 for Microsoft Mail and $495 for each of the remaining applications (Total: $2060). However, the price for the entire package was $750.[119] How can this be a profitable strategy for Microsoft? To address this question, let us consider a simple numerical example of a software company. The company owns two different applications: a word processor and a spreadsheet. Some users are mainly interested in a word processor ("writers"), some work exclusively with spreadsheets ("number crunchers"), and a third group uses both word processors and spreadsheets ("generalists").

The following table summarizes the willingness to pay for each application by each type of software user. It also indicates the number of users of each type. Based on this table, we can determine the software company's optimal price policy.

[e] A Pareto improvement is a change that makes all agents concerned better off, or at least as well off as they were initially.

User Type	No. Users	Willingness to Pay for:	
		Word Processor	Spreadsheet
Writer	40	50	0
Number cruncher	40	0	50
Generalist	20	30	30

Because the costs of producing software are all fixed (i.e., they do not depend on the number of copies sold), the software company is effectively interested in maximizing revenues.

One possible strategy for revenue maximization is to sell each application separately. If that were the case, then the optimal price would be 50. At this price, the company would sell 40 copies of each application, and revenues would be 2000 per application, or a total of 4000. The alternative price under the strategy of individual-application selling is $p = 30$. In this case, sales would be 60 per application and the revenue 1800 per application, which is less than 2000. Consider now the following alternative strategy: In addition to selling each application separately, the software company sells for 60 a package (a "suite") comprising both applications. From the perspective of the writer or the number cruncher types, this makes no difference. Each still will prefer to buy the preferred application for 50. True, for a mere extra 10 they would be able to acquire a second application but the extra utility of doing so would be zero.

The main difference with respect to the initial case is that the suite would be purchased by eclectic types who, at 50 per application, would be unwilling to buy but who, at 60 for the package, are willing. As a result, the seller now receives a total revenue of 4000 from individual-application sales plus 1200 (20 times 60) from suite sales, a 30% increase in revenue over the no-bundling case.

In summary:

> By offering different versions of the same product, or different packages of related products, a seller may be able to indirectly discriminate between different types of buyers.

DURABLE-GOODS PRICING

Nondurable goods, like groceries or bus rides, are defined by a demand flow: In each period, consumers need to purchase a certain amount. By contrast, the decision to buy a **durable good** is one in which timing is of the essence. I can buy a computer today or wait for a few months (and in the meantime, hold on to the one that I currently own). Similar reasoning applies to buying a car and other related products.

Pricing durable products involves one additional dimension of price discrimination—time. By setting different prices now and in the future, a monopolist may be able to sell both to high-valuation buyers at a high price and to low-valuation buyers at a low price—the dream of any monopolist. The idea is to set a high price today and hope that high-valuation buyers will take it. And then, in the future, once all high-valuation buyers have made their purchase, set a low price that will attract additional sales from low-valuation buyers who still have not made a purchase.

Unfortunately, the hope that high-valuation buyers will make a purchase in the first period may be just that—hope. In fact, a rational buyer should put itself in the seller's shoes and figure that it will be in the latter's interest to lower prices in the future. Because even high-valuation buyers prefer to pay low prices, the outcome of the high-price-today-and-low-price-tomorrow strategy may turn out to be that most buyers prefer to wait for the future low price. The seller's price discrimination strategy then will have backfired in several ways: First, sales are much slower; and second, average price is much lower than it would have been if the seller had simply set the monopoly price in both periods. In other words, the possibility of setting different prices in each period, at first sight an advantage to the seller, turns out to be its "curse," for total profits are lower.[f]

> When selling a durable good, sellers may want to commit to nonprice-discrimination over time. In fact, because of "strategic" purchase delays, profits may be lower under price discrimination.

There are a number of ways in which the seller can avoid the durable-goods "curse." One is to commit to not lower price in the future. Chrysler, for example, offers a "lowest-price guarantee": If, in the future, it lowers the price of a given car model, it will refund all previous buyers for the difference. The incentive to not lower price in the future is then so strong that buyers have little reason to expect prices will come down in the future; thus they have little incentive to delay purchases.[g]

Alternatively, the seller may decide not to sell the durable good, only to lease it. This is what Xerox did with its photocopiers in the late 1960s and early 1970s, at a time when it commanded substantial market power in the industry. A no-sale, lease-only policy effectively turns a durable good into a nondurable one: Buyers need to pay the lease every period that they want to use a photocopier; there is no point in delaying the time for getting a photocopier in the hope of saving on purchase price.

[f] Commenting on the sad state of the personal computer industry, someone remarked that "the industry has set a trap for itself. 'Everybody folds their arms and says, "I'll just wait for the next price cut," ' says one consultant."[120]

[g] Notice the irony of the lowest-price "guarantee": Although at first it may seem to protect the consumer, the end result is that the latter pays a higher price than it would, absent any guarantee.

10.5 IS PRICE DISCRIMINATION LEGAL? SHOULD IT BE?

As was mentioned in section 10.1, the extreme case of perfect price discrimination provides a useful framework for the welfare analysis of price discrimination. Figure 10.1, previously introduced in this chapter, represents the monopoly equilibrium with and without perfect discrimination, assuming linear demand, D, and linear costs (constant marginal cost c). A monopolist that cannot price-discriminate sets price p^M, thus selling output q^M. Under this solution, profits are given by A and consumer's surplus by B; total surplus is thus $A + B$. Consider now the case when the seller can discriminate between different buyers. The price charged to each buyer is given by the latter's willingness to pay. The monopolist thus will sell to all buyers whose willingness to pay exceeds marginal cost, that is, to all buyers from 0 to q^D. The monopolist's profit is now given by $A + B + C$, whereas consumer's surplus is zero; total surplus is therefore $A + B + C$. There are several relevant points in the comparison between the solutions, both with and without price discrimination:

• Total welfare is greater under price discrimination ($A + B + C$ as opposed to $A + B$).

• Consumer welfare is lower under price discrimination (zero as opposed to B).

• Different consumers pay different prices under price discrimination.

• More consumers are served under price discrimination. (Specifically, all consumers between q^M and q^D are served under price discrimination but not under uniform price.)

Although this is a simple, extreme example, it serves to illustrate the main trade-offs implied by price discrimination: (1) the trade-off between efficiency (which favors price discrimination) and consumer welfare (which favors uniform pricing) and (2) the trade-off between "fairness" (which favors uniform pricing) and the objective of making the good accessible to as many consumers as possible (which favors price discrimination).[h] If distribution concerns are not very important, then a case can be made in favor of price discrimination, for it increases total efficiency. However, if distribution between firms and consumers, as well as across consumers, is an important issue, then a case can be made for disallowing price discrimination.

This analysis is a bit simplistic, and several qualifications are in order. First, *it may happen that total efficiency decreases as a result of price discrimination*. For example, if perfect price discrimination is costly, it may be that the gains for the seller do not compensate the losses imposed on consumers (see exercise 10.15). Likewise, it can be shown that spatial price discrimination decreases efficiency when demand curves are linear, for example.

Second, *there are cases when price discrimination implies a strict Pareto improvement*, whereby both the seller *and* consumers are made better off (more specifically, some are equally well off and some are strictly better off as a result of price discrimination). The examples of damaged goods and bundling, presented in section 10.4, prove this point.

[h] There is no good simple term to designate this. In telecommunications, the expression **universal service** is used.

The analysis is further complicated by the fact that, both in the United States and Europe, public policy toward price discrimination has been driven by considerations that differ from the principles of economic efficiency outlined earlier.

In the United States the main concern has been to prevent price discrimination from injuring competition. In particular, the **Robinson-Patman Act** states that

It shall be unlawful for any person engaged in commerce . . . to discriminate in price between different purchasers of commodities of like grade and quality . . . where the effect of such discrimination may be substantially to lessen competition or to tend to create a monopoly in any line of commerce.

In the 1950s, Anheuser-Busch lowered the price of its Budweiser beer in the St. Louis market with respect to the price that it charged elsewhere in the United States. The Supreme Court determined that such practice violated the Robinson-Patman Act by injuring local competitors. In fact, Budweiser's market share rose from 12.5% to 39.3% as a result of the price cut. The case was remanded to the Appeals Court for further consideration. Here, the decision was made to dismiss the case on the basis that no injury to competition was made and that the primary beneficiaries of the price cut were St. Louis customers. This case illustrates one of the central dilemmas for public policy toward pricing strategies, namely, how to balance the anti-competitive effects (injury to competition, which in the limit, may lead to exit and a more concentrated industry) and the pro-competitive effects (lower prices). Chapter 15 develops this theme further.

A more recent case, which illustrates a similar trade-off, is that of the pharmaceutical industry:

Four major pharmaceutical companies have agreed to pay about $350 million to settle class-action price-fixing litigation brought against them . . . by independent U.S. pharmacies and drugstore chains. . . . The suits generally allege that a dual system of drug pricing had improperly arisen in the United States during the first half of the 1990s, with a discounted pricing system that pharmaceutical companies offered to big managed-care companies and health maintenance organizations, while a range of higher prices were offered to drugstores and big pharmacy chains.

At issue was whether the two-tiered pricing system stemmed from normal market forces, as the pharmaceutical industry has contended, or from a price-fixing conspiracy, as the plaintiffs maintain.[121]

In the European Union, a classic case of price discrimination is that of *United Brands*, who sold bananas in different European countries. Although the transportation costs to each country differed by very little, the wholesale prices charged in each country differed a great deal. At one point, the price in Denmark was more than two times the price in Ireland. United Brands argued that it only adapted its prices to what each market could bear—the essence of third-degree price discrimination. The European Commission decided that such practice was in breach of **Article 86** of the Treaty of Rome, which forbids the **abuse of dominant position**.[i] Generally, it stated that

The Commission has the firm intention of systematically applying Article 86 against undertakings in a dominant position which directly or indirectly impose discriminatory or unfair prices, . . . [on account of] the injury which these practices can cause to the user and the consumer.

The economic analysis in this chapter suggests that the grounds for the preceding justification are, at least, dubious.

A decision by the European Court of Justice seems to confirm this view. Silhouette, an Austrian maker of eyeglass frames, refused to sell its glasses to Hartlauer, a discount store chain. Hartlauer bought 21,000 Silhouette eyeglass frames in Bulgaria at a low price and announced its sale in Austria. The European Court judged that Silhouette's trademark rights extend to the point of limiting the import of its products from other countries (also known as buying in the grey market).

This decision will have important consequences. U.K. supermarket chains, for example, have sold Levi's, Adidas, and Nike products imported from countries where prices are lower.[122] This is one instance of the point made at the beginning of the chapter: If resale is easy, then price discrimination is difficult. By allowing manufacturers to limit the imports of their products into the European Union, the recent court decision essentially allows the manufacturers to price-discriminate between the European Union and the rest of the world.

In summary, it would appear that the European Union is very concerned with price discrimination within Europe but less so between Europe and the rest of the world. In fact, E.U. law dictates that a manufacturer has no right to restrict the subsequent sale of trademarked goods within the E.U. after their initial sale.

By contrast to the European Union, the U.S. Supreme Court has taken the view that, once a company sells a product, it has no right to restrict its subsequent resale unless the product is altered in a way that may mislead consumers. In other words, parallel imports are allowed. Price discrimination between the United States and the rest of the world is therefore difficult.[123]

SUMMARY

- Price discrimination, the practice of setting different prices for the same good, requires the absence of resale opportunities.

[i] This ruling was important, among other reasons, because "abuse of dominant position" is a rather vague concept for which no clear definition has been given.

- Sellers can price-discriminate either based on observable buyer characteristics (third-degree price discrimination) or by inducing buyers to self-select among different product offerings (second-degree price discrimination).

- Under third-degree price discrimination, a seller should charge a lower price in the market segments with greater price elasticity.

- Second-degree price discrimination is achieved by offering different versions of the same product, or different packages of related products.

- When selling a durable good, sellers may want to commit to not price-discriminate over time. In fact, because of "strategic" purchase delays, profits may be lower under price discrimination.

KEY CONCEPTS

- price discrimination

- arbitrage and resale

- first-, second-, and third-degree price discrimination

- selection by indicators and self-selection

- two-part tariffs and nonlinear pricing

- versioning

- bundling

- durable goods

REVIEW AND PRACTICE EXERCISES

10.1   First-time subscribers to the *Economist* pay a lower rate than repeat subscribers. Is this price discrimination? Of what type?

10.2   Many firms set a price for the export market that is lower than the price for the domestic market. How can you explain this policy?

10.3   Cement in Belgium is sold at a uniform delivered price throughout the country, that is, the same price is set for each customer, including transportation costs, regardless of where the customer is located. The same practice is also found in the sale of plasterboard in the United Kingdom.[124] Are these cases of price discrimination?

10.4   A restaurant in London has removed prices from its menu: Each consumer is asked to pay what he or she thinks the meal was worth. Is this a case of price discrimination?

10.5   In the New York Fulton fish market, the average price paid for whiting by Asian buyers is significantly lower than the price paid by white buyers.[125] What (if any) type of price discrimination does this correspond to? What additional information would you need to answer the question?

10.6   Supermarkets frequently issue coupons that entitle consumers to a discount in selected products. Is this a promotional strategy, or simply a form of price discrimination? Empirical evidence suggests that paper towels are significantly more expensive in markets offering coupons than in markets without coupons.[126] Is this consistent with your interpretation?

10.7**   A market consists of two population segments, A and B. An individual in segment A has demand for your product $q = 50 - p$. An individual in segment B has demand for your product $q = 120 - 2p$. Segment A has 1000 people in it. Segment B has 1200 people in it. Total cost of producing q units is $C = 5000 + 20q$.

a. What is total market demand for your product?

b. Assume that you must charge the same price to both segments. What is the profit-maximizing price? What are your profits?

c. Imagine now that members of segment A all wear a scarlet "A" on their shirts or blouses and that you can legally charge different prices to these people. What price do you change to the scarlet "A" people? What price do you charge to those without the scarlet "A"? What are your profits now?[127]

10.8*   Coca-Cola announced that it is developing a "smart" vending machine. Such machines are able to change prices according to the outside temperature.[128]

Suppose for the purposes of this problem that the temperature can be either "High" or "Low." On days of "High" temperature, demand is given by $Q = 280 - 2p$, where Q is number of cans of Coke sold during the day and p is the price per can measured in cents. On days of "Low" temperature, demand is only $Q = 160 - 2p$. There is an equal number of days with "High" and "Low" temperature. The marginal cost of a can of Coke is 20 cents.

a. Suppose that Coca-Cola indeed installs a "smart" vending machine, and thus is able to charge different prices for Coke on "Hot" and "Cold" days. What price should Coca-Cola charge on a "Hot" day? What price should Coca-Cola charge on a "Cold" day?

b. Alternatively, suppose that Coca-Cola continues to use its normal vending machines, which must be programmed with a fixed price, independent of the weather. Assuming that Coca-Cola is risk neutral, what is the optimal price for a can of Coke?

c. What are Coca-Cola's profits under constant and weather-variable prices? How much would Coca-Cola be willing to pay to enable its vending machine to vary prices with the weather, that is, to have a "smart" vending machine?

10.9* Suppose the California Memorial Stadium has a capacity of 50,000 and is used for exactly seven football games a year. Three of these are average games, with a demand for tickets given by $D = 150,000 - 3p$ per game, where p is ticket price. (For simplicity, assume there is only one type of ticket.) Three of the season games are not so important, the demand being $D = 90,000 - 3p$ per game. Finally, one of the games is really big, the demand being $D = 240,000 - 3p$. The costs of operating the stadium are essentially independent of the number of tickets sold.

a. Determine the optimal ticket price for each game, assuming the objective of profit maximization.

Given that the stadium is frequently full, the idea of expanding the stadium has arisen. A preliminary study suggests that the cost of capacity expansion would be $100 per seat per year.

b. Would you recommend that the University of California go ahead with the project of capacity expansion?

10.10** Your software company has just completed the first version of SpokenWord, a voice-activated word processor. As marketing manager, you have to decide on the pricing of the new software. You commissioned a study to determine the potential demand for SpokenWord. From this study, you know that there are essentially two market segments of equal size, professionals and students (one million each). Professionals would be willing to pay up to $400 and students up to $100 for the full version of the software. A substantially scaled-down version of the software would be worth $50 to consumers and would be worthless to professionals. It is equally costly to sell any version. In fact, other than the initial development costs, production costs are zero.

a. What are the optimal prices for each version of the software?

Suppose that, instead of the scaled-down version, the firm sells an intermediate version that is valued at $200 by professionals and $75 by students.

b. What are the optimal prices for each version of the software? Is the firm better off by selling the intermediate version instead of the scaled-down version?

Suppose that professionals are willing to pay up to $800(a − .5)$, and students up to $100a$, for a given version of the software, where a is the software's degree of functionality: $a = 1$ denotes a fully functional version, whereas a value $a < 1$ means that only $100a\%$ features of the software are functional. It is equally costly to produce any level of a. In fact, other than the initial development costs, production costs are zero.

c. How many versions of the software should the firm sell? Which versions? What are the optimal prices of each version?

10.11* One of the arguments used in Microsoft's defense against allegations of monopoly behavior is that it "cannot charge a monopoly price because it faces competition from . . . its own installed base." Based on the preceding discussion on durable goods, how would you qualify or extend Microsoft's defense?

10.12 In 1998, the European Commission fined Volkswagen more than $100 million for preventing its dealers in Italy from selling to foreign buyers. Is this consistent with the European Commission's policy regarding price discrimination? Is this the right decision from a social welfare point of view?

EXTENSION EXERCISES

10.13* Can coupons be used to price-discriminate? How? Empirical evidence suggests that, in U.S. cities where coupons are used more often, breakfast cereals are sold at a lower price.[129] Is this consistent with the interpretation that coupons are used for price discrimination? If not, how can the empirical observation be explained?

10.14** In September 1997, the New York State's attorney general pressed charges against Procter & Gamble over the fact that P&G eliminated the use of coupons. The argument was that P&G was colluding with rivals to eliminate coupons, for doing so "only works if everybody goes along with it."[130] What does this suggest about the practice of price discrimination in the context of oligopoly? (In the end, P&G, although not admitting any wrongdoing, agreed on a $4.2 million settlement of the charges.)

10.15* Suppose that perfect price discrimination implies a transaction cost T, incurred by the seller. Show that perfect price discrimination may be optimal for the seller but welfare-decreasing for society as a whole.

10.16[*]   Consider the model of a monopolist with two markets presented in section 10.1. Suppose that the seller has a limited capacity and zero marginal cost up to capacity (or very low marginal cost). An example of this would be an airline with two types of passengers, or a football stadium with two types of attendees.

Derive the conditions for optimal pricing. How do they relate to the case when there are no capacity constraints?

10.17[***]   Consider the model of nonlinear pricing introduced in section 10.3. Suppose there are two types of consumers, in equal number. Type 1 have demand $D_1(p) = 1 - p$, and type 2 $D_2(p) = 2(1 - p)$. Marginal cost is zero.

a. Show that, if the seller is precluded from using non-linear pricing, then the optimal price is $p = \frac{1}{2}$ and profit is $\frac{3}{8}$.

b. Show that, if the seller must set a single two-part tariff, then the optimal values are $f = \frac{9}{32}$ and $p = \frac{1}{4}$, for a profit of $\frac{9}{8}$.

c. Show that, if the seller can set multiple two-part tariffs, then the optimal values are $f_1 = \frac{1}{8}$, $p_1 = \frac{1}{2}$, $f_2 = \frac{7}{8}$, $p_2 = 0$, for a profit of $\frac{5}{4}$.

d. Show that, like profits, total surplus increases from (a) to (b) and from (b) to (c).

10.18[**]   Many retail stores set lower-than-usual prices during a fraction of the time (sale). One interpretation of this practice is that it allows for price discrimination between patient and impatient buyers.

Suppose that each buyer wants to purchase one unit per period. Each period is divided into two subperiods—the first and the second part of the period. Suppose there are two types of buyers, $i = 1, 2$. Each type of buyer is subdivided according to the part of the period they would ideally like to make their purchase. One half of the buyers would prefer to purchase during the first part of the period, one half during the second part. A buyer of type i is willing to pay $\bar{v}_i$ for a purchase during his or her preferred part of the period; and $\underline{v}_i$ for a purchase at another time.

Buyers of type 1, which constitute a fraction α of the population, are high-valuation, impatient buyers; that is, $\bar{v}_1$ is very high and $\underline{v}_1$ very low. High valuation implies that $\bar{v}_1$ is very high; impatience implies that $\underline{v}_1$ is very low: Buyers of type 1 are not willing to buy at any time other than their preferred time. Buyers of type 2, by contrast, are patient: $\bar{v}_2 \approx \underline{v}_2$. Assume that α is relatively low, specifically, $\alpha < \bar{v}_2/\bar{v}_1$. To summarize: $\bar{v}_1 > \bar{v}_2 \approx \underline{v}_2 > \alpha\bar{v}_1 > \underline{v}_1 \approx 0$.

a. Show that, under a constant-price strategy, the seller optimally sets $p = \bar{v}_2$.

b. Determine firm profits when it sets prices $p = \bar{v}_1$ and $p = \underline{v}_2$ in the first and second parts of the period, respectively.

c. Show that profits are greater under the "sales" strategy.

Vertical Relations

Although we normally think of firms as selling products and services to consumers, the fact is that most firms sell to other firms, not to final consumers. Cement producers sell cement to concrete producers, who then sell concrete to construction firms; TV set manufacturers sell TV sets to retailers, who then sell them to consumers; and so forth.

There are at least two reasons why the relation between a manufacturer and a retailer is substantially different from the direct relation between a firm and the final consumer. First, the firm that sells directly to the consumer normally controls most of the variables that determine consumer demand: price, quality, advertising, sales service, and so forth. The same is not true, however, for a manufacturer who sells through a retailer: There are many determinants of final demand that fall beyond the manufacturer's control. For example, the level of sales service and local advertising is normally controlled by the retailer. In particular, the *retail price*, an essential determinant of final demand, is set by the retailer, not the manufacturer. In summary, *the demand faced by a manufacturer depends on the price it sets (the wholesale price) and on a host of other factors, most of which it does not directly control.*

A second reason why selling to a retailer is substantially different from selling to the final consumer is that *retailers compete with each other* (whereas consumers do not). In particular, each retailer cares about the wholesale price it has to pay the manufacturer, *as well as the wholesale price paid by other retailers*. This is so because the wholesale price determines marginal cost (the retailer's marginal cost), and each firm's equilibrium profit is a function of all firms' marginal cost.[a] These two reasons justify the separate treatment of **vertical relations** between firms. By "vertical relations," we mean relations between two firms in sequence along the value chain, as in the previous examples. Normally, we will refer to the case of a manufacturer selling to one or several retailers. However, the analysis in this chapter applies generally to cases when there is an **upstream firm** (e.g.,

[a] There is a third reason why selling to intermediate firms is different from selling to consumers: The number of intermediate firms is small, whereas the number of final consumers is large; a firm that sells to the final consumer has more market power than a firm that sells to other firms. In fact, there are cases when most of the market power is on the buyer's side: Large supermarket chains, for example, have a great degree of market power with respect to suppliers.

cement producer, flour producer) selling to a **downstream firm** (e.g., concrete producer, bakery).

In each section of this chapter, we discuss reasons why an upstream firm might want to establish contractual terms different from those of a simple per-unit constant price contract. These contractual clauses are frequently known as **vertical restraints** because they normally restrain the downstream firm in some way. For example, a minimum or a maximum level may be imposed on the retail price.

Different vertical restraints may serve the same given purpose, and a given vertical restraint may serve different purposes. This makes the policy analysis of vertical restraints particularly difficult, because the use of a particular clause may be welfare-enhancing in one case and welfare-reducing in another. We consider this problem in section 11.6.

11.1 DOUBLE MARGINALIZATION AND TWO-PART TARIFFS

Consider a structure consisting of an upstream firm (M) and a downstream firm (R). Firm R is best thought of as a retailer, while firm M could be the manufacturer of the product, a wholesaler, or the supplier of an important input to firm R. For example, M could be an oil refiner and R a gas station.

Suppose there is a demand for the final product (supplied by R), given by $D(p)$. As regards the production technology, we assume the simplest possible structure: To produce one unit of output, R needs one unit of input. In fact, under the manufacturer/retailer interpretation, this is the right assumption: To sell one TV set, a retailer must get exactly one TV set from the manufacturer. Suppose that R has no costs in addition to the wholesale price, w, that it pays its supplier. Finally, firm M has a constant marginal cost c.

We begin by considering the profit-maximizing solution in a hypothetical situation where M and R are vertically integrated. In this situation, the wholesale price is a mere transfer price: What the (joint) firm maximizes is total profit $\pi = (p - c)D(p)$. Let p^M be the price that maximizes this total profit.

Consider now the case when the firms are separated. Assume that the contractual relations between M and R are confined to the determination of the wholesale price, w. In other words, M determines w, and R chooses how much to buy given w. The first point to make is that, under these circumstances, *total profits for the two firms are lower than what they would be under vertical integration*.

Under vertical separation, R chooses p to maximize $(p - w)D(p)$; in fact, w is effectively R's marginal cost. Therefore, to replicate the solution under vertical integration, M would have to offer R a wholesale price equal to marginal cost. But then M's profit would be zero. It is therefore optimal for M to set w above marginal cost. But then R sets a price greater than p^M, which is certainly not optimal for the firms as a group.

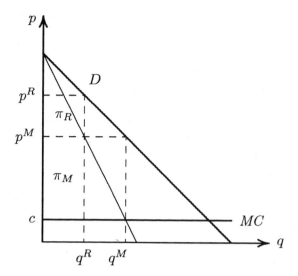

FIGURE 11.1 DOUBLE MARGINALIZATION.

This situation is illustrated in figure 11.1. In this figure, p^M is the monopoly price for a vertically integrated firm. Under vertical integration, profits are given by $(p^M - c)q^M$. Because the downstream firm is owned by the upstream firm, the latter can, for example, set the wholesale price (which is simply a transfer price) equal to p^M and order the downstream firm to set a retail price equal to the wholesale price. Under vertical separation, however, such a scheme would not work. In fact, the downstream firm would be making zero profits, whereas, by setting price greater than p^M, it would get positive profits. Specifically, the optimal price for the downstream firm would be p^R (the point where marginal revenue intersects the retailer's marginal cost, which is wholesale price p^M). If retail price is set to p^R, then manufacturer and retailer profits are given by π^M and π^R, respectively. Notice that π^M is lower than profits for the integrated firm. More importantly, $\pi^M + \pi^R$ is also lower than profits under integration. We could consider other possible values of the wholesale price, lower than p^M, but a similar inequality would result.[b]

This is known as the **double marginalization problem**. Under vertical separation, there are two monopoly pricing decisions being made. If the only contractual instrument that M and R can use is the wholesale price, then two monopoly margins will be added to marginal cost, resulting in a price that is greater than monopoly price. As a consequence, the combined profits of M and R are lower than if they were integrated.[c]

The double marginalization problem is often invoked as an argument in favor of vertical integration. However, the problem of double marginalization is not so much a problem of vertical separation as it is a problem of limited contractual options between the upstream and the downstream firms, as we will see next.

[b] As we saw earlier, if the wholesale price is equal to marginal cost, then total profits are equal to the case of vertical integration. But the upstream firm's profits would then be zero.

[c] In fact, consumer welfare is also lower under vertical separation, because price is greater than monopoly price.

Suppose that, in addition to determining a wholesale price, the upstream firm can set a fixed fee f to be paid by R in case it wants to do any business with M. As in the previous chapter, we call the pair (f, w) a **two-part tariff**. Often, the fixed fee is also called a **franchise fee** (although, in fact, franchise contracts involve more than just setting a fixed fee). Generally, by analogy with nonlinear pricing (see chapter 10), contracts of this type are an example of a **nonlinear contract**.[d]

Suppose that the manufacturer sets $w = c$ and $f = \pi^M$, where $\pi^M \equiv (p^M - c)D(p^M)$ is monopoly profits for a vertically integrated firm. There are three points to notice about this nonlinear contract: First, from the point of view of the firms, this contract is efficient, that is, it maximizes their joint profits. This is so because the marginal cost taken into consideration by the retailer (the wholesale price w) is equal to the true marginal cost (c); accordingly, the retailer sets price at the optimal level, that is, at the level that a vertically integrated monopolist would set (p^M). Second, by pricing this way, the retailer receives total gross profits $\pi = \pi^M$ (gross of the franchise fee); therefore, it is willing to pay up to $f = \pi^M$ as a fixed fee. Finally, the manufacturer receives zero in terms of variable profit (because it sells at marginal cost) but is able to recover all monopoly profits through the fixed fee.

We thus conclude:

> If nonlinear contracts are possible, then the optimal solution under vertical separation is identical to that under vertical integration.

In fact, a general point is that, *allowing for fixed fees, the upstream firm's profit maximization problem is essentially equivalent to maximizing joint profits of the upstream and the downstream firms,* and then finding the maximum fixed fee that the downstream firm is willing to pay.

This result needs to be qualified in several ways. First, we have assumed that there is no competition at each stage. If there are several downstream firms competing against each other, then the result that franchise fees are sufficient to capture monopoly profits may fail to hold. This possibility is considered in the next sections. A second qualification is that we have considered the case of complete information. If the upstream firm does not know the downstream firm's costs, then it may be optimal to set a variable fee that is greater than average marginal cost. The preceding analysis shows how a vertical restraint (a franchise fee) can be used by the upstream firm to improve its situation, in fact, to achieve the optimal solution despite vertical separation. However, franchise fees are not the only way of attaining the upstream firm's objective. An alternative vertical restraint is for the upstream firm to impose a **maximum retail price**. Specifically, the manufacturer could impose p^M as a maximum retail price and sell to the retailer at $w = p^M$. In this case, there would be no need for collecting a fixed fee.[e]

[d] Strictly speaking, the amount paid, $f + wq$, is a linear function of the quantity bought. The key point of a nonlinear contract is that price per unit ($w + f/q$ in the case of a two-part tariff) is not constant.

[e] The assumption that the retailer has no costs other than paying the wholesale price is important here. If that were not the case, the manufacturer would need to set w less than p^M or, alternatively, to *pay* the retailer for the "service" of selling its product. More on this in section 11.5.

11.2   RETAILER COMPETITION[131]

Consider now the case in which there are two downstream firms, R_1 and R_2. (All of the results we will present are equally true in the case in which there are n downstream firms.) Assume, as before, that M's marginal cost is c, whereas each R_i has no other variable cost than the wholesale price w (and no capacity constraints, that is, retailers can buy as much as they want from the manufacturer). Whereas without retailer competition setting, $w = c$ leads the retailer to set $p = p^M$, *with* retailer competition, $w = c$ would lead to a retail price below monopoly level. This is because, at $p = p^M$, each retailer would have an incentive to lower price and steal market share from the rival retailer.

Specifically, suppose that retailers compete *à la* Bertrand. Then in equilibrium retail price would be equal to the wholesale price: Recall that the wholesale price is the retailer's marginal cost. If $w = c$, as before, then $p = c$ and both manufacturer and retailers make zero profits. Under Bertrand competition, the optimal solution would be to set $w = p^M$ instead. For this wholesale price, retailers set, in equilibrium, $p = p^M$, and the manufacturer gets monopoly profits (in this case, the franchise fee would be zero).

It can be shown that, when retailers compete *à la* Cournot (an intermediate level of competition), then the manufacturer's optimal solution is to set a wholesale price (strictly) between w and p^M (see exercise 11.9). In general:

> The greater the degree of competition between retailers, the higher the optimal wholesale price.

11.3   INVESTMENT EXTERNALITIES[132]

Consider the market for consumer electronics: personal computers, stereo equipment, and so forth. Frequently, these are complex products for which sales effort is very important. In particular, consumers gain a great deal from the service provided at the point of sale. Now suppose that one retailer makes a large investment in sales effort, so that it attracts a large number of consumers to its store; suppose also that a second retailer makes no investment in sales effort but sells at a lower price than the first retailer. One possible outcome is that many price-conscious consumers will visit the first retailer to learn about the available products, and then will visit the second retailer to purchase the preferred product at a low price.

This situation entails an important **externality**:[f] The investment in sales effort by the first retailer benefits both retailers. In fact, if most consumers are price conscious, then it benefits mostly the second retailer, who *free-rides* on the first. As a consequence,

[f] We say there is an externality when an action by one agent implies a benefit or a cost to another agent. Externalities may be positive (e.g., schooling) or negative (e.g., smoking).

the incentives for investment in retailer service quality are low. Finally, the manufacturer suffers from this, for final demand depends to a great extent on sales effort.

Resale-Price Maintenance (RPM), the practice whereby the manufacturer imposes a minimum price on retailers, provides a way out of this dilemma. If the minimum price is high enough, every retailer will stick to it, that is, every retailer will price at the uniform minimum level. But then, the preceding problem no longer exists: Not even price-conscious consumers gain from purchasing from a different retailer than the first one they visit. Therefore, the benefits from increased sales accrue to the retailer who makes the corresponding investment.

Advertising provides a similar instance of an inter-retailer externality. Suppose that a car dealer pays for local TV advertising. Advertising expenditures increase demand, which in turn benefits all the car dealers selling the same car, not just the dealer who paid for the advertising costs. That is, if there is a second dealer selling the same car in the same area, then part of the increase in sales goes to that second dealer. In this case, RPM would probably not do the job of correcting the externality, but other vertical restraints might. A specific alternative is to award **exclusive territories**. This is a vertical restraint whereby each retailer is allocated a given territory that other retailers have no access to. For example, car manufacturers have an exclusive dealer in each European country. The German Fiat dealer, for instance, is not allowed to sell cars in France. Exclusive territories do the job because, if the dealer's advertising campaign is confined to its exclusive territory, then there is no longer an inter-retailer externality.

To summarize:

When retailers must make investments in sales effort that benefit several retailers, vertical restraints such as RPM and exclusive territories may help by correcting inter-retailer externalities.

11.4   INDIRECT CONTROL[133]

There are many instances wherein consumer demand depends on retailer investment. In the previous section, we considered some such examples—personal computers and stereo equipment. The list is, however, much more extensive, including many types of clothing, jewelry, sports equipment, candy, biscuits, and so forth. These are examples in which RPM has been or is observed. One difference in the latter examples with respect to consumer electronics is that the story of retailer free-riding is less convincing. For example, providing pleasant fitting rooms is an important determinant of the demand for clothing. But the idea of consumers trying on jeans at one store and then buying from another outlet that offers low prices but poor fitting rooms is not very convincing. What then is the justification for resale price maintenance?

As we have seen in section 11.1, if the manufacturer can charge retailers a fixed fee, then the manufacturer's objective is effectively to maximize industry profits (manufacturers' plus retailers' profits). Now, total profits are a function of consumer demand, which in turn is a function of retail price, p_i, and of the sales effort by retailers, s_i. Let p^* and s^* be the optimal level of price and sales effort. The problem is: Can the manufacturer induce the retailers to set p^* and s^* based on a two-part tariff (f, w)? In section 11.1, we saw that, when no investments s_i are involved, the answer is "yes." In particular, we saw that, if retailers compete with each other, then the manufacturer should set a high wholesale price and a low (or even negative) fixed fee. Would this induce the optimal level of sales effort?

Investing in sales effort leads to greater sales. For the retailer, the marginal benefit from such investment is therefore proportional to the margin it receives per unit of sales, namely $p - w$. That is, one extra sale implies an extra profit of $p - w$. If the retailer receives a low margin, then the incentives for increasing sales are small. However, from an industry-wide perspective (manufacturer plus retailers), the marginal gain from sales effort would be great. In fact, it would be proportional to $p - c$, which is greater than $p - w$ (the retail margin) because w is greater than c. We conclude that there is a conflict between the desire to induce retailers to price high (set high w) and the desire to induce retailers to invest in sales effort (set low w, so that the margin $p - w$ is high).

The manufacturer's dilemma is that it does not have enough instruments to control all of the retailers' decisions. This is where vertical restraints, in particular RPM, come in. Levi's, for example, used to impose on its retailers that they sell blue jeans above a minimum price. In fact, brand name clothing is an example where sales effort is important and inter-retailer rivalry significant.

Suppose the manufacturer sets a minimum price at the monopoly level, $\underline{p} = p^M$, and a wholesale price at the level of marginal cost, $w = c$. Because retailers compete with each other and marginal cost is low ($w = c$), each has a great incentive to undercut the rival whenever price is high. But because price must be greater than minimum price, $\underline{p}$, each retailer will set $p_i = \underline{p}$. What about investment in sales force? Because $w = c$, all of the benefits from increasing demand are captured by the retailer. The retailer will therefore choose the optimal level of s.

To summarize:

> RPM may have the virtue of preventing downstream competition that would destroy the retailers' incentives for investing in service quality and related demand-increasing efforts. This is especially important when such investments cannot be agreed upon contractually.

11.5   MANUFACTURER COMPETITION

Until now we have considered the case when there is only one manufacturer (generally, one upstream firm). However, most industries are characterized by competition at the manufacturer level, as well as at the retail level. Manufacturer competition may have various implications. First, it affects the nature of optimal contracts between manufacturers and retailers. Second, it introduces new strategic considerations for the upstream firm.

Retailer Market Power

Sometimes, the number of manufacturers is large with respect to the number of retailers. This seems especially true of grocery stores: In the Los Angeles area alone, for example, there are 15 varieties of green peas, 19 different kinds of mustard, and 12 brands of frozen pizza.[134] Most of the market power is therefore at the retailer level, not at the manufacturer level. Limited shelf space means that the opportunity cost of carrying one particular product is high. The analysis of the previous section would predict that manufacturers set a high wholesale price and a fixed fee equal to variable profits minus fixed cost. But because the resulting margin is low and fixed costs are high (the opportunity cost of shelf space is very high), the fixed fee paid by the retailer may actually be negative. In other words, it may be the manufacturer that has to pay the retailer for shelf space. In fact, **slotting allowances**, fees paid by manufacturers to obtain retailer patronage, are a common practice in these markets.[g]

Another example in which retailer market power reverses the direction of vertical restraints is the toy industry. Until recently, Toys R Us, the largest toy distributor in the United States, imposed a clause of exclusive dealing on its *suppliers*, whereby the latter were prevented from selling the same toys to Toys R Us and to other distributors.

EXTERNALITIES AGAIN

In section 11.3, we saw that vertical restraints, such as exclusive territories and RPM, may solve the problem of externalities between retailers. Externalities may also occur between manufacturers. Consider again the example of car dealerships. It is often the case that manufacturers invest resources in training salespeople who work in dealerships. Some of this training is specific to the manufacturer's cars, but some is more general (e.g., the art of car selling). If dealers were to work with more than one manufacturer, then there would be an intermanufacturer externality: Part of the training investment made by one manufacturer benefits the rival manufacturer.

One way of solving this externality is to impose on retailers the vertical restraint of **exclusive dealing**, whereby the retailer cannot work but with one manufacturer.

FORECLOSURE

Vertical restraints may be a way for manufacturers to gain market share from rival manufacturers. Consider, for example, the cola market. There are two large manufacturers,

[g] Slotting allowances are also known as *street money* or *placement allowances*.

Coca-Cola and PepsiCo, in addition to a number of small manufacturers and a large number of retailers. In this industry, and in other related ones, exclusive dealing is a common practice. Both Coca-Cola and PepsiCo have deals in colleges, restaurants, ball parks, and some retail outlets that preclude sales of rival brands—at least, sales of *the* rival brand.

Coca-Cola justifies the practice of exclusive dealing by stating that "you can't serve two masters; we pay (the distributors) a fee to supply our customers and, as such, they are our agents and an extension of the Coca-Cola Co." Supplying a competing brand would thus imply a "conflict of interest."[135] What is the justification for exclusive dealing in this case: Is it based on the objective to increase efficiency (as in the case of car dealers), or rather on the objective to increase market power? (See also exercise 11.7.)

An example in which foreclosure was more clearly the objective is that of Microsoft until 1994. Microsoft imposed contractual clauses on computer manufacturers that effectively placed rival suppliers of operating systems at a disadvantage, thus cementing the dominance of MS-DOS in the market. Box 11.1 presents the details of this example, which will be discussed further in the next section. (This case is not to be confused with the case being decided by the U.S. Department of Justice, regarding the bundling of Windows with Internet Explorer. For an analysis of this case, see chapter 5.)

To summarize:

> Manufacturers are unwilling to invest in helping their retailers if the latter sell products from rival manufacturers. Exclusive dealing solves this intermanufacturer externality. However, exclusive dealing may also imply the exit of rival manufacturers.

VERTICAL RESTRAINTS AS A COLLUSION DEVICE

As an extreme instance of manufacturer competition, consider the case when the wholesale price is set at marginal cost level: $w = c$. Suppose, moreover, that there are several retailers who compete *à la* Bertrand. Clearly, in equilibrium, retail prices are set at $p = w = c$; profits are zero (both manufacturers' and retailers' profits); and social welfare is maximized.

Suppose now that manufacturers impose (or the industry agrees on) a minimum retail price, say the monopoly price p^M. Clearly, this implies a higher level of industry profits—monopoly profits, in fact; and a lower level of social welfare. This simple example shows that vertical restraints such as RPM may be a way of softening competition between firms. Notice that in this example, there are no efficiency considerations as in the previous sections; the only effect of RPM is to increase retail price. We conclude that,

Box 11.1   Vertical Restraints by Microsoft[136]

One of the most prominent recent antitrust actions concerning vertical issues is the 1994 case against Microsoft. The case deals with the licensing of Microsoft's operating system, MS-DOS.

In the early 1980s, at the request of IBM, Microsoft developed the computer operating system MS-DOS, to be installed in IBM's newly developed PC. IBM did not impose any exclusivity clause on Microsoft. Accordingly, the latter licensed DOS to other computer manufacturers—the IBM PC "clones"—and DOS became an increasingly popular operating system (the MacIntosh Operating System (OS) being the main loser of the DOS bandwagon).

Meanwhile, rival, compatible versions of DOS were developed: The PC-DOS (by IBM), and the DR-DOS (by DRI). As of the end of 1990, Microsoft's MS-DOS held 70% of the market, IBM's PC-DOS 18%, and DRI's DR-DOS the remainder. The tendency seemed to be for an increase in the rival systems' share.

Microsoft responded to this threat by imposing a vertical restraint on downstream firms (computer manufacturers) that effectively excluded—or so it is alleged—rival upstream firms (other operating system suppliers). Basically, Microsoft imposed on computer manufacturers a fee to be paid per computer sold *regardless of whether it included the Microsoft operating system or not*. For example, if Hewlett-Packard (a downstream firm) were to sell one million PCs, then it would have to pay Microsoft one million times the fee, regardless of whether the number of HP computers shipped with Microsoft's OS was 1, 100,000, or one million. (Of course, HP had the option of not using Microsoft software at all, an unlikely event.)

As a result of Microsoft's vertical restraint, the opportunity cost of shipping a computer with the Microsoft OS was (at the margin) zero, for a fee would have to be paid regardless of whether the Microsoft OS was included or not. It was therefore likely that HP and other computer manufacturers would sell most of their computers with the Microsoft OS, to the detriment of competing operating systems. For this reason, some argued that Microsoft's clause might have had the effect of foreclosing competition at the operating systems level (the upstream level). In fact, by 1992, Microsoft's systems accounted for 81% of all shipments that included a DOS-type system.

Microsoft eventually agreed with both the U.S. and the E.U. authorities that it would stop imposing the above contractual clause on computer manufacturers. In fact, in the United States, an agreement (a consent decree) was reached on the exact same date that the case against Microsoft was filed (July 15, 1994).

in addition to efficiency motives, vertical restraints such as RPM may also be driven by market power considerations, that is,

---

Vertical restraints such as RPM may act as a collusion device.

As section 11.6 shows, this significantly complicates the public policy analysis of vertical restraints.

11.6 ARE VERTICAL RESTRAINTS LEGAL? SHOULD THEY BE?

In the previous sections, we derived a number of reasons why an upstream firm might want to impose vertical restraints. Although these contractual clauses increase profits, it is unclear whether they improve social welfare as well. For example, exclusive dealing may have the effect of foreclosing a market from upstream competitors, which in turn is likely to reduce welfare. However, exclusive dealing may also have positive efficiency effects, as we have seen. This dichotomy greatly complicates the policy analysis of vertical restraints, for there is no clear-cut rule as to which effect dominates when.

Given this lack of clear, unambiguous conclusions from the theoretical analysis, it is not entirely surprising that policy standards have varied a great deal in time and across countries. In 1967, the U.S. Supreme Court declared vertical restraints per se illegal. However, ten years later, the same Supreme Court decided that vertical nonprice restraints (e.g., exclusive territories) were to be evaluated under the Rule of Reason. A further ease of the policy toward vertical restraints came about with twelve years of deregulation economics during the Reagan–Bush administration. Since then (that is, since 1993), the trend has been, if not reversed, at least slowed down. For example, the Vertical Restraints Guidelines published by the Department of Justice in 1985, which reflected the Reagan administration's easy stance of vertical restraints, were withdrawn in 1993. Nevertheless, recent cases judged by the Supreme Court have narrowed down the case for per se illegality of vertical price restraints. Moreover, an October 1997 decision has effectively made maximum prices a legal vertical restraint.

In Europe, Article 85(1) of the Treaty of Rome prohibits vertical restraints "as incompatible with the common market." However, Article 85(3) allows for exemptions from Article 85(1) when there is a good "technical or economic" justification for the vertical restraint, and consumers receive a "fair share of the resulting benefit." Exemptions may be individual or, more commonly, block exemptions. Specifically, a 1967 block exemption allows for exclusive territories and exclusive dealing arrangements.

Another block exemption, issued in 1988, includes franchise agreements. RPM, however, is deemed illegal under Article 85(1) and no exemptions are granted under Article 85(3), although recommended minimum and maximum prices are acceptable. Although the European approach seems at first more rigorous with respect to vertical restraints, in practice it is less so than the North American one.[h]

Both in the United States and in Europe, there seems to be a tendency to be lenient in the treatment of vertical restraints, recognizing the positive efficiency effects they may have. The analysis in this chapter seems consistent with this approach.

SUMMARY

- If nonlinear contracts are possible, then the optimal solution under vertical separation may be as efficient as that under vertical integration. Otherwise, double marginalization implies suboptimal and inefficient pricing.

- If there is no competition between retailers, then the optimal wholesale price is equal to marginal cost. The greater the degree of competition between retailers, the higher the optimal wholesale price.

- Vertical restraints such as resale-price maintenance or exclusive territories may increase efficiency when (1) retailers make investments in sales effort that benefit several retailers or rival manufacturers; or (2) a two-part tariff is insufficient to simultaneously provide incentives for retail pricing and sales effort.

- Vertical restraints such as resale-price maintenance or exclusive dealing may act as a collusion device or as a means of excluding rivals.

KEY CONCEPTS

- vertical relations
- upstream and downstream firms
- double marginalization
- vertical restraints
- franchise fees
- maximum retail price

[h] The European Commission recently announced that it intends to replace the existing regulations on vertical restraints with a more flexible set of rules.[137]

- resale-price maintenance
- exclusive territories
- exclusive dealing

REVIEW AND PRACTICE EXERCISES

11.1* Assume for the purposes of this problem that, contrary to its protestations, Microsoft has a monopoly in providing operating systems, called "Windows," for personal computers. Assume also that the marginal cost to Microsoft of supplying its operating system for one more computer is zero. Denote by w the price charged by Microsoft for its operating system. (Assume that Microsoft sets a single price per computer, that is, does not employ two-part tariffs, quantity discounts, or other forms of price discrimination.)

Computer Original Equipment Manufacturers (OEMs) assemble computers. Suppose that the "bill of materials" for a computer, that is, the cost to the OEM of all the parts necessary to build a computer, adds up to $900 per machine, and that assembly costs another $100 per machine. Finally, assume (contrary to the efforts of Dell and Compaq) that computers are a homogeneous good, and the annual demand for computers is given by $Q = 50,000,000 - 10,000 \, p$, where Q is quantity and p is price as usual.

Suppose that the OEM business is perfectly competitive.

a. For any given price, w, of operating systems, what will be the price and sales of computers?

b. What price w should Microsoft set for its operating system? How much money will Microsoft make? How much money will OEMs make?' What will be the price of a computer?

(An amusing if irrelevant note: Microsoft in fact charges in the $50 to $60 range per PC for Windows98. Microsoft argued in their antitrust trial that they must not really have a monopoly or else they would be charging a lot more.)

c. How much money would a vertically integrated firm controlling both the supply of Windows and the assembly of computers make? What price would such a firm charge for computers?

d. Could Microsoft make more money by integrating downstream into computer assembly? Why or why not?

Suppose now (definitely contrary to reality) that a single firm, Compaq, has a monopoly over the assembly of computers.

e. For a given price, w, for Windows, what price, p, would Compaq set for computers, and how many computers would be sold?

f. What price, w, should Microsoft set for its operating system? How much money will Microsoft make? How much money will Compaq make? What will be the price of a computer?

g. Could Microsoft and Compaq make more money by merging? If so, how much? Would such a merger benefit or harm computer users? By how much?[138]

11.2 Empirical evidence suggests that franchiser-owned McDonald's restaurants charge lower prices than independent ones. How can this difference be explained?

11.3 Suppose that a manufacturer sells to n retailers by means of a two-part tariff (f, w), including a fixed fee f and a wholesale price w. Explain the intuition of the result that the greater the degree of retailer competition, the greater the optimal wholesale price.

11.4 The fashion (clothing), consumer electronics, fine fragrance industries are known to practice or have practiced resale price maintenance. In each case, indicate the probable motivation for RPM and the likely welfare consequences.

11.5 Vermont Castings is a manufacturer of wood-burning stoves, a somewhat complex product. One of Vermont Castings's dealers once complained about the terms of the relations between the manufacturer and dealers, stating that "the worst disappointment is spending a great deal of time with a customer only to lose him to Applewood [a competing retailer] because of price." Specifically, the dealer lamented "the loss of 3 sales of V.C. stoves . . . to people whom we educated and spent long hours with."[139]

How do you think this problem can be resolved? How would you defend your solution in an antitrust/competition policy court?

11.6 Should the European Union outlaw the practice of exclusive territories in car dealerships? Why or why not?

11.7 Beer producers are wont to impose an exclusive dealing clause on retailers. Discuss the efficiency and market power effects of this practice.

11.8* Two major music companies—Sony and Warner Music—have been subject to an antitrust inquiry by the FTC over allegations that they illegally discouraged retail discounting of compact disks. The investigation is centered on the practice of announcing suggested prices. Suggested prices are not illegal—only agreements among firms on such prices are illegal. But in practice, retailers that advertise or promote CDs at a price below the suggested price are denied cash payments by the manufacturers, in effect "forcing" such suggested prices.[140]

How would you decide on this case?

EXTENSION EXERCISES

11.9[***]   Consider the model presented in the beginning of section 11.2, but assume that retailers compete à la Cournot. Show that the optimal wholesale price is strictly between marginal cost and monopoly price.

11.10[***] Consider the following highly simplified picture of the personal computer industry.

There are many price-taking firms that assemble computer systems. Call these firms "computer OEMs." Each of these firms must buy three inputs for each computer system that it sells: (1) a variety of components that are themselves supplied competitively and collectively cost the computer OEM $500 per computer; (2) the Windows operating system, available only from Microsoft, at a price p_M, to be discussed later; and (3) a Pentium microprocessor, available only from Intel, at a price p_I, also to be discussed later. Because each computer system requires precisely one operating system and one microprocessor, the marginal cost of a computer to an OEM is $500 + p_M + p_I$. Assume that competition among OEMs drives the price of a computer system down to marginal cost; we have $p = 500 + p_M + p_I$, where p is the price of a computer system.

The demand for computer systems is given by $Q = 100,000,000 - 50,000p$.

Microsoft is the sole supplier of the Windows operating system for personal computers. The marginal cost to Microsoft of providing Windows for one more computer is zero.

Intel is the sole supplier of the Pentium microprocessors for personal computers. The marginal cost to Intel of a Pentium microprocessor for one more computer system is $300.

a. Suppose that Microsoft and Intel simultaneously and independently set the prices for Windows and Pentium chips, p_M and p_I. What are the Nash equilibrium prices, $\hat{p}_M$ and $\hat{p}_I$?

Now, suppose that Microsoft and Intel sit down to negotiate an agreement to sell Windows and Pentium chips as a package to computer OEMs for a package price of p_{MI}.

b. What package price would maximize Microsoft's and Intel's combined profits? By how much would an agreement between Microsoft and Intel boost their combined profits?

c. Would final consumers benefit from such an agreement between Microsoft and Intel, or would they be harmed? What about computer OEMs? Relate your answer to your calculations in parts (a) and (b), and explain the economic principles underlying your answer.[141]

CHAPTER 12

PRODUCT DIFFERENTIATION

The U.S. credit card industry is composed of over 4000 firms (typically, banks that issue credit cards). The good that is offered is, at least apparently, homogeneous. The number of consumers is large (75 million). The ten largest firms (credit card issuers) hold a combined 20% market share. There are no significant barriers to entry, and a fair number of firms operate at the national level, so that the geographic definition of the United States as the relevant market seems reasonable. There is no sign of an explicit price-fixing agreement between the different credit-card issuers.

Given this set of circumstances, many would feel inclined to identify the credit card industry as an example of near-perfect competition. The evidence is, however, greatly at odds with such expectation. First, interest rates are insensitive with respect to changes in the marginal cost (the money market rate), which is not consistent with perfect competition.[a] Second, during the period from 1983 to 1988, rates of return in the credit card business were three to five times higher than the normal rate of return in other lines of banking business.

One first possible explanation for this discrepancy is that credit card users are subject to **switching costs**. Many consumers obtain their first credit card through the bank they have an account with. Changing to a different card may imply a series of costs, for example, opening an account with a different bank. Moreover, before applying for a new credit card, the consumer needs to obtain information regarding the card's terms and conditions. This too is a cost of getting a new credit card (if nothing else, the time lost in finding out what the terms and conditions are).

A second explanation is that the good credit card is in fact not a homogeneous product, rather, it is a **differentiated product**. This may result from differences in quality (some credit cards offer better services) or from differences in the status that is associated with a certain credit card. For example, the services and the status associated with an

[a] As was seen in chapter 9, under perfect competition, a one-dollar change in marginal cost implies a one-dollar change in price.

American Express card are not the same as those related to a Visa card. Moreover, not all Visa cards are identical, and they are not seen by consumers as identical.[142]

In this chapter, we consider cases in which the assumptions of homogeneous product and perfect information fail to hold. Departure from these extreme assumptions has important implications for market performance. Sections 12.1 through 12.3 deal with product differentiation. Section 12.1 introduces a general framework for the analysis of product differentiation—the characteristics approach. Section 12.2, shows that introducing product differentiation in the Bertrand price competition model implies equilibrium prices above marginal cost (whereas, as seen in chapter 7, homogeneous product would imply equilibrium pricing at marginal cost level). Section 12.3 looks at the main strategic considerations involved in the decision of choosing how to design one's product. Finally, section 12.4 addresses the related issues of imperfect information and switching costs. There are a number of similarities with respect to product differentiation. There are also new results, such as the possibility of price dispersion, that is, different prices being set for the same product.

12.1 HORIZONTAL DIFFERENTIATION, VERTICAL DIFFERENTIATION, AND THE CHARACTERISTICS APPROACH

De gustibus non est disputandum (tastes are not a matter of debate), so goes the adage. Frequently, not only are competing products different, but consumers evaluate their relative merits differently. This is the case of products differing according to characteristics such as sweetness or crunchiness. In fact, consumer preferences may even be negatively correlated; that is, Consumer A prefers Firm 1's product relative to Firm 2's, whereas Consumer B prefers Firm 2's relative to Firm 1's. We refer to this situation as **horizontal differentiation**.

By contrast, there are cases in which *all* consumers prefer one product over another. For example, most if not all consumers would agree that, *everything else being equal*, a car is better the more fuel efficient it is. We refer to this situation as **vertical product differentiation**. Notice that all consumers agree that Firm 1's product is better than Firm 2's; this is consistent with the fact that some consumers are more sensitive to the difference between the products than others. For example, some consumers may find fuel efficiency an important characteristic in a car, whereas others are nearly indifferent. The important feature of vertical product differentiation is that all consumers agree that fuel efficiency is a good thing, that is, there is universal agreement that more is better.

Most, if not all, real-world examples combine elements of horizontal and vertical product differentiation. In fact, whenever products are defined by more than one characteristic, even if consumers agree that more of each characteristic is better (vertical differentiation), insofar as different consumers value different characteristics differently, we have a case of horizontal product differentiation. For example, Computer A has a fast microprocessor but small memory capacity. Computer B, by contrast, has a slow microprocessor but a large memory capacity. Every consumer agrees that a faster microprocessor and greater memory capacity make for a better computer (vertical differentiation). However, because different consumers have different preferences over memory and microprocessor speed, their ranking of the relative merits of each computer differs (horizontal differentiation).

This example points to a more general approach to consumer demand: the **characteristics approach.** This approach assumes that consumer demand is directed not toward products per se but rather toward product characteristics.[143] For example, when searching for a computer, consumers look for microprocessor speed, RAM capacity, hard disk capacity, screen size, and so forth. A consumer's valuation for a particular computer is the sum of the valuations for each particular characteristic. In other words, consumers are not interested in goods for their own sake, but for the characteristics they possess. The demand for each good is derived from the demand for characteristics.[b]

To understand the nature and usefulness of the characteristics approach, let us consider a simplified example—the demand for automobiles. As a first approximation, one might say that the main relevant characteristics in a car are (1) the ratio horse power/weight (a proxy for acceleration); (2) size; (3) extras, such as air conditioning; and (4) fuel efficiency (miles per gallon, or miles per dollar). Obviously, this leaves out a number of automobile characteristics that are difficult if not impossible to quantify (e.g., design). This means that in practice a consumer's choice depends on a number of factors that are not included in the above set of characteristics. The important thing is that, to a great extent, a consumer's preference for an auto is determined by its quantifiable characteristics.

For the sake of example, let us assume that there are only two different cars: the GM Geo and the Porsche. The approximate values of each car's characteristics are given in table 12.1. Different consumers naturally have different valuations for each of the above characteristics. In our simplified example, we assume that there are only two types of consumers: Type A ("recent college graduate") and Type B ("Chief Executive Officer"). Valuations for each characteristic j by each consumer type i are given in table 12.2. Notice that both types of consumer value the characteristic "price" at -1, that is, one extra thousand dollars in price implies that a purchase provides one unit less of net utility. This means that valuations are normalized and are valued in dollar terms (specifically, thousand-dollar terms). So for example, the number .5 in the entry "consumer A's valuation for air conditioning" means that a college graduate would be willing to pay .5 times one thousand dollars, or 500 dollars, for the characteristic "air conditioning" (a zero-one characteristic). On account of this characteristic, a college graduate is willing to pay more for a Porsche than for a Geo by a factor of 500 dollars. The number 40 in the entry "consumer B's valuation for horse power/weight" means that a CEO would be willing to pay an extra 40 thousand dollars for a car that has one extra

[b] The view that goods are bundles of measurable characteristics is reasonable in a number of different markets, such as vitamins, houses, cars, and computers. There are other examples, however, wherein such an approach would be of more limited use, such as perfumes or status goods.

TABLE 12.1 MODEL CHARACTERISTICS.

Model (j)	HP/W	Air	MP\$	Size	Price (10^3 dollars)
Geo	0.3	0	64	0.9	4
Porsche	1.0	1	12	1.2	68

TABLE 12.2 CONSUMER VALUATIONS OF CHARACTERISTICS.

Buyer (i)	HP/W	Air	MP\$	Size	Price (10^3 dollars)
A (college graduate)	5	.5	.1	1	−1
B (CEO)	40	40	0	20	−1

TABLE 12.3 NET UTILITY.

Buyer	Geo	Porsche
A	4.8	−60.1
B	26	36

unit of the "horse power/weight" characteristic. Because the Porsche has .7 more than the Geo, on account of acceleration, a CEO is willing to pay .7 times 40k = 28 thousand dollars more for a Porsche than for a Geo.

The assumption of rational consumer behavior, in the present context, implies that each consumer chooses the car that provides the highest net utility (net of price). The net utility for consumer i from buying product k is given by

$$u_{ik} = b_{i1}c_{k1} + \ldots + b_{i4}c_{k4} - p_k,$$

where b_{ij} is consumer i's valuation for characteristic j (see table 12.2) and c_{kj} is how much k has of characteristic j (see table 12.1).

These values are displayed in table 12.3, which is obtained from tables 12.1 and 12.2 by applying the preceding equation. Not surprisingly, the table indicates that a college graduate (Type A) would purchase a Geo, whereas a CEO (Type B) would prefer a Porsche. In fact, for a Type A consumer, the net utility of buying a Geo is 4.8, whereas that of a Porsche is −60.1: The consumer values the different characteristics at a low level, so that the price difference between the Geo and the Porsche dominates the choice. For a type B consumer, by contrast, the net utility from buying a Porsche is 36, whereas the net utility of buying a Geo is only 26. The Porsche's superior features in terms of acceleration and air conditioning seem to dominate in this case.

The example of demand for automobiles illustrates how the characteristics approach encompasses both horizontal and vertical product differentiation. As we consider each characteristic in isolation, we are faced with a situation of vertical product differentiation. For example, both Type A and Type B consumers agree that acceleration is a valuable characteristic and that, accordingly, the Porsche is a better car than the Geo insofar as acceleration is concerned. Likewise, both Type A and Type B consumers agree that fuel efficiency is a valuable characteristic and that, accordingly, the Geo is a better car than the Porsche insofar as fuel efficiency is concerned. Taking into account the preceding two characteristics, we conclude that a consumer of Type A thinks the Geo is a better product overall (fuel efficiency beats acceleration), whereas a consumer of Type B thinks that the Porsche is a better product overall (acceleration beats fuel efficiency).

The characteristics approach to product demand has several advantages. From a conceptual point of view, it allows for a general treatment of product differentiation that encompasses both horizontal and vertical differentiation.

From the point of view of empirical estimation of consumer demand, the characteristics approach allows for significant improvements in the use of available data. If we were to estimate the demand for n different product varieties directly—including the estimation of cross-price elasticities—we would need to estimate approximately n^2 parameters. The problem is that, if n is a large number, then n^2 is a very large number. By applying the characteristics approach, however, we need to estimate only a number of parameters in the order of n times m, where m is the number of characteristics. An application of the characteristics approach to the estimation of car demand is discussed in box 12.1.

Finally, the characteristics approach provides a useful framework for business strategy. For example, a computer manufacturer may obtain an estimate of the willingness to pay for a new computer by estimating valuations for characteristics from previous sales data. The strategy of product positioning, including the identification of a firm's close competitors, is also aided by looking at the market "map" defined by characteristics. We deal with the issue of product positioning in section 12.3.

12.2 PRODUCT DIFFERENTIATION AND MARKET POWER

In sections 12.2 through 12.4, we explore some of the implications of product differentiation for oligopoly competition. We do so by considering a model of *horizontal* product differentiation.

Consider a mile-long beach with two ice cream vendors, one at each extreme of the beach. Even if we assume both sellers offer the same product, very few consumers are

BOX 12.1 ESTIMATING THE DEMAND FOR AUTOMOBILES[144]

Excluding "exotic" models such as the Ferrari and the Rolls Royce, almost one thousand different car models were marketed in the United States during the period from 1971 to 1990. Estimating individual demands for each car model would be extremely data-demanding. By applying the characteristics approach, however, some useful results can be obtained.

The econometric model consists of assuming that each consumer chooses the model that maximizes his or her utility. Utility is a function of observable and unobservable model characteristics, as well as observable and unobservable consumer characteristics (e.g., income). For example, it is possible that two consumers with the same observable characteristics hold different views about the relative merits of two similar cars. However, if the two cars are very different, then it is unlikely that two consumers with the same observable characteristics hold different rankings.

Based on the distribution of model characteristics, prices, market shares, and consumer characteristics (in particular, income), the distribution of valuations for each characteristic can be obtained.

CONSUMER VALUATIONS FOR PRODUCT CHARACTERISTICS

Characteristic	Average	Standard Deviation
HP/Weight	≈ 0	4.628
Air conditioning	1.521	0.619
Miles per $	≈ 0	1.050
Size	3.460	2.056

Perhaps surprisingly, these results reveal that, on average, consumers don't put great weight on acceleration power or fuel efficiency. There is, however, wide disagreement among consumers regarding the value of acceleration. In fact, the estimated standard deviation is 4.628, whereas the range of values is approximately [0.15,1]. By contrast, consumers seem to agree that fuel efficiency is not a very important characteristic. In fact, although the range of values is approximately [8,65], the standard deviation is only 2.056.

The results also allow for comparisons between characteristics. For example, having air conditioning as a standard feature is worth as much as an additional $1.521/3.460 = .44$ units of size. This is approximately the difference in size between a medium-sized car and a small car.

Box 12.1   (CONTINUED)

Finally, the results can be used to produce a matrix of price elasticities for all 997 models. A selection of these is presented in the following table.

PRICE ELASTICITIES OF DEMAND FOR SELECTED AUTO MODELS

	Nissan Sentra	Ford Escort	Toyota Lexus	BMW 745i
Sentra	−6.5282	0.4544	0.0008	0.0000
Escort	0.0778	−6.0309	0.0008	0.0000
Lexus	0.0002	0.0010	−3.0847	0.0322
735i	0.0001	0.0005	0.0926	−3.5151

Notes: (1) Quantity change in row, price change in column. (2) There are 77 subcompact and compact models (including Sentra and Escort) and 24 Luxury models (including Lexus and 735i).

Not surprisingly, the results indicate that the cross elasticity between the Nissan Sentra and the Ford Escort is greater than the cross elasticity between the Nissan Sentra and the Toyota Lexus. Generally, the characteristics approach provides a quantitative idea of the relevant submarkets within a given market.

indifferent to buying from one seller or the other. If both vendors sell at the same price, a consumer who is located close to one end of the beach naturally prefers the seller who is located nearby. If, in fact, the costs of traveling to visit such a seller are lower than the costs of traveling to visit the other one, and other than travel costs, the two products are identical, even in price. The reverse is true for a consumer located near the other end of the beach. Generally, consumers do not see both vendors as the same, even though they sell products that are physically identical; different consumers value sellers differently, specifically, each consumer values sellers according to his or her location.

The situation exemplified by the ice cream example is actually more general. First, it generalizes to any situation wherein sellers and buyers are physically located at different places and a transportation cost must be paid by buyers to purchase from a specific seller (gas stations, restaurants, steel mills, etc.). Second, *by analogy*, it also applies to situations wherein sellers offer products that differ according to some characteristic, and buyers differ among themselves as to how they value such a characteristic.

For example, consider the market for corn flakes and suppose there are two brands that differ only according to sweetness: Brand 1 has no sugar added, whereas Brand 2 has large quantities of sugar added. This is analogous to two sellers at the end of a "beach," whereby one end corresponds to minimum sweetness and the other end to maximum sweetness. A consumer's location would indicate his or her preference for sweetness.

If the consumer is closely located to Brand 1's end of the "beach," then the consumer has a strong preference for no-sugar-added corn flakes. Conversely, a consumer located close to the other end of the "beach" has a sweet tooth. And a consumer located in the middle has a strong preference for corn flakes with some, but not a lot, of sugar added. Finally, the "traveling" or "transportation" cost measures the consumer's aversion to buying something different from his or her optimal degree of sweetness. To summarize: Even though we refer to location and transportation costs, the ideas developed in the context of *spatial product differentiation can also be applied to differentiation according to some other product characteristic.*

How do firms compete in prices when their products are differentiated in this way? To address this question, we consider a simple model motivated by the above examples: the **Hotelling model**.[145] The model is illustrated by figures 12.1 to 12.3. Suppose there is a large number of buyers (e.g., one million) who are distributed along a segment of length one (e.g., one mile). There are two sellers, each located at the end of the segment. Sellers simultaneously set prices, as in the Bertrand model (see chapter 7), and buyers choose which seller to buy from.

A buyer located at point x must travel a distance x to buy from Firm 1. Travel costs t per unit of distance. Therefore, the total cost for buying at Store 1 is given by p'_1, the price, plus tx, the transportation cost. The total cost for buying from Firm 1, $p_1 + tx$, is therefore a function of consumer location. Figure 12.1 depicts this total cost function for a particular value of p_1. At $x = 0$ (left axis), total cost is simply price, p'_1. As the consumer is located farther away from Firm 1, total cost increases at the rate t per unit of distance. A consumer located at Firm 2's location ($x = 1$) would need to pay a total cost $p'_1 + t$ to purchase from Firm 1.

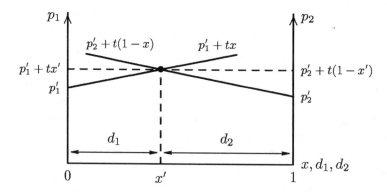

FIGURE 12.1 HOTELLING MODEL: TOTAL CONSUMER COST.

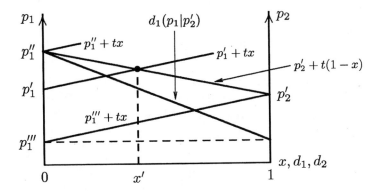

FIGURE 12.2 HOTELLING MODEL: FIRM 1'S DEMAND.

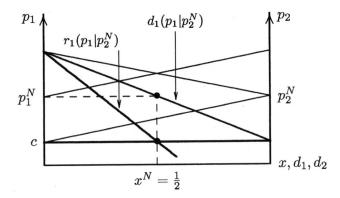

FIGURE 12.3 HOTELLING MODEL: EQUILIBRIUM.

By analogy, a buyer located at point x must travel a distance $1 - x$ to buy from Firm 2. The total cost of buying from Firm 2 is therefore given by $p'_2 + t(1 - x)$. A consumer located where Firm 2 is located ($x = 1$) would have to pay a total cost p'_2. At the other extreme, a consumer located at Firm 1's location ($x = 0$) must pay a total cost $p'_2 + t$ to buy from Firm 2. Contrary to Firm 1, the total cost of buying from Firm 2, $p'_2 + t(1 - x)$, is a downward sloping curve, that is, it is lower the farther to the right the consumer is located.

Suppose that all consumers purchase one unit. This amounts to assuming that the utility of buying one unit is high, so that the consumers' decision is not whether to buy but simply which seller to buy from. Because the products sold by Firms 1 and 2 differ only according to the firm's location, all that consumers have to do is choose the firm that minimizes their total cost, price plus transportation cost. From figure 12.1, we see that for $p_1 = p_1'$ and $p_2 = p_2'$, a consumer located at x' is indifferent between purchasing from Firm 1 and purchasing from Firm 2. A consumer located to the left of x', that is, located at $x < x'$, strictly prefers to buy from Firm 1. Finally, a consumer located to the right of x', that is, located at $x > x'$ strictly prefers to buy from Firm 2. This implies that Firm 1's demand is given by all consumers located to the left of x', whereas Firm 2's demand is given by all consumers located to the right of x'. If we assume (for simplicity) that consumers are uniformly distributed along the segment, then Firm 1's demand is given by x', whereas Firm 2's demand is given by $1 - x'$.

From figure 12.1 we can see that, although Firm 1 prices higher than its rival ($p_1' > p_2'$), it still receives positive demand. This contrasts with the Bertrand model, introduced in chapter 7, in which the firm setting the lowest price takes all of the market demand. The difference between the two models is that, in the Hotelling model, the products sold by each firm are no longer identical in the eyes of consumers. This is because of transportation costs. In fact, it can be seen from figure 12.1 that, if transportation costs are negligible (low t), then the slope of the total cost curves would be very low, and the firm with the lowest price would effectively take all of the market demand.

Generally, under the Hotelling model, each firm faces a downward-sloping demand curve. This is derived in figure 12.2. To begin, the figure reproduces the calculations from figure 12.1: If Firm 1 sets p_1' and Firm 2 sets p_2', then Firm 1 receives demand $d_1 = x'$. Suppose that Firm 1 sets p_1'' instead. At this price, the indifferent consumer is located at $x = 0$. That is, p_1 is so high that all consumers prefer buying from Firm 2. At the other extreme, suppose that Firm 1 sets p_1'''. At this price, the indifferent consumer is located at $x = 1$. That is, p_1 is so low that all consumers prefer buying from Firm 1. Generally, for p_1 between the extremes p_1'' and p_1''', we obtain the demand curve $d_1(p_1|p_2')$. Notice that the demand curve is a function of Firm 2's price. If p_2 were different from p_2', then we would obtain a different demand curve.

Having derived Firm 1's demand function, we can now identify the Nash equilibrium of the Hotelling model. As in chapter 7, we look for a pair of prices (p_1, p_2) such that no firm has an incentive to change prices. Suppose that marginal cost is constant and equal to c for both firms, and suppose that Firm 2 sets $p_2 = p_2^N$. What is Firm 1's optimal price? The solution is illustrated in figure 12.3. From Firm 1's demand curve, $d_1(p_1|p_2^N)$, we derive Firm 1's marginal revenue curve, $r_1(p_1|p_2^N)$. Firm 1's optimum results from equating marginal revenue to marginal cost, $r_1(p_1|p_2^N) = c$, which corresponds to p_1^N. Because both firms have the same marginal cost and $p_1^N = p_2^N$, we conclude that these prices constitute a Nash equilibrium.[c]

Figure 12.3 suggests a number of interesting facts about the equilibrium of the Hotelling model. First, in contrast with the Bertrand model, equilibrium price is strictly greater than marginal cost. This results from the fact that each firm faces a continuous, downward-sloping demand curve, which in turn results from the fact that consumers must incur transportation costs to make a purchase. In fact, if transportation costs are

[c] That is, the corresponding picture for Firm 2 would be identical to that for Firm 1, and so, for $p_1 = p_1^N$, Firm 2's optimal price would indeed be p_2^N.

small, that is, if the value of t is small, then each firm's demand curve is flat (see figure 12.2), and equilibrium price is close to marginal cost (see figure 12.3). A greater value of t corresponds to a greater degree of product differentiation. We thus conclude:

> The greater the degree of product differentiation, the greater the degree of market power.

In other words, product differentiation provides a solution to the Bertrand "paradox" (see chapter 7). In fact, contrary to the prediction of the Bertrand model, price competition does not necessarily lead to pricing at marginal cost level. The latter is true only under the (somewhat extreme) assumptions of homogeneous product, no capacity constraints, and no repeated interaction. In chapters 7 and 8, we saw that capacity constraints and repeated interaction may imply that firms set prices above marginal cost. We now see that product differentiation is an additional motive for positive equilibrium margins.

12.3 PRODUCT POSITIONING

In the previous section, we assumed that each firm's location is given.[d] What if firms can choose where to locate their products? **Product positioning** is an important dimension of firm strategy in many different industries. For example, music stores must decide whether to locate close to each other or far apart. Likewise, a breakfast cereal manufacturer must decide the characteristics of its products (how sweet, crunchy, etc., each cereal brand ought to be). One of the considerations in such a choice is product positioning by rival brands. In fact, "distance" with respect to competitors must be defined with respect to the rivals' choices of product characteristic. This introduces an element of strategic behavior, one that we address in this section.

In chapter 7, we looked at a situation in which each firm manages two strategic variables: capacity and price. We concluded that, in most cases, the correct model is to assume that firms first choose production capacities and then prices, given production capacities. This modeling option follows from the assumption that capacity is a long-run variable (difficult to change), whereas price is a short-run variable (easy to change). By the same token, the natural way to model pricing and product positioning is to assume that firms first (simultaneously) choose where to locate their product and then (simultaneously) choose prices, given their products' locations. The question to ask then is: What equilibrium locations will firms choose in the first stage of the two-stage game, in anticipation of the ensuing stage of price competition?

[d] In fact, we have assumed that firms are located at the extreme points of the distribution of consumer locations. However, the analysis can be extended to the case when firm locations are inside the segment.

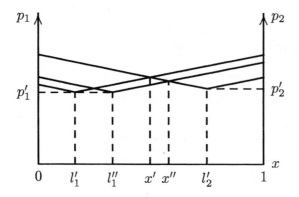

FIGURE 12.4 PRODUCT POSITIONING: DIRECT EFFECT.

Suppose, without loss of generality, that Firm 2 locates on the right half of the segment, that is, between 0.5 and 1.[e] What is Firm 1's optimal choice? Is it better for Firm 1 to locate close to Firm 2, or is it better for Firm 1 to choose a location close to 0?

There are essentially two effects (direct and strategic) to take into consideration. First, *for given prices*, the closer Firm 1 is located to Firm 2, the greater its demand is, and the greater its profits are. We refer to this as the **direct effect** of product positioning. Figure 12.4 illustrates the direct effect. For a given location by Firm 2 (l_2') and for given prices (p_1', p_2'), we consider two possible locations by Firm 1 (l_1', l_1''). As can be seen, Firm 1's demand is greater when it locates closer to l_2'. Specifically, when $l_1 = l_1''$, Firm 1's demand is given by $d_1 = x''$, whereas when $l_1 = l_1' < l_1''$, Firm 1's demand is only $d_1 = x' < x''$.

The assumption that prices are given is, however, incorrect: Prices are determined in the second period *as a function of first-period location choices*. We must therefore consider a second effect, which we refer to as the **strategic effect**: The price set by Firm 2 in the second period is a function of the location chosen by Firm 1 in the first period. What is the effect of l_1 on p_2? Consider the extreme case when $l_1 = l_2$, that is, both firms are located at the same point. In this case, the two products are effectively identical in the eyes of *every* consumer. Although consumers have to incur transportation costs, the situation is essentially that in the Bertrand model: In equilibrium, prices are set equal to marginal cost. This contrasts with the case considered in the previous section ($l_1 = 0, l_2 = 1$), where firms set positive margins. Generally, it can be shown that *the closer firms are together, the more intense price competition is*. This is not surprising: As stated in the previous section, product differentiation increases market power.

We thus have two effects of opposite sign: The direct effect induces firms to locate close to each other, whereas the strategic effect leads them to differentiate. The exact

[e] This is without loss of generality because consumers are uniformly distributed along the segment. If Firm 2 were located along the left half of the segment, then we could transpose the analysis of Firm 1's decision and get the same results.

balance of these two effects is likely to depend on the value of transportation costs and on the distribution of consumers. It seems difficult to derive general rules other than:

> If price competition is intense, then firms tend to locate far apart (high degree of differentiation). If price competition is not intense, then firms tend to locate close to the center (low degree of differentiation).

12.4 IMPERFECT INFORMATION AND SWITCHING COSTS

In the previous sections, we considered industries in which firms sell products that are similar but differentiated. Differences across products are often objective differences. For example, a Porsche is different from a GM Geo. There are cases, however, where differences are to a great extent subjective. For example, many consumers treat branded drugs differently from the corresponding generics, even though they are, physically speaking, identical.

For the purpose of studying market power, it does not matter whether products are physically differentiated or not, so long as consumers treat them as different: A similar framework to that in the previous sections would then apply. In this section, we consider the cases when consumers are imperfectly informed about prices or have to pay a cost to switch between sellers. As we will see, these are situations where, even if different sellers offer the same product, consumers treat different sellers differently, a situation akin to product differentiation.

Let us first address the case of imperfect information about prices. Consider a retail market with n competing stores and a large number of consumers. Each consumer wants to buy one unit of the good in question and is willing to pay up to u. An important assumption we now make is that consumers are not a priori informed about the prices set by each store. Specifically, to find out the price set by each store, a consumer must visit that store, which implies a cost of s for the consumer—a **search cost**.

If there were no search costs, we would have a setting identical to the Bertrand model, the result being that each store would price at marginal cost level. With a positive search cost, however, a possible equilibrium is for every firm to price at the monopoly level, $p = u$. In fact, if every firm sets $p = u$, then no firm has an incentive to reduce price: Because consumers expect every store to price at the same level and the search cost is positive, lowering the price is not going to attract any new customers; it will simply amount to a loss in revenues.[146] We thus conclude that search costs may lead to monopoly pricing even though firms compete in price and the product is homogenous.

SWITCHING COSTS

In many industries, consumers must pay a cost to switch between suppliers. For example, a MacIntosh user who switches to Windows must incur the cost of getting used to a new operating system, in addition to the cost of repurchasing software in a version that can be run with the new operating system. Sometimes, switching costs are artificially created by the sellers themselves. Frequent-flyer programs are one such instance: a frequent flyer who wishes to change airlines must incur the opportunity cost of starting the mile count from zero again.

The effect of switching costs is similar to that of search costs. In fact, the previous model can be adapted so that s is now the cost of switching between suppliers rather than the cost of searching rivals' prices. If s is large enough, then there exists an equilibrium whereby each firm sets price at the monopoly level. In fact, this is now the *only* equilibrium. Any price below monopoly level cannot be an equilibrium. If all firms were setting p lower than u, then it would pay for an individual firm to set a slightly higher price. If the price difference with respect to rival firms is less than the switching cost, then no consumer would switch. Because sales remain constant and the sale price is higher, the firm that increases price increases profits as well. We thus conclude that no price below monopoly price can be an equilibrium price.[147]

This extreme result depends to some extent on the simplistic nature of the model. However, it can be shown that, generally:

> The greater the value of search costs or switching costs, the greater the sellers' market power tends to be.

PRICE DISPERSION

Price dispersion is a widely observed phenomenon. A Braun Flex Integral shaver sells for about $90 in Spain, $103 in the Netherlands, $118 in Germany and $124 in France.[148] Similar cross-country differences are found in cars as well (see chapter 10). A Portuguese consumer magazine reports prices on the same Bruce Springsteen CD ranging from Esc 2490 to Esc 3720.[149] However, these are not necessarily examples of price dispersion in the sense considered in this section. Cross-country differences in the price of an electric shaver are more an example of price discrimination than of price dispersion. Differences in car prices result to a great extent from differences in taxation and regulation across European countries. Regarding CDs, it is difficult to compare prices across stores as different as hypermarkets and specialized music stores: The shopping experience the consumer gets is quite different in each case (the same argument applies to comparisons with internet shopping).

But consider the example of airline tickets. It is nowadays relatively easy and safe to buy tickets over the phone. Moreover, the costs of making a phone call and of posting an airline ticket are minor compared to the sale value. A recent survey suggests, however, that there is significant price dispersion for a given airline ticket (same flight, same airline, same restrictions). The main source of dispersion seems to be across European countries, but differences also can be found within the same country.[150] Can this be an equilibrium situation? Why don't consumers shop around more often?[f]

A variation of the search model presented previously can address these questions. Suppose that there are two types of consumers—one with positive search costs, and one with zero search costs. One tantalizing possibility is that, in equilibrium, some firms set a high price, while other firms set low prices. In this equilibrium, consumers with a positive search cost buy from the first store they encounter. In some cases, this will be a store charging a high price. Consumers know that there exist stores charging a lower price, but they still prefer to purchase at the first store they visit: The expected gain from searching for a lower price does not compensate the search cost. Finally, consumers with no search costs purchase at the lowest price available.

This implies that (1) stores charging a high price make sales only to consumers with positive search costs; (2) stores charging a low price sell both to consumers with positive search cost who happened to visit that store first and to consumers with zero search cost. For this to be an equilibrium, it is necessary that neither high-price stores wish to lower their price nor do low-price stores wish to increase it. This is possible because, while selling at a lower margin, low-price stores sell a greater quantity.

Models of this type are known as the **tourists–locals model**. In fact, the experience of retail trade in many cities is that some stores offer low prices while others are "tourist traps": For essentially the same product or service, large price differentials are observed. The analogy is straightforward: Tourists are consumers with high search costs, whereas locals have low search costs. Notice that this does not necessarily require the value of time to be lower for a local; in fact, the opposite may well be the case. The reason why, in fact, locals have lower search costs is that they plan to make several purchases, so that the search cost can be spread over the multiple units bought.

SUMMARY

- The greater the degree of product differentiation, the greater the degree of market power.

- If price competition is intense, then firms tend to locate far apart (high degree of differentiation). If price competition is not intense, then firms tend to locate close to where the demand is located (low degree of differentiation).

- The greater the value of search costs or switching costs, the greater the sellers' market power is.

[f] One reason for cross-country differences may be that prices quoted in different currencies increase the level of consumer confusion and make shopping comparisons more difficult. In this sense, the introduction of the European single currency (the euro) provides an interesting natural experiment: will price dispersion across European countries be reduced?

KEY CONCEPTS

- horizontal and vertical product differentiation

- characteristics approach

- product positioning

- direct and strategic effect

- search costs and switching costs

REVIEW AND PRACTICE EXERCISES

12.1* Consider a duopoly where horizontal product differentiation is important. Firms first simultaneously choose their product locations, then simultaneously set prices in an infinite series of periods.

Suppose that firms collude in prices in the second stage and anticipate this at the product-positioning stage. What do you expect this implies in terms of the degree of product differentiation?[151]

12.2 Empirical evidence suggests that, during the 1970s, a firm with an IBM 1400 was as likely as any other firm to purchase an IBM when making a new purchase; a firm with an IBM 360 was more likely to purchase an IBM than a firm that did not own an IBM 360. Software for the IBM 1400 could not run on the succeeding generations of IBM models (360, 370, 3000, and 4300); software for the IBM 360 could run on the 370, 3000, and 4300.[152] How do you interpret these results?

12.3 According to a market analyst in Brussels:

The euro [the new European single currency] will bring lower prices overall but the price differences will be more or less the ones we have right now.

Do you agree? Why or why not?

12.4 A study on retail price for books and CDs finds that price dispersion (weighted by market shares) is lower for internet retailers than for conventional retailers.[153] Discuss.

12.5 "Price dispersion is a manifestation—and indeed it is a measure—of ignorance in the market."[154] Do you agree? Compare with possible alternative explanations for price dispersion.

EXTENSION EXERCISES

12.6* Consider the model of price dispersion sketched in section 12.4. Show that there can be at most two different prices in equilibrium.

12.7* Two firms are engaged in Bertrand competition. There are 10,000 people in the population, each of whom is willing to pay at most 10 for at most one unit of the good. Both firms have a constant marginal cost of 5. Each firm is allocated half the market. It costs a customer s to switch from one firm to the other. Customers know what prices are being charged. Law or custom restricts the firms to charging whole-dollar amounts (e.g., they can charge 6, but not 6.50).

a. Suppose that $s = 0$. What are the Nash equilibria of this model? Why does discrete (whole-dollar) pricing result in more equilibria than continuous pricing?

b. Suppose that $s = 2$. What is (are) the Nash equilibrium (equilibria) of this model?

c. Suppose that $s = 4$. What is (are) the Nash equilibrium (equilibria) of this model?

d. Comparing the expected profits in (b) to those in (c), what is the value of raising customers' switching costs from 2 to 4?[155]

12.8* Twenty-five different stores sell the same product in a given area to a population of two thousand consumers. Consumers are equally likely to first visit any of the twenty-five stores. Half of the consumers have no search costs and purchase at the lowest price. The other half are willing to buy one unit of the product up to a maximum of $70 and must incur a cost of $44 to find out about the prices charged by other stores. Each store can sell up to 50 units and has a unit cost of $25.

a. Show that, in equilibrium, there exist at most two different prices.

b. Show that, if there exist two different equilibrium prices, then the higher price must be 70.

c. Show that the following is an equilibrium: 5 firms set a price of 70, and the remaining 20 firms set a price of 45.

CHAPTER 13

ADVERTISING

The pharmaceutical industry is known for its high research and development (R&D) budgets. However, advertising and promotion expenditures are even higher than R&D outlays. To be fair, this depends on how exactly we define advertising and promotion. In any event, it is unquestionable that advertising expenditures play an important role in pharmaceuticals. The same might be said of many other industries. In the soft-drink industry, for example, price competition plays a relatively secondary role with respect to advertising competition. This chapter, which concludes part IV of the book, focuses on advertising as a firm investment and strategy.

13.1   INFORMATION, PERSUASION, AND SIGNALING

PERSUASION VERSUS INFORMATION

Economists classify goods and advertising about goods in different categories. Goods can be search goods or experience goods. A **search good** is one whose features the consumer can ascertain before purchase. An **experience good**, by contrast, is one whose features can be ascertained only upon consumption.[a] The features of a personal computer (microprocessor speed, hard-disk capacity, etc.) can be determined by inspection. In this sense, a PC would be a search good. By contrast, no matter how much you are told about a given red wine, you won't know how good it is until you taste it; wine would thus be an experience good.

The distinction between search goods and experience goods leads to a parallel classification of advertising expenditures. Economists frequently distinguish between informative advertising and persuasive advertising. **Informative advertising** describes

[a] A third category might be that of **credence goods**, when quality cannot be determined even after consumption. Examples include medical and legal services.

the product's existence, its characteristics (e.g., weight, size, speed) and selling terms (e.g., price, financing interest rate). **Persuasive advertising**, by contrast, is designed to change consumers' preferences ("our product tastes better," etc.).

The distinction between information and persuasion is important in assessment of the social value of advertising. Everyone accepts that there is value in advertising messages that provide information. Most would agree, however, that there is little direct value, if any, in persuasive advertising. The question is, therefore, Which form of advertising is more important? In other words, is the average advertising message more informative or more persuasive in nature? Empirical evidence suggests that both types of advertising are important. For example, box 13.1 shows that informative advertising played an important role in the launch of a new yogurt brand. By contrast, box 13.2 suggests that persuasive advertising has been responsible for maintaining the market power of branded pharmaceuticals vis-à-vis generics manufacturers.

Box 13.1   Informative versus Persuasive Advertising[156]

The introduction of price scanners at supermarket checkout counters has allowed for the creation of datasets of unprecedented detail. A. C. Nielsen uses such datasets to follow consumer behavior patterns. By pairing this information with the monitoring of household TV viewing, one is able to relate consumption behavior to advertising exposure.

Yoplait, the second largest yogurt manufacturer in the United States, introduced Yoplait 150 in April 1987. Based on the Nielsen data described earlier, an econometric estimation can be performed of the factors that influence the decision of buying Yoplait 150 on a given shopping trip. The results are the following:

Probability of buying Yoplait 150 =

$1.85 \times$ Advertising exposure

$- 0.24 \times$ Advertising exposure $\times$ No. previous purchases

$+$ (other variables),

where "advertising exposure" is the number of 30-second ads for Yoplait 150 observed by each consumer during the week of the shopping trip. The first coefficient, positive, indicates that the more Yoplait spends on advertising, the greater the probability of a purchase. The second coefficient, negative, indicates that the more accustomed a consumer becomes to Yoplait, the less advertising expenditures will influence his or her decision. This result is consistent with the view that advertising has an informative role (in this case, information about the product's existence).

BOX 13.2   BRANDED DRUGS AND GENERICS[157]

In 1984, the U.S. Congress passed legislation that allowed drug manufacturers to receive fast Food and Drug Administration (FDA) approval for marketing generic versions of off-patent branded drugs. The idea was to limit the increase in pharmaceutical prices. In fact, since 1984, the market share of generics has grown from 18% to 42%. However, the prices of branded drugs have not decreased accordingly; quite the opposite, in fact. So much so that, although the share of generics in volume is increasing, that same share is decreasing in value.

To a great extent, these trends result from the massive direct-to-consumer advertising campaigns launched by the large pharmaceutical firms. In 1998 only, it is estimated that more than $10 billion was spent on ads and promotions. Generic drug makers, on the other hand, can hardly keep up with the marketing muscle of the large firms, in terms of both advertisement and detailing. For example, it is rare for generic drug makers to send salespeople to visit doctors as brand companies do. This is not surprising if one considers the difference in size between the large brand companies (e.g., Glaxo Wellcome, valued at $110 billion) and the generic drug companies (e.g., Mylan Laboratories, one of the leading generic drug makers, valued at $4.4 billion).

If advertising were mainly informative, we would associate it primarily with search goods. However, empirical evidence shows that the advertising/sales ratio is three times greater for experience goods than it is for search goods.[158] Observations of this kind form the basis for the popular view that "the constructive contribution [of advertising] to humanity is exactly minus zero," to quote F. Scott Fitzgerald. Economists, however, have proposed several efficiency arguments in defense of advertising. We begin with the view of persuasive advertising of experience goods as a form of (indirectly) informative advertising.

SIGNALING

In 1984, Ford Motor Co. financed an advertising campaign consisting of a series of Ford Ranger trucks being thrown out of airplanes or driven off cliffs. At about the same time, Diet Coke was introduced with an advertising campaign featuring a large concert hall full of people—including a large number of high-priced celebrities—and a simple announcement that Diet Coke was the reason for the assemblage. These are examples of ads that carry little direct information (other than the existence of the product). In fact, the most important (implicit) message seems to be "We are spending large amounts of money on this advertising campaign."[159]

The fact that these advertising campaigns provide little direct information does not preclude the possibility that they are informative—in an indirect sense. Consider the case of an experience good such as a piece of software or a bottle of wine. Suppose that time is divided into present and future. Initially, a number of new product varieties are launched in the market. Consumers know that some are high-quality products, and some are of low quality, but they don't know which ones are which: The only way to find out is to actually purchase them. If a given firm sells in the present, then its quality will be known in the future. If it does not sell, then consumers will still be uncertain about quality in the future.[b]

Suppose that firms launch high-quality products with expensive advertising campaigns. The implicit message of this "money-burning" effort can be interpreted as follows: "Because our quality is high, we can afford to spend this much money on advertising. In fact, consumers should rationally believe that our product is of high quality and purchase it. Their experience will show them that the product is indeed of high quality, the consequence of which will be that they will purchase it again in the future." If such is the case, then we conclude:

> Advertising expenditures may serve to signal product quality.

Is this a credible message? Why don't firms do the same with low-quality products, namely, spend money on advertising and sell for a high price to consumers who expect they are buying high quality? In other words, are consumers behaving rationally when they expect high advertising to mean high quality? The point is that *firms selling high-quality products have more to gain from getting consumers to try their products than firms selling low-quality products*. In fact, firms selling high-quality products will receive repeat purchases, whereas firms selling low-quality products will not. For this reason, there exists a level of advertising expenditures that firms selling high-quality products are willing to incur but firms selling low-quality products are not. This implies that, *in equilibrium*, advertising is a sure sign that the product is of high quality.

The interpretation of advertising as a signal implies a qualification on the idea of "wasteful" advertising. In equilibrium, positive advertising expenditures are a waste in the sense that they provide no direct information about product characteristics. However, the equilibrium with advertising may be more efficient than the equilibrium without advertising. If there were no advertising, it could occur that high-quality firms would not have incentive to produce, as their products are (ex-ante) identical to low-quality products. If consumers value high-quality products a great deal, then the no-advertising outcome may be worse, even considering the savings in advertising expenditure. In other words, the equilibrium with advertising may be more efficient because the indirect informative value of advertising is greater than its cost.

[b] In reality, things are not so drastic. We are considering the extreme possibilities of full information or no information for the sake of illustration only.

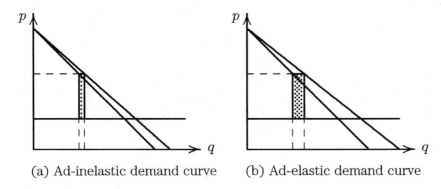

(a) Ad-inelastic demand curve   (b) Ad-elastic demand curve

FIGURE 13.1   ADVERTISING ELASTICITY AND RETURNS FROM ADVERTISING.

13.2   ADVERTISING INTENSITY

Some industries spend more on advertising than others. This can be seen, for example, by measuring advertising intensity, specifically, the **advertising-to-revenues ratio** a/R (the ratio of advertising expenditures to total sales). For example, in the salt industry, a/R is of the order 0 to .5%. For breakfast cereals, by contrast, the numbers are in the interval 8% to 13%.[160] What explains these differences in advertising intensity? In this section, we attempt to answer this question. We leave aside the issue of whether advertising is primarily informative or persuasive (see section 13.1) and simply assume that advertising expenditures imply a shift in the consumer demand curve.[c]

Figure 13.1 provides a first answer. Both graph (a) and graph (b) assume a fixed amount spent on advertising. Case (a) is the case in which advertising expenditures have little impact on demand. Cement would be an example: Construction companies are not very sensitive to cement advertising; their purchasing decisions are mostly based on price and related terms of sales. Case (b) corresponds to the case when the demand curve is sensitive to advertising expenditures. Soft drinks would be one of many examples. The main point of figure 13.1 is that *the marginal gain from advertising expenditures is greater the more sensitive the demand curve is to advertising expenditures.* As a result, other things being equal, we would expect firms to *advertise more when the demand curve is more sensitive to advertising expenditures.*

Figure 13.2 makes an additional point. In both cases (a) and (b), advertising has the same impact on quantity demanded; so, as far as the first explanation is concerned, the returns from advertising would be the same (see figure 13.1). The difference between the two cases is that the demand curve is more elastic in case (b) than in case (a). As we have seen in chapter 5, the greater the demand elasticity, the lower the optimal price. As figure 13.2 shows, this implies a lower price-cost margin when elasticity is higher. Because the price-cost margin is lower in case (b), so is the gain from advertising smaller,

[c] That is, the shift could be caused by the informative or by the persuasive nature of advertising. We do not make any particular assumption in this regard; we simply assume that there is a shift in the demand curve.

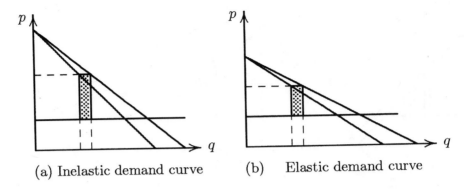

(a) Inelastic demand curve   (b)   Elastic demand curve

FIGURE 13.2 DEMAND ELASTICITY AND RETURNS FROM ADVERTISING.

even though the increase in quantity demanded is the same. In other words, *the marginal gain from advertising is greater the greater the price-cost margin.*

The ideas of Figures 13.1 and 13.2 can be summarized in the **Dorfman-Steiner formula:**[161]

$$\frac{a}{R} = \frac{p - MC}{p}\eta$$

$$= \frac{\eta}{\epsilon},$$

(13.1)

where η is the demand elasticity with respect to advertising expenditures and ϵ the price elasticity of demand. That is, η measures how much quantity demanded increases (percentwise) when advertising expenditures are increased by 1%. (Likewise, ϵ measures how much quantity demand decreases as a result of a 1% increase in price.)[d]

Thus, equation 13.1 states:

> The advertising-to-sales ratio is greater the greater the advertising elasticity of demand and the lower the price elasticity of demand (or the greater the price-cost margin).

[d] The second equality in (13.1) should be familiar from chapter 5, where it is shown that the optimal margin is inversely related to demand elasticity.

Table 13.1 displays the values of the various terms of (13.1) for a number of consumer products in Australia. Except for cigarettes and toothpaste, the value of a/R seems approximately equal to the value of η/ϵ, in accordance with the Dorfman-Steiner formula.

TABLE 13.1 ADVERTISING: OPTIMAL VALUES AND OBSERVED VALUES.[162]

Market	η/ϵ	a/R
Instant coffee	.019	.020
Bottled beer	.008	.011
Cigarettes	.019	.046
Toilet soap	.013	.012
Laundry washing powder	.019	.030
Toothpaste	.024	.059
Paint (finished coats)	.009	.019
Motor spirit	.017	.016

MARKET STRUCTURE AND ADVERTISING INTENSITY

We have seen how advertising intensity depends on the type of product, specifically, how it is a function of advertising and price elasticities of demand. A second, related, question is: How does advertising intensity vary with market structure? Do firms advertise more in industries with many small firms, or in industries with a few large ones? Equation 13.1 suggests a rephrasing of the same question in a different way: How do the firm's advertising and price elasticities vary with market structure?

The answer is easiest in the case of price elasticity: The greater the number of firms, the greater the firm's price elasticity of demand (in absolute value). The idea is that, by decreasing its price, not only is firm i increasing total demand, it is also increasing its market share; the second effect is greater the lower firm i's market share is. So, on account of the price elasticity, we would expect advertising intensity to be lower the more fragmented the industry is. In other words: The more competitive the industry is, the lower the price-cost margin; as we have seen before, the lower the price-cost margin, the lower the optimal advertising intensity.

Let us now look at the effect of market structure on the firm's advertising elasticity of demand. Let us consider two extreme cases. First, suppose that advertising increases every firm's demand equally. For example, advertising milk, with no reference to any brand name, increases the demand for every firm that sells milk. In other words, advertising milk is a **public good** for all milk sellers. In this extreme case, each firm's advertising elasticity decreases as concentration decreases. In fact, the more fragmented the industry is, the lower the benefit from advertising that is captured by the firm that pays for it.

The diamond industry provides an interesting example. For decades, DeBeers has dominated the industry, controlling more than 90% of the distribution of diamonds. DeBeers has also been the exclusive source of diamond advertising ("Diamonds are forever"). DeBeers's grip over distribution has suffered from the rise of Russian producers-turned-distributors. A further blow is expected as newly found Canadian mines begin their operations. One of the main fears held by the various industry players is that

DeBeers's reduced market share will decrease their incentive to maintain high advertising outlays, possibly to the point of leading the industry to collapse, as consumers discard the (erroneous) notion that diamonds are scarce.

Examples where advertising is a public good are rare, however. Let us then consider the opposite extreme case: Suppose total demand is fixed and independent of advertising; the only effect of advertising by firm i is to shift demand across rival firms. An example of this is prescription drugs when there is competition between a branded drug and the corresponding generic competitors: The main effect of advertising is not to make consumers buy larger quantities of the drug but rather to make them switch between generic and branded drugs. In this case, how does the advertising elasticity of demand vary with market structure? Clearly, the advertising elasticity increases as we go from one to two firms. In fact, under monopoly, the advertising elasticity would be zero (as there are no competitors), whereas under duopoly it would be positive. Generally, we might expect the elasticity to increase as market concentration decreases, *starting from high levels of concentration.*

To illustrate these ideas, consider the case of spandex, an elastic fiber used in various types of fashionable clothing (fashionable as of the end of the second millennium). Although spandex per se is a fairly homogeneous product, the industry is dominated by DuPont, whose Lycra brand name commands a market share in excess of 60% (the remainder is divided between Bayer AG, Globe Manufacturing, and other competitors).[163] One of the main reasons for DuPont's market dominance is the enormous advertising investment it made in promoting the Lycra brand name. For example, in print advertising, the Lycra logo appears jointly with major names such as Claiborne and Levi Strauss.

Spandex was invented by DuPont in 1959. If DuPont still held exclusive patent rights on spandex, would it be spending more or less on advertising? On the one hand, DuPont's advertising fosters the consumption of spandex, which benefits both DuPont and its rivals. Given this free-riding problem, we would expect DuPont to spend less when it competes against rival firms. On the other hand, one of the main reasons for DuPont's advertising effort is to keep spandex from turning into a commodity. In this sense, competition may be a factor for increased advertising.

To summarize, as the number of firms increases and industry concentration decreases, there are three effects that determine the variation in advertising intensity. First, each firm's margin decreases; second, each firm captures a lower share of the demand-increasing effect of advertising; and third, each firm captures a greater share of the demand-shifting effect of advertising. The first two effects imply a decrease in advertising intensity, whereas the third one implies an increase in advertising intensity. The net effect is ambiguous.

Not surprisingly, the empirical evidence of the effect of concentration on advertising intensity is ambiguous as well. However, there seems to be a certain *empirical regularity whereby, as concentration decreases from a high level of concentration, advertising intensity increases as concentration decreases; whereas, starting from a low level of concentration, advertising intensity decreases as concentration decreases.*

13.3 PRICE COMPETITION AND ADVERTISING

So far, we have, with few exceptions, considered the problem of advertising from a monopolist's perspective, that is, we have not explicitly considered the interaction between competing firms' advertising strategies. In principle, much of what was said about price competition can be extended to competition in advertising. In particular, the notion that duopoly (and oligopoly) competition constitutes a prisoner's dilemma is equally applicable to price competition and to competition on advertising.

In the case of price competition, both firms are better off by setting a high price. However, each firm has a unilateral incentive to cut prices; specifically, under the assumption of homogeneous product, undercutting the rival is an optimal response whenever the rival prices above marginal cost. Now, consider the extreme case when total demand is constant, and suppose that the only effect of advertising is to shift market shares across competitors. Specifically, the firm that advertises the most receives all of the market share. In this context, the joint incentive for two duopolists is to spend zero on advertising. However, whichever low level the rival spends on advertising, the optimal response is to advertise a little more. The result is that firms will advertise to the point where profits are zero, just as under Bertrand competition.

The preceding example is rather extreme: it assumes that the only effect of advertising is to shift market shares; it also assumes that the greater spender on advertising captures all of the market demand. However, the qualitative feature of the example—namely, the fact that competition leads firms to spend more on advertising than they would like—is more general (just as the "curse" of competition extends beyond the extreme assumptions of the Bertrand model).

As in the case of price competition, repeated interaction may help in alleviating the costs of excessive competition. There are, however, a few differences in advertising with respect to pricing. First, the frequency with which advertising decisions are made is normally lower than pricing decisions. For example, a gas station may change prices on a daily basis, whereas advertising budgets and advertising campaigns are normally determined on an annual or quarterly basis. Second, whereas price decisions have mostly a short-run effect, advertising expenditures frequently imply a medium- or even long-run effect. In fact, one should think of advertising expenditures as investments in the asset **brand equity**.

Both of these differences (frequency of interaction and advertising as an investment) correspond, in terms of the terminology of chapter 8, to a lower value of the discount factor. That is, other things being equal, we would expect an agreement to keep advertising expenditures at a low level to be more difficult to maintain than an agreement to maintain prices high.

In addition to comparing competition in pricing with competition in advertising, it is interesting to consider the interplay between pricing and advertising competition. We first consider how advertising competition impacts on price competition and then finish with the analysis of the reverse direction of causation.

ADVERTISING SOFTENS PRICE COMPETITION

Consider the following simple example, based on the Hotelling model (see chapter 12), but with an element of uncertainty. Suppose there are two wineries, each producing a brand of white wine. Consumers know that there exist two firms and two product varieties (one per firm); however, consumers do not know the characteristics of each product. For the sake of simplicity, suppose that the only relevant characteristic is how sweet the wine is. As we have seen in the previous chapter, this is a typical example of horizontal product differentiation: Some consumers prefer dry white wines, some sweet ones. Finally, suppose that prices p_A and p_B are observed by consumers and that the latter's preferences for sweetness are uniformly distributed in the Hotelling segment (see chapter 12).

In this context, cross-price elasticity between the two products is infinity. In other words, consumers treat the products *as if* they were identical. They are not, to be sure, but given the consumers' imperfect knowledge, it's as if they were. For this reason, if p_A is lower than p_B, then all consumers flock to Firm A, and vice versa. From the analysis of the Bertrand model (see chapter 7), we know that this leads to an equilibrium where firms price at the level of marginal cost.

Suppose now that firms advertise their location: For example, Firm A is located at l_1 and Firm B at l_2. We now have a standard Hotelling model like the one discussed in the previous chapter. As we then saw, the equilibrium consists of firms setting a price above marginal cost by an amount that is proportional to the consumers' "transportation" cost. In summary, advertising product locations transformed a Bertrand situation into a Hotelling situation.

> Generally, advertising product characteristics increases product differentiation and consequently softens competition.

An interesting example of this strategy is given by Procter & Gamble's (P&G's) recent advertising strategy for its Crest MultiCare toothpaste. See box 13.3.

In the preceding example, advertising is informative: It conveys objective information about product characteristics. Common observation, however, suggests that many advertising messages convey little or no information at all. Even in these cases, advertising seems to increase the degree of (perceived) product differentiation and soften price competition. For example, Monsanto spent vast amounts on advertising its Nutrasweet brand name and its logo while it had a monopoly on the production of aspartame. Its patents on aspartame have now expired. However, despite the fact that aspartame is a homogeneous product, Nutrasweet still holds a dominant market share. To a great extent, its dominance is due to a perceived difference between Nutrasweet and aspartame produced by rival firms. In other words, advertising may increase product differentiation

BOX 13.3   TOOTHPASTE WARS: WHY P&G'S AD PRAISES ARCHRIVAL COLGATE[164]

In June 1998, P&G paid for full-page ads in about 100 U.S. newspapers. The ads featured side-by-side comparisons between P&G's Crest MultiCare and Colgate's Total on a number of toothpaste benefits. Both brands checked on a number of items, such as "helps fight cavities" and "helps brush away plaque." However, when it came to "helps reduce and prevent gingivitis and reduce plaque," only the Colgate Total box was ticked. On the other hand, only Crest's MultiCare checked on "better taste" and "fresher feeling breath."

It is highly unusual for P&G—in fact, for any firm—to cede an advantage to a competitor in this way. P&G asserts that their "policy is to play fair, so our ad did acknowledge the competition's gingivitis claim." However, one can argue that it is in P&G's own interest to act in this way. First, praising the competitor's product makes it more difficult for Colgate to challenge the ad's claims. Second, as the analysis in the text suggests, one important effect of the ad is to increase the consumers' perception of differences between the two brands, thus softening price competition.

by informing consumers about objective product characteristics, or simply by creating a subjective sense of differentiation.

Anecdotal evidence suggests that the latter form of advertising, namely that which induces **spurious product differentiation**, is indeed very common. In addition to aspartame, one can find numerous examples, including medical drugs, cigarettes, and soft drinks. This observation forms the basis of the view that most advertising is not only wasteful, but it is anti-competitive and positively harmful. For an economist, this is a difficult question to tackle: How can consumer welfare be measured when the result of advertising is precisely to change consumer preferences? Even so, one possible efficiency defense of advertising would be that it leads to a new equilibrium with greater output. If market power is important, then it is likely that equilibrium output is below optimal output. Advertising thus improves allocative efficiency in the output market.[165]

ADVERTISING INTENSIFIES PRICE COMPETITION

Let us now examine the opposite case, namely, the case in which advertising intensifies price competition. Consider a duopoly of a homogeneous product. Each consumer is willing to pay up to u for the product. However, consumers don't know the price charged by each firm. Moreover, consumers have the time to check the price of only one of the firms, or to "visit" one of the firms. Because consumers have no information about price, their best strategy is to choose one of the firms at random, check the price, and purchase if price is not greater than u. Knowing this, both firms find it optimal to set $p = u$: A higher price would drive demand to zero; a lower price would not increase demand. In other words, demand elasticity (with respect to price decreases) is zero.

Now suppose that firms advertise their prices and that all consumers learn about prices. Because the product is homogeneous, we now have a situation like the Bertrand model, with equilibrium price equal to marginal cost. In other words, advertising price information increases demand elasticity to such an extent that firm profits go from monopoly profits to zero profits. We thus have an instance when

> Advertising prices increases price competition.

Empirical evidence from some industries seems to support this assertion. For example, it was found that the average price of eyeglasses was higher in U.S. states that imposed a ban on advertising prices (of eyeglasses) than in states that imposed no restrictions on advertising.[166]

Why would firms then spend money in advertising prices? Consider, for example, the retailing of consumer electronics. The products that are sold are essentially homogeneous (a Sony TV set, a Pioneer stereo system, etc.). Retailers frequently pay for ads in newspapers and specialized magazines. If this increases price competition, why would they do it? There are at least three explanations for this pattern of behavior.

First, advertising may have the nature of a prisoner's dilemma: All firms would be better off without spending money on advertising, but each firm prefers, unilaterally, to spend money on advertising. In fact, continuing with the model assumptions, if no firm spends money on advertising, then consumers expect all firms to set $p = u$. If one of the firms were to advertise $p = u - \epsilon$, then it would receive all of the market demand and increase its profits drastically.

A second interpretation is that not all consumers behave in the same way. In chapter 12, we looked at a model with consumers who shop and consumers who don't. Advertising prices may be part of an equilibrium wherein some firms price lower and attract shoppers. Advertising would then be a way of signaling to shoppers that the retailer is one of the low-price retailers: Even shoppers have positive search costs, and advertising reduces search costs.

A third interpretation is suggested by empirical evidence from consumer electronics retailing in the United Kingdom. Notwithstanding the large sums spent on advertising prices, the latter remain remarkably high and similar across retailers. To a great extent, this is due to resale-price maintenance and similar arrangements that keep prices high. In this context, advertising seems to be a way of announcing or reminding consumers of the retailer's existence. In other words, consumers don't gain much from shopping (because of resale-price maintenance and similar arrangements); all that consumers have to do is choose a retailer and purchase; ads play an important role in this decision. Finally, because margins are so high (because of RPM or similar arrangements), the incentive to advertise is indeed very high: One extra consumer gained accrues a large marginal revenue. In this instance, it's not so much advertising that influences price competition as the opposite: Price competition (or lack thereof) determines the incentives for advertising.

SUMMARY

- Advertising may be classified as informative or persuasive. Advertising expenditures may also serve to signal product quality.

- The advertising-to-sales ratio is greater the greater the advertising elasticity of demand and the lower the price elasticity of demand (or the greater the price-cost margin).

- Advertising product characteristics is likely to increase product differentiation and soften price competition. Advertising prices is likely to increase price competition.

KEY CONCEPTS

- search goods and experience goods
- informative advertising and persuasive advertising
- signaling
- advertising-to-revenues ratio

REVIEW AND PRACTICE EXERCISES

13.1 Explain how advertising expenditures with no direct informational content can increase market efficiency.

13.2* Empirical evidence suggests that the probability of a household switching to a different brand of breakfast cereal is increasing in the advertising intensity of that brand. However, the effect of advertising is significantly lower for households that have previously tried that brand.[167] What does this suggest about the nature of advertising expenditures (persuasion versus information)?

13.3 Consider the following industries: pharmaceuticals, cement, perfumes, fast food, and compact cars. How would you expect them to be ordered by advertising intensity? Why?

13.4 In section 13.2, it was argued that advertising intensity under duopoly should be greater than under monopoly. DeBeers, the dominant firm in the diamond industry (a cartel that in many respects is like a monopoly), spends vast resources on advertising. DeBeers has also started to advertise diamonds *and* the name DeBeers. Is this consistent with the analysis of section 13.2? What aspects of the diamond industry are not reflected in the analysis of section 13.2?

13.5 Which of the two cars, BMW series 5 or Nissan Sentra, would you expect to have a greater price elasticity? Based on this, which car would you expect to have a greater advertising-to-sales ratio? Is the empirical evidence consistent with this expectation?

13.6 Consider the values in table 13.2. In which industries do you expect advertising intensity to be higher?

TABLE 13.2 ADVERTISING, INCOME AND PRICE ELASTICITIES IN SPECIFIC INDUSTRIES.[168]

Industry	Income	Price	Advertising	
			Short-Run	Long-Run
Bakery products	.757	−.263	.223	.265
Books	2.205	−.774	.250	.348
Canning	.359	−.820	.614	.963
Cereals and grain mill products	.177	−1.469	.224	.320
Cigars and cigarettes	.001	−1.809	.408	.575
Costume jewelry	−1.407	−3.007	.282	.307
Distilled liquor	.179	−.253	.641	.745
Drugs	.719	−1.079	.663	1.042
Jewelry (precious metal)	1.792	.661	.147	.201
Malt liquor	−.184	−.562	.004	.010
Soaps	1.684	−.758	.284	.294
Soft drinks	2.008	−1.478	.567	.591
Wines	.407	−.680	.972	1.202

EXTENSION EXERCISES

13.7** Your company sells expensive, branded fountain pens. There are 100,000 people aware of your pens. Each of these 100,000 people has his or her own willingness to pay for your pens. These willingness-to-pay numbers are uniformly distributed between $0 and $500. So, your demand curve is given by $Q = 100000(1 - p/500)$. Your marginal cost per pen is $100. Well-versed in economics, you are pricing your pens at $300 each, and selling 40,000 pens, generating a contribution of $8 million.

You have just become brand manager for these fountain pens. The previous brand manager engaged in very little advertising, but you are considering running a major promotional campaign to build your brand image and visibility. You are considering two possible advertising campaigns; call them "Build Value" and "Expand Reach." (You will run either one of these campaigns or none at all; you cannot run both.)

The "Build Value" campaign will not reach any new potential customers, but will increase the willingness-to-pay of each of your 100,000 existing customers by 25%. This campaign costs $2.5 million to run.

The "Expand Reach" campaign will expand the set of potential customers by 25%, from 100,000 to 125,000. The 25,000 new customers reached will have the same distribution of willingness-to-pay as the preexisting 100,000 potential customers (namely, uniformly distributed between $0 and $500). This campaign costs $1.8 million to run.

a. If your choice were between running the "Build Value" campaign and running no campaign at all, would you choose to run the "Build Value" campaign? Show your calculations.

b. If your choice were between running the "Expand Reach" campaign and running no campaign at all, would you choose to run the "Expand Reach" campaign? Show your calculations.

c. What choice would you make in this situation: Run the "Build Value" campaign, run the "Expand Reach" campaign, or run neither?[169]

13.8** The effect of advertising expenditures can be decomposed into (a) effect on total market demand, and (b) effect on market shares. Accordingly, the following cases can be distinguished, where q_i is firm i's demand and a_i its advertising expenditure:[170]

Cooperative advertising: $\partial q_j / \partial a_i > 0$

Predatory advertising: $\partial q_j / \partial a_i < 0$

Perfectly cooperative advertising: $\partial q_i / \partial a_i = \partial q_j / \partial a_i$

Completely predatory advertising: $\partial q_i / \partial a_i + \partial q_j / \partial a_i = 0$

Empirical studies suggest the following values of demand elasticity with respect to advertising levels.[171]

Product	Advertising Elasticity	
	Own	Cross**
Coca-Cola	.25	−.06
Pepsi-Cola	.32	−.62
Saltine crackers*	.16	−.05
High-tar cigarettes	.005***	−.001***

* Long-run elasticity for major brands

** Cross elasticity is the elasticity of q_i with respect to a_j

*** NB: These are derivatives of *market share* with respect to advertising level

Based on this classification, how do you characterize advertising expenditures on cola drinks, saltine crackers, and cigarettes?

ENTRY AND EXIT

CHAPTER 14

ENTRY COSTS, MARKET STRUCTURE, AND WELFARE

One limitation of the model of perfect competition is that it says very little about the firm size distribution in a long-run equilibrium. Assuming there are constant returns to scale (i.e., average cost is constant), what is the number of firms in equilibrium? What is the size of each firm? According to the model of perfect competition, *any* number and size distribution is possible, so long as each firm is sufficiently small for the assumption of price-taking behavior to hold.[172]

Now, let us look at the empirical evidence. Figure 14.1 depicts data on market concentration (measured by C4) in a number of sectors in France and in Germany. That is, for each sector, a point is drawn such that the horizontal coordinate is the value of C4 in France and the vertical coordinate is the value of C4 in Germany. For example, if in a given sector, the four largest French firms hold 40% of the market, whereas the four largest German firms hold 60% of the market, then a point (.4,.6) appears in the diagram. Figure 14.2 represents a similar diagram, this time for France and Belgium.

If the reality of the firm size distribution were as unpredictable as the model of perfect competition suggests, then we would expect the diagrams to be just a chaotic cloud of points. However, the first diagram shows a remarkable regularity, with most points close to the 45° line. In words, for each industry, the value of C4 in France is similar to the value of C4 in Germany. This suggests that there are industry-specific factors that determine each firm's size.

By contrast with figure 14.1, figure 14.2 shows that most points are above the diagonal. Therefore, for each sector, the value of C4 tends to be greater in Belgium than in France. One important difference between the two diagrams is that, whereas figure 14.1 refers to two economies of similar size (both in population and in GDP), figure 14.2 compares two countries of very different size (France being some five times larger than

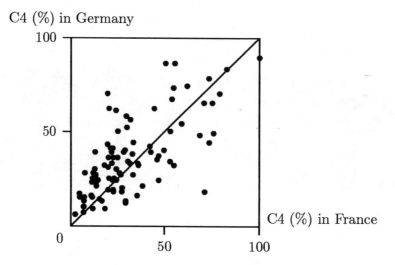

FIGURE 14.1   INDUSTRY CONCENTRATION IN FRANCE AND IN GERMANY.[173]

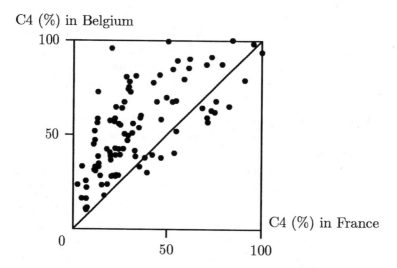

FIGURE 14.2   INDUSTRY CONCENTRATION IN FRANCE AND IN BELGIUM.

Belgium). Together, these diagrams suggest that market size, in addition to industry-specific factors, is an important determinant of market structure.

In this chapter, we focus precisely on how technology and market size influence firm size and industry concentration. First, we consider a simple model that shows how the number of firms changes as a function of market size and the nature of the production technology. We then make the important distinction between exogenous and endogenous entry costs, and see how this determines market concentration. Finally, we address the issue of whether the equilibrium number of firms in an industry is excessive or insufficient from a social perspective.

14.1 ENTRY COSTS AND MARKET STRUCTURE

Our first goal is to determine the relation between technology, market size, and industry concentration. We begin by considering a simple model in which all firms are of the same size. For this reason, determining concentration is equivalent to determining the number of firms. C4, for example, is given by $4/n$, that is, if all firms are of the same size, then the market share of the four largest firms is equal to the ratio of 4 to the number of firms. Changes in C4 can therefore be measured by changes in n.

Suppose that each firm has a cost function given by $C = F + cq_i$ and that the demand curve is given by $Q = (a - P)S$. S is a measure of market size: Doubling the value of S implies that, for a given P, Q is twice as large. It can be shown that, in equilibrium, each firm's profit is given by

$$\Pi(n) = S \left(\frac{a - c}{n + 1} \right)^2 - F.$$ **(14.1)**

A **free-entry equilibrium** is characterized by a set of active firms such that (1) no active firm wishes to leave the market, and (2) no inactive firm wishes to enter the market. Specifically, the equilibrium number of firms, $\hat{n}$, has to be such that $\Pi(\hat{n}) \geq 0$ (no active firm wishes to exit), and $\Pi(\hat{n} + 1) \leq 0$ (no inactive firm wishes to enter).[a] Equating the right-hand side of (14.1) to zero, and solving for n, we get

$$n = (a - c) \sqrt{\frac{S}{F}} - 1.$$ **(14.2)**

Hence, the equilibrium value of n is given by

$$\hat{n} = \left[(a - c) \sqrt{\frac{S}{F}} - 1 \right],$$ **(14.3)**

where $[x]$ denotes the highest integer lower than x (the characteristic function). That is, if (14.2) gives $n = 32.4$, for example, then $\hat{n} = [32.4] = 32$.

MARKET SIZE AND CONCENTRATION

Equation 14.3 states that the number of firms is an increasing function of market size (here measured directly by S and indirectly by a) and an inverse function of both fixed and variable costs (F and c). None of this is surprising. Note, however, that the relation between S and $\hat{n}$ is not proportional. In fact, *for high values of $\hat{n}$, the relation between S and $\hat{n}$ is approximately quadratic*: To duplicate the number of firms, market size must

[a] Notice that, if $\Pi(n') = 0$, then both $\hat{n} = n' - 1$ and $\hat{n} = n'$ form an equilibrium. Because $\Pi(n') = 0$ is true only "by coincidence" (i.e., nongenerically), we henceforth assume that there exists a unique solution to the system $\Pi(\hat{n} + 1) \leq 0 \leq \Pi(\hat{n})$.

increase fourfold; conversely, if market size duplicates, the number of firms increases by only 40% (specifically, by $\sqrt{2} - 1$).

What explains this nonproportional relationship? If market price were constant (with respect to the number of firms), then the relation between size and number of firms would be proportional: Double market size and you double the number of firms. However, as the number of firms increases, the market becomes more competitive, that is, the margin $p - c$ decreases. As a result, variable profit per unit of market size also decreases, which in turn limits the number of firms the market can sustain.

> Due to increased price competition, the equilibrium number of active firms varies less than proportionally with respect to market size.

Minimum Efficient Scale and Concentration

As we saw in chapter 2, one of the determinants of market structure is the firm's cost structure. In particular, the fact that most firms have a U-shaped average cost curve is an important determinant of market structure. A firm on the left-hand side of the U, that is, a firm with decreasing average cost, is said to operate under **increasing returns to scale**. (The model considered in this section, where costs are given by $F + cq$, is an extreme case in which average cost is always decreasing.)

To measure the relation between increasing returns to scale and market structure, we first need to measure the degree of increasing returns to scale. There are several ways of doing this. One way is to use the concept of **minimum efficient scale**, the minimum scale at which a firm's average cost is close to the minimum, say, within 10% of the minimum.[b] In the model considered in this section, total cost is $C = F + cq$. Average cost is therefore $AC = F/q + c$. The minimum of average cost is c. Let the minimum efficient scale (MES) be the minimum scale such that average cost is equal to c'. Equating $AC = c'$ and solving for q, we get

$$q = \frac{F}{(c' - c)} = \text{MES}.$$

It is natural to interpret changes in MES as changes in the value of F: An increase in F by a factor λ implies an increase in MES by the same factor λ. Equation 14.3 then gives the comparative statics of market structure with respect to MES (that is, F). If MES increases by a factor of 2, then the number of firms decreases by a factor of approximately $\sqrt{2}$. The intuition for this is exactly the inverse of an increase in market size by a factor of 2. In fact, if both market size and the MES increase by the same amount, then the equilibrium number of firms remains constant. For this reason, when comparing the structure of different industries, it is common to consider as an explanatory variable market size divided by MES, or MES divided by market size.

[b] In chapter 2, we defined MES as the lowest output level such that AC is minimized. The definition we consider here is slightly more general.

SCALE ECONOMIES AND CONCENTRATION

An alternative way of measuring increasing returns to scale is the coefficient of scale economies, defined as the ratio of average cost over marginal cost: $\rho \equiv AC/MC$. If this ratio is greater than one, that is, if average cost is greater than marginal cost, then we say that there are **economies of scale**; if the ratio is less than one, then we say there are **diseconomies of scale**. It can be shown that average cost is greater than marginal cost if and only if average cost is decreasing. Therefore, economies of scale or increasing returns to scale are the same thing.[c]

How does market structure depend on the degree of scale economies? As with minimum efficient scale, we would expect an industry to be more concentrated if the degree of scale economies is greater (or the MES higher). For the cost function considered above, $C = F + cq$, we have

$$\rho \equiv \frac{AC}{MC} = \frac{\frac{F}{q} + c}{c} = 1 + \frac{F}{cq}. \tag{14.4}$$

If we think of two industries that differ in the value of F, then the industry with the greatest degree of scale economies is more concentrated. In fact, from (14.4), the industry with greater F has the greater degree of scale economies; from (14.3), the industry with greater F has a smaller number of firms in the free-entry equilibrium.

> Concentration is greater the greater the minimum efficient scale (or the greater the degree of scale economies).

Both the minimum efficient scale and economies of scale are instances of **barriers to entry**. A generalization of the preceding point is, therefore, that concentration is greater the higher the barriers to entry are.

HISTORY MATTERS

The model presented at the beginning of this section makes a number of implicit assumptions regarding the entry process. It assumes that (1) all firms have access to the same unique available technology (corresponding to the cost function $C = F + cq$); (2) firms have perfect information regarding the market (in particular, they all know the demand function); and (3) the entry process itself is well coordinated; in particular, we assume that firms make their entry decisions sequentially, knowing what previous decisions earlier entrants have made.

Based on the preceding assumptions, we can exactly predict the equilibrium number of firms for given a set of parameter values that characterize the industry (i.e., the values of a, c, F, and other possible parameters in a more complex model). Notice, moreover, that the equilibrium predicted is symmetric, that is, all firms are of the same size.

[c] See exercise 14.6. See also the definition of economies of scale in chapter 2.

The evidence of most real-world industries fails to match the previous predictions. One can find examples of industries that seem to share the same set of parameters but exhibit very different market structures. Consider for example the prepared soups industry in the United States and in the United Kingdom. Although there is a difference in size between the two markets, they are very similar in terms of state of development, the composition of demand across categories (canned versus dried), and so forth. Campbell was the first entrant in the United States, having established operations in 1869. In the United Kingdom, Heinz established an initial lead in the 1930s. Although Campbell made an attempt at entering the U.K. market and Heinz the U.S. market, the current picture still is that Campbell dominates the U.S. market (63% share), while Heinz has a very small share (it mostly sells through retailers' own labels); Heinz dominates the U.K. market (41% share), while Campbell has a fairly small share (9%).[174]

One should also add that most industries include firms of different sizes. For example, the U.S. car industry is a triopoly with firms of different sizes.[d] A similar distribution of market shares is found in the European mineral water industry, which is also dominated by three firms of different sizes.

To close the gap between the predictions of the theoretical model and empirical observation, we must go beyond the assumptions listed previously. First, we must consider that often not all firms have access to the same technology. For some time, DuPont maintained a cost advantage over its rival producers of titanium dioxide. This occurred because DuPont held exclusive patent rights over a lower-cost production process. Even after those patents expired, DuPont maintained much of that advantage because of the fact that it moved down the **learning curve**; in other words, it transformed a **first-mover advantage** into a **sustainable competitive advantage**.

Even when all firms have access to the same technology, if there are several available technologies, then there may be several possible free-entry equilibria. For example, in the steel industry there are (roughly speaking) two different production processes, one with a high MES (regular mills) and one with a low MES (mini-mills). In terms of the notation of the model above, regular mills have a high F and a low c, whereas mini-mills have a low F and a high c. Unless one of the technologies clearly dominates the other one (lower F and lower c), one can find different combinations of n_1 regular mills and n_2 mini-mills that would constitute a free-entry equilibrium.[e] In the United States around 1990, operating profit per ton was approximately the same for mini-mills and major mills. This suggests that none of the technologies dominates the other one, so that the earlier assumption is satisfied.[f]

Imperfect information about market conditions may also influence market structure in ways not considered in the preceding model. For example, several oil companies built large refineries in the early 1970s. After the 1973 oil shock and subsequent demand cuts, there was excess capacity in the oil refining industry, that is, the value of n was greater than the value given by (14.3); in other words, capacity was greater that it would be if firms had known in advance about the oil shock.

Finally, in addition to forecasting mistakes, market structure may be influenced by coordination mistakes. Consider the case of commercial aircraft. In the late 1960s,

[d] A **triopoly** is a market with three firms.

[e] This possibility is illustrated in exercise 14.7.

[f] It is expected that rising labor costs will increase the comparative advantage of mini-mills, which are less labor intensive. In 1990, the market share of mini-mills in the United States was 26.5%. Estimates for year 2000 point to a value close to 40%.[175]

Lockheed and McDonnell Douglas were considering whether to enter the market for a wide-body aircraft. Because Boeing had just entered with the B747, there was room for only one more firm ($\hat{n} = 2$, according to equation 14.3), and both Lockheed and McDonnell Douglas knew it. The question was, therefore, which of the two should enter. After a long "waiting game" played between the two, both ended up entering the market, only to make huge losses from which they never recovered. In other words, the actual value of n was greater than the "equilibrium" value predicted by (14.3); an entry "mistake" led to too many firms in the market. Conversely, the current "waiting game" played between Boeing and Airbus on the superjumbo market has led (so far) to no entry by either firm, even though both seem to agree that there is enough room for one entrant. In this case, the "mistake" is too little entry with respect to the equilibrium level predicted by (14.3). (Recent events suggest that *both* firms may enter the market in the near future.)

In summary:

> The particular historical details of the evolution of an industry may in some cases determine the long-run market structure in ways that go beyond simple technology determinants.

In chapter 17, we will consider additional examples in which history has an important role in the determination of market structure.

14.2 ENDOGENOUS VERSUS EXOGENOUS ENTRY COSTS

The structure of the beer industry in Portugal is not very different from that in the United States: In Portugal, aside from some small firms, there are two firms that approximately share the market (Centralcer, Unicer). In the United States, the industry is dominated by three firms (Anhauser Bush, Miller, and Coors), one relatively large, one medium in size, and one relatively small.

Considering that the United States economy is 30 to 50 times bigger than the Portuguese economy, and based on the model presented in the previous section, one would expect a much greater difference in the equilibrium number of firms. Specifically, one would expect the number of firms in the United States to be $\sqrt{30}$ to $\sqrt{50}$ times bigger than in Portugal.

Why is the number of firms in the United States three, and not 10 or 15, as the model in the previous section would suggest? One important aspect of the beer industry that the model did not consider is *advertising*. Advertising expenditures are a large fraction of sales, both in the United States and in Portugal. In fact, the value of advertising *as a percentage of sales* is not very different between the two countries. But because the volume of sales is much higher in the United States than in Portugal, so is the volume of advertising. To enter the United States beer industry and compete with the likes of Budweiser and Miller Lite, a new entrant would need to pay a much greater entry cost than an entrant into the Portuguese beer industry. In other words, when advertising is an important part of a firm's strategy, *entry costs are endogenous*, specifically, endogenous with respect to market size.

The comparative statics of industries with **endogenous entry costs** are somewhat different from the model in the previous section. The idea of the model in the previous section is that, because of price competition, as market size increases by a factor of two, there will be room for less than twice as many firms. (In the specific case of Cournot competition, the number of firms can only increase by the square root of two as market size doubles.) If entry costs are increasing in market size, then we have an *additional* reason why the number of firms does not increase as much as market size. A bigger market induces firms to make bigger investments. Because these investments are costly, the net pie in terms of industry profits grows by less than market size. As a result, even if competition were not to increase (as in the previous section), the number of firms would increase by less than market size.

Let us consider an example that, though somewhat simplistic and extreme, serves to illustrate this point. A given country decides to deregulate its telecommunications sector. The main source of revenues in this industry is (by assumption) wireless telephony, for which a new technology has recently been developed. The government plans to allocate one license only for the right to develop this new technology, the revenues of which are estimated at S. One of the conditions for obtaining the license is that the candidate be already established as a telecommunications company; to do so, companies must pay an entry cost, F.

We will consider two different forms of allocating the license. First, assume that the winner of the license is decided by means of a lottery. (In the United States and in several countries, this method was used until recently.) If there are n potential grantees, then each gets the license in a lottery with probability $1/n$. Knowing this beforehand, each potential entrant expects a revenue of S/n (that is, S with probability $1/n$). By analogy with the previous section, the equilibrium number of entrants is given by the zero-profit condition, $\pi = S/n - F = 0$. We thus get

$$\hat{n} = \left[\frac{S}{F} \right].$$

The number of firms is proportional to market size, S. This is consistent with the result in the previous section: If there is no price competition, as we are now assuming, then twice as large a market implies twice as large a number of firms.

Consider now a different method of allocating the license: an auction. Since the late 1980s, different variations of this method have been implemented in different countries, beginning with New Zealand and including Australia, the United States, and several European and South American countries. Suppose that, upon paying the fixed cost F, each firm must bid for the right to exploit the license. Bids are submitted simultaneously, and the highest bid gets the license (and pays the proposed bid).

If there is more than one entrant, then the bidding game played between firms is similar to Bertrand competition; only now it's the highest bid, not the lowest price, that wins. Under Bertrand competition, the equilibrium is given by all firms setting prices at the level of marginal cost. By analogy, the equilibrium of the bidding game is for all firms to submit a bid equal to the value of the license, S. (If all firms were to bid less then S, then it would pay for a firm to bid just a little higher.) If there is only one entrant, then it will bid zero (or whatever the minimum bid is), and receive the license with probability one.

Just as under Bertrand competition the equilibrium profit is zero, each firm's expected payoff in the bidding game is also zero (gross of entry cost): If a firm loses the bidding, then its payoff is clearly zero; if a firm wins the license, then its payoff is S, the value of the license, minus S, the bid that it has to pay—zero payoff again. Naturally, if there is only one contender for the license, then expected payoff is S minus the value of the minimum bid admissible.

Predicting the previous outcome beforehand, no firm would be willing to enter if it expected that there would be another entrant, *regardless of market size*. In other words, the equilibrium of the entry game is for one firm only to enter, regardless of the value of S. If only one firm enters, then it will not have to bid all the way up to S to win the license, and a positive net profit will result from entry.

The reason for the result that $\hat{n} = 1$, for any value of S, is the following: Although the value of winning the license increases as S increases, so do the bids submitted by firms increase in the same amount. It follows that the value of being in the market (when $n > 1$) does not change as S increases: It is always zero.

This is in stark contrast with the case considered before (lottery allocation), wherein the number of firms was proportional to market size. The difference between the two cases lies in the assumption regarding the way the license is allocated. If a lottery is used, then the only entry cost is F, an exogenous cost. Because there is no price competition, we get the law of proportional change (of number of firms with respect to market size). If the license is auctioned, however, then total "entry" costs are given by $F + B$, where B is the bid for the license, an endogenous entry cost. The fact that B increases proportionately with S implies that the number of firms remains constant.

As mentioned earlier, this is an extreme example, in which going from exogenous to endogenous entry costs takes us from proportional change (of number of firms with respect to market size) to no change at all. In general:

> If entry costs are endogenous, then the number of firms is less sensitive to changes in market size.

Exercise 14.11 presents an example where this is the case.

Finally, we should mention that there can be various sources of endogenous entry costs. In this section, we have considered two: advertising and bidding for a government license. However, any situation in which firms engage in an "escalation war" for grabbing a share of the market (or the entire market) is likely to involve some degree of entry cost endogeneity. Another important instance of endogenous entry costs is given by research and development expenditures. For example, if firms race to be the first to patent a new medical drug that will give them a monopoly over a certain therapeutical market, then it is likely that much of the increase in the value of the market will be competed away in the patent race, so that the number of entrants does not change that much. Examples of this sort, also in the context of standardization battles, will be considered in chapters 16 and 17.

EMPIRICAL EVIDENCE

The hypothesis implied by the preceding analysis is that, when endogenous entry costs are important, the relation between market size and industry concentration should be flatter than when entry costs are exogenous. By the same token, the relation between concentration (e.g., C4) and market size should be flatter when entry costs are endogenous. (Under symmetry, C4=4/n; if n varies less with market size, so does C4.)

The ideal method for testing this hypothesis is to obtain data for a given industry in different, separated markets (e.g., different countries). However, this creates the difficulty of obtaining data for sufficiently many different separated markets. An alternative strategy is to collect data for a few markets and a few industries with similar degree of entry cost endogeneity. The problem with this alternative approach is that it implies putting apples and oranges in the same bag. However, if we believe that the main difference between industries is in the degree of scale economies (or the size of MES), then we can adjust the data and consider size divided by MES (for example) as an explanatory variable. As we saw in the preceding models, the equilibrium number of firms is a function of the ratio between S and F, which suggests that using adjusted market size when comparing different industries may be a reasonable strategy.

Table 14.1 presents data for a series of twenty industries and six countries. Based on the values of the advertising/sales ratio, we can classify the different industries into "homogeneous-product" and "advertising-intensive" industries. We can then plot the values of size/MES and concentration as in figures 14.3 and 14.4, for homogeneous-product and advertising-intensive industries, respectively. The hypothesis put forward earlier implies that the relation between concentration and size is flatter in the latter case, that is, when entry costs are endogenous. Roughly speaking, the data seem to agree with this prediction.

Notice, however, that we have presented fairly specific models of entry and competition (Cournot, license auction, etc.). The precise relation between market size and market structure will depend on the precise nature of entry and market competition. It is, therefore, not surprising that we cannot find a very precise pattern in figure 14.3. What can be shown, however, is that the lower bound of a scatter diagram with concentration

TABLE 14.1 **ADVERTISING/RETAIL SALES RATIOS FOR A SELECTION OF INDUSTRIES AND COUNTRIES (FRANCE, GERMANY, ITALY, JAPAN, UNITED KINGDOM, UNITED STATES).**[176]

High-Advertising Industries	A/RS (%)	Low-Advertising Industries	A/RS (%)
Frozen food	1.2–7.1	Salt	0.26–0.45
Soup	2.7–6.0	Sugar	0.06–0.24
Margarine	2.3–10.2	Flour	0.17–0.96
Soft drinks	1.2–5.4	Bread	0.02–0.42
RTE cereals	8.34–12.9	Processed meat	0.30–0.70
Mineral water	1.5–5.0	Canned vegetables	0.29–0.71
Sugar confectionery	1.4–6.0		
Chocolate confectionery	2.9–6.5		
R&G coffee	1.9–16.7		
Instant coffee	2.2–11.1		
Biscuits	1.9–8.0		
Pet foods	4.0–8.4		
Baby foods	0.9–4.2		
Beer	1.0–5.43		

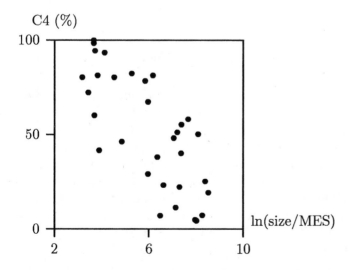

FIGURE 14.3 **INDUSTRY SIZE AND INDUSTRY CONCENTRATION, I: HOMOGENEOUS-GOOD INDUSTRIES.**

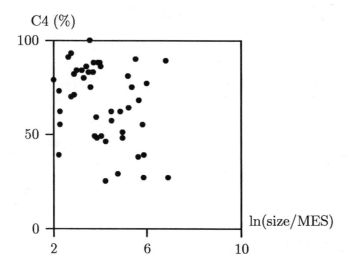

FIGURE 14.4 INDUSTRY SIZE AND INDUSTRY CONCENTRATION, I: ADVERTISING-INTENSIVE INDUSTRIES.

and size/MES in the axes is flatter when entry costs are endogenous. In this sense, the empirical evidence is quite striking: The lower bound of the plot in figure 14.4 is close to a horizontal line, whereas the lower bound of the plot in figure 14.3 is a downward-sloping line.[177]

14.3 FREE ENTRY AND SOCIAL WELFARE[178]

The model of perfect competition shows that, if there is free entry and if a number of other conditions are satisfied, then the equilibrium is socially efficient. If all of the other conditions are satisfied, then absence of free entry (e.g., barriers to entry) implies inefficiency. However, if the other conditions of the perfect competition model fail (e.g., price-taking behavior), then it is no longer necessarily the case that free entry is desirable from the perspective of economic efficiency. This point is illustrated in figure 14.5, which depicts an industry where all firms have constant marginal cost c and demand is given by $D(p)$. Suppose first that there are n active firms, each producing an output of q_n. Total output is therefore given by nq_n, whereas price is given by $p_n = D(nq_n)$. Suppose now that an extra firm enters the industry. The output produced by each firm is now q_{n+1}, so that total output is given by $(n + 1)q_{n+1}$ and price by p_{n+1}. The change in gross surplus (not including entry costs) is given by the difference between areas $[ACDG]$ and $[ABEG]$, that is, a gain given by areas $[BCI]$ plus $[CDEI]$. The gross profit earned by the new entrant is given by $(p_{n+1} - c)q_{n+1} = (p_{n+1} - c)\left((n + 1)q_{n+1} - nq_{n+1}\right) = [CDFH]$.

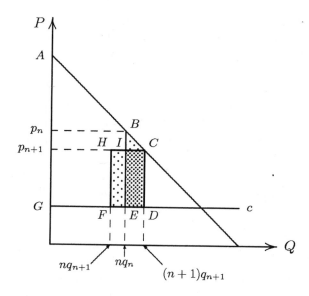

FIGURE 14.5 FREE ENTRY AND WELFARE.

The way the figure is drawn, the increase in gross surplus (area [BCI] plus [CDEI]) is smaller than the gross profit earned by the latest entrant (area [CDFH]). This implies an important potential divergence between the private and the social incentives for the entry of the $n + 1$ firm. Suppose that the entry cost, k, is such that $[BCI] + [CDEI] < k < [CDFH]$. Then entry is profitable from a private perspective (positive net profits) but not from a social perspective (the increase in gross surplus does not compensate for the entry cost). In this circumstance, *free entry would result in excessive entry*.

What is the reason for this divergence between private and social incentives for entry? The key is that part of the profits earned by the entrant are "stolen" from the incumbent firms. The area $[IEFH] = (q_n - q_{n+1})(p_{n+1} - c)$ measures (approximately) this **business stealing effect**, a transfer between firms that does not correspond to a benefit to society (although, obviously, it benefits the entrant).

Retail banking is one example where the above argument might be applied. In some European countries, because of regulation or lack of competition, margins are very high. Moreover, given the relative homogeneity of banking services and the low elasticity of demand, it is likely that the business-stealing effect is significant. For this reason, one would expect the equilibrium number of banks and bank branches to be excessive, from a social point of view. In Portugal, in the late 1980s and for a time, banks were required to pay a fee to open a new branch. Although there were different political motives underlying this measure, one possible defense in terms of economic efficiency is precisely the entry externality described previously.

PRODUCT DIFFERENTIATION, FREE ENTRY, AND EFFICIENCY

The result of excessive entry is subject to an important qualification, however. If there is product differentiation, then entry implies, in addition to a decrease in price, an increase in product variety. The entrant is normally unable to capture all of the additional willingness to pay generated by the new product. That is to say, there is a positive externality from entrant to consumers. For example, if a new car firm enters the industry with an innovative car design, many consumers will be willing to pay more for the new car than it will be priced. In other words, some of the benefits from the new car design are not captured by its designer.

The analysis of the general problem, taking product differentiation explicitly into account, is rather complex. The conclusion, however, is rather simple and intuitive:

> If product differentiation is very important, or if competition is very fierce, then free entry implies insufficient entry from a social point of view. If, conversely, product differentiation is unimportant and competition is soft, then the business-stealing effect dominates, whereby the free-entry equilibrium entails excessive entry.

FIRM HETEROGENEITY, FREE ENTRY, AND EFFICIENCY

Another qualification of the excessive entry result is that it assumes all firms are equally efficient. Empirical evidence shows that this is not a realistic assumption (see chapter 6). Moreover, empirical evidence shows that there is a significant turnover of firms in most industries: Firms that are relatively more efficient today may cease to be so in a few years' time. In this context, a *dynamic* analysis of free entry should take into account the benefits from entry in terms of increased average productivity, that is, the replacement of inefficient incumbent firms by efficient new entrants.[179] For example, average productivity in the United States telecom equipment industry increased dramatically since the industry underwent a period of deregulation. Careful accounting and econometric estimation show that most of the productivity gain was due simply to the reallocation of output between less efficient and more efficient firms (in particular, exiters and entrants). Box 14.1 explores this example in greater detail.

Box 14.1 Deregulation and Productivity in the Telecommunications Equipment Industry[180]

"Beginning in the early 1970s, the [United States] telecommunications industry entered into a period of rapid change. There were significant technological developments in telecommunications equipment and a gradual liberalization of the regulatory environment governing the provision of telecommunications services. . . .

"The conditions restricting entry were [significantly] eroded in 1975 when the FCC [Federal Communications Commission] established a registration and certification program to allow for the connection of private subscriber equipment to the network. . . . [A second important event was] the 1982 Consent Decree, . . . implemented in January 1984, [which] called for the divestiture of AT&T's regional operating companies." The decree implied that the divested regional companies were no longer "forced" to purchase equipment from AT&T's subsidiary, Western Electric, thus creating an extra factor favoring entry.

From 1963 to 1987, the number of firms increased from 104 to 481. In addition to a rapid increase in the total number of firms, there was a considerable turnover, with both high entry rates and high exit rates. For example, almost 90% of the firms active in 1987 entered after 1972. This turnover contributed to a reallocation of capacity and output between more efficient and less efficient firms. To measure how efficiently capacity is distributed among firms, we can compute the correlation between capital and productivity. A high correlation means that firms with higher levels of capital are more productive. For a given set of firms, this implies higher industry efficiency. A low (or negative) correlation means that firms with higher levels of capital are less efficient, which leads to a lower industry efficiency.

The following graph shows that, except for the period from 1981 to 1984, the correlation between productivity and capital, measured at the plant level, increased. This is consistent with the interpretation that entry and exit allowed for a more efficient allocation of capital among firms. To confirm this interpretation, it can be shown that the probability of a firm exiting is negatively correlated with its productivity. Because deregulation increased the probability of exit, it follows that deregulation increased the exit rate of low-productivity firms.

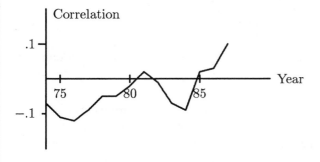

SUMMARY

- Because of increased price competition, the equilibrium number of active firms varies less than proportionately with respect to market size.

- Concentration is greater the higher the barriers to entry (greater minimum efficient scale or scale economies).

- The particular historical details of the evolution of an industry may in some cases determine the long-run market structure in ways that go beyond simple technology determinants.

- If entry costs are endogenous, then the number of firms is less sensitive to changes in market size.

- If product differentiation is very important, or if competition is very fierce, then free entry implies insufficient entry from a social point of view. If, conversely, product differentiation is unimportant and competition is soft, then the business-stealing effect dominates, whereby the free-entry equilibrium entails excessive entry.

KEY CONCEPTS

- free-entry equilibrium
- barriers to entry
- endogenous entry costs
- business stealing

REVIEW AND PRACTICE EXERCISES

14.1   Explain in words why the number of firms in a free-entry equilibrium may be less than proportional to market size.

14.2*   Suppose that two countries, initially in autarchy, decide to create a single market (i.e., a free trade agreement). For simplicity, assume that, in both economies, there is only one product. Demand for this product is given by $D_i = S_i(a - p_i)$, $(i = 1, 2)$, where S_i is a measure of country i's size. Upon the creation of a single market, total demand is given by the horizontal sum of the two initial demands.

Assuming there is free entry and that firms compete *à la* Cournot, determine the equilibrium number of firms both in autarchy and after the completion of the single market. Interpret the results.

14.3* The number of imported automobiles in California is four times higher than that in Montana, in per capita terms. The population of California is mainly urban, whereas the population of Montana is mainly rural. How do demographic differences and the model presented in section 14.1 explain the differences in consumption patterns?[181]

14.4* Retail in Switzerland is mostly dominated by highly profitable cartels. The Swiss authorities anticipate the gradual collapse of these cartels as the country becomes better integrated with the rest of Europe. The Organization for Economic Cooperation and Development, by contrast, holds a more skeptical view, claiming that the collapse of cartels does not necessarily lead to more competitive markets; rather, it adds, cartel breakdowns are frequently associated with an increase in concentration. Which prediction seems more reasonable? Are the two views inconsistent?

14.5 "Barriers to entry may be welfare improving." What particular industry characteristics might make this statement valid?

EXTENSION EXERCISES

14.6** Show that the coefficient of scale economies, AC/MC, is greater than one if and only if average cost is decreasing.

14.7*** Consider the model presented in section 14.1. Suppose that firms can choose one of two possible technologies, with cost functions $C_i = F_i + c_i q$.

a. Derive the conditions for a free-entry equilibrium.

b. Show, by means of a numerical example, that there can be more than one equilibrium, with different numbers of large and small firms.

14.8* Consider the monopolistic competition model, presented in chapter 5. According to this model, what is the relation between the degree of product differentiation and market structure?

14.9** T. Bresnahan and P. Reiss collected data for small, geographically isolated U.S. towns, on population as well as on the number of doctors, dentists, plumbers, and so forth, in each town. Based on these data, they estimated that the minimum town size that justifies the entry of a second doctor is approximately 3.96 times the required size for the first doctor to enter. For plumbers, the number is 2.12. How can these numbers be interpreted?

14.10** Derive equation (14.1).

14.11*** Consider the following model of entry into an advertising-intensive industry. To simplify the analysis, and to concentrate on the effects of advertising, suppose that there is no price competition. Specifically, the value of the market, in total sales, is given by S. (One can think of a demand curve $D(p)$ and an exogenously given price, whereby $S = pD(p)$.) S is therefore a measure of market size.

Each firm must decide whether or not to enter the industry. Entry cost is given by F. If a firm decides to enter, then it must also choose how much to invest in advertising; let a_i be the amount chosen by firm i. Finally, firm i's market share, s_i, is assumed to be equal to its share of the industry total advertising effort:

$$s_i = \frac{a_i}{\sum_{j=1}^n aj} = \frac{a_i}{A},$$

where n is the number of firms in the industry and $A \equiv \sum_{j=1}^n aj$ is total industry advertising.

a. Show that each firm i's optimal level of advertising solves

$$\frac{A - a_i}{A^2} S - 1 = 0.$$

b. Show that, in a symmetric equilibrium,

$$a = \frac{n - 1}{n^2} S.$$

where a is each firm's level of advertising.

c. Show that equilibrium profit is given by

$$\pi = \frac{S}{n^2}.$$

d. Show that the equilibrium number of entrants is given by

$$\hat{n} = \left[\sqrt{\frac{S}{F}} \right],$$

where $[x]$ means the highest integer lower than x.

e. Interpret this result in light of the previous discussion on the effects of endogenous entry costs.

STRATEGIC BEHAVIOR, ENTRY AND EXIT

EasyJet is one of the European success stories of the 1990s. Following (to a great extent) the example of Southwest Airlines, easyJet started operating low-cost, no-frills air service between different European cities, using London–Lutton as its main hub. Soon after entering the London–Amsterdam segment, KLM, which held 40% of the market, responded by matching easyJet's low fares. For KLM, this amounted most certainly to pricing below cost, and it implied serious losses for easyJet on that particular route. Although easyJet has survived this first response by an incumbent firm, it seems plausible that KLM's tactics were directed at inducing easyJet to exit the market.

This is by no means the only threat that small starting airlines must beware of. In early 1998, British Airways (BA) launched its own discount fare airline, *Go*. Although BA's move may be interpreted as taking advantage of a business opportunity (growth in demand for low-fare flights), an alternative interpretation is that Go's main goal is to "eliminate" as much as possible the competition that BA suffers from the small, low-fare airlines.[182]

In both of the preceding examples, we see that entry and exit decisions are determined by more than what the simple analysis of the previous chapter suggests. Specifically, in chapter 14 we ignored the possibility of strategic behavior at the entry stage. When making their entry decisions, firms anticipate the product market competition they will encounter if they decide to enter. But the entry decision itself (as well as the exit decision) is made in a nonstrategic way: Firms simply compare expected benefits from entering the market with the cost of entering into that market. That is, they perform a simple viability study.

In industries with a small number of players, however, entrants must take into account directed retaliation by incumbent firms. Likewise, incumbent firms should play more than the passive role of waiting for potential entrants to decide whether or not to enter the market. In this chapter, we examine situations in which entry and exit result from strategic behavior by both incumbent and entrant firms. We first consider what preemptive strategies an incumbent firm can deploy to deter entry by potential rivals. Among the possible **entry deterrence** strategies, we will consider capacity expansion, product proliferation, and long-term contracts. Second, we look at possible incumbent strategies to induce the exit of firms that have already entered, in particular, the strategy of selling at very low prices (possibly below cost). Finally, we look at mergers and acquisitions from a strategic point of view, including the strategy of entry by acquisition.

15.1 ENTRY DETERRENCE

In the early seventies, DuPont drastically increased its capacity for the production of titanium dioxide as an attempt to deter capacity expansion and/or entry by rival firms (box 15.1). Can this be an optimal strategy? In this section, we consider a simple model that addresses this question.

Consider an industry with one active firm, Firm 1, and one possible entrant, Firm 2. Firm 2 must decide whether or not to enter and, in case it enters, how much to produce. (For simplicity, we will assume throughout this section that capacity levels and output levels are identical.) Before Firm 2 makes its decisions, however, Firm 1 gets to choose its own output level. Specifically, we assume that *Firm 2 observes Firm 1's output level before deciding whether to enter and how much to produce.* Once both output levels have been chosen, price is determined as a function of total output, as in the Cournot model.

Figure 15.1 depicts three profit curves: π_1^M is Firm 1's profit in case it is a monopolist; π_1^S is Firm 1's profit in case Firm 2 enters the market. Notice that π_1^S, as depicted in the figure, is a function of q_1 only. That is, the function already assumes that Firm 2 chooses its optimal output as a function of Firm 1's initial output. In other words, π_1^S

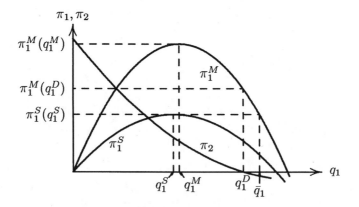

FIGURE 15.1 QUANTITY PRECOMMITMENT AND ENTRY DETERRENCE.

BOX 15.1   DUPONT AND THE TITANIUM DIOXIDE INDUSTRY[183]

Titanium dioxide (TiO_2) is a white chemical pigment employed in the manufacture of paint, paper, and other products to make them whiter or opaque. The primary raw material for the production of TiO_2 is either ilmenite ore or rutile ore. By 1970, there were seven firms in the industry: a large firm, DuPont, and six smaller ones. During the 1960s, DuPont used mainly ilmenite, whereas its rivals used mainly rutile. In 1970, a sharp increase in the price of rutile ore created a significant cost advantage for DuPont with respect to its rivals: At 1968 ore prices, Dupont had a cost advantage of 22%; at 1972 prices, this advantage averaged 44%. Moreover, stricter environmental regulation meant that several of DuPont's competitors would have to incur large costs to continue production. DuPont found itself with a competitive advantage in several dimensions. First, its production process used a cheaper input than most of its rivals. Second, its production process complied better with environmental standards. Third, because of the cost advantage, the firm was in better financial shape; thus it was better positioned to expand capacity.

A task force was formed at DuPont to study how to turn these advantages to the firm's greater benefit. The result was the strategy of expanding capacity at a pace sufficient to satisfy all of the growth in demand in the ensuing years. The idea was that *by expanding rapidly, DuPont would discourage expansion (or entry) by rival firms.* It was the task force's conviction that deterrence of competitive expansion was necessary if DuPont was to establish a dominant position: According to the plan, DuPont's market share would increase from 30% in 1972 to 56% in 1980, and perhaps 65% in 1985.

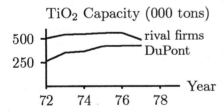

DuPont never reached the 65% target, but a market share between 55% and 60% has been maintained since the late 1970s. By 1978, market share was already close to 50%, as the preceding figure shows. By 1985, five of the firms competing with DuPont in the domestic market had exited: three by acquisition, one by complete cessation of operations, and one by shutting down its U.S. plants. These facts seem roughly consistent with DuPont's prediction when formulating the growth strategy that would materialize its "first-mover" advantage.

is the profit level that Firm 1 *expects* to earn in case Firm 2 enters and acts rationally. Finally, π_2 is Firm 2's maximum profit given what output level Firm 1 chooses initially. The value π_2 is net of entry costs.

If Firm 1 were sure it would be a monopolist, it should set output at q_1^M, earning monopoly profits $\pi_1^M(q_1^M)$. If, instead, Firm 1 were sure Firm 2 would enter, then it should set output at q_1^S, the value that maximizes $\pi_1^S(q_1)$.

Suppose that Firm 1 sets monopoly output. The problem with this strategy is that Firm 2's profits from entry are positive: $\pi_2(q_1^M) > 0$. Firm 1 should, therefore, expect that setting $q_1 = q_1^M$ induces Firm 2 to enter. But then, Firm 1's profit would be given by $\pi_1^S(q_1^M)$, a much lower value than monopoly profits. Suppose, however, that Firm 1 sets an output level greater than monopoly output. In particular, suppose that $q_1 \geq q_1^D$. For such high output levels, Firm 2's profit upon entry would be negative. If Firm 2 is rational, then an output level $q_1 \geq q_1^D$ achieves the goal of **entry deterrence**. Because Firm 1's maximum profits in case it allows Firm 2 to enter (entry accommodation) are given by $\pi_1^S(q_1^S)$, entry deterrence is optimal if and only if $\pi_1^M(q_1^D) > \pi_1^S(q_1^S)$, as is the case in figure 15.1 when $q_1 < \bar{q}_1$.

In summary, by setting an output greater than monopoly output ($q_1^D > q_1^M$), Firm 1 sacrifices profits by the amount $\pi_1^M(q_1^M) - \pi_1^M(q_1^D)$. However, if $q_1 < \bar{q}_1$, then this loss is lower than what Firm 1 would lose if it were to let Firm 2 enter, $\pi_1^M(q_1^M) - \pi_1^S(q_1^S)$.

ENTRY ACCOMMODATION AND BLOCKADED ENTRY

Firm 1's optimal strategy is not necessarily to deter Firm 2's entry. In fact, if the entry cost were very low, then it would be optimal for Firm 1 to allow entry. When the entry cost is very low, Firm 2 will enter unless Firm 1's output is very high (in which case Firm 2's prospective profit would be very low, even lower than entry cost). This situation is depicted in figure 15.2. By comparison with figure 15.1, the value of q_1^D, the minimum output by Firm 1 necessary to deter entry, is much larger. Consequently, the profit associated with the strategy $q_1 = q_1^D$ is much lower. In fact, the profit from entry deterrence, $\pi_1^M(q_1^D)$, is now lower than the profit from letting Firm 2 enter, $\pi_1^S(q_1^S)$. In words, Firm 1's optimal strategy is one of **entry accommodation**.

In the opposite situation, if entry cost is very large, then Firm 1 should ignore the threat of entry and choose monopoly output. This situation is depicted in figure 15.3. As the figure shows, even if Firm 1 were to set monopoly output, Firm 2 would find it optimal not to enter. In other words, because entry costs are very high, the threat of Firm 2's entry is not relevant. This situation is known as **blockaded entry**. To summarize:

> If entry costs are very high, then the incumbent should set monopoly capacity and ignore the threat of entry. If entry costs are very low, then the incumbent should choose capacity, taking into account the entrant's reaction curve. Finally, if entry costs are intermediate, then the incumbent should choose capacity large enough to induce the entrant not to enter.

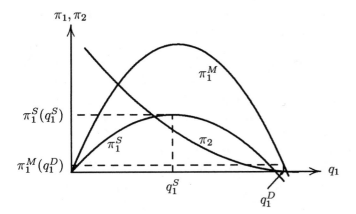

FIGURE 15.2 ENTRY ACCOMMODATION.

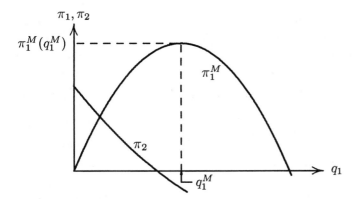

FIGURE 15.3 BLOCKADED ENTRY.

COMMITMENT, EX-ANTE OPTIMALITY, AND EX-POST OPTIMALITY[184]

Until now, we have been a bit vague about the exact nature of the incumbent's initial move. Does Firm 1 set the level of capacity, or does it set the output level instead? The distinction can be quite important. Suppose first that capacity costs are zero and that a firm may add capacity at any time. In that case, even though Firm 1 is in the market before Firm 2, Firm 1 will be able to revise its output decision even after Firm 2 enters the market (if it does). For all practical purposes, what Firm 1 is doing in the equilibrium in figure 15.1 is to announce its *intention* of producing output q_1^D in case Firm 2 enters. But then we may ask: Is this a *credible* announcement by Firm 1?

For the announcement to be credible, it must be optimal for Firm 1 to implement what it announces when the time comes for making the relevant decision. Suppose that

Firm 2, ignoring Firm 1's announcement, decides to enter and set output at the Cournot equilibrium level (as derived in chapter 7). Then Firm 1's best strategy would be to ignore its pre-announcement and choose the Cournot output as well. But the Cournot output level, q_1^N, is less than the monopoly output level, q_1^M, and a fortiori less than Firm 1's announced output level, q_1^D. Therefore, Firm 2 should reason that by entering and setting q_2 at the Cournot level, it will make positive profits net of entry costs; therefore it should enter. In other words, Firm 1's announcement that it will set output at the level q_1^D is not credible.

Now consider an alternative interpretation of the model. Before Firm 2 decides whether or not to enter, Firm 1 must choose production capacity. Capacity costs are very high and every investment in capacity is *sunk*. That is, even if Firm 1 later chooses an output lower than installed capacity, it still will not avoid the capacity cost it previously paid. Suppose, moreover, that output costs—other than capacity costs—are zero. In this context, Firm 1 has a much greater incentive to increase output than before. In fact, once capacity costs are paid, it is equally costless for Firm 1 to set any output level up to capacity. Although we would still need to look at the details of Firm 1's and Firm 2's reaction curves, an equilibrium like the one in figure 15.1 would now be possible, in fact, plausible. Notice that, in addition to the assumption that capacity costs are high, we need the assumption that they are sunk. If capacity costs were not sunk, then Firm 2 could again enter and set output at the level of Cournot; Firm 1's best reaction would be to sell capacity, recover the costs of investments previously made, and set the Cournot output level as well. We thus conclude:

Capacity preemption is a credible strategy only if capacity costs are high and sunk.

Let us return to the example of easyJet. The U.K. market for low-fare airlines comprised, as of December 1997, four main competitors: Ryanair, Virgin Express, Debonair, and easyJet. As of the third quarter of 1997, Ryanair owned 20 aircraft, Virgin Express 16, Debonair 6, and easyJet 5. According to announced expansion plans (and contracts signed with aircraft manufacturers), Ryanair will expand its fleet from 20 aircraft at the end of 1997 to 38 aircraft by the end of the year 2000. In the same period, easyJet will expand from 5 to 15. Will this deter expansion and/or entry by rival firms? (*Hint:* Does fleet expansion constitute a credible expansion strategy?)

ALTERNATIVE PREEMPTION STRATEGIES

The Italian telecommunications industry, like those of many European countries, is undergoing a process of gradual deregulation, namely entry deregulation. Telecom Italia, formerly a protected monopoly, now will have to account for possible competition from new entrants such as France Telecom. This situation seems similar to the one we considered before: an incumbent firm (the formerly protected monopolist) and a potential entrant (telecom operators from different countries).

As one looks more closely at this and related cases, however, one becomes aware of two important qualifications of the theoretical model of deterrence by capacity expansion. First, it is not only a matter of deterring versus accommodating entry. Telecom Italia is probably aware that it will be unable to avoid any type of entry at *any time* in the future. However, different strategic investments made now will likely influence the *time* at which entry will occur; different entry times will have different implications for Telecom Italia's profitability.

For example, suppose that Firm 2's maximum profits are given by $\pi_2^*(q_1, t)$. As before, the entrant's profits are a function of Firm 1's output. What is new in this formulation is that they also depend on time t. The idea is that there are different exogenous factors (technical progress, deregulation, demand expansion) that make entry more attractive as time passes (all other things being equal). That is, we assume that $\pi_2^*(q_1, t)$ is increasing in t. This implies that Firm 2 will enter at the time t_2^* when $\pi_2^*(q_1, t)$ is equal to the cost of entering the market.[a] In fact, at any time $t > t_2^*$, Firm 2 prefers being in the market to staying out. Firm 1's problem now is to choose q_1, taking into account that different values of q_1 imply different optimum entry times t_2^* for Firm 2, and consequently different profit streams for Firm 1 (monopoly profits until t_2^*, duopoly profits thereafter).

The second important difference in many real-world situations with respect to the simple model presented earlier is that incumbents have various available strategies other than capacity expansion. For example, in addition to increasing capacity, Telecom Italia probably will consider strategies such as investing in service quality, cost reduction, or brand recognition. In fact, the case of long-distance telecommunications in the United States provides a good example. Although capacity expansion has not taken AT&T very far in terms of deterring entry, its branding strategy has been fairly successful. Although the services offered by AT&T are of comparable quality to those of its rivals (MCI and Sprint, mainly), and rates are, if anything, higher for AT&T, the former monopolist still commands a very respectable market share, well in excess of 50%. Another example— discussed in greater detail in box 15.2—is that of France Telecom.

We next look at two specific important instances of an entry deterrence strategy different from capacity expansion: product proliferation and contracts.

PRODUCT PROLIFERATION[185]

The ready-to-eat breakfast cereal industry may be characterized by relatively low economies of scale and relatively low levels of technology. In other words, entry into this industry is easy, from a technological point of view. Between the 1950s and the 1970s, there was virtually no entry of new firms into the industry, even though all of the incumbent firms (Kellogg, General Mills, General Foods, and Quaker Oats) made significant profits. Finally, although the number of firms did not change, the number of brands sold by the incumbent firms increased from 25 to about 80 (and keeps increasing).

[a] If $\pi_2^*(q_1, t)$ is expressed as profit per period, then the entry cost should also be expressed in the equivalent per-period value.

BOX 15.2   FRANCE TELECOM[186]

France Telecom SA has lost only a mere 3% of its home market in the first year since the industry was open to competition (1998). This is in stark contrast with other ex-monopolies, such as Deutsche Telekom, which quickly lost about a third of its business following deregulation.

"France Telecom was probably the incumbent that did the best job at preparing for the arrival of competitors," says Philippe Germond, CEO of Cegetel, France Telecom's main rival. To begin with, the ex-monopolist made a significant effort to cut costs. From 1996 to 1998, the company shed 10% of its workforce. More than 20% changed jobs.

In parallel to the strategy of cost cutting came the strategy of price cutting. "Already in early 1997, they decreased prices by 40%." Later, when entry actually took place, France Telecom made an effort to protect its best customers, often matching the new entrants' lower prices. Altogether, France Telecom's strategy "really demotivated a lot of the competitors," concludes Germond. Bouygues Telecom, for example, dropped its plans to compete head-on with France Telecom with a fixed network, choosing to compete instead in the mobile market.

Why are profits so high and no entry is observed, even though entry seems relatively easy? Why did the number of brands increase so rapidly, while the number of firms remained constant?

Breakfast cereals are definitely not a homogeneous product. We will thus consider a simplified version of the Hotelling model (see chapter 12) to analyze this industry. Suppose for simplicity that cereals are defined by one single characteristic, say, sweetness: At one extreme, we would have something like corn flakes, at the opposite extreme Calvin's favorite chocolate-frosted sugar bombs (see *Calvin & Hobbes* cartoon strip). Finally, make the additional simplifying assumption that there is no price competition: $p_1 = p_2 = \bar{p}$, where p_1, p_2 is the price set by the first and the second firms, respectively.[b]

As in the previous section, we consider the case when there is an incumbent firm (Firm 1) that moves first and a potential entrant (Firm 2) that moves second. If Firm 1 can choose only one variety of cereal, then it will choose the location 1/2. This result was derived in chapter 12: If Firm 1 decides to locate to the right of 1/2, then Firm 2 locates immediately to the left of Firm 1; if Firm 1 locates to the left of 1/2, then Firm 2 locates immediately to the right of Firm 1. Whichever is the case, Firm 1 will receive a market share of less than 50%, whereas locating at 1/2 guarantees a 50% market share.

Let F be the cost of creating a new variety of cereal, and suppose that $F < \bar{p}/2$. Then Firm 2 will optimally decide to create a new cereal and enter the industry.[c] The

[b] Adding more characteristics or including price competition would lead to similar results, only the analysis would be more complicated.

[c] For simplicity, we assume that Firm 2 can create, at most, one variety of cereal. The results are qualitatively similar if we consider the possibility of multiple varieties.

new cereal will be located at 1/2 (or arbitrarily close to it); Firm 2 gets 50% of the market, and it receives net profits of $\bar{p}/2 - F$, the same as Firm 1.[d]

Suppose, however, that Firm 1 initially creates two varieties of breakfast cereal, one located at 1/4 and one located at 3/4. Wherever Firm 2 decides to locate, the maximum market share it can obtain is 1/4. For example, if Firm 2 locates at 1/2, it sells to all consumers whose preference is greater than 3/8 and lower than 5/8.[e] If the cost of creating a new variety is greater than $\bar{p}/4$, Firm 2 would receive negative profits, no matter what its location; it is better off staying out of the market. Firm 1, in turn, receives $\bar{p}$ times 1 (total revenues) minus $2F$ (total cost of developing two varieties of cereal) or a total of $\bar{p} - 2F$. If F is less than $\bar{p}/2$, then this is positive and greater than what Firm 1 would get from launching one variety only. In fact, profits under the two-variety strategy are $\bar{p} - 2F = 2(\bar{p}/2 - F)$, whereas profits under the one-variety strategy are only $\bar{p}/2 - F$.

The story told by this simple model seems consistent with the events in the ready-to-eat cereal industry—no entry of new firms but a large number of products launched by the incumbent. Notice that the number of varieties is greater than the incumbent would find optimal if there were no threat of entry (one variety would be optimal). Launching more varieties is only *optimal insofar as it deters entry*.

As in chapter 12, we note that the Hotelling model may be interpreted in two ways: as a model of product differentiation (e.g., breakfast cereals) or as a location model. Likewise, the strategy of product proliferation can be interpreted as a location strategy, for example, an incumbent bank opening multiple branches, or a fast-food chain opening multiple locations. In these cases, an entry deterrence strategy would imply a higher density of locations than the incumbent would find optimal, absent the threat of entry.

An example of this strategy is given by Staples, the leader in the office supplies superstore industry. Referring to Staples' investment strategy, the company's CEO states that

Staples was trying to build a critical mass of stores in the Northeast to shut out competitors. . . . By building these networks [of stores] in the big markets like New York and Boston, we have kept competitors out for a very, very long time.[187]

CONTRACTS AS A BARRIER TO ENTRY[188]

In 1985, Monsanto acquired the patent rights for aspartame, an artificial sweetener used in diet colas and other soft drinks. The patent for aspartame, which Monsanto was selling under the Nutrasweet brand name, was due to expire in 1992, thus opening the way for new entrants. In addition to other entry deterrence strategies, which are detailed in box 15.3, Monsanto anticipated patent expiry by signing long-term contracts with Coca-Cola and Pepsi-Cola. Why would the soft-drink manufacturers be interested in such contracts? Is it not better to let new entrants come in and benefit from competition between suppliers?

[d] We assume the total number of consumers is 1 (e.g., one thousand or one million).

[e] 3/8 is the midpoint between 1/4 and 1/2. A consumer located at 3/8 is indifferent between buying cereal variety 1/4 and cereal variety 1/2. The same reasoning applies to 5/8.

BOX 15.3   THE ASPARTAME MARKET[189]

Aspartame is a low-calorie, high-intensity sweetener. It was discovered (by accident) in 1965, by a research scientist at G. D. Searle & Co. who was working on an anti-ulcer drug. Use of aspartame in soft drinks was approved by the U.S. Food and Drug Administration (FDA) in 1983. Searle managed to extend the original patent to 1987 in Europe and 1992 in the United States.

In 1985, Monsanto acquired Searle—and the aspartame patent with it. The soft-drink version of aspartame is sold by Monsanto under the brand name *Nutrasweet*. The potential market for such a product is enormous, especially considering the sales volume of Diet Coke and Diet Pepsi. It is thus not surprising that, in 1986, Holland Sweetener Company (HSC), a joint venture between a Dutch and a Japanese company, began building an aspartame plant, in anticipation of Nutrasweet's patent expiry.

When HSC started selling its own version of aspartame (generic aspartame, as opposed to the branded Nutrasweet version), Monsanto dropped the price of Nutrasweet from $70, to $22–$30 per pound. This meant negative profits for HSC, but also an enormous drop in Nutrasweet's European revenues. Monsanto's reaction might seem a bit excessive, especially considering that HSC's capacity was only 5% of the world market. However, Europe is only a small fraction of the world market: The U.S. market alone is ten times the European one. One interpretation of Nutrasweet's strategy is that, by fighting entry into a small market, it may "convince" potential entrants not to attempt entering other larger markets where the same incumbent is present. Moreover, production of aspartame is subject to a steep learning curve (Monsanto managed to cut costs by 70% over a period of ten years). Nutrasweet's attack on HSC thus had the effect of slowing down HSC's move down the learning curve.

Probably as a consequence of Nutrasweet's strategy, HSC delayed its expansion plans and was not much of a competitor when the U.S. market finally opened. Monsanto, however, did not take chances: Just prior to the U.S. patent expiry, both Coke and Pepsi signed long-term contracts with Monsanto.

The analogy with monopoly pricing may help to answer this question. A profit-maximizing monopolist sets a price above marginal cost. A potential buyer with valuation lower than price but greater than marginal cost refrains from making a purchase even though it would be efficient to do so (for valuation is greater than cost). The reason for this inefficiency is that the seller cannot discriminate between buyers. By setting a price greater than marginal cost, the seller is able to extract some of the consumer's surplus—which it does at the cost of forgoing potentially profitable sales, namely, to buyers with valuation greater than cost but lower than price.

The analogy with entry deterrence is the following. By signing a contract, incumbent and buyer act, as it were, as a "monopolist" with respect to the potential entrant. The efficient solution would be for the entrant to enter if and only if its cost is lower than the incumbent's. But the incumbent/buyer "monopolist" knows that the potential entrant receives positive expected profits from entering. That is, it earns an "entry surplus." The incumbent and the buyer thus find it optimal to set an entry "price." This "price" is the fee that must be paid to the buyer for breach of the long-term contract signed with the supplier. When the entrant is very efficient, entry takes place in spite of the fee. When the entrant is more efficient than the incumbent but not much more efficient, the contract effectively deters entry. This intermediate level of entrant efficiency is analogous to the buyer whose valuation is greater than cost but lower than the price set by the monopolist.

15.2 PREDATION

If an incumbent monopolist cannot prevent entry, it can still try to gain monopoly power by inducing the exit of its rivals. Practices that have rivals' exit as the main goal are known as **predation**. Pricing below cost to injure rival firms and thus induce their exit, a practice known as **predatory pricing**, is a particularly important form of predation.

As discussed previously, the first difficulty encountered by easyJet upon entering the London–Amsterdam route was a price match by KLM, who at the time was carrying almost one half of the passengers between London and Amsterdam. Low price was the main selling point for easyJet. Having KLM (an established, well-known firm) match its fares was a big blow to easyJet's strategy. Eventually, a court case and a clever publicity campaign by easyJet's chairman, Stelio Haji-ioannou, put an end to KLM's aggressive strategy. But it is not unlikely that, the situation remaining the same for a longer period, easyJet would have found itself forced to avoid mounting losses by exiting the London-Amsterdam route.

WHAT IS PREDATORY PRICING?

There is one problem with the preceding interpretation of KLM's strategy. How can one be sure that its objective was to induce easyJet to exit the market? We have seen in previous chapters that adding more firms to a market implies a decrease in price. In fact, in a homogeneous-product market where firms do not collude, going from one to two competitors implies a price drop from monopoly price to marginal cost (see chapter 7). How can one be sure that KLM's price drop is not simply a shift from one equilibrium to another equilibrium (with exit not being at all intended)?

One possible answer is that, given its lighter structure, easyJet has lower costs than KLM. Moreover, easyJet's strategy is to charge low fares, which implies keeping low margins. For these reasons, it is likely that, by matching easyJet's price, KLM was making losses. And these losses can be justified only if KLM actually intended to drive easyJet out of the market (or, at least, increase the probability that it would exit). In particular, if KLM was pricing below cost (which is likely, but by no means clear), then the argument would gain some weight. Had KLM been sure that easyJet was going to stay in the market, it would probably not have incurred losses by pricing below cost. In summary, it is difficult to prove intent just by looking at price levels. It is very difficult to distinguish pro-competitive behavior (pricing close to cost, at a very low margin) from anti-competitive behavior (pricing below cost so that the rival exits, and price can then be brought back to a high level).

THE CHICAGO SCHOOL AND THE LONG-PURSE THEORIES OF PREDATORY PRICING

A more radical criticism of the predatory interpretation of KLM's strategy is that rational players should never exit when preyed upon; consequently, rational predators should never engage in predation. This view, associated with the Chicago school of thought, runs along the following lines. Suppose that there are two periods. In the first period, the incumbent must decide whether or not to set low prices. If it does, both incumbent and newly arrived prey make losses L in the first period. (The first period can be thought of as, say, the first year of the entrant's operation.) If the incumbent does not act aggressively, then both incumbent and entrant receive duopoly profits π^D. At the end of the first period, the entrant must decide whether or not to stay in the market. In the second period, if the entrant exits, then the incumbent receives monopoly profits π^M. Otherwise, the same situation as in the first period is repeated.

If the entrant decides to stay into the second period, then the incumbent's optimal strategy is clearly not to behave aggressively: The entrant's decision not to exit has already been made, and so, from the incumbent's perspective, it's a choice between positive profits π^D and negative profits $-L$. Let us now consider the first period. Suppose the incumbent acts aggressively. The entrant then will be making losses $-L$. Should it exit the industry? The answer is clearly "no." The incumbent's threat to keep prices low is not credible: If the entrant remains in the market, the incumbent eventually will find it optimal not to behave aggressively. So the entrant should not exit. Even if it does not have enough cash to sustain a loss of L, the entrant should borrow from a bank: Assuming that $\pi^D > L$, a bank should also see through the incumbent's incentives and conclude that staying in is a profitable strategy for the entrant; first-period losses are temporary. Finally, a rational incumbent that knows how a rational entrant behaves should avoid aggressive behavior in the first place: It does not induce any exit and costs a loss L in the first period, instead of a gain π^D.

The Chicago argument is, therefore, that no predatory behavior should be observed in practice. If an incumbent responds to entry by lowering its price, this is simply the competitive effect of a decrease in concentration—something to be welcomed, not feared.

The problem with this argument is that it relies too much on rationality and perfect information. Suppose that the entrant does not have enough cash to sustain losses in the first period. The only chance of survival in case the incumbent acts aggressively is for the entrant to borrow from a bank. According to the Chicago theory, a bank would always be willing to lend money, having seen through the equilibrium in the second period. Suppose now, perhaps more realistically, that the bank is not always willing to lend money. Specifically, the competing firms expect the bank to refuse a loan with probability ρ.

From the entrant's point of view, staying in the market while the incumbent is pricing low is a rational decision insofar as the initial loss, L, is less than what the entrant expects to gain in the future: π^D times the probability that the bank will give a loan, $1 - \rho$. That is, the entrant should be willing to stay in the market so long as $(1 - \rho)\pi^D > L$.

From the incumbent's perspective, aggressive behavior in the first period may also be an optimal strategy. By accommodating entry, the incumbent receives $\pi^D + \pi^D$, duopoly profits in each period. By behaving aggressively, the incumbent loses L in the first period; in the second period, with probability ρ, it will get π^M, for the entrant will have exited, not having obtained additional funds from the bank; and with probability $1 - \rho$ the entrant will remain active, in which case the incumbent will settle for π^D only. Simple calculations show that behaving aggressively in the first period is optimal for the incumbent if $\rho\pi^M > L + (1 + \rho)\pi^D$.

According to this alternative view, if the preceding conditions are satisfied, then (1) predation is observed in practice; (2) it is rational for the incumbent to be a predator and for the prey to resist aggressive behavior; and (3) ρ percent of the times, predation is successful in driving competition out of the market.

In this theory of predatory pricing, the important difference between firms is not so much that one is the incumbent and the other a recent entrant. What is important is that one firm is financially constrained, needing to apply for a bank loan, whereas the other is not. For this reason, the theory is known as the **long-purse** or **deep-pocket** theory of predatory pricing.[190]

OTHER EXPLANATIONS OF PREDATORY PRICING

There are at least three other explanations of why an incumbent might want to respond to entry by pricing aggressively. We now turn to these.

Low-Cost Signaling[191]

For KLM, for example, pricing low might be a way of sending easyJet the message that KLM's costs are low and that, consequently, there is no room for an additional firm to make money in the same market.

One example of this signaling theory of predation is given by the American Tobacco Company. Between 1891 and 1906, American Tobacco acquired 43 small competitors (mostly regional firms), thus establishing a quasi-monopoly. In most cases, before attempting to buy a rival, American Tobacco would engage in (allegedly) predatory pricing, effectively imposing losses on the target firm. It is estimated that the impact of these predatory actions was to lower the cost of buying rivals by up to 60%.[192] One interpretation of this number is that, by observing American Tobacco's low prices, a small regional firm would become convinced that American Tobacco's cost is low and thus the prospects of competing against it not very promising—thus the effect of settling for a lower price.

Another stylized fact derived from the analysis of the American Tobacco example is that the price paid for target firms acquired later was lower than the price paid for target firms acquired earlier by about 25% (everything else constant). This suggests that one of the effects of predation (and acquisition) is to create a reputation which in turn influences the outcome of future clashes between the large firm and small firms. To this alternative theory we turn next.

Reputation for Toughness[193]

By pricing aggressively, the incumbent may acquire a reputation for being "tough," so that in the future (or in other markets) no more entry will take place. The case of the aspartame industry, examined in detail in box 15.3, is a good example: Monsanto retaliated against Holland Sweetener's entry into the European market by lowering prices substantially. One interpretation of this strategy is that Monsanto wanted to make sure that no competitors entered the U.S. market, its most important territory, where the aspartame patent was due to expire later than in Europe.

Another example of the same explanation is given by British Airways (BA). In the 1970s, BA successfully (if at some cost) fought Laker Airways' entry into the transatlantic market.[f] In the 1980s, it took similar measures in response to entry by Virgin Atlantic, although with less successful results. In the 1990s, the "victims" have been the likes of easyJet and, again, Virgin. One possible result of this series of aggressive actions is that BA now has gained the reputation for being a tough competitor, thus discouraging future entry into its markets.[g]

Growing Markets[194]

A third explanation for predatory pricing applies to growing markets where long-term success requires a significant market share from early on. For example, in the market for operating systems, it is important to start with a good installed base of adopters, so that third-party application software developers have an incentive to write software running on the operating system; new users in turn will be attracted and a sort of snowball effect takes place. The snowball effect also works in the opposite way: Lacking a good starting installed base, an operating system may be doomed to failure.[h] In this context, predatory

[f] Laker Airways went out of business, but not before suing BA and several other airlines for conspiring to drive it out of the market. The case was eventually settled out of court.

[g] As Virgin's President Richard Branson once stated, "the safest way to become a millionaire is to start as a billionaire and invest in the airline industry." Perhaps this sentiment is a reflection of several years competing against British Airways.

A similar example in the context of the airline industry is given by the recent case of American Airlines' alleged predatory pricing against competitors in the Dallas/Forth Worth hub. See chapter 1.

[h] The dynamics of markets of this sort, that is, markets where installed base is an important determinant of long-term firm success, are examined in greater detail in chapter 17. Other examples in which initial market share is an important target are learning curves and consumer switching costs. The latter are considered in chapter 12.

pricing early on may be successful in that it prevents rivals from achieving the critical market share necessary to survive in the market.

An example of this type of predatory pricing is cable TV competition in Sacramento, California.[195] In 1983, Sacramento Cable Television (SCT) was awarded a first franchise. In 1987, a second franchise was given to Cable America. The latter started off by laying down a cable system across 700 homes, a small fraction of the market, but planning to expand to the entire Sacramento area. Cable America's initial offering was 36 channels for a monthly fee of $10, which compared favorably to SCT's $13.50 for 40 channels. However, SCT quickly responded by selectively cutting its rates in the area where Cable America had entered: The new offer consisted of three months of free service and then continued service at $5.75 a month. After seven months, Cable America threw in the towel, unable to create a critical mass of subscribers that would justify further investment in programming and laying down additional cables.

To summarize:

> Predatory pricing may be a successful strategy when (1) the prey is financially constrained, (2) low prices signal low costs or the predator's "toughness," and (3) capturing a minimum market share early on is crucial for long-term survival. In all these cases, low pricing by the predator induces the prey to exit the market.

NONPRICING PREDATORY STRATEGIES

So far, we have talked about predatory strategies in the form of price cuts. However, predatory pricing is not the only form of predation. One of the best examples for the theory presented last in the previous subsection is Microsoft's MS-DOS dominance in the market for operating systems. As was seen in chapter 11, Microsoft's strategy did not consist of directly lowering the price of MS-DOS. Rather, what Microsoft did was to impose contractual terms whereby computer manufacturers would have to pay Microsoft per computer sold, not per copy of MS-DOS shipped. This implied that the *opportunity cost* of selling a computer with MS-DOS was very small, in fact zero: A fee would have to be paid to Microsoft regardless of whether MS-DOS was included or not.

Largely based on this strategy, Microsoft was able to keep rivals DRI and IBM out of the market for DOS operating systems, and, generally, to establish MS-DOS/Windows as the dominant operating system. By the time the Department of Justice induced Microsoft to abandon its practices, the installed base of MS-DOS was already sufficiently high to create a self-sustaining advantage for Microsoft.

Another class of nonprice exclusionary strategies is **bundling** or **tying**.[i] At one point, Kodak, who held a dominant position in the market for cameras, designed its new film and camera in a format that was incompatible with other existing film formats. One interpretation of this strategy (in fact, one that Kodak was accused of) is that it forced

[i] Bundling and tying can also be a means for price discrimination. See chapter 10.

rival film manufacturers out of the market. Likewise, IBM, who for a long time dominated the computer industry, would incorporate increased amounts of storage into its central processing units to prevent sales by plug compatible memory manufacturers.[196,j]

PUBLIC POLICY TOWARD PREDATION

Predation is one of the most difficult areas of antitrust and competition policy. More than in most other areas of antitrust and competition policy, there is great disagreement among economists about general principles and about actual decisions on different cases. Why such divergence of opinion? We can identify three main reasons.

Does Predation Exist?

First, the theoretical debate as to whether predatory pricing *exists* in practice is still not completely settled. As we saw previously, a price reduction by an incumbent in response to entry can be interpreted as a competitive response to new competition, rather than as an attempt to drive that competition out of the market. However, theoretical and empirical developments are creating a consensus that there is such a thing as predatory pricing.

Identifying Predatory Behavior

This brings us to the second problem. Even if we agree that predatory pricing exists, we still have to distinguish it from simple, straightforward, competitive behavior: More competition means lower prices and possibly exit, even if no firm is attempting to drive rivals out of the market. For example, some 5000 roadside gas stations have closed down in Britain over the past eight years, while average gas prices declined significantly. An investigation by the Office of Fair Trade concluded that the price decrease resulted from increased competition between the large incumbent firms and that no predatory intent was present (box 15.4).

In the United States, a crucial step in distinguishing competition from predation is the so-called **Areeda-Turner test**: Prices should be regarded as predatory if they fall below marginal cost. But this does not solve the problem. For example, a firm might very well price below short-run marginal costs with the sole purpose of moving down its learning curve (and with no anti-competitive intent).

Alternatively, one may look for post-exit price increases. If there is predatory intent, the predator must have a reasonable expectation of recouping short-run losses in the long run, that is, after exit has taken place. In this respect, the case of Spirit Airlines versus Northwest Airlines, described in greater detail in box 15.5, is illustrative. When Spirit entered one of Northwest's markets, the latter responded by slashing its fares. Soon after Spirit exited, prices went back up, in fact, to higher levels than before Spirit's entry.[k]

Welfare Effects

Even if we are able to identify pricing with the clear intent of driving rivals out of the market, we still have to address the third question: Why should predatory pricing be

[j] There is an interesting analogy between the IBM example and the antitrust case against Microsoft; this case is discussed in chapter 5.

[k] Ironically, not too long before, Northwest (and Continental) sued American Airlines for alleged predatory pricing. Northwest and Continental claimed to have lost a total of $1 billion when forced to match the new lower fares set by American in the spring of 1992. Antitrust charges against American Airlines were cleared in the summer of 1993.[197]

BOX 15.4   GAS STATIONS IN BRITAIN: COMPETITION OR PREDATION?

Between 1990 and 1998, some 5000 roadside gas stations closed down in the United Kingdom. The Office of Fair Trade (OFT) initiated a detailed analysis of the industry and found no need to intervene to protect the losers from the gas price war.

"Excluding tax and duty, the price of ordinary unleaded gas has fallen from 15.3p per liter in February 1990 to 10.0p per liter in February 1998 . . . The key dynamic in the market is the fierce rivalry between the oil majors, such as Shell and Esso, and the large supermarket chains, . . . whose market share has grown from 5% to around 23% since 1990 . . .

Supermarkets can offer keen prices because of their high volumes and low cost base . . . Oil companies have responded by cutting their prices to match those of the supermarkets . . . Predictably, not all of the smaller independent retailers have been able to withstand the competition. As a consequence, there are around 5000 fewer gas stations in the United Kingdom today than in 1990 . . .

Does this situation constitute predatory behavior on the part of the market leaders? The weight of evidence from the marketplace suggests not . . . If successful predation had occurred, we would have seen much higher margins being earned now. In fact, between January 1991 and February 1998, gross margins in the market fell from around 6p to 4p per liter for both unleaded and leaded gas."[198]

BOX 15.5   SPIRIT AIRLINES VERSUS NORTHWEST AIRLINES

"Spirit tiptoed into the Detroit–Philadelphia market in December 1995, with one round-trip flight a day, says Vice-Chairman Mark S. Kahan. Northwest's average one-way fare when the tiny Spirit entered was more than $170. Spirit's introductory unrestricted fare: $49 one way. . . . On June 20, 1996, Northwest slashed its fares to Philadelphia to $49 on virtually all seats at all times, he says. And it poured on capacity, adding nearly 30% more seats. On September 30, Spirit abandoned the route. Says Northwest's Austin: 'We're being criticized for matching a competitor's action, which I view as pro-consumer.'

Executives at many big airlines say cutting fares and adding capacity is good for consumers. True, but only if it lasts. By the first quarter of '97—just a few months after Spirit withdrew—Northwest's average one-way fare on the route had climbed to more than $230, says Kahan. And the number of seats available from Northwest on the Detroit–Philadelphia run dropped, too."[199]

illegal? Even from a consumer's perspective, there is a trade-off to be taken into account. Predatory pricing implies that, with some probability, the prey will exit the market, leaving the predator with monopoly or near-monopoly power. But against possible higher future prices we must weigh lower short-run prices. These lower prices are not very relevant when the predator's price cuts are selective, as in the Sacramento cable TV case (only 700 customers benefited from the predator's price cuts). But consider instead the example at the beginning of the chapter: When easyJet entered the London–Amsterdam route, KLM retaliated by cutting fares. easyJet survived this attack. In the end, both easyJet and KLM lost the price war episode. Who gained in the process? Clearly, consumers.

Skepticism about the (alleged) negative effects of predatory pricing is especially relevant in industries with important **network externalities**. This concept, which will be examined in greater detail in chapter 17, refers to the case when consumers benefit from there being other consumers who are buying the same product. The MacIntosh operating system is worth little to a consumer when few other users adopt the same operating system. For one, it is more difficult to exchange files when the other party is based on a different platform. More importantly, as we saw earlier, having few buyers of the MacOS implies that little software will be developed for it. In the context of network industries, like operating systems, preventing predatory behavior may be a mixed blessing. On the one hand, a competitor is saved for the industry; on the other hand, less standardization is achieved, with the obvious negative consequences.

In practice, the U.S. Supreme Court has clarified two conditions for illegal predatory pricing.[200] The first condition is that price is below cost. The second is that a firm pricing below cost is sufficiently likely to recoup its short-run losses, that is, predation is a rational strategy. At the same time, the Court has repeatedly shown its skepticism about cases of predatory pricing: "Predatory pricing schemes are rarely tried, and are even more rarely successful."[201]

The analysis in this section suggests that the Court's view is flawed when it implicitly assumes that predation is an unlikely event. Not only do we observe predation in practice, but we can also find convincing and rational explanations for its occurrence. However, distinguishing predation from competitive behavior is difficult. Moreover, the welfare analysis of predation reveals that its effects are ambiguous, even if we restrict it to consumer welfare. For this reason, the Courts may be right in not giving much weight to cases of alleged predation—although for different reasons.

The European legal tradition regarding predation is less rich than the North American one. Predation normally would be considered an infringement of Article 86 of the Treaty of Rome, which forbids the abuse of a dominant position. In one important case, AKZO Chemie BV, a Dutch chemical firm, was fined by the European Commission for ten million ECU as a result of alleged predatory action directed against Engineering and Chemical Supplies Ltd. (ECS), a small British firm.

It should be noted that, a few years earlier, AKZO had threatened ECS that it would cut prices in ECS's market unless ECS exited from the markets it had recently entered, markets that were dominated by AKZO. There was good evidence of this, because AKZO actually convened a meeting with ECS for this effect. The European Commission seems to have put a lot of weight on this past occurrence, as well as on the fact that AKZO is a much larger firm than ECS. By contrast, there was hardly any investigation of whether AKZO priced below cost or imposed any significant damage on ECS. Many critical analysts claim it did not.

This case is interesting in that it illustrates the difficulty of judging cases of alleged predation. In terms of evidence of intent, an element on which policymakers seem to put a lot of weight, the case could hardly be more clear-cut: AKZO even convened a meeting with ECS for the purpose of announcing its intention. Do such announcements, together with actual price cuts, amount to (illegal) predatory pricing? Should they be illegal?

15.3   MERGERS AND ACQUISITIONS

In the previous section, we looked at firm strategies that induce exit by current competitors. An alternative way of eliminating competition is simply to acquire the rival firm. In fact, the strategy of American Tobacco, described earlier as an example of predatory behavior, eventually led to the acquisition of the prey firms, rather than their exit. Generally, mergers and acquisitions implicitly imply "exit" (of the merging firms, or at least of the acquired firm) and "entry" (of the newly formed firm, in case of a merger).

What are the causes of mergers and acquisitions? A brief look at a few examples will show that the causes are manifold.

- In the 1980s, Sony purchased the film studio Columbia with the objective of creating "synergies" between two complementary producers. Columbia's collection of quality movies was seen as a guarantee of a minimum supply of "software" to complement the "hardware" offered by Sony (e.g., video players).

- Philip Morris and Kraft possess a large number of food products sold through supermarket chains. Creating a new firm of greater size allowed Philip Morris and Kraft to increase their bargaining power with respect to retailers. This is important, for example, when it comes to obtaining shelf space for the launch of a new product.

- When Nestlé acquired Rowntree, its main goal was to enter the British market for chocolates. Rowntree owned a vast number of well-known brands (Smarties, After Eight, Kit Kat, etc.). Buying Rowntree allowed Nestlé to save the high costs of launching new brands.

- Another example involving Nestlé is the joint venture with General Mills for the production and distribution of breakfast cereals in Europe. The main goal of this joint venture was to exploit the synergies between two complementary firms: Nestlé's distribution skills (especially in Europe) and General Mills's production skills.

In addition to these examples, in which some strategic or efficiency effect is envisaged by the merger, there are a number of cases where mergers and acquisitions are done mainly for financial or tax reasons. For example, acquiring firms from different industries is equivalent to holding a diversified investment portfolio, thus reducing the overall risk for the parent company.

In this section, we focus on **horizontal mergers**, that is, mergers or acquisitions between two firms within the same industry. From the previous list, both Phillip Morris and Nestlé would qualify as examples of horizontal mergers—not so the example of Sony (or the examples where mergers result from financial or tax reasons).

THE IMPLICATIONS OF MERGERS

Consider an industry with n firms that compete as in the Cournot model. Suppose that all firms have the same marginal cost, c, and fixed cost, F. What happens when, for example, firms 1 and 2 merge? The newly formed firm, 1&2, has marginal cost c and fixed cost F. After firms have had time to adjust their quantities, we will converge to a new equilibrium that, effectively, corresponds to the same Cournot equilibrium, but now with $n - 1$ firms instead of the initial n.

As was seen in previous chapters, the equilibrium price under Cournot equilibrium is (strictly) decreasing with respect to the number of firms. Going from n to $n - 1$ competitors implies an increase in price. Generally, an increase in concentration implies an increase in price. In other words, market price increases as a result of the merger. Consequently, if product differentiation is not very important—so that market price is the only concern for consumers—then mergers imply a decrease in consumer welfare.

Suppose that n is a large number, so that n is approximately equal to $n - 1$. Then, under Cournot competition, profits are approximately the same with n competitors or with $n - 1$ competitors. But then the merger between two firms from the initial set of n competitors would seem unprofitable: Initially, the two firms earn a total of 2 times $\pi(n)$, where $\pi(n)$ is equilibrium profits when there are n competitors. After the merger, the combined firm earns $\pi(n - 1)$. If $\pi(n)$ is approximately equal to $\pi(n - 1)$, then postmerger profits are little more than one half of premerger profits.

Horizontal mergers do occur in practice. If we assume that firms and firm managers are concerned with firm value, then it must be the case that (at least some) horizontal mergers are profitable, that is, they increase the combined value of the merging firms. This suggests that the preceding analysis is missing something. One important aspect that is missing is **synergies**, in particular, **cost efficiencies**. We have assumed that both the fixed and the marginal cost of the merged firm would be the same as before the merger. However, the examples at the beginning of this section suggest that this is not such a good assumption. For example, the joint venture between Nestlé and General Mills combines complementary skills that lead to a lower marginal cost of producing and distributing breakfast cereals. The recent merger between Daimler and Chrysler is

BOX 15.6 THE DAIMLERCHRYSLER MERGER

"Now that the creation of DaimlerChrysler is officially going ahead, efforts to save $3 billion a year will go into high gear. Here is where savings are expected to come from:

- **Advanced technologies.** Eliminate overlapping research into fuel cells, electric cars, and advanced diesel engines.

- **Finance.** Reduce back-office costs, and coordinate tax planning and other activities.

- **Purchasing.** Consolidate parts and equipment buying. DaimlerChrysler is expected to follow Chrysler's system of working with suppliers.

- **Joint production.** Build Daimler sport utility vehicles at a plant in Austria where Chrysler makes Jeeps and minivans.

- **New products.** Possibly cooperate on future products such as minivans.

- **New markets.** Cooperate in emerging markets such as Latin America and Asia, perhaps with joint distribution."[202]

expected to create cost savings of $3 billion a year. To a great extent, these are derived by avoiding duplication of fixed costs (box 15.6). Be it marginal costs or fixed costs, mergers normally create efficiencies. We thus have two main effects:

Mergers normally imply an increase in prices and a reduction in costs.

As we will see later, these two effects correspond to the main trade-off faced by policy-makers when it comes to merger analysis.

The preceding analysis notwithstanding, mergers do not necessarily need to create significant cost efficiencies to be profitable. We have so far assumed that the mode of competition remains the same after the merger (e.g., Cournot before and Cournot after, though with a more concentrated industry). However, one of the implications of the merger may be precisely to change the mode of competition in the industry. Specifically, a more concentrated industry (the result of the merger) may allow for a greater degree of collusion among competitors. We will return to this point when discussing public policy toward mergers.

We stated earlier that total output tends to decrease as a result of a merger. In particular, *the combined output of the merged firms normally decreases*. Why? Before the merger, if firm i were to decrease output by one unit, it would (1) lose $p - MC$, its selling margin; and (2) gain $q_i \Delta p$, where q_i is its output and Δp the increase in price that results from the output decrease. Because we start (before the merger) from an equilibrium situation, it must be the case that no firm would have an incentive to decrease (or increase) output. In other words, the positive and the negative effect of an output reduction exactly cancel out.

Consider now the situation after the merger between firms i and j. Starting from the same output levels as before the merger, the newly formed firm *i&j* stands to gain from a reduction in output. In fact, although the loss in terms of lower output is still $p - MC$, the gain from an increased price is now $(q_i + q_j)\Delta p$. In other words, when firm i lowers output, it now takes into account not only the effect of a higher price on its profits but also the effect on firm j's profits. Therefore, unless the merger implies a significant reduction in the marginal cost of the combined firm *i&j*, total output of the merging firms goes down.

Not every firm decreases its output as a result of a merger. In fact, for the *nonmerging firms*, the opposite is true. Before the merger, if firm k were to decrease output by one unit, it would (1) lose $p - MC$, its selling margin; and (2) gain $q_k \Delta p$. After the merger, (2) remains the same but (1) is now greater. If firm k was indifferent between decreasing and increasing output before the merger, it now strictly prefers to increase.

In fact, nonmerging firms are the main beneficiaries from the merger: Without having to incur any costs, they see the number of their competitors decrease by one. The nonmerging firms are, as it were, free-riding on the output reduction (and price increase) initiated by the merging firms. As a well-known author put it, "the promoter of a merger is likely to receive much encouragement from each firm—almost every encouragement, in fact, except participation."[203]

This is not true in general, however. For example, if the merged firm becomes very efficient, specifically, if its marginal cost is substantially lower than before the merger, then it may happen that nonmerging firms see their profits decrease. In terms of the preceding analysis, recall that we (implicitly) made the assumption that marginal cost remains unchanged as a result of the merger. Otherwise, effect (1) of an output reduction would increase and the merging firm *i&j* would no longer find it profitable to reduce output. The situation is then inverted: nonmerging firms reduce their market share and profits as a result of the merger.

> The value of nonmerging firms may decrease or increase as the result of a merger, depending on the cost efficiencies generated by the merger.

Three examples show that both situations are possible in practice.

1. In August 1998, "British Petroleum PLC said it would buy Amoco Corp. in the largest industrial merger ever. . . . The accord has helped push up stock prices of most major oil companies. Mobil Corp., [for example,] was up $2.625 late Thursday at $69.375."[204]

2. Meanwhile, responding to the announcement of a proposed merger between British Airways and American Airlines, Virgin Atlantic—a smaller competitor in the London–U.S. routes—painted its aircraft with the clear message "BA/AA No Way."[1]

3. In the European defense industry, the merger between rivals GKN plc and Alvis plc is putting the pressure on Vickers, a third competitor. "Together, GKN and Alvis will be in a far better position to call the shots as Europe undergoes defense and aerospace consolidation. . . . Some analysts have warned that could shut the door on Vickers."[205]

MERGER WAVES

One stylized fact of merger activity is that mergers occur in waves: Periods of intense merger activity in a given industry alternate with periods of relative stability. There are several explanations for this phenomenon. In particular, some explanations emphasize exogenous causes, and others put an emphasis on endogenous effects.

Take, for example, the airline industry. First in the United States, then in Europe and the rest of the world, the industry is undergoing a process of deregulation. One consequence of this is that many airlines have been forming alliances, in an effort to survive in an increasingly competitive industry. Currently, there are more than 500 alliances worldwide.[206] Although these alliances have been formed in sequence, it would be incorrect to say that the nth alliance was triggered by the $n - 1$st alliance. More likely, they are both the result of the (exogenous) change in government regulation.

To understand how a sequence of mergers may be endogenously determined, consider the following simple example. Suppose that firms compete as in the Cournot model; demand is given by $Q = 150 - P$, marginal cost is constant and equal to 30, and fixed cost is 120 (the same for all firms). Profits per firm as a function of the number of competitors are then as follows:

No. Firms	Profit per Firm
2	680
3	330
4	168

[1] In the case of Virgin Atlantic, an additional concern with the BA/AA merger is that Virgin Atlantic's relative size would be even smaller. As we saw in the preceding section, predatory practices are not unknown in this industry. A greater asymmetry in size between competitors may increase the likelihood of such an event.

Suppose that there are initially four firms. A merger between Firms 1 and 2 would not be profitable: Before the merger, the two firms combined for $2 \times 168 = 336$, whereas following the merger, they would get only 330. Suppose, however, that Firms 3 and 4 merge. The reason for this merger might be that there is a special synergy that only the merger between 3 and 4 would generate; or, it could be that the managers of Firms 3 and 4 have personal ambitions of running a very large firm, to the point that they decide to merge even if firm value is not increased. Whichever the reason for the merger between Firms 3 and 4 is, the "initial" situation is now an oligopoly with three firms only: 1, 2, and 3&4. Now, it does pay for Firms 1 and 2 to merge: Without the merger, they earn a combined $2 \times 330 = 660$, whereas by merging, total profits would be 680.

In other words, the gains from merger between a given pair of firms increase when two rival firms merge. Although this is not always true, it is an intuitive result: As we saw before, nonmerging firms free-ride on merging firms by increasing output when the latter decrease output upon merging. This results in a lower gain for the merging firms. If the number of nonmerging firms is smaller, then the free-riding effect is lower and the merging firms are able to reap more of the benefits from increased concentration. In the previous example, starting with four firms, we have two free-riding firms, whereas starting with three firms, there is only one free-riding firm. For this reason, a merger between two firms (e.g., Firms 3 and 4) may trigger the merger between two other firms (e.g., Firms 1 and 2). Generally, this may be the source of the merger waves to which we alluded earlier.

> Merger waves may result from exogenous events (e.g., industry deregulation) or from endogenous events (e.g., a merger between two large firms).

Real-world examples of sequences of mergers in particular industries suggest that both exogenous and endogenous effects are present. For instance, the U.S. supermarket business is undergoing a rapid process of consolidation, "driven by a desire to cut costs and remain competitive with Wal-Mart Stores Inc., which has invaded the grocery business with its low-cost distribution model."[207] As several firms merge together, the pressure to cut costs becomes greater, which in turn leads to further mergers, as firms strive to achieve cost efficiencies. In September 1999 alone, "Kroger has made a $13 billion offer for Fre Meyer; . . . Safeway has announced plans to buy Dominick's Supermarkets for $1.8 billion; and Canada's Empire has said it would buy a rival chain, Oshawa, for $900 million. [In the previous month], Albertson's snapped up American Stores for $12 billion. Meanwhile Kmart, a discount retailer, said this week that it needs to find a supermarket chain to be its partner."[208]

Another example is provided by the European telecommunications industry. "Telecoms and media alliances have mushroomed in recent months and will continue to do so this year. . . . The trend is being driven by market-opening measures within the bloc, pressure to remain at the forefront of technology and the alliance between AT&T Corp. and British Telecommunications plc, which observers say has altered Europe's telecom equilibrium."[209] Of the three reasons pointed out, the first one corresponds to an exogenous event, whereas the third one would be better classified as an endogenous event (a merger that induces additional mergers).

PUBLIC POLICY TOWARD MERGERS

There are essentially three interested parties in a merger: the merging firms, the nonmerging firms, and consumers. The previous analysis suggests that, in general, consumers lose from the merger. Nonmerging firms may gain or may lose. Merging firms, finally, are expected to gain from the merger, at least in expected terms (or else they wouldn't merge).

The task for public policy is to evaluate the relative weight of each gain and loss and then to make an assessment of the overall effect of the merger (taking into account the relative weight given to firm profits and consumer welfare). This task is especially hard when it comes to estimating the cost savings implied by the merger. In fact, most of the information necessary for such evaluation lies with the merging firms. The merging firms have a strategic incentive to distort such information, in the hope of convincing policymakers that the overall effect of the merger is positive.

One of the few general rules for merger policy is that the greater the price increase, the less desirable the merger is. The idea is simple: A higher price implies a loss for consumers that is less than compensated by the gain to firms (the difference being the allocative inefficiency caused by the gap between price and marginal cost). Moreover, policymakers normally give more weight to consumer welfare than to firm profits. So, even if there were no allocative efficiency loss, a higher price would imply a transfer from consumers to firms, a negative effect (from a policymaker's perspective).

How can the policymaker estimate the likely increase in price following the merger? From chapter 9, we know that, for a given mode of competition, the greater the market concentration the greater the price. A merger between two large firms is therefore likely to imply a greater increase in price than a merger between two small firms. Moreover, collusion is more likely in concentrated industries; it is therefore possible that the merger implies a switch to a more collusive situation.

It is important to distinguish these two channels of price increase. The first one, known as the **unilateral effect** of the merger, is essentially a function of the increase in concentration (see chapter 9). The second one, the **collusion effect**, also depends on the *distribution* of market shares. An example will help to clarify this issue. In February 1992, the food products manufacturer Nestlé made a bid for Perrier S.A., Europe's leading producer of mineral water. Market shares prior to the merger were as follows: Perrier, 35.9%; BSN, 23%; Nestlé, 17.1%; others, 24%. The Nestlé/Perrier merger thus would create a leading producer with 53% of the market and a second firm with only 23%. Nestlé anticipated that the European Commission would not be very keen on such an increase in concentration, in particular on having a single firm with such a large market share. It therefore proposed to the Commission that, together with the merger, it would transfer Volvic, one of the Nestlé/Perrier water sources, to rival BSN. Taking this asset transfer into account, the foreseeable postmerger market shares would be Nestlé/Perrier, 38%; BSN (with Volvic), 38%; others, 24%.

The Commission approved the merger with the conditional asset transfer. The idea is that anti-competitive concerns are less significant in a 38-38 dominant duopoly than they are in a 53-23 one. However, such presumption is far from obvious. In particular, the argument can be made that collusion between Nestlé/Perrier is made much easier when they hold symmetric market shares than when they are very different in size.[210] Although the unilateral effect of the merger (increased concentration and price) is likely to be greater without the asset transfer, the collusion effect (increased collusion) is likely to be greater with the asset transfer.

How does one go about estimating the price effect of a merger? One possibility is to estimate the impact of the merger on concentration and then apply a formula like equation 9.1, which relates concentration to price. The practical problem of this approach is that, to compute the concentration index, one first needs to compute market shares; in order to compute market shares, one first needs to define the market; the latter is far from trivial.

For example, in 1996, Staples and Office Depot, the two largest chains of office-supplies superstores, proposed to merge. The merger was eventually disallowed by the U.S. District Court, ruling in favor of the Federal Trade Commission, which argued that the merger would increase market power in the industry, to the detriment of consumers. In fact, if the relevant market definition is "office superstores," then Staples and Office Depot would combine for a market share of more than 70%. However, if the relevant industry definition is "stores that sell office supplies," then the combined market shares of the two firms would be much lower.

Disagreement between firms and merger authorities concerning market definition is common. It shows how difficult and inexact the science of market definition is. For this and other reasons, anti-trust authorities such as the U.S. Federal Trade Commission have come to favor the more direct approach of estimating the impact of a merger on consumer prices. For example, in examining the Staples/Office Depot proposed merger, the FTC concluded that prices in cities with little or no competition between superstore chains are up to 15% higher than in cities where there is competition. This provides a benchmark estimate of how much prices would increase, as a result of the merger, in cities where only Staples and Office Depot operate (of which, as it turns out, there is a fair number).

A second general rule for merger policy is that the smaller the relative size of the merging firms, the more likely that the overall impact of the merger will be positive. There are two reasons for this rule. First, the smaller the merging firms are, the lower the price increase caused by the merger. For example, going from 20 to 19 firms implies a lower increase in price than going from 3 to 2 firms.

The second reason is that a merger between small firms indicates that efficiency gains are likely to be significant. We saw before that, under Cournot competition, the greater the number of nonparticipating firms, the greater the free-riding effect (whereby nonmerging firms increase output in response to the merging firms' output decrease). Because the merging firms get together of their own volition, it must be that efficiency gains are significant enough to compensate for the negative effect caused by free-riding. This lower bound on the extent of efficiency gains is greater the greater the number of nonparticipating firms, or, in other words, the smaller the relative size of the merging firms.[211]

The smaller the size of the merging firms, the more likely the total effect of a merger is positive.

There are many other considerations to take into account in the public-policy analysis of a merger. For example, policymakers are naturally more lenient toward mergers in industries where entry is easy. The idea is that, in such industries, the price effect (increase in price as a result of the merger) cannot be very significant, or else entry would take place and would counteract the negative effect of the merger.

Most government authorities responsible for merger analysis have a set of rules or guidelines, which include the preceding ideas and other related ones—the 1992 Merger Guidelines in the United States, or the Regulation 89/90 in Europe, for example. Ultimately, what matters is the relative weight given to each of the interested parties, for there are always winners and losers.

SUMMARY

- An incumbent firm's capacity choice may influence entry decisions by new firms. If entry costs are high, then the incumbent should set monopoly capacity and ignore the threat of entry. If entry costs are low, then the incumbent should choose capacity, taking into account the entrant's reaction curve. Finally, if entry costs are intermediate, then the incumbent should choose capacity large enough to induce the entrant not to enter.

- Capacity preemption is a credible strategy only if capacity costs are high and sunk.

- Predatory pricing may be a successful strategy when (1) the prey is financially constrained, (2) low prices signal low costs or the predator's "toughness," and (3) capturing a minimum market share early on is crucial for long-term survival. In all these cases, low pricing by the predator induces the prey to exit the market.

- Mergers normally imply an increase in prices and a reduction in costs for the merging firms. The value of nonmerging firms may decrease or increase as the result of a merger, depending on the cost efficiencies generated by the merger. The total effect of a merger is more likely to be positive the smaller the size of the merging firms.

- Merger waves may result from exogenous events (e.g., industry deregulation) or from endogenous events (e.g., a merger between two large firms).

KEY CONCEPTS

- preemption

- entry deterrence, entry accommodation, and blockaded entry

- product proliferation

- predation

- horizontal mergers

- unilateral effect and collusion effect

REVIEW AND PRACTICE EXERCISES

15.1* LC Burgers is currently the sole fast-food chain in Linear City, a city that is one mile long and consists of one street, with one thousand consumers distributed uniformly along the street. The price for the BigLC, the only product sold by the LC Burger chain, is set nationally at $4, so that the local Linear City manager's decision is limited to choosing the number and location of its stores.

Each store costs $600,000 to open and lasts indefinitely. Each consumer buys one burger per week at the current price of $4. However, no consumer will walk for more than a quarter of a mile to buy a burger. Operating costs are $1 per burger. The interest rates is 0.1% per week. The market conditions are unchanging, so present discounted profits can be regarded as level perpetuities.

a. Suppose that LC Burgers faces no competition and no threat of entry. How many stores should LC Burgers open, and at what locations?

CS Burgers is contemplating entering Linear City. CS Burgers' costs and prices are the same as those of LC Burgers. Moreover, consumers regard the products at both chains as equally good; so, if both brands are in town, each consumer buys from the closest store.

b. At what locations should CS Burgers open stores, given that LC Burgers has opened the locations found to be optimal in part (a)?

c. Recognizing the threat of entry by CS Burgers, at what locations should LC Burgers open stores?

d. Would your analysis of these product-location decisions be affected if you also considered the possibility of pricing competition, that is, if prices were then set independently, given the locations of the stores (rather than taking prices as fixed, as was done previously)?

e. Moving beyond this particular model, does product positioning involve a first-mover advantage or a second-mover advantage, or does this depend upon particular aspects of the market in question?

15.2   Less than one year after the deregulation of the German telecommunications market at the start of 1998, domestic long-distance rates have fallen by more than 70%. Deutsche Telekom, the former monopolist, accompanied some of these rate drops by increases in monthly fees and local calls. MobilCom, one of the main competitors, fears it may be unable to match the price reductions. Following the announcement of a price reduction by Deutsche Telekom at the end of 1998, shares of MobilCom fell by 7%. Two other competitors, O.tel.o and Mannesmann Arcor, said they would match the price cuts. VIAG Interkom, however, accused Telekom of "competition-distorting behavior," claiming the company is exploiting its (still remaining) monopoly power in the local market to subsidize its long-distance business.[212]

Is this a case of predatory pricing? Present arguments in favor of, and against, such assertion.

15.3   "The combined output of two merging firms decreases as a result of the merger." True or false?

15.4*   One of the efficiencies created by mergers in the paper industry results from reorganization of production. A machine is more efficient the narrower the range of products it produces, among other reasons because the length of each production run can be made longer.

The paper industry underwent a wave of mergers in the 1980s. Of the firms that merged, about two thirds increased their market share as a result of the merger.

Assuming that (1) firms compete by setting production capacity, and (2) paper products are relatively homogeneous across firms, explain how the previous paragraph explains the pattern of changes in market shares. Which firms would you expect to increase their market share?[213]

15.5 "The renewed prospect of a link-up between British Aerospace PLC and the Marconi defense arm of General Electric Co. PLC of the United Kingdom has led to revived talks between the top defense companies in Germany and France."[214] Discuss.

EXTENSION EXERCISES

15.6 Consider a homogeneous product industry with inverse demand given by $p = 100 - 2Q$. Variable cost is given by $C = 10q$. There is currently one incumbent firm and one potential competitor. Entry into the industry implies a sunk cost of F.

a. Determine the incumbent's optimal output in the absence of potential competition.

b. Suppose the entrant takes the incumbent's output choice as given. Show that the entrant's equilibrium profit is decreasing in the incumbent's output.

c. What output should the incumbent firm set to deter entry?

d. Assuming that the incumbent firm decides to deter entry, determine the Lerner index as a function of F. Discuss the result.

e. Determine the lowest value of e such that the incumbent firm prefers to deter entry.

15.7*** A large fraction of industry entry corresponds to acquisition of incumbent firms. For example, from a sample of 3788 entry events, about 70% were acquisitions.[215] Econometric analysis suggests that entry by acquisition is more common in more concentrated industries.[216] Can you explain this observation? *Suggestion:* Consider a Cournot oligopoly with n symmetric firms. Determine the maximum that an entrant would be willing to pay for one of the incumbent firms. Determine also the minimum that an incumbent would require from a buyer, *knowing that the alternative to selling the firm is for the entrant to create a new firm.* Show that the difference between the two values above is greater when the industry is more concentrated.[217]

What other factors would you expect to influence the "build or buy" decision when entering an industry?

PART **SIX**

TECHNOLOGY

CHAPTER 16

RESEARCH AND DEVELOPMENT

Imagine that H. G. Wells' time machine actually works. Assume, moreover, that you are given a $100,000 prize and the option of remaining in the year 2000, or, alternatively, traveling to 1900. Were you to decide to move back to 1900, $100,000 would make you a very wealthy person: You would be able, for example, to afford a large mansion with many servants. By contrast, $100,000 in 2000 won't get you much of a mansion—at most a very small apartment in London or New York. Does that mean you would be better off by moving back in time?

There are many issues involved in the decision of what century to live in. In particular, the set of available goods would normally play an important role. For example, no matter how much money you have in 1900, you won't be able to buy a CD player. If you live in the United States, you will be able to buy a telephone, but there won't be many people you can call with it.

These examples suggest that technical progress is an important part of economic development. In chapter 15, we emphasized the fact that industries change as a result of entry of new firms and exit of existing ones. In this chapter, by contrast, the emphasis is on the fact that industries change with the introduction of new products and production processes, and on the fact that new products and production processes result primarily from Research and Development (R&D) effort.

Table 16.1 lists the top spenders on R&D, also indicating the importance of R&D expenditures as a percentage of total sales. At $7.97 billion, General Motors's R&D budget is at the level of a university of considerable size. Equally impressive, Pfizer's investment in R&D exceeds 15% of its revenues. It is also noticeable that the relative importance of R&D expenditures varies considerably across firms and across industries.

From an economics point of view, the values in table 16.1 suggest a number of interesting questions. Why are R&D expenditures so much higher in some industries

TABLE 16.1 THE WORLD'S BIGGEST SPENDERS IN RESEARCH AND DEVELOPMENT.[218]

Firm	Billions of Dollars	Percent (of sales)	Firm	Billions of Dollars	Percent (of sales)
General Motors	7.97	4.9	NTT	2.46	3.7
Ford Motors	6.16	4.1	Volkswagen	2.38	3.9
Siemens	4.40	7.6	Intel	2.29	9.4
IBM	4.19	5.5	Hoechst	2.16	7.7
Hitachi	3.76	5.9	Bayer	2.14	7.2
Toyota	3.38	3.7	Sony	2.11	5.2
Matsushita	3.25	5.7	Northern Telecom	2.08	13.9
Daimler-Benz	3.06	4.6	Johnson & Johnson	2.08	9.5
Hewlett-Packard	2.99	7.2	Bell Canada Enterprises	1.98	8.8
Ericsson Telefon	2.98	14.5	Philips	1.95	5.3
Lucent Technologies	2.94	11.5	Roche	1.94	15.5
Motorola	2.67	9.2	Honda Motor	1.87	4.7
Fujitsu	2.64	7.8	Pfizer	1.87	15.8
NEC	2.61	7.0	Microsoft	1.87	16.9
Asea Brown Boveri	2.58	8.5	Boeing	1.87	4.2
EI du Pont de Nemours	2.53	5.8	Glaxo Wellcome	1.84	14.4
Toshiba	2.48	6.1	Alcatel Alsthom	1.78	6.8
Novartis	2.46	11.8	Robert Bosch	1.76	7.0

than in others? Does industry structure have a significant effect on the extent to which firms engage in R&D? Are today's R&D leaders likely to remain the leaders in the future? More generally, what is the impact of R&D competition on market structure? These are some of the question we will address in the first part of this chapter. In the last section, we will address some public policy issues related to R&D: What can public policy do to favor investment in R&D? Should agreements between firms pertaining to R&D be allowed?

16.1 MARKET STRUCTURE AND INCENTIVES FOR R&D

In most of the previous chapters, we have looked at the causes and consequences of market power. In particular, we have examined the consequences of market power in terms of producer's and consumer's surplus. To put it simply, market power implies a loss of allocative efficiency. In this sense, an optimal market structure is one that minimizes the extent of market power: perfect competition (or, absent perfect competition, government regulation that decreases the extent of market power).

When technical progress is taken into consideration, the question is somewhat different. Which market structure induces the greatest incentives for investment in R&D? Or, to put it somewhat differently: Do firms invest more in fragmented industries where each firm is of relatively small size and product market competition is very intense; or, rather, in industries where a few firms command significant market power? In a classic essay, Joseph Schumpeter argues that

As soon as we go into the details and inquire into the individual items in which progress was most conspicuous, the trail leads not to the doors of those firms that work under conditions of comparatively free competition but precisely to the doors of the large concerns.

Later, he adds that

Perfect competition is not only impossible but inferior, and has no title to being set up as a model of ideal efficiency.[219]

Had Schumpeter lived a few decades longer, he would have had the pleasure of confirming his view in examples like that of AT&T, a monopolist until the 1980s: The Bell Labs, AT&T's research branch, were responsible for some of the most important discoveries in the twentieth century, including the transistor and the laser.

The argument can be made, however, that it is precisely in competitive industries that each firm has greater incentives to engage in R&D. Consider a process innovation that allows a firm to reduce marginal cost from $\overline{c}$ to $\underline{c}$. For a monopolist, such innovation is worth approximately q^M (monopoly output) times $(\overline{c} - \underline{c})$, the cost savings implied by the innovation. This is given by area A in figure 16.1. Consider, however, a competitive,

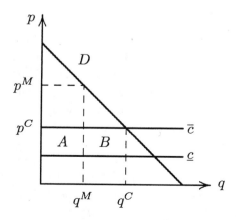

FIGURE 16.1 GAINS FROM COST REDUCTION UNDER MONOPOLY AND UNDER COMPETITION.

price-setting, industry with many firms producing at marginal cost $\overline{c}$. In the initial, pre-innovation, situation, a firm earns a profit of zero. By reducing cost to $\underline{c}$, the innovator is able to set a price just below $\overline{c}$ and capture the entire market (no other firm would be willing to match such a price, as it would imply pricing below marginal cost). The innovator's profit is therefore given by q^C times $\overline{c} - \underline{c}$, the area $A + B$ in figure 16.1. Because the initial profit was nil, we conclude that $A + B$ is the value of the cost-reducing innovation, greater than that under monopoly.

In other words, one important difference between monopoly and competition is that, in the former case, one must account for the "monopolist's disincentive created by his preinvention monopoly profits," whereas under competition such pre-innovation profits do not exist.[220] This is known as the **replacement effect**. Generally, the replacement effect would indicate that firms with more market power have a lower incentive to innovate because they have more to lose than firms with little market power, who have little or nothing to lose from innovation. For example, the U.S. Justice Department has recently filed an antitrust lawsuit against the United States' two largest credit card networks, Visa and MasterCard, accusing them of stifling competition (Visa and MasterCard are jointly owned). Joel Klein, the head of the Justice Department's antitrust division, believes the lawsuit could eventually lower interest rates if, by stripping Visa and MasterCard of market power, it creates a competitive incentive to develop new products and services.[221] Implicit in this reasoning is the idea that market power reduces the incentives to innovate.

Are the two preceding views—the Schumpeter hypothesis and the replacement effect—inconsistent with each other? Not necessarily. The view that large firms are the main source of R&D and technological progress is primarily based on the observation that large firms have more resources to invest than small firms. But why should that be important, one might ask. After all, if the gains from innovation for a small firm are very large, why doesn't the firm borrow money to invest in R&D? The answer is that capital markets are not perfect, especially when it comes to R&D investments. Suppose that a small firm has a great idea but no money to finance it, and a venture capitalist (VC) has money to finance ideas but no ideas. This might seem like a perfect match between supply and demand. The problem is that, to convince the VC that the idea is good, the firm needs to reveal it, risking to lose the idea without getting the funding. Nondisclosure agreements (NDAs) are an attempt to solve this problem, but they seldom work with VCs. By signing an NDA, a VC commits to not disclosing or using the information received from the NDA holder. But many VCs are unwilling to sign such an agreement. They claim they see too many similar ideas every week to have their tongues tied by any single one.[222] And so the problem persists. In fact, this problem is one of the reasons why a large fraction of total R&D investments are self-financed, and it indirectly explains why most R&D expenditures originate in large firms. Additional reasons why large firms may be better positioned to perform R&D include economies of scale and economies of scope in performing R&D;[a] also, large firms can more easily spread the risks from R&D.

By contrast, the idea that one should expect more R&D in more competitive industries results from the *incentives* for investing in R&D, not the *capacity* to do so. A

[a] Regarding economies of scope, one important aspect is that technological advances in one area frequently are used in a different area. A large firm that covers both areas is better positioned to exploit the full benefits from its R&D.

firm with market power increases its profits by innovating. A firm with no market power changes from a situation with no profits to one with positive profits. Even if the latter are lower than monopoly profits, the *increase* is likely to be larger, and it is the increase that matters from the perspective of incentives.

Notice, moreover, that the model illustrated in figure 16.1 is not entirely consistent with the assumptions of the perfect competition model. We have assumed that innovation lowers cost, allowing the innovator to undercut its rivals and capture the entire market. That is, effectively, the innovator is a monopolist ex-post, a monopolist protected by the legal or practical inability of its rivals to imitate it. If there were perfect competition, then, following innovation, every other firm would imitate the innovator, and perfect competition would drive profits down to zero, leaving little compensation for the innovator's effort.

In this sense, the preceding analysis is not entirely dissimilar from the second part of the Schumpeter hypothesis (see the earlier quotation). From a Schumpeterian point of view, the optimal market structure is not likely to be perfect competition, but rather a form of dynamic competition that involves some degree of monopoly power. Or, to put it the other way around, a form of monopoly that involves some degree of competition—not competition from currently existing firms, but rather potential competition from new products or production processes that may displace the current monopolist's product or production process. This is, in Schumpeter's words, the process of **creative destruction**.

In other words, following Schumpeter, many economists and policymakers subscribe to the view that perfect competition implies efficient resource allocation in a static sense, but that optimality breaks down when one takes dynamic efficiency into consideration. This is not to say that monopoly is the market structure that leads to the highest level of dynamic efficiency. Rather, it implies that the optimal system is one of dynamic competition where, in the short run, there always will be some degree of market power—temporary market power, however.

16.2   THE DYNAMICS OF R&D COMPETITION

Consider an industry with market "leaders" (large firms) and "followers" (small firms). Which of these have the greater propensity to invest in R&D? Does R&D contribute to the leveling of the field (smaller firms catching up with larger ones), or, on the contrary, is it a force toward increasing dominance, whereby the leaders tend to solidify their positions?

THE EFFICIENCY EFFECT AND THE PERSISTENCE OF MONOPOLY

To address the previous questions, consider a simple model with two firms: an incumbent ("monopolist") and a potential competitor ("rival"). Suppose, moreover, that there is a third player, an R&D lab, which has just discovered and patented an innovation. The R&D lab is unable to market its innovation directly, so it wants to sell the patent to the firm that is willing to pay the most. Which firm, monopoly or rival, is willing to pay the most for the innovation? Although neither firm is directly engaged in R&D, answering this question provides an indication as to which firm has the greater incentive to invest in R&D.

The monopolist is receiving monopoly profits π^M. If it acquires the patent, it will remain as a monopolist and receive the same monopoly profits, π^M (gross of the payment to the R&D lab), whereas the rival firm gets zero. If the rival firm obtains the rights to the patent, then it will be able to enter the market and compete with the monopolist, in which case each firm receives profits π^D.

In this context, the monopolist is willing to pay up to $\pi^M - \pi^D$ for the patent—the difference between profits in case it acquires the patent and profits in case it doesn't. The rival firm, in turn, is willing to bid up to $\pi^D - 0 = \pi^D$, again the difference between profits if it acquires the patent and profits if it doesn't. The condition that the monopolist is willing to pay more than the rival is therefore that $\pi^M - \pi^D > \pi^D$, or simply $\pi^M > 2\pi^D$. In other words, the monopolist is willing to pay more than the rival firm if and only if monopoly profits are greater than two times duopoly profits. But two times duopoly profits is simply industry profits under duopoly, so the condition requires that industry profits are greater under monopoly than under duopoly.

Unless the rival were to bring a substantially differentiated product to the market, we would expect the preceding condition to hold. In fact, if the products offered by the two firms are identical and marginal cost is constant, then profits under duopoly are surely lower than profits under monopoly. This implies that *the monopolist's incentives to invest in R&D are greater than the rival's*. The intuition for this important result is that *the monopolist has more to lose from not winning the bid for the patent (the difference between monopoly profits and duopoly profits) than the rival has to gain from winning it (duopoly profits)*. As a result, the monopolist's dominance over the industry will tend to persist over time. In other words, industry structure will move in the direction that total industry profits are higher (monopoly), a feature known as the **efficiency effect**.

Behavior in the plain-paper copier (PPC) market in the early 1970s illustrates the pattern predicted by the preceding model. In this market, Xerox was the leader ("monopolist") in the late 1960s: it had invented the plain-paper photocopier and was holding a monopoly position in that segment. Another firm, namely IBM, started to invest in R&D with a view toward discovering an alternative, or better, technology than Xerox's. But it was precisely Xerox who invested the most in R&D. See box 16.1 for details.

Another example is given by the insulin industry. Advances in biology during the 1970s, in particular the development of the technique of "gene-splicing," opened the possibility of producing medically useful substances. One obvious candidate was insulin, a protein that is used in the treatment and control of diabetes. The U.S. insulin market was then dominated by Eli Lilly & Co. If a new firm were to enter the market with synthetic human insulin, it would be competing against Eli Lilly. As it turned out, it was precisely Eli Lilly that made the greatest effort to secure dominance over the new production process. In May 1976, the pharmaceutical giant convened a conference with experts in recombinant DNA technology to study the possibility of developing the new technique. From then on, Eli Lilly maintained contacts with the various labs working on the project. On August 24, 1978, Genentech finally completed all of the steps required for

Box 16.1 Xerox's Plain Paper Copier[223]

One of the great inventions of the 1960s was Rank Xerox's technology of electrostatic copying ("xerography"). This technology allowed for copying onto plain paper at a substantially lower cost than photography-based methods. It was also much better in terms of quality than the older technology of "coated paper" copying.

With a view toward protecting its near-monopoly, Xerox patented not only the process of xerography but also every imaginable feature of its copier technology. As claimed in the suit later filed against it by the SCM Corporation, Xerox maintained a "patent thicket" wherein some innovations were neither used nor licensed to others. It would appear that the only purpose of these "sleeping patents" was to prevent competitors from inventing a technology similar to Xerox's.

The result was that, when IBM and Litton entered the market in 1972, Xerox sued them under literally hundreds of patents. More than 25% of IBM's budget at the time was devoted to patent counsel, not R&D. As a result of mounting complaints against Xerox's exclusionary strategy, the Federal Trade Commission eventually ordered Xerox to license its patents to all entrants at nominal cost. Within a few years, prices of plain-paper copiers were cut in half. Xerox's market share dropped from 100% in 1972 to less than 50% in 1977.

the synthesis of human insulin (ahead of three other rival labs). One day after Genentech's last experiment, Eli Lilly signed an agreement with the recently formed biotech firm.[224]

Still another example is given by the pharmaceutical industry. In April 1998, Pfizer Inc. launched Viagra, one of the biggest-selling drugs in the world. Viagra's success has attracted the attention of several competitors, some of which have started developing their own version of the drug. More importantly, Pfizer is itself developing an improved version of Viagra, in the hope that this will maintain the firm's dominant position, one step ahead of potential competitors.[225]

The Replacement Effect and Creative Destruction

Consider the following variation on the previous model: With probability ρ, the rival does not bid for the patent at all; however, at the time when bids are submitted, the monopolist does not know whether the rival is submitting a bid or not. This is not an unrealistic assumption: In fact, it is generally difficult to identify potential competitors and to assert how credible their intentions are.

Suppose moreover that, if neither the monopolist nor the rival submits a bid, then the new patent remains unused and the monopolist continues as initially. What is the monopolist's willingness to pay now? If the monopolist bids and acquires the patent, then it will continue to receive monopoly profits π^M. If it does not bid, with probability $1 - \rho$

the rival bids and the now ex-monopolist receives profits π^D; with probability ρ, however, the rival does not bid and the monopolist receives profits π^M (as initially). This implies that the monopolist is willing to bid up to $\pi^M - \left((1-\rho)\pi^D + \rho\pi^M\right) = (1-\rho)(\pi^M - \pi^D)$. The rival, in turn, is still willing to bid up to π^D. We conclude that, *if there is significant uncertainty about the presence of a rival (high ρ), then the monopolist is willing to pay less for the innovation than the rival.*[b]

The intuition for this result can be found in the replacement effect, to which we alluded in the previous section. With probability ρ, the rival is not a binding constraint to the monopolist. This implies that acquiring the patent brings the monopolist few benefits—in fact, no benefits at all. The monopolist is replacing initial monopoly profits π^M with monopoly profits π^M from the new product. In other words, the monopolist is *cannibalizing its own monopoly profits.*

Box 16.2 presents an example of this—videogame machines in the late 1980s. In this example, Nintendo was the monopolist, Sega the rival firm. Although there was not a patent bidding process as considered earlier, the outcome of the game played between Nintendo and Sega was that the latter was the first to introduce a new, improved machine. Although Nintendo had the possibility of following the same route, the firm decided against it, based on the idea that introducing the better machine would have the effect of eating into the market share of its old machine.

So far, we have considered the case of a **gradual innovation**, that is, an innovation that does not displace the existing product. In other words, we have assumed that even if the rival enters the market with the new product, the monopolist is still able to make positive profits.[c] Consider now the case of a **drastic innovation**, that is, an innovation that renders the existing product obsolete. In this case, if the rival acquires the patent and enters the industry, the monopolist's profits are zero, whereas the rival itself makes monopoly profits.

Let us redo the above calculations but assuming now a drastic innovation. If the monopolist bids and acquires the patent, its profits will be π^M. If the monopolist does not bid, then with probability $1 - \rho$ the rival bids and the monopolist receives zero profits; with probability ρ, however, the rival does not bid and the monopolist receives profits π^M (as initially). This implies that the monopolist is willing to bid up to $\pi^M - \left((1-\rho)0 + \rho\pi^M\right) = (1-\rho)\pi^M$. The rival, in turn, is now willing to bid up to π^M, which is greater than $(1-\rho)\pi^M$. We conclude that *the monopolist is willing to pay less for a drastic innovation than the rival is.*

We can summarize the preceding results as follows:

[b] Specifically, the condition is that ρ be greater than $(\pi^M - 2\pi^D)/(\pi^M - \pi^D)$.

[c] For simplicity, we have assumed that, upon entry, the rival makes the same profits as the monopolist, but we could easily have considered the case when the rival's profits are greater than the monopolist's; the same intuitions would still apply.

> Incumbent firms have a greater incentive than entrants to perform R&D toward a gradual innovation. If, however, there is uncertainty regarding the threat of entry or if the innovation is sufficiently drastic, then outsiders may have a greater incentive to perform R&D than incumbents.

Box 16.2 Sega versus Nintendo[226]

Video games are a big business. Nintendo, one of the success stories of the 1980s, finished the decade with a market value exceeding Sony's and Nissan's. Nintendo's main product was then an 8-bit machine and a series of games featuring the popular Mario. Sega, although an older firm, was by then a distant second in terms of market share.

Since the late 1980s, Nintendo had been developing a faster, 16-bit machine. Nintendo, however, was not in a hurry to launch the new product: "The Nintendo philosophy is that we haven't maxed out the 8-bit system yet." In fact, by the late 1980s, Nintendo's 8-bit machine was at the peak of its sales. Launching the 16-bit machine might significantly cannibalize the market for the slower system.

Sega did not have to worry about such trade-offs. In October 1988, it introduced its 16-bit Mega Drive home video-game system. The advantage of having a more powerful machine is that it allows for better image and sound, as well as the possibility of displaying multilayered images. A better system coupled with aggressive marketing led Sega to significantly increase its market share during the early 1990s.

Eventually—in September 1991, that is, three years later—Nintendo introduced its own 16-bit machine. A fierce price war ensued, with Nintendo and Sega sharing the market in approximately equal shares. In the transition from the 8-bit system to the 16-bit system, Nintendo lost its position of near-monopoly, having to share the market with Sega. However, it is not clear whether Nintendo could have done better than it did. Although an early launch of the 16-bit system might have protected its market share, it might not have increased the firm's total profits if we include those from sales of 8-bit machines.

RISK CHOICE

Very often, choosing an R&D strategy is choosing not just how much to invest but also how to invest. Specifically, firms must consider the strategic choice of risk of their R&D strategies. The trade-offs involved in the choice of risk are typically the following: A low-risk strategy is one that implies a low-value innovation with a high probability, whereas a high-risk strategy is one that implies a high-value innovation with a low probability.

The conventional wisdom from sports competition states that a team that is behind in a race should adopt a riskier strategy, the idea being that such team has "little to lose." Consider, for example, the Superbowl or the World Cup. To lose by one point or to lose by several points makes little difference. This is the sense in which a trailing team has little to lose. By contrast, the trailing team has a lot to gain from reversing the relative positions of the two teams. It should, therefore, adopt a high-risk strategy,

TABLE 16.2 THE EVOLUTION OF ANTIDEPRESSANTS.[227]

Class	Date Introduced	Brand Names
MAO inhibitors	1950s	Nardil, Parnate
Tricyclics	1950s	Elavil, Tofranil, Pamelor
Selective serotonin reuptake inhibitors	1987	Prozac, Zoloft, Paxil
Substance P receptor blocker	Under development	No products named yet

like passing on a fourth-down (American football) or sending the goalie to score on a corner kick (soccer). The leading team, in turn, faces the exactly opposite incentives: It has little to gain from moving further ahead in the score (winning by one point is not very different from winning by several points), but it stands to lose a lot if the score is reversed. Accordingly, the leading team has a great incentive to play a safe strategy, one that is unlikely to increase its lead but that will maintain the lead with a high probability.

A similar intuition applies in the context of R&D competition. Consider an industry where, by means of R&D investment, firms attempt to move up a product-quality ladder (e.g., microprocessor speed) or down a cost ladder (e.g., steel production cost). In this context, a safe strategy is one that implies a small step up the ladder with a high probability, whereas a risky strategy is one that leads to a large jump with a low probability. Take the example of the market for antidepressants, the evolution of which is briefly summarized in table 16.2. As of the early 1990s, a pharmaceutical firm could select between two alternative strategies:

1. Invest in the development (or improvement) of an antidepressant based on the selective serotonin reuptake inhibitor approach. This would be a relatively safe strategy. The technology is relatively well known and the probability of success is accordingly high. However, the extent of success is probably limited as the new drug would imply at best a modest improvement over the existing ones.

2. Invest in the development of an antidepressant based on the substance P receptor blocker approach. This would be a relatively risky strategy. Because no drugs have been developed according to this approach, there is a significant probability that problems will arise that will turn the project into a flop. However, conditional on success, the payoff will likely be high because major improvements over the current drugs are a distinct possibility.

Based on the intuition from sports competition, one would expect market leaders to invest primarily in improvements to their current products (safe strategy), whereas market laggards (and outsiders) would primarily invest in the new class of products.

Generally, one would expect market leaders to be primarily responsible for small, incremental innovations; small firms and outsiders would tend to be primarily responsible for large, radical innovations.

LEARNING-BY-DOING AND MARKET DOMINANCE

Many industries are characterized by a steep **learning curve**, that is, a significant negative relation between production cost and cumulative output (or some other measure of past production experience). The learning curve can be understood as an instance of complementarity between R&D and production, that is, a form of R&D that involves production. Typical industries in which the learning curve is important include shipbuilding, aircraft manufacturing, and manufacturing of semiconductors. For example, it has been estimated that the production cost of a semiconductor drops by about 20% following each doubling of cumulative production. Learning effects may be related to a particular product or to a class of products, such as the Boeing 7xx line of aircraft.

The learning curve provides an additional source of persistent dominance, or even increasing dominance, by the market leader: By selling more, the leader lowers its cost faster, which in turn makes it more competitive, which in turn makes it sell more, and so on.[228] Boeing's dominance of the wide-body market (with the B747) is attributed, to a great extent, to its ability to move down the learning curve faster than its rivals (McDonnell Douglas DC10 and Lockheed 1011) and to take advantage of the "snowball" effect that this implied.

The computer memory industry provides another interesting example. Erasable Programmable Read Only Memories (EPROMs) and Dynamic Random Access Memories (DRAMs) are two types of memory. One important difference between EPROMs and DRAMs is that production economies of scale play an important role in the latter, whereas the learning curve is particularly important for EPROMs.[229] Table 16.3 presents data on the leading suppliers of a series of generations of computer memory chips. The first part pertains to EPROMs, the second to DRAMs. The data seem roughly consistent with the idea that the learning curve contributes to a greater persistence in market dominance: The top positions in the EPROM market seem much more stable than in the DRAM market.

ORGANIZATIONAL VERSUS STRATEGIC CONSIDERATIONS[230]

The photolithographic alignment industry produces machines that are used by semiconductor manufacturers in the production of DRAMs and other solid-state devices. Over the past forty years, the industry has been subject to a fast rate of technical progress. However, innovation has consistently been of an incremental nature in the sense that— as considered earlier—noninnovating incumbents have managed to maintain a positive market share. The innovators have been in some cases incumbent firms, in other cases new entrants.

A closer look at the industry reveals some interesting patterns. Although all of the innovations have been gradual from a *market* perspective (i.e., noninnovating incumbents remain active), the same is not true from an *organizational* point of view. Each

TABLE 16.3 MARKET LEADERS IN VARIOUS GENERATIONS OF EPROMs AND DRAMs.[231]

EPROMs

8K		32K		512K	
Intel	22	Intel	18	Intel	42
Texas Inst.	17	Texas Inst.	17	AMD	26
National	16	AMD	11	Texas Inst.	16
AMD	13	NEC	10		

DRAMs

4K		1M		4M	
Intel	46	Toshiba	22	Samsung	13
Texas Inst.	25	Samsung	14	NEC	12
Mostek	14	NEC	10	Hitachi	11
		Mitsubishi	10	Toshiba	11

firm's R&D "production function" consists of a series of capabilities that are best suited for the type of research the firm has conducted in the past. In this organizational sense, some of the innovations in the industry were radical; that is, some of the innovations, if introduced by an incumbent, would imply a significant change in that firm's R&D process and would render previous R&D capabilities obsolete. It turns out that all of the radical innovations (in this organizational sense) were introduced by entrants, whereas incumbents mostly introduced gradual innovations (both in the market sense and in the organizational sense). Incumbents did try to invest in more radical innovations, but they were much less productive than entrants in doing so.

This example suggests a number of observations. First, it confirms the prediction that incumbents tend to invest relatively more in gradual innovations, while entrants are the main source of drastic innovations. Second, it shows that there may be a difference between the amount each firm invests in R&D and the actual rate of innovation; in other words, firms may differ in their R&D productivity. Third, and more importantly, the example suggests that strategic considerations may not be the only driver of R&D and industry structure. In fact, a detailed analysis of the photolithographic alignment industry suggests that **organizational inertia** may be as important or more important than strategic considerations in determining the patterns of R&D investment.

16.3 PUBLIC POLICY

As hinted at the beginning of the chapter, economic growth and welfare result to a great extent from technical progress. Not surprisingly, governments are eager to foster the rate at which firms invest in R&D. The most direct way of doing so—though not necessarily the most efficient—is to subsidize R&D by firms (and by other institutions, such as universities and research laboratories). In this section, we consider two areas of public policy that indirectly affect the extent to which firms engage in R&D: patent protection and policy toward interfirm agreements pertaining to R&D.

PATENTS

The primary purpose of the patent system is to reward innovators. However, because patents grant their holders monopoly rights, patents imply an efficiency cost, the allocative inefficiency from monopoly pricing. This is the first basic trade-off faced by the policymaker: Granting more valuable patents increases the incentives for R&D, which in the long run results in a higher rate of technical progress. But it also increases market power, resulting in a lower degree of economic efficiency.[232]

There are several dimensions, in addition to length, along which patents can be made weaker or stronger. Sections 102 and 103 of the U.S. Patent Code, for example, impose the requirements of "novelty" and "nonobviousness" for a patent application to be accepted. To give a simple example, it would be difficult to obtain a patent on the process of combining tea and ice cubes to produce a refreshing drink (iced tea). In fact, it would be difficult to argue that (1) iced tea is a novel product (after all, it is just tea served at a lower temperature) and (2) the production process is not obvious (combining ice with an existing drink is a fairly obvious idea).

Aside from extreme examples, there is inevitably room for discretion in determining the extent of the novelty and nonobviousness requirements. Ultimately, it is up to the courts to determine the strength of the protection provided by the system of intellectual property rights. To give an example of actual patent litigation that took place in the 1980s: Does a protein produced with recombinant DNA infringe a patent on the same protein produced synthetically?

A related issue is that of **patent breadth**. In fact, the example just given can be thought of as one of patent breadth: Did the original patent on the protein cover only the protein when produced synthetically (narrow breadth), or did it extend to other production processes as well (wide breadth)? Another example of the issues involved with patent breadth is given by tennis rackets. For a long time, tennis rackets were designed with the standard size of 70 square inches. Then came Howard Head of Prince Manufacturing, inventor of the oversized racket. In the United States, Prince was granted patent protection for rackets ranging from 85 to 130 square inches. The same breadth of patent protection did not apply, however, in other countries, such as England, Germany, or Japan. The different treatment received in the United States is consistent with the

American "doctrine of equivalents," whereby a product serving the same purpose as a patented one may infringe the latter's patent.[233]

The concepts of novelty requirement and breadth of protection are also of great importance in the context of **copyright** protection. Copyrights are not the same as patents. The latter apply to products, processes, substances, and designs. Copyrights, in turn, apply to artistic works and works of authorship when these are fixed in a tangible medium, such as a book or a CD ROM. Despite this difference, the same principles of public policy that apply to patents apply to copyrights as well. In particular, an interesting issue regarding the copyright of software is the breadth of the copyright, or, alternatively, the novelty requirement imposed on subsequent works of software. Did the Windows operating system infringe on Apple's MacIntosh OS copyright? Did the Nintendo's computer game system infringe on Atari's copyright? Generally, does the software copyright protect the code itself or the "look and feel" of the software's operation? Previous court decisions on these and related cases have been mixed, but tend to recognize copyright protection for the "look and feel" of the software. It remains an issue, however, how similar the "look and feel" must be before infringement is declared.

To summarize, both patent protection and copyright protection come in degrees. Changing the breadth or the novelty requirement—generally, changing the *strength* of protection—makes patents and copyrights more or less valuable. What then is the optimal policy? As seen earlier, when it comes to the optimal duration of a patent, the trade-off is simple: A longer patent is more valuable and thus provides a greater incentive for innovation; however a longer patent also implies longer-lasting monopoly power, which in turn lowers the market's allocative efficiency. A similar trade-off applies with respect to the strength of patent protection: The stronger the patent is, the greater the incentive for innovation; however, a stronger patent also implies less competition in the postinnovation market, that is, a lower likelihood that additional competitors will appear.

However, having two instruments to play with (length and strength of protection), we are now faced with a new trade-off: Given a certain desired level of patent protection, should that value be achieved by means of stronger patents, or rather by means of longer ones? One first answer to this question is suggested by figure 16.2.[234] A strong patent would give its owner monopoly profits for the duration of the patent: This is given in figure 16.2 by the area $q^M(p^M - c)$, where q^M and p^M are monopoly output and price, respectively, and c is marginal cost (which, for simplicity, we assume to be constant). Suppose, however, that we make patents slightly weaker, so that the patent holder is subject to some competition and is unable to charge more than p^L, where $p^L < p^M$. One way of implementing such a weaker patent would be to force the patent holder to license the patent for the value $p^L - c$, a value that is lower than the monopoly margin. Assuming that competition takes place as in the Bertrand model, licensing for a fee $p^L - c$ would effectively drive prices down to p^L.

Under this weak patent system, the monopolist is actually indifferent between selling directly to the consumer or receiving license fees from rival competitors. Specifically,

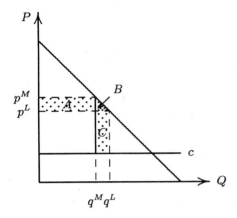

FIGURE 16.2 PATENT STRENGTH AND PATENT VALUE.

with respect to the strong patent case, the patent holder loses profits corresponding to area A and gains profits corresponding to area C. If the weak patent is just a little weaker than the strong patent—that is, if the license fee is just a little lower than p^M minus c—then areas A and C are approximately equal. In other words, the patent holder suffers very little from a slight weakening of the patent.[d]

From the point of view of allocative efficiency, however, even a slight weakening of the patent system has a significant effect. In fact, with respect to the strong patent system, the weak patent system increases total welfare by an amount equal to areas B plus C.

Thus, in terms of postinnovation value, society has much more to gain from a weakening of the patent system than the monopolist has to lose. This contrasts with changing the duration of the patent: In terms of postinnovation value, what a monopolist has to gain from a longer patent is proportional to what society has to lose. Double the patent life and you double both the patent value and total allocative inefficiency. Putting these facts together suggests that an optimal patent system should make patents very long but very weak. This would seem to be the best compromise between making patents valuable and minimizing the allocative inefficiency that they induce.

This is not the end of the story, however. One of the purposes of patents, in addition to giving incentives for innovation, is to publicize the relevant information regarding the product or process in question. In fact, it is a requirement for a patent that it should contain "a written description . . . in such full, clear, concise and exact terms as to enable any person skilled in the art . . . to make and use the same" (U.S. Patent Code, Section 112). Among other things, this allows the information possessed by one party to be available to everyone else, thus accelerating the aggregate rate of innovation.

The disclosure requirement may, however, create the wrong incentives for R&D investors. Suppose that a laboratory has made a basic innovation, one that can be used as a basis for several other derived innovations. For example, a technique for locating and purifying human genes (basic innovation) may be used in the development of a

[d] This is a consequence of the fact that profits are a concave function of price, and p^M, the monopoly price, is the value that maximizes profits. In the neighborhood of the optimal solution, the derivative of profit with respect to price is approximately equal to zero: A slightly lower (or higher) price leads to an approximately equal profit.

series of medical drugs (derived innovations). If patent protection is very weak—in the sense described previously—then the inventor will have little incentive to patent. In fact, by keeping its invention secret, it will have a better chance at winning the race to develop the derived innovations that flow from the basic one. But, from a social point of view, such delay in making information public may be costly. In fact, it implies that only one firm—as opposed to several firms—will be engaged in research directed at derived innovations.[235] An optimal patent system should trade off this effect against the allocative efficiency effect considered in the preceding discussion.

To summarize:

> An optimal patent system balances the benefits from greater incentives for R&D against the costs of increased market power implied by patent rights.

R&D Agreements

Government authorities are normally defensive when it comes to agreements between firms. As we have seen in chapter 8, firms have much to benefit from softening product market competition, consumers being the main losers in the process. What about agreements with respect to R&D?

The answer to this question depends, to a great extent, on the degree of **spillovers** across firms. No man is an island; likewise, no firm performs R&D in isolation. Some of the R&D results obtained by firms become public knowledge, thus benefiting other firms as well. Some other results are leaked out because workers leave the firm to join rival firms, or simply because researchers share their latest achievements at scientific conferences, with little or no concern for the commercial implications of their actions. Whichever the reason, it is generally agreed that $1 of R&D expenditure by firm i benefits firm j to the same extent as if firm j had spent γ dollars on R&D, where γ is a number between zero and one.

Let us consider the extreme situation when γ is close to one, that is, very high spillovers. In this case, R&D expenditures are like a public good among all firms in the industry. It is a well-known result that the private provision of public goods leads to underinvestment. In other words, society would be better off if firms were to invest more in public goods. When a firm invests, it does not take into account that its expenditure benefits not only the investor but also a number of other firms. In this context, R&D agreements between firms may serve to alleviate the **free-rider problem** associated with public goods.

An additional reason why efficient R&D investment levels may require cooperation between firms is the sheer size and risk of some R&D projects, such as developing a new aircraft, designing a new microchip, or initiating a new line of pharmaceutical research. In these cases, allowing for interfirm cooperation—or even the merger between competing firms—may be necessary for the research project to be undertaken at all.

Consider, however, the extreme case when γ is close to zero, that is, spillovers are very low. Suppose moreover that (1) R&D competition takes the form of a race with a fixed prize; (2) the social value of innovation is much higher than the private value;[e] and (3) when firm i's expenditure increases, the probability that firm i is the first to innovate increases, the probability that innovation occurs at all increases, and the probability that firm j is the first to innovate decreases. In this case, the externality between firms is the other way around: When firm i increases its R&D expenditures, it does not take into account the fact that firm j decreases the probability of winning the race. In other words, part of the gain from increased R&D expenditures is a loss for a rival firm. Consequently, if firms i and j were to choose their R&D budgets jointly—the essence of an R&D agreement—they would end up choosing lower levels. And this would be bad from a social point of view: Given the difference between private and social value from innovation (the second assumption earlier), society would be better off if firms were to increase R&D expenditures, not reduce them.

> Interfirm R&D agreements may have the virtue of alleviating the free-rider problem. However, they may also lead to an undesirable reduction in total R&D expenditures.

The latter possibility notwithstanding, public policy toward R&D agreements tends to be far more tolerant than that regarding other interfirm agreements. In the European Union, Paragraph 1 or Article 85 of the Treaty of Rome prohibits interfirm agreements that distort competition. However, a block exemption was issued in 1984 for agreements pertaining to R&D (Regulation No. 418/85). In justifying such exemption, the European Commission argued that

In many cases, the synergy arising out of cooperation is necessary because it enables the partners to share the financial risks involved, and in particular, to bring together a wider range of intellectual and mental resources and experience, thus promoting the transfer of technology.[236]

In the United States, the relevant legislation is the National Cooperative Research Act of 1984. This Act mandates that research agreements, if challenged under the U.S. antitrust laws, be judged under a rule of reason. Specifically, one should investigate whether the alleged restraint of trade was necessary for achieving the ends of the research agreement. This falls short of the E.U. block exemption, which essentially provides a

[e] For example, it may be the case that regulation prevents firms from setting very high prices, whereby the ratio between consumer and producer surplus is very high.

"safe harbor" for R&D agreements. Although an exemption was proposed in the United States, it was felt that

The principal difficulty with this proposal lay in its elimination of any threat of private enforcement to ensure that market power is not unreasonably exercised.[237]

This contrast between Europe and the United States is in fact typical, with the U.S. legislator preferring to err on the side of promoting competition, the European Union on the side of promoting cooperation.

SUMMARY

- Incumbent firms have a greater incentive than entrants to perform R&D toward a gradual innovation. If, however, there is uncertainty regarding the threat of entry, or if the innovation is sufficiently drastic, then outsiders may have a greater incentive to perform R&D than incumbents.

- An optimal patent system balances the benefits from greater incentives for R&D against the costs of increased market power implied by patent rights.

- Interfirm R&D agreements may have the virtue of alleviating the free-rider problem. However, they may also lead to an undesirable reduction in total R&D expenditures.

KEY CONCEPTS

- creative destruction
- replacement effect and efficiency effect
- gradual and drastic innovations
- organizational inertia
- spillovers and free-riding
- patent and copyright protection

REVIEW AND PRACTICE EXERCISES

16.1   "Perfect competition is not only impossible but inferior, and has no title to being set up as a model of ideal efficiency." Do you agree? Why or why not?

16.2   "R&D competition implies a dynamic system whereby industries tend to become more and more concentrated." Do you agree? Why or why not?

16.3   Two firms are engaged in Bertrand competition. There are 10,000 people in the population, each of whom is willing to pay at most 10 for at most one unit of the good. Currently, both firms have a constant marginal cost of 5.

a. What is the equilibrium in this market? What are the firms' profits?

b. Suppose that one firm can adopt a new technology that lowers its marginal cost to 3. What is the equilibrium now? How much would this firm be willing to pay for this new technology?

c. Suppose the new technology mentioned in (b) is available to both firms. The cost to a firm of purchasing this technology is 10,000. The game is now played in two stages. First, the firms simultaneously decide whether to adopt the new technology or not. Then, in the second stage, the firms set prices simultaneously. Assume that each firm knows whether or not its rival acquired the new technology when choosing its prices. What is (are) the Nash equilibrium (equilibria) of this game? (What does your answer suggest about why firms engage in patent races?)[238]

16.4*   In 1984, the U.S. Congress passed legislation that allowed generic drug makers to receive fast marketing approval from the Food and Drug Administration (FDA). Since then, the market share of generic drug companies has increased considerably (in volume). Branded drug companies have attempted different tactics to protect their market share. In some cases, large pharmaceutical firms have paid generic firms to keep off the market. Ivax Corp. and Novartis AG, for example, have agreed not to market a generic competitor to Abbott Laboratories' hypertension drug Hytrin. In exchange, Abott pays quarterly fees totaling several million dollars.[239]

Compare this example to the discussion on the persistence of monopoly power.

16.5   Patent life is 17 years in the United States and 20 years in Europe. From the perspective of social welfare, do you find this period too short or too long? Explain

16.6   Should firms be allowed to enter into agreements regarding R&D?

CHAPTER 17

NETWORKS AND STANDARDS

For a consumer in the 1990s, life without telephones may be difficult to imagine. But let us mentally go back to the 1880s and ask ourselves the question: How much would having a telephone be worth? The likely answer is "not very much," as the number of other telephone owners was then rather small. To take a more recent example, consider electronic mail. Ten or fifteen years ago, outside of the military and academic worlds, there were few benefits to having an e-mail address because the number of people with whom one could exchange messages was minimal.

Both of these are examples of **network externalities**, the situation whereby the benefit a consumer derives from owning a product increases when the number of other consumers increases. This is true for both telephones and e-mail. In fact, these two means of communication have one additional aspect in common: Both are examples of *direct* network externalities, those that arise when the different buyers form a network of users who communicate with each other. However, direct network externalities are by no means the only relevant instance when consumers care about the number of other consumers. The benefit from buying a Windows-based computer, for example, is greater the greater the number of other buyers of the same operating system: Even if a computer user does not directly communicate with others, the fact that there are many of them implies that a great variety of software will be written for the popular operating system.

In this chapter, we look at a number of issues of competition with network externalities. In section 17.1, we introduce the simple economics of demand with network effects, including the concepts of consumer expectations and critical mass. In section 17.2, we present a simple model of the competition between two different, incompatible versions of a new technology (for example, two versions of Digital Versatile Disks). In section 17.3, we consider the case when a new version competes against an old version of the same technology (e.g., 3.5-in floppies vs $5\frac{1}{4}$-in floppies). Strategic compatibility decisions are addressed in section 17.4. Finally, section 17.5 considers some issues of public policy in the context of networks and standards.

17.1   CONSUMER EXPECTATIONS AND CRITICAL MASS

The demand for products subject to network externalities has some peculiarities that are not present in "normal" demand curves. The utility each consumer derives from the product depends on how many other consumers there are who purchase the same product—the size of the network of users. Or, to be more precise, demand depends on what each consumer *expects* the size of the network will be. The previous sentence points to an important element in the determination of demand under network effects: **consumer expectations**.

To illustrate this point, suppose there are one million consumers for a new technology subject to network effects. Each consumer's valuation for the product is given by n, where n is the number of other adopters (if the number of adopters is large, then this is approximately network size). In other words, the greater the value of n, the greater the valuation each potential buyer has for the product. Specifically, each consumer is willing to pay up to n^e for the product, where n^e is the *expected* size of the network.

Suppose that each consumer expects no other consumer will join the network, that is, $n^e = 0$. Then no consumer is willing to pay a positive value to join the network, for the net benefit would be negative. It follows that, for any positive price, it is a Nash equilibrium for no consumer to join the network of technology adopters. We may refer to this as a **fulfilled-expectations equilibrium**, to emphasize the fact that the equilibrium value of n is equal to the expected value n^e.

Suppose now that every consumer expects every other consumer to join the network. This implies that each consumer is willing to pay up to 999,999 for the new technology. Suppose that the price is less than 999,999. Then we have a second Nash equilibrium, namely for every adopter to join the network of technology adopters. To summarize, for prices greater than zero and lower than 999,999, there exist two Nash equilibria, one where every consumer buys the new technology and one where no consumer buys the new technology. In other words:

> Network effects may imply multiple demand levels for a given price. Which value takes place depends on consumers' expectations regarding network size.

What can we say about this "chicken-and-egg" problem? For example, if the price is 900,000, which equilibrium would we expect to prevail—zero adopters or one million adopters? What if price is 900? Strictly speaking, both equilibria are possible in both cases. However, intuitively, the low-adoption equilibrium seems more likely in the case when price is high; the high-adoption equilibrium seems more likely in the low-price case. Suppose that price is 900,000. In this case, consumers would go ahead and purchase the technology only if they were sure at least 900,000 other consumers (out of a million) would do the same. If, however, price is 900, then it suffices for each consumer to believe 900 other consumers (out of a million) would do the same.

In practice, games of technology adoption are played over time, not in a single period. Suppose that price is 900. Even if most consumers are pessimistic about the chances of converging to the high-adoption equilibrium, it is likely that 900 out of one million (less than .1%) will indeed purchase the technology. Once this happens, it becomes a dominant strategy for the other consumers to purchase as well (because 900 consumers have already bought, the future network size is at least 900). We would thus expect the market to rapidly converge toward the high-adoption equilibrium. In other words, convergence to the high equilibrium depends on passing a given threshold (900 adopters in the case when price is 900). Once that threshold is crossed, demand will continue increasing in a self-reinforcing process that ends in the large-network equilibrium. This threshold level is usually referred to as the **critical mass** of buyers that leads to the buildup of the network. Finally, from the preceding analysis, we also conclude that the lower the price, the greater the likelihood that the threshold is crossed, that is, the critical mass is achieved.

These observations have a number of implications. In a competitive market, where price depends primarily on cost considerations, and technical progress drives costs down over time, we would expect the initial equilibrium to be a high price and a very small or nonexisting network (zero adoption equilibrium). As time passes, cost goes down and so does price. Eventually, the critical threshold is crossed, and demand converges to the high-network equilibrium. As an illustration, figure 17.1 depicts the evolution of the

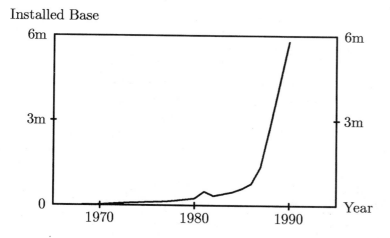

Installed Base

FIGURE 17.1 FAX MACHINES IN THE UNITED STATES: INSTALLED BASE, BY YEAR.[240]

installed base for fax machines over the 1980s, the decade when demand took off in the United States. The figure suggests that, around 1986, a critical-mass threshold was crossed, leading to a rapid convergence toward a large-network equilibrium.

In markets that are monopolized or wherein one firm holds significant power to set prices, the preceding observations suggest that a successful strategy might be to set a low introductory price to get the "snowball rolling," that is, to get demand past the critical mass and onto the high-network equilibrium. The Bell company was one of the first firms to adopt this strategy, when telephones were first introduced in the United States in the 1890s. Additional examples of introductory pricing are presented in section 17.3.

In markets with strong network effects, a large installed base of users is an asset that must be maintained with care, for there is always the danger of tilting toward a low-adoption equilibrium. Take the example of eBay. Founded in 1995 as a person-to-person internet auction site, eBay has grown at an incredibly fast rate: By the end of 1999, it counted more than nine million registered users. Online auction houses like eBay provide a good example of network effects: The more users sell through eBay, the greater the variety of items that can be found, and the greater the value of buying through eBay. Likewise, the greater the number of buyers, the greater the number and value of bids, and the greater the value of selling through eBay. eBay's revenues are collected from listing fees charged to sellers who post their items in the company's website. In 1999, eBay reduced a planned fee increase in response to strong negative reaction from its customers. It seems eBay is aware of the danger that a number of its customers will "defect" and start selling through rival auction sites (Amazon.com, Yahoo!, and so forth). Such a move might create a "snowball" effect that would end up destroying eBay's current competitive advantage of a large installed base of users.[a]

17.2   PATH DEPENDENCE[241]

The classic model of economics is an ahistorical model. The equilibrium in a given industry, the value of firms, and so forth, are determined by the forces of long-run supply and demand. Yes, there can be other factors that have a transitory effect—a storm, a fad—but sooner or later, the forces of supply and demand take the economy back to its equilibrium state. In mathematical terms, we say that the economy is an *ergodic* system: The state of the economy at time $t + k$ does not depend on the state of the economy at time t, if k is large enough. In other words, historical events may have an effect, but that effect vanishes as time goes by.

Network externalities provide an interesting challenge to this view of the world. Why is VHS, not Betamax, the accepted standard for consumer videocassette recorders? Why does Windows, not MacOS, dominate the market for operating systems? Generally, why is English, not Italian, the *lingua franca* of the modern world? In all of these cases, the answer must be based on the historical process that led to the cur-

[a] As of November 1999, eBay was receiving more than 1.2 million visitors a day, whereas Yahoo! Auctions and Amazon Auctions had only 105,000 and 70,000, respectively.

rent equilibrium as opposed to an alternative equilibrium. In other words, there is no argument that makes one equilibrium necessarily more compelling than the other ones.[b]

To understand the importance of historical events in the development of an industry with network externalities, let us consider a simple model. There are two versions of a new technology, say a videocassette recorder (VCR). The two versions (e.g., Betamax and VHS) are incompatible with each other, so the network benefits accrue only to buyers of the same version. The prices of each version are exogenously given. For simplicity, suppose they are the same.

Consumers arrive in the market sequentially. That is, in each period, a new consumer must make a decision of which version of the new technology to choose, A or B. Some consumers have a preference for A, some for B. However, every consumer prefers to buy a version that has a large installed base. Specifically, "A fans" derive a utility of $u + n_A$ from an A machine and a utility n_B from a B machine, where n_A and n_B represent the size of the installed base of A and B machines, respectively. u is the utility that an A fan derives from product A even if no other consumer buys the same product, also known as *standalone utility*; as can be seen, an A fan derives no standalone utility from machine B (in fact, this difference is the reason why it is called an "A fan"); finally, n_i ($i = A, B$) is the network-related component of utility, the same for both machines (conditional on network size, of course). Analogously, "B fans" derive a utility of $u + n_B$ from a B machine and a utility n_A from an A machine.

Notice that, if $n_A = n_B$, then A fans buy A and B fans buy B. However, if one of the technologies has a sufficiently greater installed base, then both types will buy the same technology. Specifically, if $u + n_A < n_B$, then even A fans prefer to buy technology B. That is, if $n_B - n_A > u$, then both types buy technology B. By analogy, if $n_A - n_B > u$ then both types buy technology A.

This situation is depicted in figure 17.2. On the horizontal axis, we plot the sequence of consumers arriving in the market, one in each period. On the vertical axis, we plot the difference in installed base between technologies A and B. As long as the difference is within the band $[-u, u]$, each consumer will choose his or her preferred technology. However, once we go out of these barriers, every consumer will choose the leading technology, *which in turn reinforces the choice by subsequent consumers*. In other words, we are in the presence of a **self-reinforcing process**. The barriers u and $-u$ are **absorbing barriers**. Once we pass these barriers, we say that the industry is **locked-in** to one of the technologies.

This model, simple as it is, allows us to derive a number of implications. First, notice that, sooner or later, the industry is bound to become locked-in to a given standard.[c] A second implication is that, in this world, *the best does not always necessarily win*. To understand this, suppose that there are more A fans than there are B fans. Because the utility functions are symmetric, it would be optimal for the market to choose technology A. At least, it would certainly be suboptimal to be locked-in to technology B. However, the latter outcome is clearly possible: Even though, on the whole, there are more A fans than there are B fans, it is quite possible that B fans will be represented more than proportionately among the first series of adopters.

[b] Some countries drive on the right while others drive on the left. This example, which also features network externalities (if in an extremely dramatic way), suggests that there can be more than one equilibrium, and that no particular equilibrium dominates the other one.

[c] We should remark, however, that the strength of this conclusion depends crucially on the assumption that utility is linear, not concave, in the size of the network. If utility were concave and the size of u large in relation to the value of network externalities, then it would be conceivable that the industry would maintain the two technologies indefinitely. See exercise 17.6.

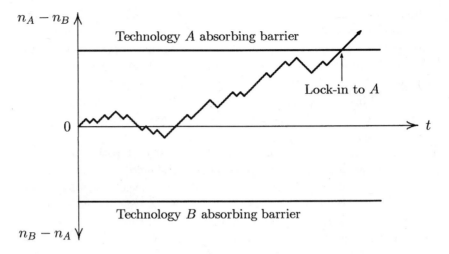

FIGURE 17.2 TECHNOLOGY ADOPTION WITH NETWORK EXTERNALITIES.

This last remark points to a third important characteristic of the model of sequential technology adoption: The eventual outcome, in terms of which technology the industry gets locked-in to, will depend on the outcome of a limited, possibly small, number of initial adoptions. In other words, the first consumers' decisions may turn out to be very important *small historical events*. Dynamic processes that have this property are said to be **path dependent**.

The battle between Betamax and VHS illustrates several of these points. (See box 17.1 for a more detailed analysis.) In this industry, the main source of network externalities is that rental store availability of videos in a given format (Betamax, VHS) depends to a great extent on the number of owners of a machine for that format. If there are very few Betamax owners in a given neighborhood, then it is unlikely that a video store will have an interest in stocking tapes recorded in that format. As the model would predict, the industry did indeed get locked-in to one of the technologies, VHS. The possibility of an industry getting locked-in to an inferior technology is illustrated by this case: Many experts claim that the quality of the Betamax technology was (and continues to be) superior to VHS. Finally, the fate of a multibillion dollar industry was decided at a time (late 1970s to early 1980s) when the number of adopters was still relatively small. Their decisions turned out to be important small historical events.

Another example, if a somewhat controversial one, is given by typewriters' keyboard layout. The design that is currently used, the QWERTY design, was patented in 1868 by Christopher Sholes. The main advantage of QWERTY with respect to previous designs is that it solved the key-jamming problem, that is, the problem that the type bars frequently jammed when certain key sequences were struck quickly. QWERTY avoided the problem by setting those keys far enough apart that the speed of typing would be

BOX 17.1 THE BATTLE BETWEEN VHS AND BETAMAX[242]

Sony has a historical reputation of leadership in consumer electronics. It led Japanese producers in the development and marketing of the audiotape recorder and the microtelevision, among many other products. The 1974 launch of the Betamax videotape recording system continued Sony's record of technological leadership.

By the mid 1970s, different competing standards of videocassette recording (VCR) were being developed. Its reputation notwithstanding, Sony was aware that it would be unable to set an industry standard by itself. In 1974, seven months before the launch of Betamax, Sony chairman Akio Morita showed his machine to executives from Matsushita, JVC, and RCA, in a effort to get support for the Betamax design. Sony's attitude was that of presenting Betamax as the undisputed standard: "We completed this one, so why don't you follow," he seemed to imply.

Sony's arrogant tone did not go over well with its potential partners. Months later, when Sony invited JVC and Matsushita to inspect the Betamax production facilities, JVC replied that it intended to proceed alone with its VCR development, and so it would be unfair to see any more of Sony's technology. Konosuke Matsushita, in turn, was unhappy he had not been consulted before Sony committed to a design, and decided to withhold his company's participation in Sony's standard. The fact that JVC was (partly) owned by Matsushita also played a role in this decision.

Two years later, JVC introduced the Video Home System (VHS), an incompatible alternative to Sony's Betamax. Sony had the head start: By the time VHS was introduced, more than 100,000 Betamax machines had already been sold. But the machine JVC introduced in September 1976 was, in some respects, a better product than the Betamax. In particular, its tapes could record two hours, twice as long as the Betamax. In fact, one of the reasons for JVC's refusal to adopt the Betamax standard was precisely the limitation in play time.

Another important difference with respect to Sony is that JVC followed from the start a much more open policy with respect to bringing other firms on board. Says Morita: "We didn't put enough effort into making a family. . . . The other side, coming later, made a family." By 1984, the VHS group included 40 companies, whereas the Beta group featured only a dozen. A greater "bandwagon" of supporting firms had two effects. First, it gave the VHS standard greater credibility. Second, it induced a faster pace of product improvement at the crucial time when the market was deciding which standard to adopt. (There were actually six VCR designs developed in the 1970s. However, for technical and/or marketing reasons, four of these were never serious candidates to set the industry standard. The battle was therefore between Betamax and VHS.)

(continued)

BOX 17.1 (CONTINUED)

Because of its (slight) technological advantage over Betamax, VHS took off at a faster pace than Betamax. By 1980, VHS's share of the installed base was already greater than 50% (see the following chart).

In comparison with the installed based in the late 1980s, the numbers in the late 1970s do not amount to much. Thus VHS had the larger share by the late 1970s, but this was a large share of a very small total (less than 10 million adopters).

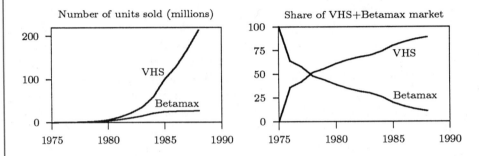

But this advantage proved to be crucial in the 1980s, when sales of VCRs accelerated. In contrast with the 1970s, the consumer in the 1980s used VCRs mainly to watch prerecorded cassettes (mostly movies). This created a snowball effect whereby VHS's initial advantage gradually multiplied, to the point of effectively killing the Betamax standard. As Fortune magazine put it in a 1985 article, "Betamax keeps falling further behind. . . . As consumers perceive Betamax faltering, they flock in even greater numbers to VHS, worried that those who produce movie cassettes for VCRs might desert Betamax."

In 1988, Sony started production of VHS recorders.

reduced. The event that led to the QWERTY design was a "small historical event" in the sense that today's computers still incorporate the original keyboard design, even though bar jamming is no longer an issue. Did the industry get locked-in to an inefficient equilibrium? Claims have been made that an alternative keyboard—the Dvorak keyboard—would enable an increase in typing speed,[243] although recent research casts doubts on these claims.[244] However, the suspicion remains that the QWERTY keyboard performs worse than the optimal keyboard from the perspective of maximum typing speed.

Network externalities may imply multiple equilibria, whereby an industry locks-in to one technology or another. Which technology ends up being chosen depends to a great extent on the actions of early adopters. The eventual winner need not be the superior or most-preferred technology.

17.3   EXCESS INERTIA AND EXCESS MOMENTUM[245]

In the previous section, we considered the case of two alternative versions of a new product or technology. The battle between VHS and Betamax was given as an example; a more recent one would be recordable Digital Versatile Disks, where the alternatives are the DVD-RAM and the DVD+RW systems. In some cases, however, the option is not between two new versions but rather between an old and a new version of a given product or technology: color versus black-and-white TV, FM versus AM broadcasting, Office 97 versus Office 95, and so forth. What determines whether (and when) a switch between an old and a new technology takes place?

To address this and related issues, we consider a simple stylized model. Suppose there is an old technology, denoted O, and a new one, denoted N. For simplicity, assume there are only two adopters, both of whom are current O users. These adopters must sequentially decide whether or not to switch to technology N. Potentially, an adopter may be an O fan (i.e., a "conservative") or an N fan. An adopter knows its own type, but not the other adopter's type. The crucial element of the game is that, when deciding whether or not to switch to the new technology, the first adopter does not know what the future adopter will do. And because of network externalities, the benefits from switching to a new technology depend on whether the other adopter does the same.

Specifically, figure 17.3 depicts, for each type of adopter, the payoff from adoption of technology O or N (no switch, switch), depending on what the other adopter does. For example, if an N-type decides not to switch and the other adopter does switch, then the N-type receives a payoff of 10. As can be seen, the strategy N gives N fans a greater payoff if the other adopter also chooses N. However, N's best overall outcome is to choose the same technology as the other adopter. For a conservative adopter, in turn, choosing the new technology is a dominated strategy: No matter what the other adopter does, an O fan is always better off sticking to the old technology.

Suppose that the probability that an adopter is of the N type is 80%. What is the equilibrium of the adoption game? Let us first consider the second adopter's decision. Clearly, if it is an O type, then it will always choose technology O, for the reasons explained before. If, however, it is an N type, then it will switch to N if and only if the first adopter switched to N.

	O	*N*
O	12	10
N	−10	17

N type

	O	*N*
O	10	9
N	−20	−8

O type

FIGURE 17.3 SIMULTANEOUS TECHNOLOGY ADOPTION DECISIONS: PAYOFF FOR A GIVEN TYPE OF AGENT (*CHOICE IN ROW*) AS A FUNCTION OF THE OTHER AGENT'S CHOICE (*COLUMN*).

Let us now consider the first adopter's choice, taking into account the expected second period outcomes. We will argue that the optimal choice for the first adopter is always to choose *O*, that is, not to switch to the new technology even if it is an *N* type. We do this by comparing the expected benefit that an *N* fan would get from each possible choice. The expected benefit from choosing technology *N* is $20\%(-10) + 80\%(17) = 11.6$. With probability 20%, the second adopter is of the *O* type, in which case it will choose *O*; the first adopter gets stranded as the only adopter of the new technology, which in turn leads to a payoff of −10. With probability 80%, the second adopter is of the *N* type and switches to technology *N*; in this case, our first adopter enjoys a utility of 17, the highest value possible.

Not switching to the new technology implies, however, a higher expected payoff for the first adopter, namely 12. In other words, *even though (a) the prior belief is that adopters prefer the new technology with a high probability; and (b) both adopters actually favor the new technology; it turns out that the only equilibrium is for the new technology not to be adopted.*

This feature of adoption games, known as **excess inertia**, highlights the important difference between complete and incomplete information, even when the latter is "almost complete." The first adopter knows that "almost surely" the second adopter favors the new technology. Moreover, it is common knowledge that, if both adopters prefer the new technology, then both are better off switching to the new technology. However, the possibility that the second adopter does not switch, remote as it might be, acts as an important deterrent to adopting the new technology.

It is unlikely that a stylized model such as the one presented earlier can depict the exact details of technology adoption in real-world situations. However, the problem of excess inertia is very much a real problem. The switch from AM to FM broadcasting in the late forties provides an example (see box 17.2). Most people saw FM as a superior technology. However, fear of getting stranded with a useless (and expensive) FM receiver kept consumers from making the switch, which in turn kept broadcasters from making the switch, which in turn kept manufacturers from making the switch. A similar failure

Box 17.2 AM VERSUS FM[246]

In 1945, Paul W. Kesten, then Executive Vice President of Columbia Broadcasting Systems, wrote:

I believe that FM is not merely one aspect of the future of audio broadcasting—but that it contains in itself almost the whole future of audio broadcasting.

In fact, FM was generally viewed as a superior technology to AM. FM eliminates static, has higher fidelity because of the use of wider channels, has a constant effective service area, and allows for closer geographical proximity on the same frequency without interference.

The early optimism notwithstanding, FM did not succeed in supplanting AM during the initial postwar years. In fact, FM's market penetration fell well below expectations. This is especially surprising in light of the fact that, between 1946 and 1948, a large number of broadcasting licenses were issued and a significant number of FM stations went on air.

Why didn't consumers follow the trend set by broadcasters? One reason is that the U.S. Federal Communications Commission (FCC) shifted the frequencies to be used by FM from those that had been assigned before the war. This created uncertainty on the consumer's side, namely the fear of getting stranded with an obsolete receiver in case the FCC were to change frequencies again. Moreover, the additional cost of an AM/FM receiver was not insignificant (the transistor had yet to be invented). Finally, the FCC policy of allowing 'simulcasting' (broadcasting in AM and FM) further reduced the perceived benefit from investing in an FM receiver.

When all of these ingredients were put together, it is not entirely surprising that the industry got stuck to AM. This example of "excess inertia" resulted from a partial chicken-and-egg problem: Consumers did not buy FM receivers for fear that other consumers would not adopt and/or the technical features would change in a way that would make their receivers worthless. As a consequence, manufacturers eventually ceased to produce FM receivers and radio stations reverted back to AM broadcasting.

to move to a superior technology is given by the flop of quadraphonic sound in the 1970s, a case that is described in greater detail in box 17.3.

Excess inertia is only a possibility. That is, the market is not necessarily too slow in adopting new technologies. In some cases, a switch to a new technology may take place

BOX 17.3 QUADRAPHONIC SOUND[247]

In the early 1970s, it was the general opinion that the era of stereo sound was coming to an end. Quadraphonic sound—an audio system that records four channels—was considered the next logical development in the industry. Early studies on quadraphonic sound claimed that up to 80% of the sound perceived by listeners at live concerts is reflected from the walls and ceiling, with the remaining 20% traveling directly from the orchestra to the listener's ears. For this reason, quadraphonic sound allows for a more realistic recreation of the "concert-hall experience" at home.

Two different approaches to quadraphonic sound were developed—the matrix system and the discrete system. The matrix system had the advantage that record production was as simple as the production of stereo records, but suffered from problems in the complete separation of the four channels. The discrete system allowed for a better separation of the four channels, but implied higher production costs and a more complex record player.

In 1971, Columbia Records introduced its quadraphonic system, the SQ, based on the matrix approach. That same year, JVC launched a rival system based on the discrete approach. In January 1972, RCA—Columbia's main rival in record production—announced that it was backing an improved version of JVC's standard. The "quad war" was on.

From the onset, both players were aware there was no room for two incompatible technologies in the market. They were also aware that whichever technology the consumer favored would eventually be adopted. Influencing consumer expectations was therefore an important part of Columbia's and RCA's strategy. This consisted as much of praising the qualities of their own technology as of bashing the rival one. Columbia depicted RCA as a "spoiler" to the establishment of a standard. RCA, in turn, responded that the matrix system was "a Mickey-Mouse approach that only simulates four channels." Columbia countered that its system was already as good as having four separated channels (however, by May 1973, SQ had already gone through five different generations).

The early market performance of quadraphonic sound was optimistic. By the beginning of 1974, quad hardware accounted for 25 to 30% of sales in value, with forecasts as high as 70% by the end of the year. Expert studies predicted that by the end of the 1980s, quadraphonic would already have replaced stereo.

This optimism was short-lived, however. Consumers were afraid of getting stranded with the wrong piece of equipment, and the existence of multiple standards confused them. Even though both systems were backward compatible (i.e., they could play stereo records), matrix and discrete were not compatible with each

Box 17.3 (CONTINUED)

other (i.e., one would get stereo sound only from quadraphonic records of a different format). Retailers reflected the customers' uneasiness about quadraphonic, and thus were not keen on pushing the new technology. Beginning in the second half of 1974, disillusionment over quadraphonic sound gradually set in. Despite a final effort by manufacturers to boost sales, stocks of quadraphonic sound equipment continued to pile up.

In 1976, all new products launched in the market were based on stereo. The "quad war" had ended—with no winner.

too quickly. Consider the same game structure as before but with payoffs as in Figure 17.4. Suppose, moreover, that the probability that an adopter is of the N type is now only 1%. Inspection of the payoff tables reveals that both types of adopters prefer compatibility to incompatibility (i.e., network valuations dominate standalone valuations). N types *marginally* prefer the situation when both switch to the new technology, whereas O types *greatly* prefer that no one switch to the new technology.

Because O types have a great preference for maintaining the status quo and the probability that an adopter is of the O type is very high, we would like the equilibrium to be for a switch never to occur. However, as we will see, a switch will occur whenever the first adopter is of the N type. In fact, a first adopter correctly anticipates that a switch to N will be followed by another switch to N *regardless of the second adopter's type*. This is true because an O type, its preference for the status quo notwithstanding, still prefers compatibility more strongly than technology O. Knowing that, a first adopter, if of the N type, will switch to the new technology, eventually receiving a payoff of 13 instead of 12.

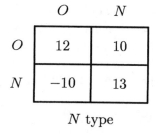

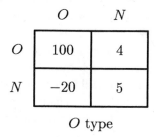

FIGURE 17.4 SIMULTANEOUS TECHNOLOGY ADOPTION DECISIONS: PAYOFF FOR A GIVEN TYPE OF AGENT (*CHOICE IN ROW*) AS A FUNCTION OF THE OTHER AGENT'S CHOICE (*COLUMN*).

Although this is a marginal gain compared with the loss for an *O*-type second adopter (a loss of 95), the first adopter is not concerned with the second adopter's payoff, only with the second adopter's action.

In other words, the phenomenon of network externalities may lead to a **bandwagon effect**, whereby initial adoptions trigger subsequent ones.[d] In some circumstances, preferences are such that the industry would be better off if no switch to the new technology were to take place. In this case, if a switch does take place, then we say the market exhibits **excess momentum**.

Software updates are sometimes an example of excess momentum. Many users of Office 95 were quite satisfied with their version of the software. However, when a number of key players adopted Office 97, owners of Office 95 had an incentive to switch to Office 97 for reasons of compatibility. This does not mean that, in the end, these users were made better off. They would probably prefer the initial situation when every user worked with Office 95. However, the new situation (everyone with Office 97) is better than sticking to Office 95 while the rest of the world switches to Office 97. Switching to Office 97 is then the lesser evil, as it were.

Network externalities may imply *excess inertia*, whereby a new technology is not adopted even though it would be in most people's interest to do so. But network externalities may also imply *excess momentum*, whereby a switch to a new technology occurs even though most people would prefer it not to happen.

17.4 COMPATIBILITY

In section 17.2, we looked at the case when two versions of a new technology battle for market dominance. The battle is of particular importance because of network externalities: Consumers' valuations of Betamax VCRs, for example, depend on how many other consumers own a Betamax VCR. In this particular example, the reason for network externalities is that the more people own a Betamax VCR, the greater variety of Betamax tapes will be available at video rental stores. But suppose that VHS VCRs can play VHS-format tapes *and* Betamax-format tapes as well. Then the relevant size of the network, from the perspective of a Betamax buyer, is the *total* number of VCRs. In fact, the variety of tapes available on Betamax format will now be a function of the total number of VCRs—both Betamax and VHS—for both play Betamax tapes.[e]

This example highlights the importance of **compatibility** between different technologies. From the consumers' point of view, compatibility seems to be a good idea (assuming that compatibility does not imply an increase in price or a reduction in qual-

[d] The terms domino effect and snowball effect also are used in this context.

[e] This is certainly the case when Betamax machines can also read VHS-format tapes. If that were not the case—that is, if compatibility were one way—then the problem would be slightly more complicated.

ity). What about producers? On the one hand, compatibility implies a lower degree of product differentiation, which normally leads to a greater degree of price competition (see chapter 12). On the other hand, compatibility implies greater consumer benefits. If producers can capture a significant share of those added benefits, the balance may be in favor of compatibility (from the producers' point of view).

To get a better understanding of some of the trade-offs involved in strategic compatibility decisions, let us consider a simple two-stage game. In the first stage, firms decide whether or not to make their technologies compatible. If no agreement is reached, then a "standardization battle" takes place, following which one of the technologies is adopted as a standard. In the second stage, product market competition takes place. If a compatibility agreement was previously reached, then each firm earns duopoly profits π^D. If no agreement was reached in the previous stage, then whichever firm won the standards battle gets monopoly profits π^M, whereas the other one gets zero. In which case are firms better off on average—with or without compatibility?

Consider a first possible scenario: The compatibility battle is a battle to attract customers. To do so, firms need to spend resources. The firm that is prepared to spend the most wins the battle. For example, in the quest to attract customers to its satellite-based digital TV system, U.K.'s BSkyB is subsidizing customers willing to purchase the decoder required to receive Sky's broadcast signal.

The prize from winning the standards battle is π^M, the second-stage profit for a standard setter. The standards battle is essentially like an auction: Whoever pays the most wins the auction. The result, analogous to Bertrand competition, is that firms will escalate their offers up to the value π^M. In the end, winning this auction will not produce great satisfaction: The prize π^M just compensates the resources spent to get there. Both winner and loser end up with a *net* payoff of zero.[f] No matter how low duopoly profits π^D are, firms would be better off if they had reached a compatibility agreement.

Now consider a second possible scenario: The choice of the prevailing standard results from a series of events that firms have no direct control over. For example, consumers happen to like one of the technologies better, start buying it, and the snowball effect described in section 17.2 does the rest; or, alternatively, a series of government regulations and other policy measures give one of the standards an initial edge which, again, is cemented by self-reinforcing dynamics. For the purpose of the model, suppose that incompatibility implies that each of the technologies is chosen as the industry standard with probability 50%.

What are the equilibrium payoffs now? If firms choose compatibility, then, as before, they end up each getting duopoly profits π^D. What if they do not agree on making their technologies compatible? Then one of the technologies is chosen as a standard with probability 50% and enjoys monopoly profits π^M, while the other gets zero. On average, each firm gets 50% π^M. We conclude that incompatibility is better if and only if 50% π^M is greater than π^D, or simply if $\pi^M > 2\,\pi^D$, a condition that generally holds: It is better

[f] This result is based on the assumption that only the winner pays the bid. This would be the case if the only relevant strategy was the level of adoption subsidies, for example. In practice, an important part of the "bids" is paid regardless of whether or not the bid is a winning bid. In this case, it is possible that the loser ends up with a negative net payoff.

to be a monopolist half of the time than a duopolist all of the time.[g] This is especially true if product market competition is very intense, so that π^D is much lower than π^M. In summary:

> If standards competition is very intense, then firms prefer compatibility. If product market competition is very intense, then firms prefer incompatibility.

Standards competition was modeled previously in a fairly specific context. But the intuition would normally apply in other contexts as well. In particular, one likely effect of standards competition is to reduce the size of the product market. Box 17.3 describes one such example, the (failed) adoption of quadraphonic sound, wherein two incompatible standards battled with each other to the point of eliminating the market (leaving consumers with the [inferior] standard of stereo sound). The main reason for the failure of quadraphonic sound was that consumers became very confused over which standard to choose, thus preferring not to choose any at all.

A related example is the failed introduction of digital audio tapes. The two competing technologies were Philips' Digital Compact Cassette and the Japanese electronics industry's Digital Audio Tape. Both failed to reach any significant degree of market penetration.

Quadraphonic sound and digital audio tapes have one aspect in common: Both are new technologies that attempted to replace existing technologies (stereo and analog audiotape, respectively). The fact that consumers had the "easy" option of staying with an inferior but sure technology implied—in both cases—that excess inertia prevailed.[h] In terms of the preceding model, the existence of a reasonable status quo technology means that the potential costs from a standardization battle are very high—not so much because firms need to spend large amounts of resources (as modeled earlier) but because the probability that *both* will lose the race is high.[i]

17.5 PUBLIC POLICY

Externalities are one of the few instances where economists agree there may be a role for public policy. Does this apply to network externalities as well? If so, what should governments do, that is, how can public policy correct for the externality in question?

As was discussed in section 17.2, compatibility between different technologies, or standardization, implies that the relevant network of consumers is increased, which in turn implies a greater benefit for consumers. In other words, if technology A, with n_A users, and technology B, with n_B users, become compatible, then an A adopter's

[g] This condition was also introduced in chapter 16 in a slightly different context.

[h] Compare with the AM versus FM battle, discussed in section 17.3, wherein a similar phenomenon took place.

[i] We could then change the preceding model and assume that, under a scenario of standards competition, the probability that a given firm's standard prevails is $\alpha < 50\%$. If α is sufficiently low, then the same result follows: Firms would be better off with compatibility.

value increases from $v(n_A)$ to $v(n_A + n_B)$, where $v(\cdot)$ is the network benefit function. A tantalizing implication is that standardization is a good thing, something that public policy should actively pursue.

Unfortunately, the answer is not so simple. Consider the contrast between Europe and the United States in standards-setting for second generation mobile telephony. In 1988, the European Parliament established ETSI, the European Telecommunications Standards Institute. Members of ETSI include European telecom operators, as well as equipment manufacturers. Although participation in ETSI is voluntary and decisions are not binding, ETSI decisions are normally turned into (binding) European norms by the European Parliament. This process of decision making has contributed to a great degree of standardization in European mobile telephony: All European countries adhere to the GSM standard, which implies that roaming (using a handset from country A to make calls in country B) is possible across Europe.

No such centralized process exists in the United States. As a result, four different standards coexist in the market. At an initial stage, this created a situation that was inferior to that in Europe, especially because of the limitations it imposed on roaming within the country. Currently, each standard's coverage of the U.S. territory is complete or near complete; that is, roaming is now as good in the United States as it is in Europe. Moreover, competition between different standards has led to sharp reductions in price and to significant technological progress. For example, recently developed software allows handset makers to deliver phones compatible with all major standards.[248] In the end, the American consumer seems better off than the European consumer.

The fast pace of technical progress in the (not-standardized) North American camp suggests that the benefits from competition may override the benefits from standardization.[j] An additional benefit, one that was not considered in the previous discussion, is product variety.[k] Finally, one should add the non-negligible fact that competition implies lower prices.

But standardization wars have social costs, too. Consider the example of Digital Versatile Disks (DVDs).[249] The DVD, a new type of CD, can store up to nine gigabytes of information on each side—compared with 650 megabytes on a standard CD-ROM—and is expected to supplant videotapes in the home, compact disks in the stereo, and floppy disks in the personal computer. In the early 1990s, Sony Corp. and Philips Electronics NV began joint development of a video-on-disk system. Meanwhile, Toshiba Corp. approached the U.S. media conglomerate Time Warner Inc., proposing a rival system. Open warfare started in 1994, with both sides trying to impose their system. Eventually (in December 1995), an agreement was reached on a design, one that drew heavily on the Toshiba–Time Warner design. But in the process, industry squabbling cost producers and consumers a delay of at least 18 months in market introduction. As an IBM manager put it, "competition on a format is not good for the end user or for the companies involved."

[j] In fact, when it came to deciding on a standard for third-generation wireless, Europe opted for Qualcomm's CDMA, a technology developed in nonstandardized America.

[k] Centrally planned economies, like that of the former Soviet Union, were characterized by a high degree of standardization, a fact from which consumers derived limited benefits.

To summarize:

> The benefits from standardization must be weighed against the costs of lower competition and product variety.

If deciding whether or not to favor standardization is a difficult question, deciding which technology or standard to favor is an even more difficult one. In this context, one problem faced by public policy is that of *information and timing*. If the government acts too early, then it must do so based on very limited information about the relative merits of each standard. If, on the other hand, the government waits too long, then the industry will already have locked-in to a particular standard, possibly the inferior one (as shown in section 17.2). What is the optimal "time window" for government intervention? Is there a window at all?

Finally, we saw in section 17.3 that one of the possible effects of network externalities is to cause excess inertia, too slow a switch from old to new technologies. An obvious role for public policy in this context is to act as a coordinating device between the different agents in play, so as to avoid the chicken-and-egg problem that leads to excess inertia. For example, the U.K. government has determined that no analog TV broadcasting will be allowed after the year 2008. This may be what it takes for the industry—in particular, viewers—to make the switch.[1] But even if the U.K. government's policy proves effective in inducing a switch, the question remains whether the switch—and the timing of the switch—are optimal from a social point of view. This is, in fact, a general point about public policy: Whenever the government supersedes the workings of the market, the question must be asked whether the former has all of the information contained in the latter, which normally is not the case.

[1] Contrast this case with the failed switch from AM to FM, in which the U.S. Federal Communications Commission (FCC) allowed for the possibility of simulcast, simultaneous broadcasting in AM and FM.

Another example of government policy in this context is given by the Australian government's announcement that all analog cellular phones must migrate to digital. The initial deadline was set to 1997, then was changed to 1998, then to 2000. This suggests that even the government has difficulties in establishing a credible commitment.

SUMMARY

- Network effects may imply multiple demand levels for a given price. Which value takes place depends on consumers' expectations regarding network size.

- Network externalities may imply multiple equilibria, whereby an industry locks-in to one technology or another. Which technology ends up being chosen depends to a great extent on the actions of early adopters. The eventual winner need not be the superior or most-preferred technology.

- Network externalities may imply *excess inertia*, whereby a new technology is not adopted even though it would be in most people's interest to do so. But network externalities may also imply *excess momentum*, whereby a switch to a new technology occurs even though most people would prefer it not to happen.

- If standards competition is very intense, then firms prefer compatibility. If product market competition is very intense, then firms prefer incompatibility.

- The benefits from standardization must be weighed against the costs of lower competition and product variety.

KEY CONCEPTS

- network externalities
- consumer expectations
- self-reinforcing process
- lock-in
- path dependence
- excess inertia
- excess momentum
- bandwagon effect
- compatibility

REVIEW AND PRACTICE EXERCISES

17.1* You have created a business-to-business (B2B) Internet venture directed at an industry with exactly fifty (50) identical firms. Your services allow these firms to do business with each other more efficiently as members of your trading network. You plan to sell access to your service for a price p per member firm. Each firm's benefit from the service is given by $2n$, where n is the number of other firms joining the B2B network as a member. So, if 21 firms join your service, each places a value of 2×20 or 40 on membership in your network.

Suppose for part (a) that you set the price, p, and then firms simultaneously and independently decide whether or not to join as members.

a. Show that, for a price greater than zero and lower than 98, there exist exactly two Nash equilibria in the simultaneous-move game played by firms deciding whether or not to join the network as members.

Suppose for part (b) that you are able to persuade 10 firms to join your network at an initial stage as "Charter Members." At a second stage, you set a price for the remaining 40 firms. These 40 firms then simultaneously decide (as in part [a]) whether to join your network as regular members.

b. For each price p, determine the equilibria of the game played between the remaining 40 firms in the second stage.

Finally, for part (c), consider the same situation as in part (c), but suppose that, when there are multiple Nash equilibria, firms behave conservatively and conjecture that the low-adoption Nash equilibrium will be played. (Note that, by the definition of Nash equilibrium, this conjecture is self-fulfilling.)

c. How much would you be willing to pay (in total to all 10 early adopters) to persuade the first 10 firms to join the network as Charter Members?

17.2 Empirical evidence suggests that, between 1986 and 1991, consumers were willing to pay a significant premium for spreadsheets that were compatible with the Lotus platform, the dominant spreadsheet during that period.[250] What type of network externalities is this evidence of?

17.3 People are more likely to buy their first home computer in areas where a high fraction of households already own computers or where a large share of their friends and family own computers: A 10% greater penetration in the surrounding city is associated with a 1% higher adoption rate.[251] How can this be explained by network externalities? What alternative explanations are there?

17.4** In the early days of Automated Teller Machines (ATMs), there were very few interbank networks, that is, each bank's network was incompatible with that of other banks. Empirical evidence shows that banks with a larger network of branches adopted ATMs earlier. To what extent can network externalities explain this observation?[252]

17.5 How would you respond to the following quotation:

Apple Computer, the company that brought you the idiot-friendly Macintosh, is staring at bankruptcy. Meanwhile, the great army of technocrats at Microsoft, which only last year managed to reproduce the look and feel of a 1980s Mac, lumbers on, invincible.

A bad break for Apple? A rare exception to the Darwinian rules in which the best products win the hearts and dollars of consumers?[253]

17.6[*]   Consider the model of technology adoption presented in section 17.2. Suppose that the utility derived by an A fan from technology A is given by $u + n_A$ if n_A is less than $\bar{n}_A$, and $u + \bar{n}_A$ for values of n greater than $\bar{n}_A$. Likewise, utility from buying technology B is as before except that for n_B greater than $\bar{n}_B$ we get $\bar{n}_B$. Analogous expressions apply for B fans. In other words, network externalities are bounded: Once the network reaches a certain size, no additional benefits are gained from a larger network.

Show that, under these circumstances and for certain values of u, n_A, n_B, three different outcomes are possible: (1) the industry becomes locked-in to technology A; (2) the industry becomes locked-in to technology B; or (3) the two technologies survive in the long run.

17.7   Explain why the market adoption of a new technology may be too fast or too slow.

17.8   Company A has just developed a new technology. Company B approaches Company A, stating it has developed its own version of the technology and proposing a compromise that would make the two technologies compatible with each other. What advice would you give Company A?

17.9   A standardization battle is currently under way in the recordable DVD industry, with Philips and Sony on one side, Matsushita and Toshiba on the other side. In an effort to coordinate on a standard, an industry group was set up: the DVD Forum. In April 1997, the forum's ten members voted eight-to-two to standardize around the Matsushita-backed format, leaving Philips and Sony stranded with their losing format. Within a few weeks, Philips and Sony announced they would start selling their own format.

What role can you see for public policy in this case?

EXTENSION EXERCISES

17.10[*]   You are marketing a new wireless information device (WID). Consumers differ in their willingness to pay for the device. (No one needs more than one.) All consumers value owning a WID more highly, the larger is the total number of consumers using such devices. Denote the expected total number of WID users by n^e, which we also can call the "expected size of the WID network." If all consumers expect the size of the WID network to be n^e, and the price of the device is p, then the number of users who will want to buy the device (i.e., the total quantity demanded) is given by $n = 100 - p + vn^e$, where $0 < v < 1$. (Note that this is a standard linear relationship between price and unit sales for any given level of expected network size, n^e.)

a. Interpret the parameter v. What factors influence v?

Suppose that your marginal cost per WID is 20. Suppose also that consumers are quite sophisticated and form accurate expectations about the size of the WID network, for any price p that you might set, so that n must equal n^e.

b. What is the profit-maximizing price of WIDs? How many are sold, and what profits do you earn?

Suppose that you could improve the performance of your WID communications network and thus enhance the network effects, raising v from 1/3 to 1/2.

c. How much would you pay to develop this enhancement? [254]

17.11[*] Two firms, Compress and Squeeze, offer incompatible software products that encrypt and shrink the size of large data files for safe storage and/or faster transmission. This software category exhibits strong network effects, because users seek to send files to each other, and a file saved in one format cannot be retrieved using the other format. The marginal cost of serving one customer is $40 for either firm.

To keep things simple, suppose that there are only two customers, "Pioneer" and "Follower," and two time periods, "This Year" and "Next Year." As the name suggests, Pioneer moves first, picking one format, This Year. Pioneer cannot change her choice once it is made. In contrast, Follower picks Next Year. Follower will be aware of Pioneer's pick when the time comes for Follower to pick. The annual interest rate is 20% for Compress and Squeeze and Pioneer.

Pioneer regards Compress and Squeeze as equally attractive products. Pioneer values either product at $100 during This Year (before Follower enters the market), and at $100 during Next Year if Follower does not pick the same product. If Follower does pick the same product Next Year, Pioneer's value during Next Year will be $136. (In other words, the network effect is worth $36 to Pioneer.) Follower has very similar preferences. If Follower picks the same product Next Year as Pioneer did This Year, Follower values that product at $136. Alternatively, if Follower picks a different product Next Year than Pioneer did This Year, the value to Follower of that product will be only $100.

Finally, suppose that Compress and Squeeze simultaneously set prices This Year at which they offer their products to Pioneer. (One could just as well say that they bid for Pioneer's business.) Then Compress and Squeeze simultaneously set prices Next Year at which they will offer their products to Follower.

For simplicity, assume that Pioneer will pick Compress if Pioneer is just indifferent between Compress and Squeeze, and that Follower will pick the same product as Pioneer if Follower is indifferent between Compress and Squeeze, given the values they offer and the prices they charge.

a. What prices will Compress and Squeeze set Next Year in bidding to win Follower's business if Compress wins Pioneer's business This Year?

b. What prices will Compress and Squeeze set This Year in bidding to win Pioneer's business?

c. What product will Pioneer buy, and what product will Follower buy?

d. What are the resulting payoffs of Compress, Squeeze, Pioneer, and Follower?

e. Describe in words the advantages of early or late adopters identified in this problem.

f. How does all of this change if there is rapid technological progress so that costs Next Year are much lower than costs This Year?

g. How does your analysis change if the (marginal) cost of serving a customer is only 20 rather than 40?[255]

17.12* Technological progress (of a sort) has led to the WalkDVD. As the name suggests, this is a miniature DVD player. It is attached to a pair of headphones and special viewing glasses that, together, allow for highly realistic sound and image effects, as well as easy mobility. Three firms, Son, Tosh, and Phil, are planning to launch their WalkDVD players. There are two possible formats to choose from, S and T, and the three competitors have not agreed on which standard to adopt. Son prefers standard S, whereas Tosh prefers standard T. Phil does not have any strong preference other than being compatible with the other firms. Specifically, the payoffs for each player as a function of the standard they adopt and the number of firms that adopt the same standard are given by table 17.1. For example, the value 200 in the Son row and S2 column means that if Son chooses the S standard and two firms choose the S standard, then Son's payoff is 200.

Suppose that all three firms simultaneously choose which standard to adopt.

a. Show that "all firms choosing S" and "all firms choosing T" are both Nash equilibria of this game.

b. Determine whether there are any other Nash equilibria in this simultaneous-move game.

Son has just acquired a firm that manufactures DVDs for the S format. For all practical purposes, this implies that Son is committed to the S format. It is now up to Tosh and Phil to simultaneously decide which format to choose.

TABLE 17.1   PAYOFFS IN STANDARD SETTING GAME.

Firm	S1	S2	S3	T1	T2	T2
Son	100	200	250	40	80	110
Tosh	40	80	110	100	200	250
Phil	60	100	120	60	100	120

c. Write down the 2x2 payoff matrix for the game now played by Tosh and Phil. Find the Nash equilibrium of this game.

d. Do you think Son's move was a good one? How would your answer differ if Phil had a slight preference for the T format (e.g., assume that payoffs for T1, T2, and T3 are 70, 110, and 130, respectively)?

Suppose now that all firms' payoffs are like Phil in the preceding table. You are Son.

e. If you could choose, would you rather move before Tosh and Phil, or after them? Contrast your answer to what you have learned from the answers to parts (c) and (d).

17.13*** Consider the market for a given piece of hardware—a photocopier of brand x, for example—that needs after-sale servicing. Suppose that there is free entry into this after market. Servicing photocopiers implies a fixed cost of F and a marginal cost of c per unit of service provided. Total demand for servicing is given by $D = S(a - p)$, where p is price and S the number of photocopier owners. Finally, suppose that firms in the after market compete *à la* Cournot.

Show that consumer surplus (per consumer) in the after market is given by

$$U = \frac{1}{2} \left(a - c - \sqrt{\frac{F}{S}} \right)^2,$$

an increasing, concave function of S. (*Hint:* apply the results on Cournot competition with free entry derived in chapter 14. Take into account the fact that consumer surplus per consumer is given by $(a - p)^2/2$.)

Relate this result to the discussion on indirect network externalities (at the beginning of the chapter).

NOTES

CHAPTER 1

1. Stigler, George J. *The Organization of Industry.* Homewood, Illinois: R. D. Irwin, 1969, p. 1.
2. *Chemistry and Industry News* (http://ci.mond.org/9708/970806.html).
3. *The People's Pharmacy* (http://homearts.com/depts/health/kfpeop18.htm).
4. *The Scientist,* 9, no. 14 (July 1995): 3.
5. Harberger, Arnold C. "Monopoly and Resource Allocation," *American Economic Review* 44 (1954): 77–87.
6. Baumol, William, John Panzar, and Robert Willig. *Contestable Markets and the Theory of Industry Structure.* New York: Harcourt Brace Jovanovich, 1982.
7. Hall, Robert E. "The Relationship between Price and Marginal Cost in U.S. Industry," *Journal of Political Economy* 96 (1988): 921–947.
8. *The Wall Street Journal Europe,* November 14, 1996.
9. *The Wall Street Journal Europe,* May 6, 1999.
10. *The Wall Street Journal Europe,* June 3, 1999.
11. *Financial Times,* May 24, 1999.
12. Hicks, John. "Annual Survey of Economic Theory: The Theory of Monopoly," *Econometrica* 3 (1935): 1–20.
13. *The Wall Street Journal,* November 24, 1999.
14. Schumpeter, Joseph. *Capitalism, Socialism, and Democracy* (2nd ed.). New York: 1950, pp. 82 and 106.
15. *The Wall Street Journal Europe,* May 28–29, 1999.
16. *The Wall Street Journal Europe,* June 10, 1998.
17. *The Economist,* August 31, 1996.
18. This framework is based on the seminal work by Mason and Bain. See Mason, Edward S. "Price and Production Policies of Large-Scale Enterprise," *American Economic Review* 29 (1939): 61–74. Mason, Edward S. "The Current State of the Monopoly Problem in the United States," *Harvard Law Review* 62 (1949): 1265–1285. Bain, Joe S. *Barriers to New Competition.* Cambridge, MA: Harvard University Press, 1956. Bain, Joe S. *Industrial Organization.* New York: John Wiley & Sons, 1959.
19. Porter, Michael E. *Competitive Strategy.* New York: The Free Press, 1980.
20. Nickell, Stephen J. "Competition and Corporate Performance," *Journal of Political Economy* 104 (1996): 724–746.

CHAPTER 2

21. This example is adapted from Hermalin, Benjamin E. "The Parable of Red Pens and Blue Pens," W. Haas School of Business, University of California, Berkeley, 1997.
22. Adapted from Ball, Sir James. "Redsyke Quarry," London Business School Case Study, 1988.
23. Adapted from Haas School of Business economics problem sets.
24. Data provided by British Rail to the Mergers and Monopolies Commission.
25. Adapted from Haas School of Business economics problem sets.

26. *The Wall Street Journal Europe*, September 22, 1998.

27. Adapted from Haas School of Business economics problem sets.

28. Adapted from Haas School of Business economics problem sets.

CHAPTER 3

29. This section is partly based in Holmstrom, Bengt R. and Jean Tirole. "The Theory of the Firm," in R. Schmalensee and R. D. Willig (Eds.), *Handbook of Industrial Organization*. Amsterdam: North-Holland, 1989.

30. This box adapts results from Hermalin, Benjamin E. and Michael S. Weisbach. "The Determinants of Board Composition," *Rand Journal of Economics* 19 (1988): 589–606; and Hermalin, Benjamin E. and Michael S. Weisbach. "Endogenously Chosen Boards of Directors and Their Monitoring of the CEO," *American Economic Review* 88 (1998): 96–118.

31. *The Wall Street Journal*, December 13, 1999.

32. Adapted from Schranz, Mary S. "Takeovers Improve Firm Performance: Evidence from the Banking Industry," *Journal of Political Economy* 101 (1993): 299–326.

33. The theory presented in this section is based on Williamson, Oliver E. *Markets and Hierarchies*. New York: The Free Press, 1975; and on Grossman, Sanford J. and Oliver D. Hart. "The Costs and Benefits of Ownership: A Theory of Vertical and Lateral Integration," *Journal of Political Economy* 94 (1986): 691–719.

34. This case is described in detail by Klein, Benjamin, R., A. Crawford, and A. A. Alchian. "Vertical Integration, Appropriable Rents, and the Competitive Contracting Process," *Journal of Law and Economics* 21 (1978): 297–326.

35. Schmalensee, Richard. "Inter-Industry Studies of Structure and Performance," in R. Schmalensee and R. Willig (Eds.), *Handbook of Industrial Organization*. Amsterdam: North-Holland, 1989.

36. Mueller, Dennis. *Profits in the Long Run*. Cambridge: Cambridge University Press, 1986.

37. Rumelt, Richard P. "Towards a Strategic Theory of the Firm," in R. Lamb (Ed.), *Competitive Strategic Management*. Englewood Cliffs, NJ: Prentice Hall, 1984. Three other important references for this and the topics to follow are Penrose, E. T. *The Theory of the Growth of the Firm*. Oxford: Blackwell, 1959; Wernerfelt, B. "A Resource-Based View of the Firm," *Strategic Management Journal* 5 (1984): 171–180; Dierickx, I. and K. Cool. "Asset Stock Accumulation and Sustainability of Competitive Advantage," *Management Science* 35 (1989): 1504-1511.

38. Rumelt, Richard P., op. cit.

39. Adapted from Haas School of Business economics problem sets.

40. Adapted from Haas School of Business economics problem sets.

41. *The Wall Street Journal Europe*, November 5, 1998.

42. Adapted from Haas School of Business economics problem sets.

43. See, for example, Affuso, Luisa. "An Empirical Study on Contractual Heterogeneity within the Firm: The "Vertical Integration-Franchise Contracts" Mix," University of Cambridge, 1998.

44. Watts, Christophe F. "The Determinants of Organisational Choice: Franchising and Vertical Integration," M.Sc. dissertation, University of Southampton, 1995.

CHAPTER 4

45. Nash, John. "Non-Cooperative Games," *Annals of Mathematics* 54 (1951): 286–295.

46. Selten, Reinhard. "Spieltheoretische Behandlung eines Oligopolmodells mit Nachfragetragheit," *Zeitschrift für die gesamte Staatswissenschaft* 121 (1965): 301–324, 667–689.

47. This exercise is adapted from Dixit, Avinash K. and Barry J. Nalebuff. *Thinking Strategically*. New York: W. W. Norton, 1991.

48. This game was first proposed by Rosenthal, Robert. "Games of Perfect Information, Predatory Pricing and the Chain-Store Paradox," *Journal of Economic Theory* 25 (1981): 92–100.

CHAPTER 5

49. Shephard, William G. *The Economics of Industrial Organization*. (4th ed.). Upper Saddle River, NJ: Prentice Hall, 1997, Table 1.

50. MacAvoy, Paul W. *The Failure of Antitrust and Regulation to Establish Competition in Long-Distance Telephone Services*. Cambridge, MA: MIT Press, 1996, Table 5.2.

51. Adapted from "Big Friendly Giant," *The Economist*, January 30, 1999; and Mark Boslet. "Economist Calls Microsoft a Monopoly," *The Wall Street Journal Europe*, January 6, 1999.

52. This section is partly based on Armstrong, Mark, Simon Cowan, and John Vickers. *Regulatory Reform: Economic Analysis and British Experience*. Cambridge, MA: MIT Press, 1994.

53. Cabral, Luís and Michael H. Riordan. "Incentives for Cost Reduction under Price Cap Regulation," *Journal of Regulatory Economics* 1 (1989): 93–102.

54. Adapted from several articles in *The Wall Street Journal Europe*, December 28, 1998; January 8–9, 1999.

55. Willig, Robert. "The Theory of Network Access Pricing," in Trebing (Ed.), *Issues in Public Utility Regulation,* Michigan State University Public Utilities Papers, 1979. Baumol, William. "Some Subtle Issues in Railroad Regulation," *Transport Economics* 10 (1983): 341–355.

56. Laffont, Jean-Jacques and Jean Tirole. "Creating Competition through Interconnection: Theory and Practice," *Journal of Regulatory Economics* 10 (1996): 227–256.

57. *The Wall Street Journal Europe*, March 17, 1999.

58. Armstrong, Mark, Chris Doyle, and John Vickers. "The Access Pricing Problem: A Synthesis," *Journal of Industrial Economics* 44 (1996): 131–150.

59. Adapted from Haas School of Business economics problem sets.

60. Ward, Michael R. "Measurements of Market Power in Long Distance Telecommunications," Federal Trade Commission, Bureau of Economics Staff Report, 1995.

61. Adapted from Haas School of Business economics problem sets.

62. Adapted from Haas School of Business economics problem sets.

CHAPTER 6

63. Lucas, Robert. "On the Size Distribution of Business Firms," *Bell Journal of Economics* 9 (1978): 508–523.

64. Mueller, Dennis. *Profits in the Long Run*. Cambridge: Cambridge University Press, 1986.

65. Cable, John and Joachim Schwalbach. *International Comparisons of Entry and Exit,* in Geroski and Schwalbach (Eds.), *Entry and Market Contestability*. Oxford: Blackwell, 1991.

66. Cable and Schwalbach, op. cit.

67. Van Ark, Bart and Erik Monnikhof. "Size Distribution of Output and Employment: A Data Set for Manufacturing Industries in Five OECD Countries, 1960–1990," OECD Economics Department Working Paper No. 166., 1996.

68. Several models have been proposed to account for the main stylized facts (including those presented in section 6.2). The model we present here is adapted from Jovanovic, Boyan. "Selection and Evolution of Industry," *Econometrica* 50 (1982): 649–670. Other important contributions include Lippman, Stephen and R. Rumelt. "Uncertain Imitability: An Analysis of Interfirm Differences in Efficiency under Competition," *Bell Journal of Economics* 13

(1982): 418–438; Hopenhayn, Hugo. "Entry, Exit, and Firm Dynamics in Long Run Equilibrium," *Econometrica* 60 (1992): 1127–1150; and Ericson, Richard and Ariel Pakes. "Markov-Perfect Industry Dynamics: A Framework for Empirical Work," *Review of Economics Studies* 62 (1989): 53–82.

69. Ericson, Richard and Ariel Pakes, op. cit.

70. Chamberlin, Edward H. *The Theory of Monopolistic Competition*. Cambridge, MA: Harvard University Press, 1933.

71. Adapted from Haas School of Business economics problem sets.

CHAPTER 7

72. *The Wall Street Journal*, November 16, 1999.

73. The Bertrand model was first introduced by Bertrand, J. "Théorie Mathématique de la Richesse Sociale," *Journal de Savants* (1883): 499–508.

74. Davidson, Carl and Raymond Deneckere. "Long-run Competition in Capacity, Short-run Competition in Price, and the Cournot Model," *Rand Journal of Economics* 17 (1986): 404-415. Herk, Leonard F. "Consumer Choice and Cournot Behavior in Capacity-constrained Duopoly Competition," *Rand Journal of Economics* 24 (1993): 399–417.

75. Kreps, David M. and José A. Sheinkman. "Capacity Precommitment and Bertrand Competition Yield Cournot Outcomes," *Bell Journal of Economics* 14 (1983): 326–337.

76. Cournot, A. *Recherches sur les Principes Mathématiques de la Théorie des Richesses* (1838). English translation edited by N. Bacon. New York: Macmillan, 1897.

77. *The Wall Street Journal*, August 17, 1999.

78. This example is adapted from Shapiro, Carl and Hal Varian. *Information Rules: A Strategic Guide to the Network Economy*. Cambridge, MA: Harvard Business School Press, 1998.

79. Adapted from Haas School of Business economics problem sets.

CHAPTER 8

80. See Box 8.5 and Fuller, John. *The Gentlemen Conspirators: The Story of the Price-Fixers in the Electrical Industry*. New York: Grove Press, 1962.

81. These kinds of equilibria, as they apply to oligopoly competition, were first proposed by Friedman, James. "A Noncooperative Equilibrium for Supergames," *Review of Economic Studies* 28 (1971): 1–12. The general underlying idea is, however, very old and of unknown origin. For this reason, the main results are referred to as **folk theorems**.

82. This subsection follows the analysis proposed by Green, Ed and Robert Porter. "Noncooperative Collusion under Imperfect Price Information," *Econometrica* 52 (1984): 87–100. These authors in turn follow the seminal work by Stigler, George. "A Theory of Oligopoly," *Journal of Political Economy* 72 (1964): 44–61.

83. Adapted and quoted from Porter, Robert H. "A Study of Cartel Stability: The Joint Executive Committee, 1880–1886," *Bell Journal of Economics* 14 (1983): 301–314.

84. Rotemberg, Julio and Garth Saloner. "A Supergame-Theoretic Model of Price Wars during Booms," *American Economic Review* 76 (1986): 390–407.

85. See Box 8.2 and Porter, op. cit. See also Ellison, Glenn. "Theories of Cartel Stability and the Joint Executive Committee," *Rand Journal of Economics* 25 (1994): 37–57.

86. *Aviation Week and Space Technology*, January 11, 1993. For econometric evidence on this claim, see Busse, Meghan R. "Firm Financial Conditions and Airline Price Wars," Yale School of Management, 1997.

87. *Financial Times,* February 1, 1995.

88. Levenstein, Margaret C. "Price Wars and the Stability of Collusion: A Study of the Pre-World War I Bromine Industry," *Journal of Industrial Economics* 45 (1997): 117–137.

89. The following analysis draws partly on Bernheim, B. Douglas and Michael D. Whinston. "Multimarket Contact and Collusive Behavior," *Rand Journal of Economics* 21 (1990): 1–26.

90. Adapted from Evans, W. N. and I. N. Kessides. "Living by the 'Golden Rule': Multimarket Contact in the U.S. Airline Industry," *Quarterly Journal of Economics* 109 (1994): 341–366.

91. Adapted from Stuart, Toby. "Cat Fight in the Pet Food Industry," Harvard Business School Case No. 9-391-189.

92. Adapted from Porter, Michael. "General Electric vs. Westinghouse in Large Turbine Generators," Harvard Business School Case No. 9-380-129, 1980.

93. Text and data adapted from Albæk, Svend, Peter Møllgaard, and Per B. Overgaard. "Government-Assisted Oligopoly Coordination? A Concrete Case," *Journal of Industrial Economics* 45 (1997): 429–443.

94. Smith, Adam. *The Wealth of Nations*, chapter X, Part II.

95. *The Wall Street Journal Europe*, June 11–12, 1999.

96. Adapted from Haas School of Business economics problem sets.

97. Morrison, Steven A. and Clifford Winston. "Causes and Consequences of Airline Fare Wars," *Brookings Papers on Economic Activity* (Microeconomics), 205–276, 1996.

98. *The Wall Street Journal Europe*, August 12, 1998.

99. *The Wall Street Journal*, October 11, 1999.

100. Dick, Andrew. "If Cartels Were Legal, Would Firms Fix Prices?" Antitrust Division, U.S. Department of Justice, 1997.

101. *The Economist*, December 5, 1998.

102. Fernández, Nerea and Pedro Marín. "Market Power and Multimarket Contact: Some Evidence from the Spanish Hotel Industry," *Journal of Industrial Economics* 46 (1998): 301–315.

103. USIA *EPF513 04/03/98, written by USIA Staff Writer Bruce Odessey.

104. See Schmitz, John and Stephen W. Fuller. "Effect of Contract Disclosure on Railroad Grain Rates: An Analysis of Corn Belt Corridors," *The Logistics and Transportation Review* 31 (1995): 97–124.

CHAPTER 9

105. A more general and rigorous statement of this result may be found in Novshek, William and Hugo Sonnenshein. "Cournot and Walras Equilibrium," *Journal of Economic Theory* 19 (1978): 223–266.

106. One of the first contributions was Bain, Joe. "Relation of Profit Rate to Industry Concentration: American Manufacturing, 1936–1940," *Quarterly Journal of Economics* 65 (1951): 293–324.

107. For a survey, see Schmalensee, Richard. "Inter-Industry Studies of Structure and Performance," in Schmalensee and Willig (Eds.), *Handbook of Industrial Organization*. Amsterdam: North-Holland, 1989.

108. Demsetz, Harold. "Industry Structure, Market Rivalry, and Public Policy," *Journal of Law and Economics* 16 (1973): 1–9.

109. Porter, Michael. *Competitive Strategy*. New York: Free Press, 1980.

110. A survey of applications of the framework above and of similar ones can be found in Bresnahan, Timothy F. "Empirical Studies of Industries with Market Power," in Schmalensee and Willig (Eds.), *Handbook of Industrial Organization*. Amsterdam: North-Holland, 1989.

111. For an analysis of a dynamic model of this type, see Porter, Robert H. "A Study of Cartel Stability: The Joint Executive Committee, 1880–1886," *Bell Journal of Economics* 14 (1983): 301–314.

CHAPTER 10

112. See Stigler, George. *Theory of Price.* New York: McMillan, 1987.

113. See Tirole, Jean. *The Theory of Industrial Organization.* Cambridge, MA: MIT Press, 1989, pp. 137–143.

114. This classification is due to Pigou, A. C. *The Economics of Welfare* (4th ed.). London: McMillan & Co., 1932. See also Varian, Hal. "Price Discrimination," in R. Schmalensee and R. D. Willig (Eds.), *Handbook of Industrial Organization.* Amsterdam: North-Holland, 1989, p. 600.

115. This box is based on Verboven, Frank. "International Price Discrimination in the European Car Market," *Rand Journal of Economics* 27 (1996): 240–268.

116. This term is due to Shapiro, Carl and Hal Varian. *Information Rules: A Strategic Guide to the Network Economy.* Cambridge, MA: Harvard Business School Press, 1998.

117. Quoted by Ekelund, R. B. "Price Discrimination and Product Differentiation in Economic Theory: An Early Analysis," *Quarterly Journal of Economics* 84 (1970): 268–278.

118. This box is based on Deneckere, Raymond J. and R. Preston McAfee. "Damaged Goods," *Journal of Economics and Management Strategy* 5 (1996): 149–174.

119. *The New York Times*, October 15, 1993.

120. *The Wall Street Journal,* September 5, 1985.

121. *The Wall Street Journal Europe*, July 15, 1998.

122. *The Wall Street Journal Europe*, July 17–18, 1998.

123. *The Economist*, June 13, 1998.

124. Philips, Louis. *The Economics of Price Discrimination.* Cambridge: Cambridge University Press, 1983, pp. 23–30.

125. Graddy, Kathryn. "Testing for Imperfect Competition at the Fulton Fish Market," *Rand Journal of Economics* 26 (1995): 75–92.

126. Levedahl, J. W. "Marketing, Price Discrimination, and Welfare: Comment," *Southern Economic Journal* 3 (1984): 886–891.

127. Adapted from Haas School of Business economics problem sets.

128. *Financial Times*, October 28, 1999.

129. Nevo, Aviv and Catherine Wolfram. "Prices and Coupons for Breakfast Cereals," University of California, Berkeley, and Harvard University, 1999.

130. *The Economist*, August 1, 1997.

CHAPTER 11

131. This section is partly based on Rey, Patrick and Jean Tirole. "A Primer in Vertical Foreclosure," University of Toulouse, 1997.

132. This section is partly based on Mathewson, Frank and Ralph Winter. "An Economic Theory of Vertical Restraints," *Rand Journal of Economics* 15 (1984): 27–38.

133. This section is based on Winter, Ralph A. "Vertical Control and Price versus Nonprice Competition," *Quarterly Journal of Economics* 108 (1993): 61–76.

134. Shaffer, Greg. "Slotting Allowances and Resale Price Maintenance: A Comparison of Facilitating Practices," *Rand Journal of Economics* 22 (1991): 120–135.

135. *The Wall Street Journal*, May 15, 1998.

136. This box is partly based on Comanor, William S. and Patrick Rey. "Competition Policy towards Vertical Restraints in Europe and the United States," *Empirica* 24 (1997): 37–52.

137. *The Wall Street Journal*, December 22, 1999.

138. Adapted from Haas School of Business economics problem sets.

139. See Judge R. Posner's opinion, cited in Mathewson, Frank and Ralph Winter. "The Law and Economics of Resale Price Maintenance," *Review of Industrial Organization* 13 (1998): 57–84.

140. *The Wall Street Journal*, December 16, 1999.

141. Adapted from Haas School of Business economics problem sets.

CHAPTER 12

142. These stylized facts may be found in Ausubel, Lawrence M. "The Failure of Competition in the Credit Card Market," *American Economic Review* 81 (1991): 50–81, who also suggests additional explanations.

143. This approach dates back at least to Lancaster, K. J. *Consumer Demand: A New Approach.* New York: Columbia University Press, 1971. See also Anderson, Simon P., de Palma, Andre, and Thisse, Jacques-Francois. *Discrete Choice Theory of Product Differentiation*, 1971. Cambridge, MA: MIT Press, 1992.

144. Adapted from Berry, Steven, James Levinson, and Ariel Pakes. "Automobile Prices in Market Equilibrium," *Econometrica* 63 (1995): 841–890.

145. Hotelling, Harold. "Stability in Competition," *Economic Journal* 39 (1929): 41–57. See also D'Aspremont, Claude, J. Jaskold Gabszewicz, and Jacques-François Thisse. "On Hotelling's 'Stability of Competition,'" *Econometrica* 47 (1979): 1145–1150.

146. Diamond, Peter A. "A Model of Price Adjustment," *Journal of Economic Theory* 3 (1971): 156–168.

147. See Klemperer, Paul. "Competition When Consumers Have Switching Costs: An Overview with Applications to Industrial Organization, Macroeconomics, and International Trade," *Review of Economic Studies* 62 (1995): 515–539.

148. *International Herald Tribune*, December 28, 1998.

149. *ProTeste*, No. 123 (February 1993).

150. BBC, *The Money Programme*, December 20, 1998.

151. See Friedman, James W. and Jacques-François Thisse. "Partial Collusion Fosters Minimum Product Differentiation," *Rand Journal of Economics* 24 (1993): 631–645.

152. See Greenstein, Shane M. "Did Installed Base Give an Incumbent Any (Measurable) Advantages in Federal Computer Procurement?" *Rand Journal of Economics* 24 (1993): 19–39.

153. Brynjolfsson, E. and M. Smith. "Frictionless Commerce? A Comparison of Internet and Conventional Retailers," Working Paper, MIT, 1999.

154. Stigler, George. "The Economics of Information," *Journal of Political Economy* 69 (1961): 213–225.

155. Adapted from Haas School of Business economics problem sets.

CHAPTER 13

156. Adapted from Ackerberg, Daniel A. "Empirically Distinguishing Informative and Prestige Effects of Advertising," mimeo, Boston University.

157. Adapted from *The Wall Street Journal Europe*, November 19, 1998.

158. Nelson, Phillip. "Advertising as Information," *Journal of Political Economy* 81 (1974): 729–754.

159. See Milgrom, Paul R. and John Roberts. "Price and Advertising Signals of Product Quality," *Journal of Political Economy* 94 (1986): 796–821.

160. Sutton, John. *Sunk Costs and Market Structure.* Cambridge, MA: MIT Press, 1992. See also table 14.1.

161. Dorfman, R. and Peter O. Steiner. "Optimal Advertising and Optimal Quality," *American Economic Review* 44 (1954): 826–836.

162. Source: Metwally, M. M. "Advertising and Competitive Behavior of Selected Australian Firms," *Review of Economics and Statistics* 47 (1975): 417–427.

163. *The Wall Street Journal*, October 11, 1999.

164. Adapted from *The Wall Street Journal Europe*, June 30, 1998.

165. Dixit, Avinash and Victor Norman. "Advertising and Welfare," *The Bell Journal of Economics* 9 (1978): 1–17.

166. Benham, Lee. "The Effect of Advertising on the Price of Eyeglasses," *Journal of Law and Economics* 15 (1972): 337–352. For a more elaborate argument that price advertising reduces prices, see Butters, Gerard R. "Equilibrium Distributions of Sales and Advertising Prices," *The Review of Economic Studies* 44 (1977): 465–491.

167. Shum, Matthew. "Advertising and Switching Behavior in the Breakfast Cereals Market," University of Toronto, 1999.

168. Comanor, William S. and Thomas A. Wilson. *Advertising and Market Power.* Cambridge, MA: Harvard University Press, 1974.

169. Adapted from Haas School of Business economics problem sets.

170. Friedman, James. "Advertising and Oligopolistic Equilibrium," *Bell Journal of Economics* 14 (1983): 464–373.

171. Roberts, Mark and Larry Samuelson. "An Empirical Analysis of Dynamic, Nonprice Competition in an Oligopolistic Industry," *Rand Journal of Economics* 19 (1988): 200–220. Gasmi, F., Jean-Jacques Laffont, and Quang Vuong. "Econometric Analysis of Collusive Behavior in a Soft-Drink Market," *Journal of Economics, Management and Strategy* 1 (1992): 277–312. Slade, Margaret E. "Product Rivalry with Multiple Strategic Weapons: An Analysis of Price and Advertising Competition," *Journal of Economics, Management and Strategy* 4 (1995): 445–476.

CHAPTER 14

172. Lucas, Robert E. "Adjustment Costs and the Theory of Supply," *Journal of Political Economy* 75 (1967): 321–334.

173. Source: Bruce Lyons (U. East Anglia) and Kate Matraves (U. Texas A&M).

174. Sutton, John. *Sunk Costs and Market Structure.* Cambridge, MA: MIT Press, 1992.

175. "Battle of the Minis," *PaineWebber World Steel Dynamics*, 12/89. Barnett, Donald F. and Robert W. Crandall. *Up from the Ashes: The Rise of the Steel Minimill in the United States.* Washington, DC: Brookings Institution, 1986.

176. Sutton, op. cit.

177. Sutton, op. cit.

178. This section is partly based on Mankiw, N. Gregory and Michael D. Whinston. "Free Entry and Social Inefficiency," *Rand Journal of Economics* 17 (1986): 48–58.

179. See Vickers, John. "Entry and Competitive Selection," Oxford University, December, 1995.

180. Adapted and quoted from Olley, G. Steven and Ariel Pakes. "The Dynamics of Productivity in the Telecommunications Equipment Industry," *Econometrica* 64 (1996): 1263–1297.

181. Adapted from an exercise written by T. Bresnahan.

CHAPTER 15

182. This example was taken from Sull, Don. "easyJet: The $500 Million Gamble," *European Management Journal* 17 (1999): 20–38.

183. This box is adapted from Ghemawat, Pankaj. "Capacity Expansion in the Titanium Dioxide Industry," *Journal of Industrial Economics* 33 (1984): 145–163; Hall, Elizabeth A. "An Analysis of Preemptive Behavior in the Titanium Dioxide Industry," *International Journal of Industrial Organization* 8 (1990): 469–484.

184. This section is adapted from Dixit, A. "The Role of Investment in Entry Deterrence," *Economic Journal* 90 (1980): 95–106.

185. This section is partly based on Schmalensee, Richard. "Entry Deterrence in the Ready-to-eat Breakfast Cereal Industry," *Bell Journal of Economics* 9 (1978): 305–327.

186. Adapted from David Woodruff. "France Telecom Stays on Top of the Game," *The Wall Street Journal Europe*, January 8–9, 1999.

187. Stemberg, Thomas G. *Staples for Success: From Business Plan to Billion-Dollar Business in Just a Decade.* Santa Monica, CA: Knowledge Exchange, 1996.

188. This subsection is adapted from Aghion, Philippe and Patrick Bolton. "Contracts as a Barrier to Entry," *American Economic Review* 77 (1987): 38–401.

189. Adapted from Nalebuff, Barry J. and Adam M. Brandenburger. *Co-opetition.* London: Harper-Collins, Business 1996.

190. For a rigorous analysis of the theory of predation based on financial contracting see Bolton, Patrick and David S. Scharfstein. "A Theory of Predation Based on Agency Problems in Financial Contracting," *American Economic Review* 80 (1990): 93–106.

191. This view on predatory pricing was developed by Saloner, Garth. "Predation, Mergers, and Incomplete Information," *Rand Journal of Economics* 18 (1987): 165–186.

192. Burns, Malcolm R. "Predatory Pricing and Acquisition Cost of Competitors," *Journal of Political Economy* 94 (1986): 266–296.

193. This view on predatory pricing was developed by Kreps, David M. and Robert Wilson. "Reputation and Imperfect Information," *Journal of Economic Theory* 27 (1982): 253–279, and Milgrom, Paul R. and John Roberts. "Predation, Reputation and Entry Deterrence," *Journal of Economic Theory* 27 (1982): 280–312.

194. This view on predatory pricing is developed in Cabral, Luís and Michael H. Riordan. "The Learning Curve, Market Dominance, and Predatory Pricing," *Econometrica* 62 (1994): 1115–1140, and Cabral, Luís and Michael H. Riordan. "The Learning Curve, Predation, Antitrust, and Welfare," *Journal of Industrial Economics* 45 (1997): 155–169.

195. This example is adapted from Hazlett, T. W. "Predation in Local Cable TV Markets," *Antitrust Bulletin* (1995): 609–644.

196. Whinston, Michael D. "Tying, Foreclosure, and Exclusion," *American Economic Review* 80 (1990): 837-859.

197. *Financial Times*, August 11, 1993.

198. Office of Fair Trading, *Fair Trading*, Issue 20 (1998).

199. *Business Week*, March 16, 1998.

200. *Brook Group Ltd. v. Brown & Williams Tobacco Corp.*, 113 S. Ct. 2578 (1993).

201. *Matsushita Electric Industrial Co. v. Zenith Radio Corp.*, 106 S. Ct. 1348 (1986).

202. *The Wall Street Journal Europe*, September 21, 1998.

203. George Stigler. "Monopoly and Oligopoly by Merger," *American Economic Review Proceedings* 40 (May 1950): 479–489.

204. *The Wall Street Journal Europe*, August 14–15, 1998.

205. *The Wall Street Journal Europe*, September 16, 1998.

206. *The Economist*, June 25, 1998.

207. *The Wall Street Journal Europe*, October 28, 1998.

208. *The Economist*, October 31, 1998.

209. *The Wall Street Journal Europe*, September 7, 1998.

210. Compte, Olivier, Frederic Jenny, and Patrick Rey. "Capacity Constraints, Mergers and Collusion," University of Toulouse, 1997.

211. This point was formalized by Farrell, Joseph and Carl Shapiro. "Horizontal Mergers: An Equilibrium Analysis," *American Economic Review* 80 (1990): 107–126.

212. *International Herald Tribune*, December 29, 1998.

213. Pesendorfer, Martin. "Horizontal Mergers in the Paper Industry," Department of Economics, Yale University, September, 1998.

214. *The Wall Street Journal Europe*, January 15–16, 1999.

215. Porter, Michael. "From Competitive Advantage to Corporate Strategy," *Harvard Business Review* (May–June 1987): 43–59.

216. Caves, Richard E. and Sanjeev Mehra. "Entry of Foreign Multinationals into U.S. Manufacturing Industries," in M. Porter (Ed.), *Competition in Global Industries*. Cambridge, MA: Harvard Business School Press, 1986.

217. This exercise is adapted from Gilbert, Richard and David Newbery. "Alternative Entry Paths: The Build or Buy Decision," *Journal of Economics and Management Strategy* 1 (1992): 127–150.

CHAPTER 16

218. *International Herald Tribune*, July 4–5, 1998, p. 15, and author's calculations.

219. Schumpeter, Joseph. *Capitalism, Socialism, and Democracy* (2nd ed.). New York: 1950, pp. 82 and 106.

220. Arrow, Kenneth J. "Economic Welfare and the Allocation of Resources for Invention," in National Bureau of Economic Research. *The Rate and Direction of Inventive Activity*. Princeton: Princeton University Press, 1962, p. 622.

221. *The Wall Street Journal Europe*, October 8, 1998.

222. *The Wall Street Journal*, November 3, 1999.

223. Adapted from Bresnahan, Timothy. "Post-entry Competition in the Plain Paper Copier Market," *American Economic Review* 75 (1985): 15–19.

224. Adapted from Barese, Paul, Adam Brandenburger, and Vijay Krishna. "The Race to Develop Human Insulin," Harvard Business School Case No. 9-191-121, 1992. See also Hall, Stephen S. *Invisible Frontiers: The Race to Synthesize a Human Gene*. New York: Atlantic Monthly Press, 1987.

225. *The Wall Street Journal Europe*, June 16, 1998.

226. Adapted from Nalebuff, Barry and Adam Brandenburger. *Co-opetition*. London: Harper-Collins Business, 1996.

227. *The Wall Street Journal Europe*, August 14–15, 1998.

228. Cabral, Luís and Michael H. Riordan. "The Learning Curve, Market Dominance, and Predatory Pricing," *Econometrica* 62 (1994): 1115–1140.

229. Gruber, Harald. *Learning and Strategic Product Innovation: Theory and Evidence for the Semiconductor Industry*. Amsterdam: North Holland, 1992.

230. This subsection is adapted from Henderson, Rebecca. "Underinvestment and Incompetence as Responses to Radical Innovation: Evidence from the Photolithographic Alignment Equipment Industry," *Rand Journal of Economics* 24 (1993): 248–270.

231. Gruber, Harald. "Learning by Doing and Spillovers: Further Evidence for the Semiconductor Industry," *Review of Industrial Organization* 13 (1998): 697–711.

232. For a formal analysis of this trade-off, see Nordhaus, William. *Invention, Growth and Welfare: A Theoretical Treatment of Technological Change.* Cambridge, MA: MIT Press, 1969.

233. Klemperer, Paul. "How Broad Should the Scope of Patent Protection Be?" *Rand Journal of Economics* 21 (1990): 113–130.

234. The following argument is similar to that in Gilbert, Richard and Carl Shapiro. "Optimal Patent Length and Breadth," *Rand Journal of Economics* 21 (1990): 106–112.

235. Matutes, Carmen, Pierre Regibeau, and Katharine Rockett. "Optimal Patent Design and the Diffusion of Innovations," *Rand Journal of Economics* 27 (1996): 60–83. See also Scotchmer, Suzanne and Jerry Green. "Novelty and Disclosure in Patent Law," *Rand Journal of Economics* 21 (1990): 131–146.

236. European Commission. *Fourteenth Report on Competition Policy.* Brussels, 1995, pp. 37–38.

237. U.S. Senate, Committee of the Judiciary. The National Cooperative Production Amendments Act of 1993, Antitrust and Trade Regulation Report, 1993, pp. 725.

238. Adapted from Haas School of Business economics problem sets.

239. *The Wall Street Journal Europe*, November 19, 1998.

CHAPTER 17

240. Source: Dataquest. See also Economides, Nicholas and Charles Himmelberg. "Critical Mass and Network Size with Applications to the U.S. Fax Market," New York University, Stern School of Business Discussion Paper No. EC-95-11, 1995.

241. This section is adapted from Arthur, W. Brian. "Competing Technologies, Increasing Returns, and Lock-in by Historical Events," *The Economic Journal* 99 (1989): 116–131.

242. Adapted from Cusumano, Michael A., Yiorgos Mylonadis, and Richard S. Rosenbloom. "Strategic Maneuvering and Mass-Market Dynamic: The Triumph of VHS over Beta," *Business History Review* 66 (1992): 51–94. Nayak, P. Ranganath and John M. Ketteringham. *Breakthroughs!* New York: Rawson Associates, 1986. Smith, Lee. "Sony Battles Back," *Fortune*, April 15, 1985.

243. David, Paul A. "Clio and the Economics of QWERTY," *American Economic Review* 75 (1985): 332–337.

244. Liebowitz, Stan and Stephen Margolis. "The Fable of the Keys," *Journal of Law and Economics* 33 (1990): 1–25.

245. This section is adapted from Farrell, Joseph and Garth Saloner. "Standardization, Compatibility, and Innovation," *Rand Journal of Economics* 16 (1985): 70–83.

246. Adapted from Besen, Stanley M. "AM versus FM: The Battle of the Bands," *Industrial and Corporate Change* 1 (1992): 375–396.

247. Adapted from Postrel, Steven. "Competing Networks and Proprietary Standards: The Case of Quadraphonic Sound," *Journal of Industrial Economics* 39 (1990): 169–185.

248. *The Wall Street Journal*, November 24, 1999.

249. This example is adapted from Homer, Steve. "Electronics Giants Square Off over Videodisk Standards," *The Wall Street Journal Europe*, Convergence, Summer, 1998.

250. Gandal, Neil. "Hedonic Price Indexes for Spreadsheets and an Empirical Test for Network Externalities," *Rand Journal of Economics* 25 (1994): 160–170.

251. Goolsbee, Austan and Peter J. Klenow. "Evidence on Learning and Network Externalities in the Diffusion of Home Computers," University of Chicago, 1998.

252. Saloner, Garth and Andrea Shepherd. "Adoption of Technologies with Network Effects: An Empirical Examination of the Adoption of Automated Teller Machines," *Rand Journal of Economics* 26 (199?): 479–501.

253. *The New York Times Magazine*, May 5, 1996.

254. Adapted from Haas School of Business economics problem sets.

255. Adapted from Haas School of Business economics problem sets.

INDEX

Page numbers followed by "f" refer to figures; page numbers followed by "b" refer to boxes; page numbers followed by "t" refer to tables; page numbers followed by "fn" refer to footnotes.